The Best
TV Pub
Quiz Book
Ever!

Senior Art Editor: Zoe Mercer
Editorial Assistants: Heather Dickson, Sam Wigand
Production: Garry Lewis

Printed and bound in Great Britain

The Best TV Pub Quiz Book Ever!

DR JEREMY SIMS

CARLTON

Contents

HARD

Introduction

Television is one of those things that unites all of humanity. There aren't many of them, either. Alcohol is another one, barring the occasional tee-totaller. So it is perfectly natural that *The Best Pub TV Quiz Book Ever!* came into being. Frankly, the human psyche demanded it. Everyone watches TV at least sometimes, and most of us watch it a lot more than that. Where else can you get the same breadth of experience and depth of emotion over such a wide range of areas in just one evening? It's impossible. For better or for worse, TV has become a vital and entrenched fixture of modern life. It has the extra added benefit of being a topic that everyone knows something about, so it's an ideal subject to quiz people on, particularly after they've had a couple of pints.

Inside *The Best Pub TV Quiz Book Ever!* , you'll find more than 9,000 questions covering a stunning range of programs and program-related areas, divided into easy, medium, and hard sections. The quizzes are divided into themes, but you'll want to allow some slack. To keep things interesting, the different topics are used in a broad sense rather than a narrow one, so as to make sure that even subject-area experts stay on their toes. Similarly, composition varies between difficulty levels... the possible questions to be asked in some areas are just harder than others!

At the back of the book, you'll also find a comprehensive set of guidelines on how to prepare for and run a successful quiz of your own down the local, and some handy answer sheet templates to photocopy and give out to contestants. Running a pub quiz can be a lot of hard work, but it's also very rewarding, even if not usually particularly lucrative! There is one important guideline you should always remember when running a quiz of course, and that is never, ever, under any circumstances, give out your own pens.

More importantly than that though – seriously for a minute – when you are going to be running a quiz, prepare properly beforehand. Don't just take this book along and read out of it (because apart from anything else, some other wise guy might have bought a copy too, and be checking the answers). Note down all the questions and all the answers, and make sure you've got everything. If an answer makes you think "hang on a moment, is that right?" then double-check it to make sure that it is not only correct, but it is the only correct answer. While every possible effort has been undertaken to make absolutely sure that every answer is accurate, there is a slight possibility that an error may have crept in, and the answer is wrong. Nothing is more humiliating than telling people who are right that they are wrong in front of a lot of witnesses who will remember it and tease you about it mercilessly for the next three years. If you've made sure of your answers, you'll be absolutely 100% safe, not just 99.9% safe.

So there you go. Take your book in hand, put on your TV Challenge hat, wade in, and have fun. After all, that's what it's all about.

📺 Easy Questions

The whole point of these questions is that they are, well, easy. As in not hard. That means that they shouldn't give you any problems, or indeed anyone else who has looked at a television set more than once in the last thirty years. If you get these questions right, that's really not much to be proud of. In fact, it's close to the truth that getting these questions wrong is something to be worried about. If you find yourself doing badly on these questions, there are many possible reasons. The first thing to check is that you're looking at the correct answer block. If you've made that mistake, it'll throw your results right out. Alternatively, you may be extremely drunk. If reading this short introduction is proving tricky, that could be the cause. Try again later. Another possible cause is that you might only be three or four years old – again, try again later, only make it much later. Finally, you may have been born in the wilds and have spent your life being raised by a friendly family of finches, in which case you can be forgiven for your ignorance. They're nice creatures, but they're really not much cop when it comes to Coronation Street.

So, when you're devising a quiz for people, you might like to soften them up with a few of these questions, preparing them for something nasty. If nothing else, it'll make sure that even the bloke in the corner who's so hammered he can't stand will get one or two points, and save face. Tomorrow, he may even be grateful enough to buy you a drink for being so considerate. It's worth a shot, so to speak...

Answers: see Quiz 2, page 10   LEVEL 1

1. What is the name of Popeye's girlfriend?

2. Where do the Wombles live?

3. Which cartoon character yells "Yab-a-dab-a-doo"?

4. What kind of puppet animal is *Basil Brush*?

5. Herman was the Frankenstein-like father of which ghoulish family?

6. What is the real-life relationship between the children's comedy duo, *The Krankies*?

7. Which cartoon animal superhero has a pal called Spotty Man?

8. Who is Yogi Bear's smaller than the average bear pal?

9. Where would you find Ermintrude the cow and a rabbit called Dylan?

10. Which series featured International Rescue?

11. What is the name of the family *Paddington Bear* lives with?

12. What colour are Rupert Bear's checked trousers?

13. What is the symbol used by *Blue Peter*?

14. In *The Muppets*, what kind of animal is Fozzie?

15. How many human pals does *Scooby Doo* have?

16. What was the numberplate on *Postman Pat*'s van?

17. Who is Rod Hull's temperamental puppet friend?

18. What is the name of Keith Harris's duck friend who wishes he could fly?

19. What programme would you have been watching if "It's Friday....It's five o'clock ... and it's..."?

20. In *Batman*, which villain left riddles at the scenes of his crimes?

21. Which newspaper does Superman's alter ego Clark Kent write for?

22. What was the name of the Lone Ranger's horse?

23. What was Bagpuss?

24. What letter did Zorro cut with his sword at the beginning of each episode of his series?

25. What was the name of Fred Flinstone's pet dinosaur?

26. Name the *Flowerpot Men*.

27. Who is Sooty's canine sidekick?

28. What sort of creatures were *Pinky and Perky*?

29. Gomez and Mortitia are the husband and wife of which creepy TV family?

30. What is Casper?

Answers: see Quiz 1, page 9

LEVEL 1

1. Which news programme does Trevor McDonald present?
2. On which channel is *Panorama*?
3. Who presented *TV Eye*?
4. What time does *Newsround* start?
5. Which ex-newsreader presented *The Clothes Show*?
6. Who was the ITV commentator for the 1998 Football World Cup Final?
7. What nationality is Clive James?
8. Who presented *Crime Beat*?
9. What is BBC2's evening news programme called?
10. Who presented *Whickers World*?
11. Which Kate is an international correspondent for BBC television?
12. Which Dimbleby presented *Question Time*?
13. Which Brian had a Sunday lunchtime political programme?
14. Who is the presenter of *The Late Show*?
15. Who swore while being interviewed by Bill Grundy?
16. Which is *The Shopping Channel*?
17. Who was the Chief Executive of the newly created *TV-AM*?
18. On which sport is John McCrillick a commentator?
19. Which royal event in 1953 had the largest television audience?
20. Which organisation researched ITV's viewing figures?
21. What was the subject of *Triumph of The Nerds*?
22. What was C4's series on addictive pleasures?
23. Who presented BBC2's *Vintner's Tales*?
24. Who presented *Quest For The Lost Civilisation*?
25. What was the subject of the documentary series *Absolute Truth*?
26. Who was the subject of the documentary *A Very Singular Man*?
27. Which Docu-soap featured yachtswoman Tracy Edwards?
28. Who circumnavigated the globe in 79 days and 7 hours?
29. What was the first global TV programme?
30. What was the first British fly on the wall documentary series?

Answers: see Quiz 4, page 12   LEVEL 1

1. In *Goodnight Sweetheart* where does Gary time travel to?
2. Who is agoraphobic in *Game On*?
3. What was Mavis Wilton's maiden name in *Coronation Street*?
4. Which Channel 4 sporting coverage is introduced by Derek Thompson?
5. Which series featured Tara King and Mother?
6. Which Australian series was subtitled *The McGregor Saga*?
7. Which soap featured the character Rick Alessi?
8. What is the name of Roy Clarke's sitcom about a snobbish woman and her embarrassing relations?
9. Who plays Foggy in *Last Of The Summer Wine*?
10. Who played a woodwork teacher in *The Beiderbeck Tapes*?
11. Who was the voice of cricket and did television commentaries?
12. What was the family business in *Nearest and Dearest*?
13. In which series did the characters David Addison and Maddie Hayes appear?
14. Who hosts *Watercolour Challenge*?
15. Which BBC2 chat show is hosted by Desmond Wilcox's wife?
16. Which series has been hosted by Eamonn Andrews and Michael Aspel?
17. On which series were Mark Lamarr and Ulrika Jonsson team captains?
18. Which S.F. series featured Martin Landau as John Koenig?
19. Which Williams hosts his own chat show?
20. Who presents *The Pepsi Chart Show* on Channel 5?
21. Who hosted the 1998 game show *The Moment of Truth*?
22. Which S.F. series features the character Jack Logan?
23. In which feelgood series did Victor French play Mark?
24. What is the children's Saturday morning programme featuring Otis?
25. Which action show had a super-helicopter hidden by its pilot, Stringfellow Hawke?
26. Which comedian succeeded Bruce Forsythe as host of *The Generation Game*?
27. Which channel shows *Xena: Warrior Princess* and *Hercules: The Legendary Journeys*?
28. Whose *Tales of The City* were a Channel 4 series?
29. Who presented *In Suspicious Circumstances*?
30. Which Knight presents his *Sunday Morning Breakfast Show*?

Answers: see Quiz 3, page 11

LEVEL 1

1. Which Placido is one of the *Three Tenors*?
2. Who presented the original *Opportunity Knocks*?
3. Which BBC programme presents the pop charts?
4. Chart toppers Berlin sang the theme music to which film starring Tom Cruise?
5. On which channel was the *Saturday Chart Show* broadcast?
6. Which two of the Osmonds hosted their own TV series?
7. On which night is *...Night At The Palladium* screened?
8. Former *Generation Game* hostess Rosemarie Ford introduced which evening dance series on BBC1?
9. Which TV entertainer sang *Tie Me Kangaroo Down* and *Two Little Boys*?
10. What nationality is TV entertainer Barry Humphries?
11. David Nixon was famed for what kind of TV act?
12. Who presents *This Is Your Life*?
13. Matthew Kelly, Sarah Kennedy, Henry Kelly and Jeremy Beadle formed the quartet which presented which madcap weekend show?
14. Which 1990s BBC2 series showcased famous ballets?
15. Which former DJ presented his chat show three times a week?
16. Which former BBC impressionist has the initials M.Y.?
17. Who hosts TFI Friday?
18. How many Monkees were there?
19. Which singer won the Eurovision Song Contest with *Puppet On A String*?
20. What colour was the *Whistle Test*?
21. In 1994 who sang the theme tune *Crocodile Shoes*?
22. Who was the British lead singer of *The Monkees*?
23. Which singer was televised singing in the Wimbledon rain in 1996?
24. Channel 4's *The Tube* was presented by which Paula?
25. Who hosts ITV's *Stars In Their Eyes*?
26. *It'll Be All Right On The Night* is hosted by who?
27. Which televised pop concert raised money for famine relief in Ethiopia?
28. Which TV duo topped the charts with *Unchained Melody*?
29. What was the title of Mr Blobby's first No 1 single?
30. Which Irish singer won the Eurovision Song Contest with *All Kinds Of Everything*?

Answers: see Quiz 6, page 14

LEVEL 1

1. Who starred as Sid in *Bless This House*?
2. What is the first name of Mrs Bucket in *Keeping Up Appearances*?
3. Who is Gary's best friend in *Men Behaving Badly*?
4. Who is Wayne's wife in *Harry Enfield and Chums*?
5. Who is Gareth Hale's comedy partner?
6. Who was the comic with the "short fat hairy legs"?
7. Who are Monica, Rachel, Phoebe, Chandler, Joey and Ross?
8. What is *Frasier's* surname?
9. Who was the cafe owner, played by Gordon Kaye, in *'Allo, 'Allo*?
10. What was Del Boy's surname in *Only Fools And Horses*?
11. Who was the star of *Sez Les*?
12. In which cartoon series do Itchy and Scratchy appear?
13. What is the English version of *All In The Family*?
14. Which comedy series is set in a Torquay hotel?
15. In which series is the character Sally Smedley?
16. Who is the star of *Spin City*?
17. Who was the last barman in *Cheers*?
18. Who was Ronnie Barker's comedy partner in *The Two Ronnies*?
19. In *Porridge* who was Lennie Godber's cellmate?
20. Which actor played Ernie Bilko?
21. Who played Eric Sykes' twin sister in *Sykes*?
22. Who was Stan's sister in *On The Buses*?
23. In *Absolutely Fabulous* who was Edina's best friend?
24. Who created Gizzard Puke?
25. Who played Barbara in *The Good Life*?
26. In which series was the character Frank Spencer?
27. Who portrays *Ellen*?
28. Who was Ritchie's flatmate in *Bottom*?
29. In *Goodnight Sweetheart* what is Nicholas Lyndhurst's character?
30. In which series is Dorian the next door neighbour?

Answers: see Quiz 5, page 13

1. Who succeeded Jeremy Beadle as host of *You've Been Framed*?
2. Which character replaced Oscar Blaketon as the sergeant in *Heartbeat*?
3. What was the BBC2 drama series about young lawyers?
4. What was the title of Joanna Lumley's desert island documentary?
5. Who presented *Wipeout* after Paul Daniels?
6. Which children's programme features Katy Hall as one of three presenters?
7. Who plays Elizabeth in *Hawkeye*?
8. Which quiz about events on one particular day is presented by Martin Lewis?
9. Who plays DC Isobel de Pauli in the crime series *Liverpool One*?
10. Which chat show hostess has the christian name Sally?
11. Who had a girlfriend Clare in *Game On*?
12. In which series is Reg a 1940's policeman?
13. Which soap features the character Toadfish?
14. Which series features Darryl and Chris as convicted armed robbers?
15. Which series starred Rudolph Walker and Jack Smethhurst?
16. Which character was Gordon Brittas's wife in *The Brittas Empire*?
17. Which children's series had a postmistress named Mrs. Dingle?
18. Which soap has an omnibus edition on a Saturday Evening?
19. What does the H stand for in *M*A*S*H*?
20. What nationality is Ulrika Jonsson?
21. In which sitcom does Roger Lloyd Pack portray a plumber named Jake the Klingon?
22. Which star of *Ballykissangel* appeared in *Goodnight Sweetheart*?
23. Which series features DCI Jack Meadows?
24. Which series set in Alaska features the characters Holling, Maurice and Ed?
25. On which channel would you have found *He-Man and The Masters of the Universe*?
26. Which technology programme is presented by Peter Snow and Philippa Forrester?
27. Who presented *The X Creatures* on BBC1?
28. Which US crime series features detectives Pembleton and Bayliss?
29. Which animated series features Hank, Peggy and Bobby?
30. Who starred in *Ruby Does The Season*?

Answers: see Quiz 8, page 16
                                                              LEVEL 1

1. Who did Mike Baldwin marry in 1986?
2. Which TV series starred Tyne Daly and Sharon Gless?
3. Where did the Robinson family become lost?
4. On which channel is *NYPD Blue* transmitted?
5. What rank is Mitch Buchanan in *Baywatch*?
6. Which series featured WDC Viv Martella?
7. Where was *Harry's Game* set?
8. Which Superhero is portrayed by Dean Cain?
9. What is the house in *The House of Cards*?
10. Which character was the butler in *Upstairs Downstairs*?
11. Which country was the location for *Jewel In The Crown*?
12. Who played Paris in *Mission Impossible*?
13. In which series does Robbie Coltrane portray Fitz?
14. Who plays the character of *Maisie Raine*?
15. Which 19th century hero does Sean Bean play?
16. What was the sequel to *Band of Gold*?
17. Who was Dr. Finlay's partner in practice?
18. Which character is played by George Clooney in *ER*?
19. What is Seigfried Farnon's occupation?
20. Which *Charlie's Angel* played Mrs. King?
21. Who was Dempsey's sidekick?
22. Which series featured the character Pug Henry?
23. Who played Jesus of Nazareth?
24. Who played Barlow?
25. Which western series featured Big John and Blue?
26. What was *Lou Grant's* occupation?
27. Which detective did Angie Dickenson portray?
28. Which of *Randall and Hopkirk* was not a ghost?
29. Who played Rowdy Yates in *Rawhide*?
30. Who presented *Tales of the Unexpected*?

ANSWERS

Soaps 1 (see Quiz 8)
1. The Queen Vic. 2. Four times per week. 3. A cat. 4. The patio. 5. A magazine. 6. *Emmerdale Farm*. 7. *Dynasty*. 8. *Knott's Landing*. 9. *Crossroads*. 10. *Let The Blood Run Free*. 11. Alf Roberts. 12. *Crossroads*. 13. *Soap*. 14. Yorkshire. 15. The Woolpack. 16. Cindy Beale. 17. Tinhead. 18. He isn't married. 19. *Brookside*. 20. Kim. 21. The Rover's Return. 22. Dot Cotton. 23. Mike Read. 24. Mike Baldwin. 25. Fred Elliott. 26. Yorkshire TV. 27. *Dynasty*. 28. Jack Duckworth. 29. *Dallas*. 30. *Peyton Place*.

QUIZ 8 Soaps 1

Answers: see Quiz 7, page 15

LEVEL 1

1. What is the name of the pub in Albert Square?
2. How many times each week is *Coronation Street* broadcast?
3. What animal appears on the opening credits of *Coronation Street*?
4. What was Trevor Jordache buried under in *Brookside*?
5. In the 1960s series *Compact*, what was Compact?
6. What was Emmerdale previously called?
7. In which US soap did Joan Collins star?
8. In which Landing did some of the Ewings settle after *Dallas*?
9. Which ITV soap featured actress Noelle Gordon and the character Amy Turtle?
10. Which is the Australian spoof medical soap?
11. Alf Roberts was mayor of Wetherfield in which ITV soap?
12. Which soap was set in a Birmingham motel?
13. Which comedy spoof series finished its weekly introductory plot summary with the words "Confused? You will be after the next exciting episode of … "?
14. *Emmerdale* is set in which UK county?
15. What is the name of the pub in *Emmerdale*?
16. Who left *Eastenders* for France with two of her children?
17. Who is the metal-headed character in *Brookside*?
18. In *Coronation Street*, who is Ken Barlow married to?
19. Did the TV astrologer Russel Grant appear in *Brookside* or *Eastenders*?
20. Who was Frank Tate's murdered wife in *Emmerdale*?
21. Which pub sells Newton & Ridley beer?
22. June Brown plays which dotty character in *Eastenders*?
23. Which bespectacled comedian plays a major character in *Eastenders*?
24. Who owns the factory in *Coronation Street*?
25. Who is the Street's repetitive butcher?
26. Which TV company produces *Emmerdale*?
27. The Carringtons featured in which US soap?
28. Bill Tarmey plays which character in *Coronation Street*?
29. In which soap was JR shot?
30. Which Place was an early TV Soap?

Drama 1 (see Quiz 7)

1. Susan Barlow. 2. *Cagney and Lacey*. 3. Space. 4. Channel 4. 5. Captain. 6. *The Bill*. 7. Northern Ireland. 8. *Superman*. 9. The Houses of Parliament. 10. Hudson. 11. India. 12. Leonard Nimoy. 13. *Cracker*. 14. Pauline Quirke. 15. Richard Sharpe. 16. Gold. 17. Dr. Cameron. 18. Doug Ross. 19. Vet. 20. Kate Jackson. 21. Makepiece. 22. *The Winds Of War*. 23. Robert Powell. 24. Stratford Johns. 25. *The High Chaparral*. 26. Newspaper Editor. 27. Pepper Anderson. 28. Randall. 29. Clint Eastwood. 30. Roald Dahl.

ANSWERS

16

Answers: see Quiz 10, page 18

LEVEL 1

1. Which series featured Dale Robertson as a railroad detective?
2. Who played Chicken George in *Roots*?
3. Who was the presenter of *Don't Forget Your Toothbrush*?
4. Which Clive chaired *Whose Line is it Anyway*?
5. In which US city did *Cheers* take place?
6. Which doctor set aside his Casebook in the 90s revival of the series?
7. Which character in *Absolutely Fabulous* was Edina's secretary?
8. Which American sitcom, set in Miami, was made into a British version *Brighton Belles*?
9. What was the sequel from *And Mother Makes Three*?
10. In which series were Gavin and Tim gay lovers?
11. Which series highlights technological milestones from *Tomorrow's World*?
12. Who was Henry's son in *Home To Roost*?
13. What was the computer game programme hosted by Dominic Diamond?
14. What was the name of the spoof TV station in the series starring Angus Deayton?
15. Which sport was featured in the sitcom *Outside Edge*?
16. In *Neighbours*, Erinsborough is a suburb of which city?
17. Who played Elizabeth Darcy in *Pride and Prejudice*?
18. Who starred as the host in *Knowing Me – Knowing You ....With Alan Partridge*?
19. What was the name of the series about dustmen starring Edward Woodward and Roy Hudd?
20. What is Commander Riker's christian name in *Star Trek: The Next Generation*?
21. Where is the drama series *Roughnecks* set?
22. In which series does Michael Culver play Prior Robert and Sean Pertwee play Hugh Beringer?
23. Which comedy series featured *The Veterinarians Hospital*, a place for old jokes?
24. On which night does *Noel's House Party* take place?
25. What was the full title of the comedy starring Rowan Atkinson set in Regency times?
26. Who played Barry The Brummie in *Auf Weidersehen Pet*?
27. Which medical series featured the characters Dr. Andrew Collin and Dr. Rajah?
28. What is the name of the hamlet near *Camberwick Green*?
29. In *Roughnecks* what is the nickname of the cook played by Ricky Tomlinson?
30. Which series featured Arkwright's corner shop?

Answers: see Quiz 9, page 17

1. Who is the star of *Suddenly Susan*?
2. Which series about New York cabbies starred Danny De Vito?
3. What was Harry in *Harry and the Hendersons*?
4. Who was Lurcio in *Up Pompeii!*?
5. Who was the punk in *The Young Ones*?
6. Which comedy series featured the *River Police*?
7. Which Nick is the chairman of *They Think It's All Over*?
8. Who is the star of *Chef*?
9. Which character was the *Man About The House*?
10. Who does Tony fancy in *Men Behaving Badly*?
11. Who are TV's rag and bone men?
12. In *The Good Life* who is Margo's husband?
13. In *Only Fools And Horses* who is Del's brother?
14. Who plays *Roseanne's* husband?
15. In *Friends* who is Monica's brother?
16. What is *Seinfeld's* christian name?
17. Which series featured Maplins Holiday Camp?
18. Who was 'The One With the Glasses'?
19. Where is *Spin City* set?
20. Who plays Victor Meldrew?
21. Where does *Ellen* work?
22. Who plays Larry Sanders?
23. Who was the female star of *Moonlighting*?
24. Who played Jeeves to Hugh Laurie's Bertie Wooster?
25. What is *Seinfeld's* job?
26. Which family feature in *Til Death Us Do Part*?
27. Which comedy show is the TV version of radio's *News Quiz*?
28. Who plays Mrs Slocombe in *Are You Being Served*?
29. What is Homer Simpson's middle initial?
30. What is Basil Fawlty's wife's name?

Answers: see Quiz 12, page 20   LEVEL 1

1. What position does Odo hold in *Deep Space 9*?

2. What relation to *Doctor Who* was his original travelling companion, Susan?

3. Who was the female communications officer aboard the first USS Enterprise?

4. What exalted position was attained by Sheridan on *Babylon 5*?

5. Which US official body do agents Scully and Mulder belong to?

6. Which series featured Moonbase Alpha?

7. What race is Lt. Worf in *Star Trek: The Next Generation*?

8. Who were *Captain Scarlet's* enemies?

9. Who is the captain of the USS *Voyager*?

10. Who was Sapphire's partner?

11. On which show did you find Lori Singer travelling in cyberspace?

12. "Only David Vincent knows" – about whom?

13. Who is "faster than a speeding bullet"?

14. Who is Batman's assistant?

15. Which Flash fought the evil Emperor Ming?

16. *The Hitch-Hiker's Guide* was a guide to what?

17. Who was assisted by robots called Tweaky and Theo?

18. According to the series title how many were in Blake's crew?

19. Who are flung from one dimension to the next at the end of each show?

20. Which spaceship did Lorne Green command?

21. Which space opera series was created by writers Morgan and Wong of X-files fame?

22. How many characters form the crew of *Red Dwarf*?

23. Which show about invading aliens had a one-letter title?

24. In which programme would you find an intelligent computer called KITT?

25. How was Number Six known?

26. Which alien plants invaded following a comet's blinding appearance?

27. "Anything can happen in the next half-hour" on which show?

28. What type of vehicle was *Streethawk*?

29. What colour was the *Incredible Hulk*?

30. Which lamborghini-driving crime-fighter was generated by a computer?

Answers: see Quiz 11, page 19

1. In which Star Trek spinoff does 'Q' most frequently make an appearance?
2. Which team have won *University Challenge* two years running?
3. Who is Jennifer Paterson's colleague on *Two Fat Ladies*?
4. Which drama series was set on the oil rig Osprey Explorer?
5. Which series featured Mr. Clamp the greengrocer and Mr. Antonio the ice cream seller?
6. Who was the star of *Sean's Show*?
7. Who last role was as a supermarket manager in *Tripper's Day*?
8. In which children's series where the characters Mickey Murphy the Baker and PC McGary?
9. Which character did Ralph Waite portray in *The Waltons*?
10. Which drama features Claude Jeremiah Greengrass?
11. Who in *Eastenders* are Beppe, Bruno and Gianni?
12. What is *Jimmy's*?
13. On which children's programme did the characters Hartley Hare and Pig appear?
14. On which programme did Susan Stranks take-over from Jenny Handley?
15. On which variety show was *Name That Tune* a feature?
16. Who had an elephant called Bimbo?
17. Which Jimmy introduced the first *Top of The Pops*?
18. What were Rita Garnett's parents called?
19. Who is the American female commentator on BBC's coverage of Wimbledon?
20. Which showjumping commentator's first name was Dorien?
21. Which company produces *Neighbours*?
22. Which sport did Ron Pickering commentate on?
23. What was the drama series about a family in wartime Liverpool?
24. Which ITV sports programme featured Jimmy Hill?
25. Which 80s drama centered on Liverpudlian Yosser Hughes?
26. Which animals did Barbara Woodhouse usually appear with?
27. What is Charlie Fairhead's job at Holby City Hospital?
28. What was James' wife called in *All Creatures Great and Small*?
29. What is Lance Corporal Jones occupation in *Dads Army*?
30. Which was Britain's first pop TV show?

QUIZ 13 Children's TV 2

Answers: see Quiz 14, page 22

LEVEL 1

1. Which mouthy puppet rat first appeared on breakfast TV?
2. Who lived at Mockingbird Heights, 1313 Mockingbird Lane?
3. Kermit, Gonzo, Miss Piggy are all what?
4. Which country did *Paddington Bear* come from?
5. Which programme began with the words "Here is a house. Here is a door. Windows: one, two, three, four"?
6. In *Sesame Street*, what was the name of the grumpy creature who lived in a trash can?
7. What sort of animal was Skippy?
8. Who is Wile E Coyote always trying to catch?
9. Which Superhero does Princess Diana of Paradise Island become?
10. Which show featured the tallest, fastest, biggest and other outstanding achievements?
11. What did *Top Cat* sleep in?
12. Which program featured Parsley the Lion and Lady Rosemary?
13. Which Gerry and Sylvia pioneered Supermarionation?
14. What was the name of Mork's Earthling girlfriend?
15. What was the surname of *The Beverley Hillbillies*?
16. Who was the Caped Crusader?
17. *Animal Magic* was presented by who?
18. How was Granny Smith better known?
19. On *The Magic Roundabout*, what kind of creature is Brian?
20. What was *Worzel Gummidge*?
21. Which Mike drove the *Supercar*?
22. Which cartoon cat yells "I hate those meeces to pieces!"?
23. Which programme has been presented by John Noakes, Peter Purves, Janet Ellis, Simon Groom and Lesley Judd as well as many others?
24. *Pebbles And Bam Bam* was a spin-off from which other cartoon series?
25. Which former *Minder* played *Just William*?
26. The Fat Controller, Gordon, Bertie the Bus are all characters in which series?
27. Tucker, Zammo, Stu Pot and Roly all went to which school?
28. Musky and Vince were pals of which law-enforcing cartoon dog?
29. Who was Shari Lewis' famous puppet?
30. ITV's 80s kid's interest program was named after which acquisitive bird?

ANSWERS **Drama 2 (see Quiz 14)**

1. Frank Marker. 2. Terry McCann. 3. Fred Dryer. 4. *Elizabeth R.* 5. *The Fall Guy*. 6. Starsky.
7. *Murder She Wrote.* 8. Michael Elphick. 9. Patrick McGoohan. 10. Diana Rigg. 11. *Tenko.*
12. Barrister. 13. Ian McShane. 14. *Heartbeat*. 15. Sarah Lancashire. 16. *Prisoner Cell Block H.*
17. Pauline Quirke. 18. *The Untouchables*. 19. *ER* . 20. *Casualty*. 21. *Upstairs and Downstairs.*
22. Susannah Harker. 23. *Soldier Soldier*. 24. Alan Davies. 25. Edward Woodward. 26. Craig
McClachlan. 27. Robert Wagner. 28. *The Professionals* . 29. Don Johnson. 30. Cagney.

Answers: see Quiz 13, page 21

1. Which character was the *Public Eye*?
2. Who was Arthur Dailey's first minder?
3. Who was *Hunter*?
4. What was Glenda Jackson's royal role?
5. Which series featured Colt Seevers?
6. Which TV cop is played by Paul Michael Glaser?
7. Which mystery series stars Angela Lansbury?
8. Who played *Boon*?
9. Who was *The Prisoner*?
10. Who played Mrs Peel in *The Avengers*?
11. Which series featured women in a Japanese prison camp?
12. What was Horace Rumpole's profession?
13. Who plays *Lovejoy*?
14. Which series starred Nick Berry as a policeman?
15. Which ex-*Coronation Street* star appeared in *Where the Heart Is*?
16. What is the Australian series about a women's detention centre?
17. Who played *The Sculptress*?
18. In which series was the character Elliot Ness?
19. In which series are Peter Benton and Carol Hathaway?
20. Which series features Baz, Megan and Charlie?
21. Which drama series, set in the Edwardian era, featured the wealthy Bellamy family?
22. Which actress links *House of Cards* to *Ultraviolet*?
23. In which series did Robson and Jerome first appear together?
24. Who plays Jonathan Creek?
25. Who starred as *The Equaliser*?
26. Which ex-*Neighbours* actor starred in *Bugs*?
27. Who played Jonathan in *Hart To Hart*?
28. Who were Bodie and Doyle?
29. Who played Crockett in *Miami Vice*?
30. In *Cagney and Lacey* who was the sergeant?

Comedy 3

Answers: see Quiz 16, page 24

LEVEL I

1. Which series featured Blanche Deveraux?
2. In which series is the character Baldrick?
3. Who is Harry Enfield's writing partner on *Harry Enfield and Chums*?
4. In which series are Julia Sawalha and June Whitfield related?
5. Which characters were *Just Good Friends*?
6. What was Mrs Boswell's christian name in *Bread*?
7. Who played *The New Statesman*?
8. Which comedy series featured Ted Bovis?
9. Who played Sir Humphrey in *Yes, Minister*?
10. Where does BooBoo live?
11. Who is the female star of *Game On*?
12. What is Agent Smart's christian name in *Get Smart*?
13. Who plays Jeannie in *I Dream Of Jeannie*?
14. Who is Barbara's husband in *The Good Life*?
15. What is Tim Taylor's programme in *Home Improvements*?
16. Who was Lucy in *I Love Lucy*?
17. From which country does *Kids In The Hall* originate?
18. What was Alan Alda's role in *M*A*S*H*?
19. Which comedy series featured the Dead Parrot Sketch?
20. Which strange family had a niece named Marilyn?
21. To which family is Lurch the butler?
22. In which country is *'Allo, 'Allo* set?
23. Which sitcom features Bill and Ben Porter?
24. Who played Edmund Blackadder?
25. Who is *Caroline In The City*?
26. Who plays Sam Malone in *Cheers*?
27. Which sitcom is about catholic clergy on remote Craggy Island?
28. Which TV series was the forerunner of *The Naked Gun* films?
29. What is *Frasier's* profession?
30. Who is the star of *The Fresh Prince Of Bel Air*?

Pot Luck 5 (see Quiz 16)

1. Joan Bakewell. 2. They were both *Cheers* bartenders. 3. Farmer Barleymo. 4. He was run over by a tram. 5. Jimmy Smits. 6. Doctors. 7. *Murder One*. 8. Kathryn. 9. James Martinez. 10. BBC 2. 11. Albert Hall. 12. Woodentop. 13. Roland Rat. 14. *The Air Show*. 15. *You've Been Framed*. 16. Hawaii. 17. Maureen Holdsworth. 18. *Knight Rider*. 19. *Murder She Wrote*. 20. Ted Danson. 21. James Garner. 22. Hillsborough. 23. Grizzley. 24. Tony Stamp. 25. John Le Carre. 26. *Alias Smith and Jones*. 27. Greengrass. 28. Dervla Kirwan. 29. Neely Capshaw. 30. *L.A. Law*.

ANSWERS

Answers: see Quiz 15, page 23

LEVEL 1

1. Who presented *Heart of The Matter* and *Late Night Line-up*?
2. What did Coach and Woody have in common?
3. What was the farmer's name in *Bod*?
4. How did Alan Bradley die in *Coronation Street*?
5. Who played Victor Sifuentes in *LA .Law*?
6. What profession do the characters Mark Greene and Kerry Weaver follow?
7. Which series featured the lawyer Theodore Hoffman?
8. What is Captain Janeway's christian name in *Voyager*?
9. Who is Greg Medavoy's partner in *NYPD Blue*?
10. Which channel shows *The Sky At Night*?
11. Where is *The Last Night Of The Proms* broadcast from?
12. What was the original title for *The Bill*?
13. Which rodent was the star of *Good Morning Britain*?
14. Which BBC2 series features aviation topics?
15. What is the series featuring viewers' amusing home video clips?
16. Where was *Magnum P. I.* set?
17. Who was Maude Grimes' daughter in *Coronation Street*?
18. Which series starred a black Pontiac TransAm as a hero?
19. Which series featured the character Jessica Fletcher?
20. Who was the star of *Gullivers Travels*?
21. Who played Woodrow in *Streets of Laredo*?
22. What was the name of the drama documentary about a football stadium disaster?
23. What was the nickname of mountain man James Adams?
24. Which character does Graham Cole portray in *The Bill*?
25. Who was the author of *Tinker Taylor Soldier Spy*?
26. Which series featured the character Hannibal Hayes?
27. Who in *Heartbeat* had a dog named Alfred?
28. Who played Assumpta Fitzgerald in *Ballykissangel*?
29. What is Geena Lee Nolin's character in *Baywatch*?
30. Which series starred Susan Dey as Grace Van Owen?

ANSWERS

Comedy 3 (see Quiz 15)
1. *The Golden Girls.* 2. *Blackadder.* 3. Paul Whitehouse. 4. *Absolutely Fabulous.* 5. Vince and Penny.
6. Nellie. 7. Rik Mayall. 8. *Hi De Hi!* 9. Nigel Hawthorne. 10. Jellystone Park. 11. Samantha Janus.
12. Maxwell. 13. Barbara Eden. 14. Tom Good. 15. *Tooltime.* 16. Lucille Ball. 17. Canada.
18. Hawkeye Pierce. 19. *Monty Python's Flying Circus.* 20. The Munsters. 21. The Addams Family.
22. France. 23. *2 Point 4 Children.* 24. Rowan Atkinson. 25. Lea Thompson. 26. Ted Danson.
27. *Father Ted.* 28. *Police Squad.* 29. A psychiatrist. 30. Will Smith.

QUIZ 17 Soaps 2

Answers: see Quiz 18, page 26

1. Who was Bobby Ewing's first wife in *Dallas*?
2. What was Tom Howard's business in *Howards Way*?
3. Who is Toyah's sister in *Coronation Street*?
4. Who is Ricky Butcher's wife in *Eastenders*?
5. In *Neighbours*, whose daughter was Julie Martin?
6. Who is Ailsa's husband in *Home And Away*?
7. Which pub did Alan Turner run in *Emmerdale*?
8. Which TV writer created *Brookside*?
9. In which Western state of the USA is *Knots Landing* set?
10. Which 60's US soap starred Mia Farrow and Ryan O'Neal?
11. Who was famed for his allotment in *Eastenders*?
12. Which character did Michelle Gayle portray in *Eastenders*?
13. Who was Bet Gilroy's estranged husband in *Coronation Street*?
14. What is Susan Kennedy's occupation in *Neighbours*?
15. Who was Bobby Ewing's mother in *Dallas*?
16. Who is Jacqui's dad in *Brookside*?
17. Which character in *Coronation Street* was married to Samir Rashid?
18. Who owned The Meal Machine in *Eastenders*?
19. Which character does John James portray in *The Colbys*?
20. In which establishment was the office of Ozcabs in *Eastenders*?
21. Who in *Coronation Street* was Gail Platt's late husband?
22. Who is Michael Ross's wife in *Home And Away*?
23. Name Debbie Martin's younger sister in *Neighbours*.
24. Who is Pete Beale's sister in *Eastenders*?
25. Which Hartman did Kimberley Davies portray in *Neighbours*?
26. Who sold her baby to the Mallets in *Coronation Street*?
27. Who is Max's wife in *Brookside*?
28. Which BBC1 soap was created by Tony Holland and Julia Smith?
29. Which Sean owned the Bookmakers in Rosamund Street around the corner from *Coronation Street*?
30. In *Coronation Street*, where did Rita find her dead husband, Ted Sullivan?

ANSWERS

Sport I (see Quiz 18)

1. Boxing. 2. James Hunt. 3. Denis Compton. 4. *Superstars*. 5. Snooker. 6. Soccer. 7. *World of Sport*. 8. Ford. 9. Italy. 10. Darts. 11. Statto. 12. Keith Wolstenholme. 13. Sue Barker. 14. *Football Italia*. 15. Snooker. 16. A ski-jumper. 17. *American Gladiators*. 18. Greenwich. 19. The University Boat Race. 20. Aintree. 21. ITV. 22. Terry Wogan. 23. Brut. 24. The Summer Olympics. 25. Bob Wilson. 26. *Grandstand*. 27. Emlyn Hughes. 28. Ian St John and Jimmy Greaves. 29. Football. 30. Rory McGrath.

Answers: see Quiz 17, page 25

LEVEL I

1. On which sport was Reg Gutteridge a commentator?
2. Which late motor racing world champion commentated on Formula One?
3. Who was a footballer for Arsenal and a cricket player and commentator?
4. Which competition pitted champions of differing sports against each other?
5. For which sport is John Spencer a commentator?
6. For which sport is Barry Venison a pundit?
7. Which television sports programme was introduced by Dickie Davies?
8. Which company sponsored Monday Night Football on Sky TV in 1998?
9. From which country is Channel 4's Sunday football coverage?
10. For which sport is Eric Bristow renowned?
11. Who wears pyjamas on *Fantasy Football League*?
12. Who said, "They think it's all over – it is now" in 1966?
13. Who is the chairperson of *A Question Of Sport*?
14. On which sports programme does Joe Jordan appear?
15. What sport did Ted Lowe commentate on?
16. Who was Eddie The Eagle?
17. *Gladiators* was based on which US TV show?
18. In which park does the London Marathon start?
19. Which annual event features the crews of Oxford and Cambridge?
20. Where is The Grand National run?
21. Which channel took over Formula One coverage from BBC?
22. Who presents *Auntie's Sporting Bloomers*?
23. Henry Cooper advertised which aftershave?
24. Which multi-athletic event is screened in the summer every four years?
25. Which former Arsenal goalkeeper has presented football on both the BBC and ITV?
26. What is the name of the long running Saturday afternoon sports programme on BBC1?
27. Which former Liverpool football club captain was also captain on *Question of Sport*?
28. Who are *Saint and Greavsie*?
29. *The Manageress* was about a female manager in which sport?
30. Name Gary Lineker's hairy comic partner from *They Think It's All Over*.

Answers: see Quiz 20, page 28

LEVEL 1

1. What was the theme tune of *Minder*?
2. Which series of interviews was conducted by John Freeman?
3. What is the name of the holographic doctor in *Voyager*?
4. Which of the lads in *Auf Weidersehen Pet* came from Bristol?
5. In which series was the character Mrs Miggins?
6. On which show did Caron Keating stand in for Judy Finnegan?
7. Which series featured Howard Cunningham?
8. Which program featured Neil the hippy?
9. Who shared a theatre box with Statler in *The Muppet Show*?
10. Who conceived and starred in *The Nanny*?
11. Who does Christopher Ellison portray in *The Bill*?
12. Which character was first played by Loretta Swit in a pilot episode?
13. Who portrays Dr. Mark Greene in *ER*?
14. What was the name of Bruce Willis's character in *Moonlighting*?
15. Which series starred Barry Evans as an English teacher?
16. In which series was The Master an enemy?
17. What was Jack Duckworth's first job at The Rovers Return?
18. In which other bar in Walford did Lofty work apart from the Queen Vic?
19. Who was Doug's wife in *Neighbours*?
20. Which soap featured a special video episode entitled *The Lost Weekend*?
21. Who was Peter Cook's partner in *Not Only But Also*?
22. Who presented the *Trouble-shooter* series on TV?
23. Which game show has been presented by both Lily Savage and Les Dawson?
24. Which *Mrs* presents her own chat show?
25. Which cop show featured an Arsenal footballer in a 1998 Christmas special?
26. What TV drama series was based on the novels set in Cornwall by Winston Graham?
27. John Archer was killed by what?
28. Which delivery man had a cat named Jess?
29. Which character does Michael Starke portray in *Brookside*?
30. Which TV detective was created by R.D. Wingfield?

Crime 1 (see Quiz 20)

1. George Carter. 2. Hutch. 3. Sun Hill. 4. Morse. 5. William Shatner. 6. Miss Marple. 7. John Watt. 8. Cornwall. 9. D.I. Frost. 10. *Hill Street Blues*. 11. *The Cops*. 12. Raymond Burr. 13. Chuck Norris. 14. Mary Beth. 15. A Mountie. 16. Oscar Blaketon. 17. *Between The Lines*. 18. Andy. 19. California. 20. *Due South*. 21. Tubbs. 22. *Magnum P.I.* 23. A Boxer. 24. Adam Faith. 25. Hercule. 26. Wiggum. 27. Amanda Burton. 28. *Columbo*. 29. *Kojak*. 30. *Cracker*.

1. Who is Regan's sergeant in *The Sweeney*?
2. Who is Starsky's partner?
3. What is *The Bill's* local nick?
4. Which detective's patch is Oxford?
5. Who played *TJ Hooker*?
6. Who is Agatha Christie's foremost lady sleuth?
7. Who was Charlie Barlow's sergeant in *Z Cars*?
8. Where is *Wycliffe* set?
9. Which cop does David Jason play?
10. Which police series was set on the Hill?
11. Name the BBC's gritty police drama, launched in 1998.
12. Who played Perry Mason?
13. Who plays *Walker – Texas Ranger*?
14. What are Lacey's christian names in *Cagney and Lacey*?
15. What is Constable Benton Fraser?
16. Which character was Nick Rowan's sergeant in *Heartbeat*?
17. Which series featured Tony Clark and Harry Taylor?
18. What is Sipowicz's first name in *NYPD Blue*?
19. In which American state was *L.A. Law* located?
20. Which series featured Diefenbaker?
21. Who is Crockett's partner in *Miami Vice*?
22. Which series set in Hawaii stars Tom Selleck?
23. What was Terry's previous profession in *Minder*?
24. Who played *Budgie*?
25. What is Poirot's first name?
26. What is the name of the Police Chief in *The Simpsons*?
27. Who was the star of *Silent Witness*?
28. What was the name of Peter Falk's scruffy detective?
29. Whose first name was Theo?
30. In which series was there a female detective named Penhaligon?

Comedy 4

Answers: see Quiz 22, page 30

LEVEL 1

1. Who is *Ellen's* best friend?
2. Who did Shelley Long portray in *Cheers*?
3. Who played Brenda in *Baghdad Cafe*?
4. Whose daughters were Darlene and Becky?
5. Rose Marie and Morey Amsterdam starred in which comedy series?
6. What were the names of the two families in *Soap*?
7. Which character does Christopher Ryan play in *Bottom*?
8. Who is Connie Booth's character in *Fawlty Towers*?
9. What was Kim Hartman's character in *'Allo, 'Allo*?
10. By what name was Daisy Moses better known in *The Beverley Hillbillies*?
11. Who runs a catering business in *2 Point 4 Children*?
12. Who is Saffron's brother in *Absolutely Fabulous*?
13. Which hospital comedy starred Peter Bowles, James Bolam and Chrisopher Strauli?
14. What is *Chef* Lenny Henry's character first name?
15. Which sitcom was the song *My Little Horse* entered for a contest?
16. Who has a brother Niles?
17. Who plays Dave Lister in *Red Dwarf*?
18. In which show would you hear the catchphrase "suits you, sir"?
19. What rank is Ernie Bilko in *The Phil Silvers Show*?
20. Who was the star of *Police Squad*?
21. Who presents *Shooting Stars*?
22. *Threes Company* was the American version of which British sitcom?
23. Who plays Charlie in *Babes in The Wood*?
24. Who is Tim Taylor's assistant in *Tool Time*?
25. What is *Caroline in The City's* occupation?
26. Which two of the *Friends* were an item?
27. Which series features Martin and Mandy as tenants?
28. Whose neighbours are the Leadbetters?
29. Which 1960s series featured Ricky Ricardo?
30. Which series starred Larry Hagman and Barbara Eden?

QUIZ 22   Pot Luck 7

Answers: see Quiz 21, see page 29

LEVEL 1

1. Which song was a hit for Letitia Dean and Paul Medford?
2. On which sport was John Rickman a commentator?
3. Which screen hero was a thriller writer in *Department S*?
4. What was the subject of the children's programme *Lift-Off*?
5. Which Pam won *Opportunity Knocks* in the 1970s?
6. What is the name of BBC TV's listings magazine?
7. Who wrote the series *GBH*?
8. Which consumer programme was presented by Mike Brewer and Richard Sutton?
9. Who had a *Football Scrapbook* television programme?
10. Who was Uncle Arthur in *Dads Army*?
11. Which *Eastenders* character emigrated following an extra-marital affair?
12. Who gets killed in every *South Park* episode?
13. Who was Mike in *Only Fools And Horses*?
14. Which garden-revamping program stars Alan Titchmarsh?
15. On which game show did Anne Aston keep the scores?
16. Who do the magazine *Private Eye* refer to as Trevor Barbados?
17. In which country was *El Dorado* set?
18. Who played Vincent's father in *Beauty and The Beast*?
19. Who is Gomez & Morticia's super-hairy cousin in the *Addams Family*?
20. Which Renault advertising character frequently met her father in compromising situations?
21. Which series featured the character Young Mr. Grace?
22. Who is Eriq La Salle's character in *ER*?
23. Which game show is based on snooker?
24. Who is Andy's partner in *NYPD Blue*?
25. Which surreal US cop show only lasted one series in the early 1990s?
26. In which show were Una Stubbs and Lionel Blair team captains?
27. What animals are Ren and Stimpy?
28. Which actors had a hit with *Whispering Grass*?
29. What race is Dr Spock?
30. Which program is set in a Brixton barbers?

ANSWERS   Comedy 4 (see Quiz 21)

1. Paige Clark. 2. Diane Chambers. 3. Whoopi Goldberg. 4. *Roseanne*. 5. *The Dick Van Dyke Show*. 6. Tates & Campbells. 7. Dave Hedgehog. 8. Polly Sherman. 9. Helga. 10. Granny Clampett. 11. Bill Porter and Rona. 12. Serge. 13. *Only When I Laugh*. 14. Gareth. 15. *Father Ted*. 16. Frasier Crane. 17. Craig Charles. 18. *The Fast Show*. 19. Master Sergeant. 20. Leslie Neilson. 21 Vic Reeves & Bob Mortimer. 22. *Man About The House*. 23. Karl Howman. 24. Al. 25. Cartoonist. 26. Ross and Rachel. 27. *Game On*. 28. Tom and Barbara Good. 29. *I Love Lucy*. 30. *I Dream of Jeannie*.

Answers: see Quiz 24, page 32

LEVEL 1

1. Who presented *Models Close Up*?
2. Who presented *The Day The Universe Changed*?
3. Which programme was presented by Professor Robert Winston?
4. Who presented his *Postcard From Rio*?
5. Who presents *Countryfile*?
6. Which airline does Jeremy Spake work for in *Airport*?
7. On which channel was *Liberty! The American War Of Independence*?
8. Which documentary series starred Prince Edward?
9. Which hospital was featured in *Jimmy's*?
10. Which comedian completed a *World Tour Of Scotland*?
11. Who presented the opening programme on BBC Choice?
12. What is the first name of the presenter of *Portillo's Progress*?
13. What is the title of C4's Italian Football magazine?
14. What is Katie Derham's occupation?
15. Who presents *Cricket Monthly*?
16. Which sports show is presented by Danny Kelly?
17. Which C5 game show is hosted by Junior Simpson?
18. Who won the 1998 Eurovision Contest?
19. On which night is BBC2's *The Money Programme*?
20. On which programme is Oz Clarke a wine expert?
21. Which ex-England player presents *Football Focus*?
22. Who is Carol Barnes?
23. What does Sian Davies present?
24. *The People's Princess* was a tribute to whom?
25. Which current affairs programme is presented by Juliet Morris?
26. Which newsreader is Peter Snow's brother?
27. What is *Top Gear* presenter Willson's christian name?
28. On which day of the week was the World Cup Final 1998?
29. On which channel does Kirsty Young read the news?
30. Who co-presents *On The Ball* with Gabby Yorath?

ANSWERS

Drama 3 (see Quiz 24)

1. *Boys From The Blackstuff.* 2. Emma Thompson. 3. America. 4. A stunt man. 5. The police force. 6. Robbie Coltrane. 7. *Millennium*. 8. Lawyer. 9. Richard Chamberlain. 10. Larkin. 11. Peter Bowles. 12. *Reilly - Ace of Spies*. 13. Nerys Hughes. 14. John Thaw. 15. A novelist. 16. *The Singing Detective*. 17. The fire service. 18. A fashion house. 19. Lady Chatterley. 20. *Peak Practice*. 21. *Sharpe*. 22. Ben Elton. 23. *A year In Provence*. 24. *Cardiac Arrest*. 25. Charles Dickens. 26. George Eliot. 27. McGann. 28. Jane Austen. 29. Elizabeth I. 30. Shipping.

Answers: see Quiz 23, page 31

LEVEL 1

1. Alan Bleasdale wrote the script for the 80's series *"Boys From The…"* what?
2. TV and film actor Kenneth Branagh was married to which actress?
3. *Bonanza* was set in which country?
4. What dangerous occupation did *The Fall Guy* have?
5. In which public service did *Juliet Bravo* serve?
6. Who stars as *Cracker* in the UK?
7. Which programme featured a man who could see into the minds of criminals?
8. What was the profession of most of the characters in *This Life*?
9. Who starred as *Doctor Kildare*?
10. Pam Ferris and David Jason played Ma and Pa who in *Darling Buds Of May*?
11. Which Peter starred in *The Irish RM* and with Penelope Keith in *To The Manor Born*?
12. In the series name, Reilly was Ace of what?
13. Which former *Liver Bird* played *The District Nurse*?
14. Which actor connects *The Sweeney*, *Morse* and *Kavanagh*?
15. What was the profession of Mary Fisher in *The Life and Loves Of A She Devil*?
16. The mystery drama written by Dennis Potter was called *The Singing…* what?
17. *London's Burning* follows the drama in which emergency service?
18. What kind of house was *The House Of Elliot*?
19. Which Lady, based on DH Lawrence's classic, was first televised in 1993?
20. What kind of Practice stars Kevin Whately as a rural GP?
21. Sean Bean stars as which 19th century British officer?
22. Which *Man From Auntie* comedian wrote *Stark*?
23. In the BBC series, John Thaw and Lindsay Duncan spent how long in Provence?
24. The BBC 2 medical drama was called *Cardiac* what?
25. Who wrote the classic *Martin Chuzzlewit*, dramatised by the BBC in 1994?
26. Which Victorian female author wrote *Middlemarch*?
27. Which family of four brothers starred in the historical drama, *The Hanging Gale*, set in 19th century Ireland?
28. The 1995 drama series *Pride And Prejudice*, was based on whose novel?
29. The MP Glenda Jackson starred on TV as which female British monarch?
30. What kind of transportation featured in *The Onedin Line*?

Answers: see Quiz 26, page 34
LEVEL 1

1. What was Frank Furillo's ex-wife's name in *Hill Street Blues*?
2. On which channel is *News at Ten*?
3. Which series features Denzil and Trigger?
4. Which title by Jules Verne was re-enacted by Michael Palin?
5. Which show featured Animal and Gonzo?
6. Who is in charge of the 15th squad of detectives in *NYPD Blue*?
7. Which programme featured the character Deep Throat?
8. What was Rebecca's surname in *Cheers*?
9. Which soap featured Malcolm McDowell in a guest role?
10. Who played Michael Murray in *GBH*?
11. Which Ray presents his World of Survival on BBC2?
12. Who played Laura in *The Dick Van Dyke Show*?
13. Who is Bart Simpson's oldest sister?
14. Which character did Joan Collins play in *Dynasty*?
15. Who first played *Robin of Sherwood*?
16. Who was Tom Howard's wife in *Howard's Way*?
17. Who was Barry Grant's mother in *Brookside*?
18. On which programme did Statto and Jeff Astle appear?
19. What was the name of the quiz where the guests sat in boxes?
20. Which Radio 4 'peoples' show does John Peel introduce?
21. In *Jonathon Creek* where does Jonathon live?
22. What are Lancelot, Guinevere and Arthur?
23. Who recorded *Anyone Can Fall In Love*?
24. Which show features video clips sent in by members of the public?
25. What is the pub in *Neighbours*?
26. Who wrote *Butterflies*?
27. What does Gary Imlach introduce?
28. Who was Callan's informer?
29. What was the policeman's name in *'Allo, 'Allo*?
30. Who presented *Stars on Sunday*?

QUIZ 26 Comedy 5

Answers: see Quiz 25, page 33

LEVEL 1

1. Which series featured Col. Blake and Major Burns?
2. Who plays Gary in *Men Behaving Badly*?
3. In which series did Tony Randall play Felix Unger?
4. Who is David Jason's character in *Only Fools and Horses*?
5. Who had a sister named Brenda Morgenstern?
6. Who was the ...*Teenage Witch*?
7. Who were *The Two Ronnies*?
8. Who was George Roper's wife in *Man About The House*?
9. Who is playwright Jack Rosenthal's wife?
10. In which series did Eamonn Walker play Winston the home help?
11. Whose neighbours are Pippa and Patrick?
12. Which character in *Absolutely Fabulous* is a fashion magazine executive?
13. Who was the accident prone deputy manager of Whitbury Leisure Centre?
14. Who played the president of the U.S.A. in *Whoops Apocalypse*?
15. What was the sequel to *No Honestly* featuring Lisa Goddard?
16. Where was Dawn French the vicar of?
17. Which comedian and star of Jolson played an ex-con in *Time After Time*?
18. Which *Doctor Who* appeared in *The Two Of Us*?
19. Which sitcom starred Nicola MacAuliffe and Duncan Preston as surgeons?
20. Who was Julian in *Terry and Julian*?
21. What was the sitcom starring Judy Loe and Roger Rees set around a singles bar?
22. Who played the butler in *Two's Company*?
23. *Home James* was a spin off from which sitcom starring Jim Davidson?
24. Who played Clarence the short sighted removal man?
25. Which series was a sequel to *The Growing Pains of P.C. Penrose*?
26. Which American actress starred in *Shirley's World*?
27. Which sequel to *Are You Being Served* was set in a large country house?
28. Which *Steptoe and Son* actor's last series was *Grundy*?
29. What was the sequel to *Happy Ever After* starring June Whitfield and Terry Scott?
30. Which character in *Red Dwarf* was played by both Norman Lovett and Hattie Hayridge?

ANSWERS

Pot Luck 8 (see Quiz 25)

1. Fay. 2. ITV. 3. *Only Fools And Horses*. 4. *Around The World In 80 Days*. 5. *The Muppet Show*. 6. Lt. Fancy. 7. *The X-Files*. 8. Howe. 9. *Crossroads*. 10. Robert Lindsay. 11. Mears. 12. Mary Tyler Moore. 13. Lisa. 14. Alexis. 15. Michael Praed. 16. Jan. 17. Sheila. 18. *Fantasy Football League*. 19. *Celebrity Squares*. 20. *Home Truths*. 21. In a windmill. 22. Lottery draw machines. 23. Anita Dobson. 24. *You've Been Framed*. 25. The Waterhole. 26. Carla Lane. 27. American Football. 28. Lonely. 29. Officer Crabtree. 30. Jess Yates.

Answers: see Quiz 28, page 36 LEVEL 1

1. Which family live at No. 10 Brookside Close?
2. What was the surname of Alexis's third husband, Dex, in Dynasty?
3. Who was Pam and Bobby Ewing's son?
4. Who told her husband in Eastenders she was dying in an attempt to stop him from leaving her?
5. What had been the occupation of Betty Turpin's husband in Coronation Street?
6. In Soap who preceded Saunders as the Tate's butler?
7. Which character in The Colbys was played by Charlton Heston?
8. What was the name of Dot Cotton's husband?
9. Who is Ricky's boss at the Arches in Eastenders?
10. In Neighbours who was Daphne's husband?
11. Where in Emmerdale is The Woolpack located?
12. Who in Eastenders had two sons, David and Simon?
13. Who was Danni and Brett's mother in Neighbours?
14. In Coronation Street which of Liz McDonald's sons has been in prison?
15. Who owns a hairdressers in Brookside?
16. What was the name of Joe Mangel's son in Neighbours?
17. Who is Roy's son in Eastenders?
18. Which Channel 4 soap shows a map of Chester in its opening credits?
19. Who was Jim Robinson's entrepreneurial mother-in-law in Neighbours?
20. Which character in Dallas was portrayed by Priscilla Presley?
21. Which character did pop star Peter Noone play in Coronation Street?
22. What was Punk Mary's surname in Eastenders?
23. What was Don Brennan's trade in Coronation Street?
24. What was the name of Mavis Riley's budgie in Coronation Street?
25. Whose mother's name was Mo in Eastenders?
26. Which character does Brooke Satchwell play in Neighbours?
27. Who is Mark's wife in Eastenders?
28. Which character does Judy Nunn portray in Home And Away?
29. Who did Sarah Beaumont have an adulterous affair with in Neighbours?
30. Who is butcher Fred Elliot's nephew in Coronation Street?

Pot Luck 9 (see Quiz 29)
1. Ena. 2. Alan. 3. The Sullivans. 4. Paul Henry. 5. Sylvia Costas. 6. Anita Harris. 7. Bless This House. 8. Local Heroes. 9. Michael Newman. 10. Arnie Thomas. 11 Weather presenters. 12. Camelot. 13. 625. 14. Astra. 15. Esther Rantzen. 16. Les Dawson. 17. Kermit the Frog. 18. Five 19. A chat show host. 20. Oprah. 21. Basil Brush. 22. Magpie. 23. Derek Nimmo. 24. Wilma. 25. Gordon Kaye. 26. Barcelona. 27. Mel Smith. 28. Mrs. Slocombe. 29. Peter Sellers. 30. Wilson.

Answers: see Quiz 27, page 35

LEVEL I

1. What was Mrs Sharples' christian name in *Coronation Street*?
2. What was the first name of interviewer and presenter Whicker?
3. What was the first Australian soap shown in the U.K.?
4. Who recorded *Benny's Theme*?
5. Who is Andy Sipowicz married to in *NYPD Blue*?
6. Who starred in *Anita In Jumbleland*?
7. In which series did Robin Stewart play Sally Geeson's brother?
8. Which series is presented by Adam Hart-Davis?
9. Which character on *Baywatch* plays himself?
10. What was Tom Arnold's character in *Roseanne*?
11. What are Suzanne Charlton and John Kettley?
12. Who runs *The National Lottery*?
13. How many lines are transmitted in terrestrial television?
14. What satellites beam BSkyB programmes?
15. Who presented *That's Life*?
16. Who appeared with Roy Barraclough as Cissie and Ada?
17. Which Muppet is adored by Miss Piggy?
18. How many channels are available on analogue terrestrial television?
19. What is David Letterman?
20. What is chat show host Ms Winfrey's first name?
21. Which fox is a puppet?
22. Which programme did Mick Robertson and Douglas Rae present?
23. Who played Noote in *All Gas And Gaiters*?
24. Who is Fred Flintstone's wife?
25. Who plays Rene Artois in *'Allo, 'Allo*?
26. Where does Manuel come from in *Fawlty Towers*?
27. Who is Griff Rhys-Jones's comedy partner?
28. Who was worried about her pussy in *Are you Being Served*?
29. Which of *The Goons* was an international film star?
30. Which character is a sergeant in *Dad's Army*?

Soaps 3 (see Quiz 27)
1. The Corkhills. 2. Dexter. 3. Christopher. 4. Angie Watts. 5. A police sergeant. 6. Benson. 7. Jason Colby. 8. Charlie. 9. Phil Mitchell. 10. Des Clarke. 11. Beckindale. 12. Pat Wicks. 13. Cheryl Stark. 14. Steve. 15. Jacqui Dixon. 16. Toby. 17. Barry Evans. 18. *Hollyoaks*. 19. Helen Daniels. 20. Jenna Wade. 21. Stanley Fairclough. 22. Smith. 23. Taxi driver. 24. Harriet. 25. Frank Butcher. 26. Anne Wilkinson. 27. Ruth Fowler. 28. Ailsa. 29. Karl Kennedy. 30. Ashley Peacock.

Answers: see Quiz 30, page 38   LEVEL I

1. Which series often featured Man At Arms and his daughter Teela?
2. Which *Dr Who* became *Worzel Gummidge*?
3. Former *Blue Peter* presenter Caron Keating is the daughter of which Irish-born female TV host?
4. How many days each week was *Play School* broadcast?
5. On which day did *Tiswas* appear?
6. On which channel was the *Multi-coloured Swap Shop*?
7. What colour was the *Pink Panther*'s sports car?
8. What colour are the *Smurfs*?
9. What was unusual about Clarence the lion in *Daktari*?
10. What kind of locomotive was Thomas?
11. How many *Teletubbies* are there?
12. Who played the *Knight Rider*?
13. Who is the female presenter of The *Gladiators*?
14. What was James T. Kirk?
15. In which series did the mute woman Marina appear?
16. Who said "time for bed"?
17. Which children's series featured Ant and Dec?
18. Who was *Grange Hill*'s headmistress?
19. Which cartoon series featured Fred and Barney?
20. Which series features a Christmas Appeal?
21. How was *Top Cat* known to his close friends?
22. Which cartoon series features a Great Dane?
23. Which Polish programme, shown on Channel 4, featured Toyah Wilcox and Nigel Kennedy narrating the English version, and a wooden main character?
24. What was *Ace Ventura*?
25. Who lives in Jellystone Park?
26. What was Flipper?
27. Who played *Batman* in the 1960s TV series?
28. Which postman had a black and white cat?
29. Who in *Thunderbirds* owned a pink Rolls Royce?
30. In *Grange Hill* what was Stebson's nickname?

Answers: see Quiz 29, page 37

LEVEL 1

1. On which day is *Football Focus* broadcast?
2. Willy Carson was a *Question Of Sport* captain, true or false?
3. Which duo present *Fantasy Football League*?
4. On which night did Jimmy Hill first present *Match of the Day*?
5. Peter Aliss commentates on which sport?
6. Ian Botham was a captain on which TV sports quiz?
7. Which British motor racing champion was BBC Sports Personality of the Year in 1994?
8. Which former England captain presents rugby on ITV?
9. At what time is Sky's *Sports Centre* normally broadcast?
10. Who retired as host of *A Question Of Sport* in 1997?
11. *They Think It's All Over* is presented by who?
12. Which female champion swimmer was a Gladiator?
13. Fatima Whitbread was televised winning Olympic gold in which athletic discipline?
14. Which sport does Brendan Foster commentate on?
15. Desmond who presents sport on BBC?
16. Which boxer became BBC Sports Personality Of The Year in 1970?
17. Dan Maskell commentated on which sport?
18. On what day was *Match Of The Day Extra* broadcast?
19. Which Steve presents *Grandstand*?
20. Mark Lawrenson and Trevor Brooking are regulars on which football show?
21. Which late night series shows highlights of Nation-wide Football league matches?
22. On Channel 4 which impressionist, Alistair, hosted his *Football Backchat*?
23. Which channel hosts *Sports Review Of The Year*?
24. Ex-footballer Jeff Astle sings on which show hosted by Skinner and Baddiel?
25. Ski Sunday is broadcast on which channel?
26. Which channel broadcasts *Football Italia*?
27. With what form of transport is the Tour de France contested?
28. How many contestants are there in each episode of *Gladiators*?
29. Frank Bough hosted which Saturday afternoon sports programme?
30. Which BBC football presenter played for Leicester City and Tottenham Hotspur?

Answers: see Quiz 32, page 40

LEVEL 1

1. Who was the star of *Further Up Pompeii*?
2. Who is Rowan Atkinson's hapless silent character?
3. Which *Heartbeat* actor was *The Gaffer*?
4. Which spin off from *Man About The House* featured Brian Murphy and Yootha Joyce?
5. From which sitcom was *Going Straight* the sequel?
6. A sequel to *Last of The Summer Wine* featured the characters in their younger days. What was its title?
7. Who starred with Julia Mackenzie, as her husband, in *French Fields*?
8. In which county was Arkwright's corner shop?
9. Who played Tony Britton's son in *Don't Wait Up*?
10. What was the UK's first dedicated (non-terrestrial) comedy channel?
11. A pilot show entitled *Prisoner and Escort* became which sitcom?
12. The credits of which sitcom feature a tortoise?
13. Where did the Boswells live?
14. What was the series featuring Nicholas Lyndhurst and Clive Francis as inept spies?
15. Who wrote and sang the theme for *No Honestly*?
16. The nautical TV series *HMS Paradise* was based on which comedy radio show?
17. In which series did John Gordon Sinclair play a journalist?
18. Which sitcom featured Nellie and Eli Pledge?
19. What was the sequel to *The Likely Lads*?
20. What was the sitcom about servants and masters written by Jimmy Perry and David Croft?
21. Which Russ ran his *Madhouse* on TV?
22. Who starred as *Blackadder*'s sidekick Baldrick?
23. Which comic presents *In Bed With MeDinner*?
24. Who is Sid Little's comedy partner?
25. What are the first names of Fry and Laurie?
26. The painter and decorator Jacko appeared in which comedy series?
27. Which comedy's theme tune began with the words "I'm H-A-P-P-Y"?
28. In which town is *Fawlty Towers* set?
29. Which former Goon presented the religious programme *Highway*?
30. In *Only Fools And Horses* Del Boy's van had how many wheels?

Answers: see Quiz 31, page 39

LEVEL I

1. What was the name of *Frasier's* wife?
2. Who was Ellie Mae's pa in *The Beverley Hillbillies*?
3. Who did Karl Howman play in *Brushstrokes*?
4. What is the clown's name in *The Simpsons*?
5. What type of programme was *Dungeons & Dragons*?
6. Who is the headmaster in *Home and Away*?
7. Who is Madge's husband in *Neighbours*?
8. Which green duck is a puppet?
9. What is Superman's earthly name?
10. Who is Sooty's female friend?
11. Which private detective was portrayed by Buddy Ebsen?
12. Which character had three sons, Adam, Hoss and Little Joe?
13. Which *Doctor Who* starred in the very first *Carry On* film?
14. Which sattelite channel is famous for re-running old programmes?
15. What was *The Fugitive's* profession?
16. Who did James Arness portray in *Gunsmoke*?
17. Who played Jonathan in *Highway To Heaven*?
18. Who played Paladin in *Have Gun Will Travel*?
19. Which post did Michael Hayes hold?
20. Which character was the D.J. in *Midnight Caller*?
21. Who created *Neighbours*?
22. Which James was 'in the pits' for ITV's Formula One coverage in 1998?
23. Who was the first British winner of *The World's Strongest Man*?
24. What was *Catweazle*?
25. Who played Jack in *On The Buses*?
26. On which show would you hear the catchphrase "Cheque, please"?
27. In which series is the character Dave Hedgehog?
28. Who played Booker in *Roseanne*?
29. Who in *Drop The Dead Donkey* is Henry's co-presenter?
30. Which landlady, in *Coronation Street*, was mugged on her way home from The Rovers Return?

Answers: see Quiz 34, page 42
LEVEL I

1. In which south-western county was the 1970s series *Poldark* set?
2. What kind of bouquet featured Frank Finlay and Susan Penhaligon amidst family tensions in the 1970s?
3. Gemma Jones starred as *The Duchess* of which street on the BBC?
4. Richard O'Sullivan played which infamous 18th century highwayman in the 1980s ITV series?
5. Gordon Jackson was a butler in which 1970s series about an Edwardian family?
6. Robson and Jerome starred together in which ITV series about the army?
7. Pamela Anderson starred in which series about a beach lifeguard unit?
8. What does *ER* stand for?
9. In which drama series did Clive Russell play Archie, one of the rig crew?
10. Who played Dr. Claire Maitland in *Cardiac Arrest*?
11. Which medical emergency team were stationed at Cooper's Crossing, Australia?
12. Which star of *Tenko* appeared in *Waiting For God*?
13. In which series is the fictional village Aidensfield?
14. Which policeman in *The Bill* ran down and killed a pedestrian?
15. Which drama series featured the character Recall?
16. Anton Rodgers plays vet Noah Kirby in which series?
17. Who played Ma Larkin in *The Darling Buds Of May*?
18. What was the spin off series from *Beverley Hills 90210*?
19. In which country was the drama series *Amongst Women* set?
20. Which drama series features Glen Murphy as George?
21. Who played Cecil Rhodes in BBC's *Rhodes*?
22. Which actor was *The Chancer*?
23. In which series did Jack Davenport portray lawyer Miles?
24. In which series is Jake Henshaw a vet?
25. In which swashbuckling series did Pete Postlethwaite play Obadiah Hatesworth?
26. Who played Owen Springer in *Reckless*?
27. Which series features Dana and Fox?
28. Which Leslie Charteris character was portrayed by Ian Ogilvy?
29. Which spy series starred Ray Lonnen and Roy Marsden?
30. Which series starred Bill Cosby as a criminologist?

Answers: see Quiz 33, page 41

LEVEL I

1. Who had flying ducks on her wall in *Coronation Street*?
2. What was the name of Frank Butcher's eldest daughter in *Eastenders*?
3. In which soap did Joanna Lumley play Eileen Perkins?
4. Which family runs the Italian restaurant in *Eastenders*?
5. Who is Anne and Lance's mother in *Neighbours*?
6. Who is Sarah Louise's mother in *Coronation Street*?
7. In *Coronation Street* which bar did Minnie, Martha and Ena frequent in The Rovers Return?
8. Who was Pete Beale's brother in *Eastenders*?
9. Who in *Dynasty* had a son 'Little Blake'?
10. Which Ena was the caretaker at the Glad Tidings Mission in *Coronation Street*?
11. What is the name of Emily Nugent's nephew who stood for the Wetherfield council?
12. Which 1930's US family included Jim Bob and Olivia?
13. In *Neighbours*, what was the name of Kerry Bishop's daughter?
14. Which business was the main concern of the Ewings of *Dallas*?
15. Who is Zoe's brother in *Emmerdale*?
16. What is Jacqui Corkhill's husband's name in *Brookside*?
17. Who is Grant Mitchell's wife in *Eastenders*?
18. Which character does Barbara Knox portray in *Coronation Street*?
19. In which mountains of Virginia was Walton's Mountain?
20. In which two soaps has David Easter appeared?
21. In which decade was *Neighbours* first shown in the U.K.?
22. Which Dot was the laundrette manageress in *Eastenders*?
23. Which two writers, Hazel and Peter, created *Crossroads*?
24. In *Eastenders*, who did Den Watts meet while in Venice with Angie?
25. In *Soap* what was the name of Mary Campbell's gay son?
26. Percy who established a Neighbourhood Watch Scheme in *Coronation Street*?
27. Which *Coronation Street* taxi driver did Ivy Tilsley marry in 1988?
28. In *Coronation Street* who ran a haberdashery emporium in Rosamund Street?
29. In which Channel 4 soap did the Finnegans try to take over a night club?
30. Who owned a budgie called Randy in the *Coronation Street*?

Drama 4 (see Quiz 33)
1. Cornwall. 2. *A Bouquet Of Barbed Wire*. 3. *The Duchess of Duke Street*. 4. *Dick Turpin*. 5. *Upstairs, Downstairs*. 6. *Soldier, Soldier*. 7. *Baywatch*. 8. *Emergency Room*. 9. *Roughnecks*. 10. Helen Baxendale. 11. *The Flying Doctors*. 12. Stephanie Cole. 13. *Heartbeat*. 14. PC Tony Stamp. 15. *London's Burning*. 16. *Noah's Ark*. 17. Pam Ferris. 18. *Melrose Place*. 19. Ireland. 20. *London's Burning*. 21. Martin Shaw. 22. Clive Owen. 23. *This Life*. 24. *Noah's Ark*. 25. *Sharpe*. 26. Robson Green. 27. *The X-Files*. 28. *The Saint*. 29. *The Sandbaggers*. 30. *The Cosby Mysteries*.

Answers: see Quiz 36, page 44

LEVEL I

1. Which S.F. series featured Sam Beckett?
2. Which series centred around the doctors of St. Elygius Hospital, Boston?
3. Who co-starred with Michael Douglas in *The Streets Of San Francisco*?
4. Which series starred Robert Carlyle as a Scottish policeman?
5. Which crime series of the sixties featured tales of the 65th Precinct of New York?
6. Who plays *Quincy*?
7. What kind of programme was *Mary Hartman, Mary Hartman*?
8. Who played Kid Curry in *Alias Smith and Jones*?
9. Which series featured the character Father Peter Clifford?
10. Who portrays Lois Lane in *The New Adventures of Superman*?
11. Which series featured the IMF team?
12. Which series centred around the inhabitants of Cicely, Alaska?
13. Which character did Judi Trott portray in *Robin Of Sherwood*?
14. Which ex-baseball star ran the *Cheers* bar?
15. Which series featured Tim Healy, Kevin Whately and Jimmy Nail as site workers in Germany?
16. Which series featured Rob and Laura Petrie?
17. Who was Samantha's husband in *Bewitched*?
18. Where is Frasier's radio station?
19. How many sons does Rab C Nesbit have?
20. Which of the *Golden Girls* was a southern belle?
21. Who is Dorothy's boyfriend in *Men Behaving Badly*?
22. Who is *Father Ted*'s housekeeper?
23. Who starred as *Murphy Brown*?
24. What was Ron Howard's character in *Happy Days*?
25. Who is the creator of *ER*?
26. Who lived at Nelson Mandela House, Peckham?
27. Who is Tony Hill's sister in *Eastenders*?
28. Which soap is set in Weatherfield?
29. In which series did Erika Eleniak play a lifeguard?
30. Which series of interviews was introduced by John Freeman?

Answers: see Quiz 35, page 43

LEVEL I

1. Football commentator Trevor Brooking spent his playing career with which club?
2. Commentator Nigel Starmer-Smith is associated with which sport?
3. Julian Wilson, Richard Pitman, Peter Scudamore are associated with which sport?
4. Hamilton Bland commentates on which sport?
5. David Vine presented which Winter sports programme on BBC2?
6. *Football Italia* is broadcast on which afternoon?
7. Which Manchester United and Wales footballer provided tips on soccer skills on Channel 4?
8. Which Yorkshireman Geoff played and commentated on cricket?
9. On which channel is *The Big Match* broadcast?
10. Tony Lewis introduces coverage of what?
11. What nationality is sports presenter Hazel Irvine?
12. *My Granny Could've Done Better* documents the history of which football cup?
13. Which Channel 5 sports quiz, with a cliché for a title, is hosted by Jeremy Nicholas?
14. Rugby Union star Jeremy Guscott co-presents which ITV physical challenge series?
15. For what sporting event did the BBC use the theme *Tokyo Melody* in 1964?
16. What was Alan Weeks a specialist commentator on?
17. Which event did Eddie The Eagle compete in during the Winter Olympics?
18. In 1998, from where was the final test match for cricket televised?
19. What sport is Bill McLaren a commentator on?
20. Which Media Tycoon's company made a bid £635 million for Manchester United?
21. Which channel broadcasts Women's NBA?
22. Who introduces live Premiership football?
23. Which cricket commentator was sacked in 1998?
24. Does *No Balls Allowed* ever feature football?
25. Which is the only terrestrial channel *not* to broadcast live football?
26. Who introduces ITV's Champions League coverage?
27. Who contested the 1998 FA Cup final?
28. In which sport do teams contest the Superbowl?
29. Does Michael Owen host his own show?
30. Which channel broadcasts *Eurogoals*?

1. What were the surnames of the famous comedy duo Eric and Ernie?
2. Frank Windsor starred as a sergeant in which army comedy series?
3. *The Fall And Rise...* of whom did we see on TV?
4. Which actress starred as the main character in *After Henry*?
5. The comedy *Bread* was set in which city?
6. Which Sid, of *Carry On* fame, starred in *Bless This House*?
7. What does Hank Hill sell in *King of the Hill*?
8. In *Fawlty Towers*, he was from Barcelona. Who was the character?
9. Maureen Lipman starred in which sitcom about an agony aunt?
10. Whose characters include an offensive drunk and a pathetic chat-show host?
11. Dudley Moore was one half of a famous comedy duo. Who was the other half?
12. Who starred in *Alas Smith And Jones*?
13. Richard Gordon wrote *Doctor In The ... what*?
14. Whose catchphrase was "Oooh, no Mrs!"?
15. Which comedian and comic writer starred in Sykes alongside Hattie Jacques?
16. Which comedian sang about *Ernie, The Fastest Milkman In The West*?
17. *I Love Lucy* starred American comedienne Lucille who?
18. Warren Mitchell stars as which grumpy pensioner in *In Sickness And In Health*?
19. What do the following have in common: Jimmy Tarbuck, Lilly Savage, Ken Dodd and Stan Boardman?
20. Which 1980s BBC comedy was set in a holiday camp?
21. Granddad, Uncle Albert, Boysee and Trigger all appeared in which classic BBC series?
22. Which Paul is the creator of *The Fast Show*?
23. Who played Captain Mainwaring in *Dad's Army*?
24. Which of Fry and Laurie appeared as the Prince in *Blackadder the Third*?
25. Richard briers and Felicity Kendall lived what kind of life according to the title of their self-sufficient comedy?
26. Who hosts *Tibs And Fibs*?
27. In which comedy did the female agent warn Rene "I will say this only once"?
28. What are the Christian names of the comic duo *Wood and Walters*?
29. The comedy *Surgical Spirit* was set in what kind of building?
30. What is the setting for *Drop The Dead Donkey*?

Answers: see Quiz 37, page 45

LEVEL I

1. Which series was described as a story about six terraced houses, a shop and a pub?
2. On which sport was John Rickman a pundit?
3. Which puppet has been presented by father Harry and son Matthew?
4. Which Royal Event was televised on July 29th 1981?
5. Which children's programme featured Patch and Petra?
6. Who plays Compo in *Last of The Summer Wine*?
7. What was Alf's wife's name in *Til Death Us Do Part*?
8. Who was the host of *Odd One Out*?
9. Which country failed to score in the *Eurovision Song Contest*?
10. Who are referred to as 'The Management'?
11. What was Sid Little's nickname?
12. Which character does Helen Mirren play in *Prime Suspect*?
13. What is the name of Olive Oyl's brother?
14. Which puppeteer created a muppet for *Sam and Friends*?
15. Who is the last remaining original character in *Brookside*?
16. Which cartoon featured Mr. Copper?
17. Which character in *Spitting Image* commented on the peas?
18. Which party game was *Give us a Clue* based on?
19. Who called Pike 'You stupid boy' in *Dads Army*?
20. What was the comedy series about a concert party in India?
21. Who presented *Juke Box Jury*?
22. Who was Ludicrus Sextus's servant in *Up Pompeii*?
23. Which sport does Stuart Storey commentate on?
24. Who in *Eastenders* was known as Tricky Dicky?
25. In *Chef* what is Gareth's surname?
26. Who is Homer Simpson's boss?
27. What was Sid Hooper's occupation in *Crossroads*?
28. On which channel was *Mastermind* broadcast?
29. Whose catchphrase is 'I'm free' on *Are You Being Served*?
30. Who played Arthur Dailey in *Minder*?

Answers: see Quiz 40, page 48   LEVEL I

1. In *Doctor Who*, who was K-9?

2. What was *Black Beauty*?

3. In *Happy Days* who was Ritchie's sister?

4. Who was the bird in cartoons with Sylvester?

5. Which series featured Miss Piggy?

6. Who were Herman and Lily?

7. On which programme was there a cat named Jason?

8. Which program featured Big Ted and Little Ted?

9. Who played *The Incredible Hulk*?

10. To which team did Face and Mad Murdock belong?

11. Who was the voice of *Mr. Magoo*?

12. Who is Huey, Dewey and Louie's uncle?

13. Which series about a secret helicopter starred Jan Michael Vincent?

14. Which sitcom featured Arnold and Willis Jackson?

15. Which US series featured Josh Saviano as Paul Pfeiffer?

16. Which colourful feline cartoon character has his own series?

17. In which series was Baron Silas Greenback the arch villain?

18. Which cartoon series featured Kanga and Piglet?

19. In which S.F. series does Maximillian Arturo appear?

20. Which character in *The Cosby Show* did Malcolm Jamal Warner portray?

21. Which pop music show featured *Legs and Co*?

22. What was the name of the boy doctor who had his own series?

23. Which popular children's soap is set in the North East?

24. The puppet Muffin was what kind of creature?

25. On *Watch With Mother*, who was the puppet baby clown?

26. *Sooty* is a puppet what?

27. What colour are Sweep's ears?

28. What are the twins called in *Rugrats*?

29. What was the surname of the famous Billy, a tubby schoolboy created by Frank Richards?

30. What did Bill and Ben live in?

Drama 5 (see Quiz 40)

1. *Ultraviolet.* 2. *Supply And Demand.* 3. Nadim Sawalha. 4. Trinity. 5. She was electrocuted. 6. Harriet. 7. Robert Pastorelli. 8. *Dark Skies.* 9. Lou Grant. 10. Ricardo. 11. *Rumpole of The Bailey.* 12. Jonathan Brandis. 13. Kyle McLachlan. 14. *The Fugitive.* 15. Hamish Macbeth. 16. Los Angeles Tribune. 17. *The Vanishing Man.* 18. Adam Faith. 19. *The Bill.* 20. *Mission Impossible.* 21. *Northern Exposure.* 22. *ER.* 23. Lotus Seven. 24. Silent. 25. Station Officer. 26. *Crocodile Shoes.* 27. *Hart To Hart.* 28. *Vegas.* 29. *All Creatures Great And Small.* 30. Roger Moore.

Answers: see Quiz 39, page 47

LEVEL 1

1. Which thriller series starred Jack Davenport as DS Michael Colefield?
2. In which Linda La Plante series did Larry Lamb play Simon Hughes?
3. In *Dangerfield* the father of actresses Nadia and Julia plays Dr. Shabaan Hamada. Who is he?
4. In which town is Lucas Buck the sheriff in *American Gothic*?
5. How did Assumpta die in *Ballykissangel*?
6. What was Makepiece's christian name in *Dempsey And Makepiece*?
7. Who plays Gerry Fitzgerald in *Fitz*?
8. In which drama S.F. series were the characters John Loengard and Kimberley Sayers?
9. Which spin off from *The Mary Tyler Moore Show* was a drama series?
10. What is Tubbs' first name in *Miami Vice*?
11. In which Drama series did Judge Guthrie Featherstone appear?
12. Who plays Lucas in *Seaquest DSV*?
13. Who played Special Agent Dale Cooper in *Twin Peaks*?
14. In which series did Lt. Gerard pursue a doctor?
15. Which drama series featured Wee Jock and The Clan McLopez?
16. Where did *Lou Grant* work in LA?
17. In which drama series does Neil Morrissey play Nick Cameron?
18. Which former pop singer starred in *Love Hurts*?
19. In which drama series does Colin Tarrant play Inspector Monroe?
20. Which series featured Barbara Bain as Cinnamon?
21. In which series was the character Marilyn Whirlwind a doctor's receptionist?
22. In which series was Anna Del Amico a hospital doctor?
23. What car did *The Prisoner* drive in the opening credits?
24. In the series starring Amanda Burton what kind of Witness were her cadavers?
25. In *London's Burning* what rank was Nick?
26. What was the title of a Jimmy Nail series and his hit record?
27. In which series were Jonathan and Jennifer crime fighters?
28. Where was Dan Tanna a private eye?
29. The characters Siegfried and Tristan Farnon appeared in which series?
30. Which suave UK actor links Simon Templar and Maverick?

QUIZ 41 Pot Luck 13

Answers: see Quiz 42, page 50

LEVEL I

1. What was the name of the android in *Red Dwarf*?
2. Who replaced Nigel LeVaillant as *Dangerfield*?
3. Which comedy series featured the Clampetts?
4. Who presents *The Sky At Night*?
5. Who was Krystle Carrington's husband in *Dynasty*?
6. In *Steptoe And Son* what is the father's name?
7. What was *Quincy*?
8. Which series featured BA Baracus?
9. Who played the title role in *Faith in the Future*?
10. Which Irishman presents *The Eurovision Song Contest*?
11. Which TV comedy star recorded *Splish-Splash*?
12. To which singing group do Donny, Marie and Jimmy belong?
13. Who was Dick Grayson's alter-ego?
14. What is the name of *Rab C Nesbitt's* youngest son?
15. What was the name of Granada's weekly review of the press?
16. What was the prequel of *The Fenn Street Gang*?
17. Which series starred Paula Wilcox and Richard Beckinsale?
18. Who was the quizmaster on *The Sky's The Limit*?
19. What was the name of ITV's Saturday sports programme?
20. Name the two high-voiced puppet pigs.
21. Where is *Coronation Street*?
22. In which city are the *Neighbours*?
23. Who presents *This Morning with Richard Madeley*?
24. What is the name of Hank Hill's wife?
25. What is the name of the 'big' kid in *South Park*?
26. Which soap is set in Summer Bay?
27. Who plays Guinan in *Star Trek: The Next Generation*?
28. What is *Dr. Who's* time machine called?
29. What do Jeremy Clarkson and Quentin Willson present?
30. Who plays CJ in *Baywatch*?

Comedy 8 (see Quiz 42)

1. *Keeping Up Appearances*. 2. Victor Meldrew. 3. *Agony Again*. 4. *The Two Ronnies*. 5. *An Actor's Life For Me*. 6. *Brass Eye*. 7. Husband and wife. 8. *Terry and June*. 9. *Porridge*. 10. *Rising Damp*. 11. A corner shop. 12. *Citizen Smith*. 13. Mel Smith. 14. *The Golden Girls*. 15. Eric Morecambe and Ernie Wise. 16. Nora Batty. 17. Jennifer Saunders. 18. In prison. 19. Glasgow. 20. *Stressed Eric*. 21. Les Dawson. 22. Jessica. 23. *Happy Days*. 24. *Frasier*. 25. Pamela Stephenson. 26. A dog. 27. Springfield. 28. Three. 29. *Monty Python*. 30. Roman Empire.

QUIZ 42 Comedy 8

Answers: see Quiz 41, page 49   LEVEL 1

1. Mrs Bucket, played by Patricia Routledge, appears in which BBC comedy?
2. Whose catchphrase is "I don't believe it!"?
3. What was the sequel to *Agony* starring Maureen Lipman, shown in 1995?
4. The opening credits to which duo's programmes featured two pairs of glasses?
5. Which 1990s BBC sitcom starred John Gordon Sinclair as an aspiring actor?
6. Chris Morris created and was the star of which Channel 4 comedy series that fooled celebrities with spoof news stories?
7. How were George and Mildred related in the ITV comedy?
8. Terry Scott and June Whitfield starred as which married couple?
9. Ronnie Barker played the lead role in which BBC comedy about prison inmates?
10. What was Rising in the ITV series starring Leonard Rossiter as a scheming landlord?
11. What kind of establishment did Arkwright run in *Open All Hours*?
12. Robert Lindsay played the role of which citizen?
13. Who plays *Mr Bean*?
14. *Brighton Belles* was the UK version of which hit US comedy?
15. Eric Bartholomew and Ernie Wiseman were better known as what?
16. Which Nora is renowned for her sharp tongue in *Last of the Summer Wine*?
17. Which comedienne wrote and starred in *Absolutely Fabulous*?
18. In *Birds Of A Feather*, where are Sharon and Tracy's husbands residing?
19. In which Scottish city does *Rab C Nesbitt* live?
20. Which adult cartoon character was stressed on BBC2?
21. Which late TV comedian was famed for playing the piano badly?
22. What was the name of Frank Spencer's daughter?
23. In which series did The Fonz appear?
24. Psychiatrists the Crane brothers feature in which Channel 4 Friday night comedy?
25. Billy Connolly is married to which *Not The Night O'clock News* comedienne?
26. Which programme features the bar "where everybody knows your name"?
27. In which town do *The Simpsons* live?
28. How many children did *Roseanne* have in her series?
29. According to the series title who had a *Flying Circus*?
30. *Up Pompeii* was set in the time of which empire?

ANSWERS

Pot Luck 13 (see Quiz 41)
1. Kryten. 2. Nigel Havers. 3. *The Beverley Hillbillies.* 4. Patrick Moore. 5. Blake. 6. Albert.
7. A pathologist. 8. *The A Team.* 9. Lynda Bellingham. 10. Terry Wogan. 11. Charlie Drake.
12. The Osmonds. 13. Robin. 14. Gash. 15. *What The Papers Say.* 16. *Please Sir!* 17. *The Lovers.*
18. Hughie Green. 19. *World of Sport.* 20. *Pinky and Perky.* 21. Weatherfield. 22. Melbourne.
23. Judy Finnegan. 24. Peggy. 25. Eric Cartman. 26. *Home and Away.* 27. Whoopi Goldberg.
28. Tardis. 29. *Top Gear.* 30. Pamela Anderson Lee.

50

QUIZ 43 — Soaps 5

LEVEL 1

Answers: see Quiz 44, page 52

1. Which Rita owns The Kabin in *Coronation Street*?
2. In *Coronation Street* who was married to Derek Wilton?
3. What is Des Barnes' job in the Street?
4. Which landlady did Alec Gilroy marry in *Coronation Street*?
5. Who is Phil Mitchell's brother in *Eastenders*?
6. Who took over the fruit and veg stall from his uncle in *Eastenders*?
7. Who is the landlady of the Queen Vic?
8. In which city is Brookside Close?
9. Which Tate is in a wheelchair in *Emmerdale*?
10. In which US series were the characters Blake and Alexis?
11. What is Ricky Butcher's job in *Eastenders*?
12. Which of the Robinsons did Philip Martin marry in *Neighbours*?
13. Who was Vicky Fowler's publican father in *Eastenders*?
14. In *Crossroads* who did Benny call 'Miss Diane'?
15. In *Dynasty* who was Alexis's sister?
16. Which famed *Chariots Of Fire* composer recorded the *Brookside* theme?
17. In *Coronation Street* who was Des Barnes wife?
18. Which Beale had her husband shot in *Eastenders*?
19. Which *Neighbours* star sang *I Should be so Lucky*?
20. Who was Miss Bettabuy 1991 in *Coronation Street* and went on to marry Curly?
21. Which Karl is the G.P. in Ramsey Street?
22. Who was Terry Sullivan's best mate in *Brookside*?
23. Who was pub landlady Annie Walker's husband?
24. In *Dallas*, who was J.R.'s father?
25. In *Dynasty*, which actress Heather played Sammy Joe?
26. What is name of the headmaster in *Home And Away*?
27. In *Emmerdale*, who did Annie Sugden finally marry?
28. In *Eastenders*, which Frank had a car business called Deals on Wheels?
29. What is the name of Judy Malet's husband in the Street?
30. Who did Scott Robinson marry in *Neighbours*?

Pot Luck 14 (see Quiz 44)

1. Feltz. 2. *The Big Breakfast.* 3. The Worthington Cup. 4. Astro. 5. Miss Boathook. 6. *Game For A Laugh.* 7. The Great Sorprendo. 8. Delia Smith. 9. Heathrow. 10. *Emmerdale.* 11. Reverend Jim. 12. Fred Savage. 13. Channel 4. 14. *Voyager.* 15. Gary Coleman. 16. *This Life.* 17. 100 acre wood. 18. 15. 19. Liverpool Docks. 20. Dennis Potter. 21. Fly on the wall documentary. 22. Denise Van Outen. 23. David Attenborough. 24. Jean-Paul Gaultier. 25. Live TV. 26. Swithinbank. 27. Chris Tarrant. 28. Geoff Hamilton. 29. Ainsley Harriot. 30. Jeremy Spake.

ANSWERS

Answers: see Quiz 43, page 51

LEVEL 1

1. Which Vanessa had her own chat show?
2. Which morning programme was co-presented by Johnny Vaughn?
3. What did the Coca-cola Cup change its name to in 1998?
4. What was the name of The Jetsons' dog?
5. Who was Colonel K's secretary in *Dangermouse*?
6. Rusty Lee and Jeremy Beadle co-presented which programme?
7. Which magician is married to Victoria Wood?
8. Which TV cook's first series was *Family Fare*?
9. What was the setting for *Airport*?
10. In which series is the fictional village Beckingdale?
11. In *Taxi* what was Jim Ignatowski's nickname?
12. Who played Kevin Arnold in *The Wonder Years*?
13. Which channel broadcasts *Cutting Edge* documentaries?
14. Which S. F. series features the character Neelix?
15. Who played Arnold in *Diff'rent Strokes*?
16. In which programme would you find Milly and Egg?
17. Where do Winnie The Pooh and his friends live?
18. How many contestants start the quiz programme hosted by William G. Stewart?
19. From where was *This Morning* originally broadcast?
20. Which playwright created *Blackeyes*?
21. What type of programme was *Lakeside*?
22. Which breakfast time presenter appeared in *Babes In The Wood*?
23. Which presenter and programme maker has a brother Lord Dickie?
24. Which dress designer co-presented *Eurotrash*?
25. On which channel would you find *The Weather In Norwegian*?
26. Which Anne presented *Gardens of The Caribbean*?
27. Who presented *Man-O-Man*?
28. Which late TV personality had a garden at Barnsdale?
29. Which TV Chef presented *Party Of A Lifetime*?
30. Who was the Aeroflot customer care manager featured on *Airport*?

Answers: see Quiz 46, page 54

LEVEL 1

1. In which series would you find the character Tosh Lines?
2. Which Victorian detective did Jeremy Brett portray?
3. Which series starred John Hannah as a pathologist?
4. Which TV detective was played by Mark McManus?
5. Which Chief of Detectives was in a wheelchair?
6. Which series featured Jack Lord as Steve McGarrett?
7. In which series did Jack Warner play a beat bobby?
8. Which detective was famous for sucking lollipops?
9. Which Jersey detective was played by John Nettles?
10. Who does Kevin Whately portray in *Inspector Morse*?
11. Paul Michael Glazier and David Soul starred as which crimefighting duo?
12. Who shot Mr Burns in *The Simpsons*?
13. Which Agatha Christie sleuth lives in St Mary's mead?
14. Which policeman worked in Dock Green?
15. What is TV detective Columbo's first name?
16. *Murder, She Wrote* stars which *Bedknobs and Broomsticks* actress?
17. Which crimefighter had a boss called Devon Miles, played by Edward Mulhare?
18. Which former Dr Who also played Sherlock Holmes?
19. Which Nick presents BBC's *Crime Watch*?
20. The original Saint was played by which Bond man?
21. Which BBC crime series featured the main character Inspector Jean Darblay?
22. Who starred in *Cracker*?
23. Which writer with the initials PD created Detective Chief Superintendent Dalgleish?
24. Who is Agatha Christie's Belgian sleuth?
25. Helen Mirren starred as Detective Chief Inspector Jane Tennison in which series?
26. In which city was *Thief Takers* set?
27. What was *In The Sky* according to the crime series starring Richard Griffiths?
28. Which ITV police detective is based in Cornwall?
29. Who stars as *Rumpole of the Bailey*?
30. Which Don plays *Nash Bridges*?

Answers: see Quiz 45, page 53

LEVEL 1

1. Who risks life and limb in *The Cook Report*?
2. Who introduces programmes with the words "Hello, good evening and welcome"?
3. Which news service won awards for its coverage of the Gulf War?
4. ITN provides the news service for which channels?
5. What special device was used by John Snow during BBC television coverage of elections to show voting swings?
6. Which famous Royal event was screened around the world in 1953?
7. On which channel is the current affairs programme, *Panorama*?
8. Angela Rippon read the news for which TV company?
9. Sir David Attenborough is famed for presenting what type of documentary on TV?
10. The news and current affairs programme, *Newsnight*, is broadcast on which channel?
11. Which programme ends with 'And Finally'?
12. Which BBC interviewer is nicknamed Parkie?
13. John Craven presented news for children on which channel?
14. Which Harty presented chat shows on TV?
15. Who presents *The South Bank Show*?
16. Which Jeremy presents *Top Gear* on BBC2?
17. Which Knight presented *Life On Earth*?
18. What is the BBC's dedicated news channel called?
19. Which chairman of *Question Time* was famed for his bow ties?
20. Which BBC science series shows a baby swimming underwater in its opening credits?
21. Channel 4's archaeology series *Time Team* was presented by which comic actor?
22. Presenter Robert Kilroy-Silk appears on which channel?
23. Which Miriam is a TV doctor?
24. Jilly Goolden and Oz Clarke sample wine together on which BBC2 series?
25. Barry Norman presented profiles of films on which channel before moving to Sky?
26. Which Lorraine presented *GMTV*?
27. Who replaced the late Geoff Hamilton as presenter of *Gardener's World*?
28. Ruby Wax interviewed which Duchess on TV?
29. Eamonn Holmes presents which breakfast-time programme?
30. On which day does Sir David Frost present a breakfast programme?

Answers: see Quiz 48, page 56 LEVEL 1

1. Which *Eastender* is now one of the *Hello Girls*?
2. According to the title of the comedy how many children does Belinda Lang have?
3. True or false: *The Good Life*'s Paul Eddington also played the Prime Minister?
4. Who is Stephanie Cole waiting for in the BBC comedy about a retirement home?
5. Which irreverent cartoon features Cartman and the ill-fated Kenny?
6. *Parker Lewis Can't...* do what, according to the title of the US high-school comedy?
7. What is the name of Hank Hill's son in *King Of The Hill*?
8. Which letter do the stars of *Absolutely Fabulous* all start their first names with?
9. Which sitcom was the song *My Little Horse* entered for a contest?
10. What is the name of the drunk in *The Simpsons*?
11. How many humans are there in *Red Dwarf*?
12. Who plays the husband in *Roseanne*?
13. What rank is Ernie Bilko in *The Phil Silvers Show*?
14. Who was the star of *Police Squad*?
15. What type of Product did Mark Thomas offer on Channel 4?
16. *Three's Company* was the American version of which British sitcom?
17. Who plays Charlie in *Babes in The Wood*?
18. Who is Tim Taylor's assistant in *Tool Time*?
19. What is *Caroline in The City*'s occupation?
20. Has Sylvester Stallone ever appeared on *Friends*?
21. Which series features Martin and Mandy as tenants?
22. Whose neighbours are the Leadbetters?
23. Which 1960s series featured Ricky Ricardo?
24. Which series starred Larry Hagman and Barbara Eden?
25. Which series featured Col Blake and Major Burns?
26. Who plays Gary in *Men Behaving Badly*?
27. In which series did Tony Randall play Felix Unger?
28. Who is David Jason's character in *Only Fools and Horses*?
29. Which character from *The Fast Show* said "This week, I have been mostly eating... "?
30. Which spoof news bulletin starred Steve Coogan and Chris Morris?

Answers: see Quiz 47, page 55

LEVEL 1

1. Anya Sitaram, Jez Nelson and Craig Doyle are reporters on which technology programme?
2. Who starred in *Oktober* and *Ballykissangel*?
3. Which fly on the wall documentary comes from Alder Hay, Liverpool?
4. Where did one Nigel replace another?
5. Which daytime programme became *Late Lunch*?
6. Which Laurie Lee book has been made into an ITV film version?
7. Who presents *World of Survival* on BBC2?
8. Who presented *The Private Life Of Plants*?
9. Who presents *How To Cook* on BBC2?
10. Which daytime TV programme does Dr. Chris Steele appear on?
11. Which actor played Louie de Palma in *Taxi*?
12. Who runs the post office in *Heartbeat*?
13. Who did Don Brennan kidnap in his taxi in *Coronation Street*?
14. Which Fern presents *Ready Steady Cook*?
15. Who plays Dr. Jonathan Paige in *Dangerfield*?
16. In which drama series were Sicknote and Vaseline members of Blue Watch?
17. Who lives in the flat above Gary and Tony in *Men Behaving Badly*?
18. Which *Knight Rider* became a lifeguard?
19. Which bigoted character supported West Ham?
20. Which George portrayed Arthur Dailey in *Minder*?
21. Who played Peggy the chalet maid in *Hi De Hi*?
22. Which character in *Eastenders* was played by Letitia Dean?
23. Which former *Neighbours* actress had a hit with *The Locomotion*?
24. Which programme does Jill Dando present in the winter?
25. Which channel is dedicated to the House of Commons?
26. What is the U.S. version of *Cracker* called?
27. In which year was *Neighbours* first broadcast in Britain?
28. On which sport did Jack Kramer commentate?
29. What is the presenter of *Local Heroes* form of transport?
30. Who was the first male presenter of *How Do They Do That*?

Answers: see Quiz 50, page 58

LEVEL I

1. What rank was Ted Roach in *The Bill*?
2. Which series featured reporters Joe Rossi and Billy Newman?
3. In which series were the characters Caleb and Merlyn Temple?
4. Which courtroom drama series featured Soapy Sam Ballard?
5. Who played Dr. Kristin Westphalen in *Seaquest DSV*?
6. Who is Zoe, a star of *Love Hurts*?
7. Who was Makepiece's American partner?
8. Who gave the last rites to Assumpta in *Ballykissangel*?
9. Which character does Edward James Olmos portray in *Miami Vice*?
10. Which acting Sutherland appeared in *Twin Peaks*?
11. Which TV Role has been played by both Julia Foster and Alex Kingston?
12. What was Taggart's invalid wife's name?
13. Which play about homelessness was made by Ken Loach?
14. Who played Lady Bellamy in *Upstairs Downstairs*?
15. Which TV Doctor played John Blackthorne?
16. What was Doyle's christian name in *The Professionals*?
17. Who played Anna Fairley in *Reckless*?
18. In which series set in Cumbria featured the character Danny Kavanagh?
19. Which drama series featured Miles and Ferdy?
20. In which series did David Bowie play a special agent?
21. Who created Adam Dalgliesh?
22. Who directed *Staggered* and starred in it as a toy salesman left on a remote island after his stag night?
23. Which Catherine Cookson drama starred Robson Green as Rory Connor?
24. Which series featured district nurses Ruth and Peggy?
25. In which series did Helen Baxendale portray Cordelia?
26. Who played DCI Nick Hall in *Thief Takers*?
27. In which series did Fitzpatrick and Drysdale appear as servicemen?
28. Whose ghost visited Mountie Fraser?
29. Which star of *If* appeared in *Our Friends In The North*?
30. Which character did John Nettles portray in *Midsomer Murders*?

ANSWERS

Quiz & Games I (see Quiz 50)

1. Bruce Forsyth. 2. Melinda Messenger. 3. Blind Date. 4. Bullie. 5. *Blockbusters*. 6. Two.
7. *Treasure Hunt*. 8. Leslie Crowther. 9. Black. 10. Four. 11. Lily Savage. 12. *15 To 1*. 13. Clive
Anderson. 14. Les Dennis. 15. Pop music. 16. Craig Charles. 17. Challenge TV. 18. Noel
Edmonds. 19. Cricketer. 20. *The Century*. 21. *Junkyard*. 22. David Coleman. 23. *Now Get Out Of
That*. 24. Paul Daniels. 25. Angus Deayton. 26. Gaby Roslin. 27. *Ready Steady Cook*. 28. Lloyd
Grossman. 29. Jilly Goolden. 30. *Supermarket Sweep*.

Answers: see Quiz 49, page 57

LEVEL 1

1. Which Bruce presented *The Generation Game?*
2. Who presents *Fort Bayard?*
3. Which programme does Cilla Black use for matchmaking?
4. Which cartoon character appeared in *Bullseye?*
5. Which show was famously hosted by Bob Holness?
6. How many contestants are there each day on *Countdown?*
7. Kenneth Kendall and Anneka Rice hosted which Channel 4 quiz in which contestants had to seek and answer clues?
8. Who first hosted *The Price Is Right?*
9. What colour was the famous contestant's chair on *Mastermind?*
10. How many contestants faced the challenge of the *Krypton Factor* in each episode?
11. Who hosts *Blankety Blank?*
12. What are the odds of winning the Channel 4 afternoon quiz hosted by William G Stewart?
13. Which barrister presents Channel 4's *Whose Line Is It Anyway?*
14. Who hosts *Family Fortunes?*
15. What is the subject of *Never Mind The Buzzcocks?*
16. Who hosts *Robot Wars?*
17. Which channel is dedicated to gameshows?
18. Who hosts *Telly Addicts?*
19. *They Think It's All Over* team captain David Gower was a captain in which sport?
20. Nicolas Parsons hosted an Anglia TV gameshow called *The Sale Of...* what?
21. In which show did Robert Llewellyn make teams build devices out of scrap?
22. Which chairman of *A Question Of Sport* retired in 1997?
23. Which program featured Bernard Falk putting contestants in sticky situations?
24. Who presents *Every Second Counts?*
25. Which movie quiz did Michael Aspell host in the 1970s?
26. Which Gaby presented *Whatever You Want?*
27. Which show features a 'trolly dolly?
28. Who nosed around stars homes in *Through The Keyhole?*
29. *The Great Antiques Hunt* is presented by which female wine connoisseur?
30. Dale Winton hosts what kind of Sweep?

ANSWERS

Drama 6 (see Quiz 49)

1. Detective Sergeant. 2. *Lou Grant.* 3. *American Gothic.* 4. *Rumpole of The Bailey.* 5. Stephanie Beacham. 6. Wanamaker. 7. Dempsey. 8. Father Peter Clifford. 9. Lt. Castillo. 10. Kiefer. 11. *Moll Flanders.* 12. Jean. 13. *Cathy Come Home.* 14. Rachel Gurney. 15. Richard Chamberlain. 16. Ray. 17. Francesca Annis. 18. *The Lakes.* 19. *This Life.* 20. *Twin Peaks.* 21. P.D. James. 22. Martin Clunes. 23. *The Gambling Man.* 24. *Where The Heart Is.* 25. *An Unsuitable Job For A Woman.* 26. Nicholas Ball. 27. *Soldier, Soldier.* 28. His father. 29. Malcolm McDowall. 30. Detective Inspector Barnaby.

Answers: see Quiz 52, page 60

LEVEL 1

1. In which children's series were Mr. Carraway the fishmonger and Mr. Crockett the garage owner?

2. Which 60's series featured the refuse disposal crew of Thunderbird Three?

3. Which character did the late Gary Holton play in *Auf Weidersehen Pet*?

4. Who is Lesley Joseph's character in *Birds Of A Feather*?

5. Which comedy set in a newsroom featured Damien Day and George Dent?

6. Lieutenant B'Elanna Torres appears in which S.F. series?

7. Which actor played both Selwyn Froggitt and The Gaffer?

8. In which sitcom does Ryan Stiles play Lewis?

9. What is Dr. Maddox's christian name in *Casualty*?

10. What series was the prequel to *French Fields*?

11. Which programme has been presented by Mike Scott and Derek Grainger?

12. Which programme featured Dick Dastardly and Muttley?

13. What was Gladys Emmanuel in *Open All Hours*?

14. In which series are Sgt. Nick Schultz and Dash McKinlay?

15. Who was the star of *And Mother Makes Five*?

16. What was the comedy series set in a Tailors shop?

17. Whose body was discovered in the first episode of *Eastenders*?

18. Who worked in Miami Modes in *Coronation Street* with Dot Greenhalgh?

19. What is Mr. Rumbold's christian name in *Are You Being Served*?

20. Who was Richie Rich's minder?

21. What is the pub in *Heartbeat*?

22. What is the name of Patrick Moore's astronomy programme?

23. Which TV series featured the characters from radio's *Take It From Here*?

24. Who played Diana Weston's mother in *The Upper Hand*?

25. On which interior design programme does Andy Kane appear?

26. Which channel broadcast *The Phil Silvers Show*?

27. Who hosted *Never Mind The Buzzcocks*?

28. Which odd series featured celebs trying to complete various trials supposedly set by the Rangdo, leader of the planet Arg, who usually appeared as an Aspidestra?

29. Which character in *Dynasty* was played by both Pamela Sue Martin and Emma Sams?

30. Which *Dallas* character died in 1982?

Soaps 6 (see Quiz 52)

1. *Coronation Street*. 2. Three. 3. Four. 4. A wooly hat. 5. *Take The High Road*. 6. *Triangle*. 7. Phil Redmond. 8. Walford. 9. *Heartbeat*. 10. June Brown. 11. The Kabin newsagent. 12. *Crossroads*. 13. Chester. 14. Steve and Liz MacDonald. 15. Grant Mitchell. 16. Shortland Street. 17. *Prisoner*. 18. *Neighbours*. 19. Ramsey Street. 20. Sunday. 21. Sunset. 22. Shortland Street. 23. *Emmerdale*. 24. *Eastenders*. 25. *Home And Away*. 26. Platt. 27. *Brookside*. 28. Baldwin. 29. Mike Reid. 30. H.

Answers: see Quiz 51, page 59

LEVEL 1

1. Hilda Ogden was a major character in which series?
2. How many JRs were there in *Dallas*?
3. How many feet appeared in the closing credits of *The Bill*?
4. What was Benny's trademark item of clothing?
5. Complete the name of the Scottish TV soap set in the Highlands: *Take The...?*
6. Kate O'Mara featured in which short-lasting 1980s soap about a North Sea ferry company?
7. Which writer created both *Grange Hill* and *Brookside*?
8. *Eastenders* is set in which fictitious district of London?
9. Nick Berry went from *Eastenders* to a PC in which ITV Sunday evening series?
10. Who plays Dot Cotton in *Eastenders*?
11. Rita Sullivan runs which shop in *Coronation Street*?
12. Noelle Gordon was the manageress in which soap?
13. In which Cheshire city is Channel 4's *Hollyoaks* set?
14. Which couple in *Coronation Street* have sons named Andy and Steve?
15. Which character does Ross Kemp play in *Eastenders*?
16. Which New Zealand soap centres around a hospital?
17. Which Australian soap follows the trials and tribulations of a women's prison?
18. Which soap featured the Ramseys and the Robinsons?
19. In which street is *Neighbours* set?
20. On which day is the omnibus edition of *Brookside* aired?
21 What kind of Beach is broadcast on Channel 5?
22. The characters Rangi, Lionel and Nick appear in which street down under?
23. Seth Armstrong was the gamekeeper in which ITV series?
24. In which soap did Michelle Fowler gain a BA degree?
25. Shane and Angel were characters in which Aussie soap?
26. What is Gail and Martin's surname in *Coronation Street*?
27. Which soap is set in Liverpool?
28. The lingerie factory in *Coronation Street* is owned by Mike who?
29. Which comedian plays Frank Butcher in *Eastenders*?
30. In which cell block is *Prisoner* set?

Pot Luck 16 (see Quiz 51)

1. *Camberwick Green*. 2. *The Dustbinmen*. 3. Wayne. 4. Dorien. 5. *Drop The Dead Donkey*. 6. *Star Trek: Voyager*. 7. Bill Maynard. 8. *The Drew Carey Show*. 9. Sean. 10. *Fresh Fields*. 11. Cinema. 12. *Wacky Races*. 13. A Nurse. 14. *The Blue Heelers*. 15. Wendy Craig. 16. *Never Mind The Quality, Feel The Width*. 17. Reg Cox. 18. Elsie Tanner. 19. Cuthbert. 20. Eddie Catflap. 21. *The Aidensfield Arms*. 22. *The Sky At Night*. 23. The Glums. 24. Honor Blackman. 25. *Changing Rooms*. 26. BBC2. 27. Mark Lamarr. 28. *The Adventure Game*. 29. Fallon. 30. Jock Ewing.

ANSWERS

Answers: see Quiz 54, page 62

LEVEL 1

1. Who was George Roper's wife in *Man About The House*?
2. Who is playwright Jack Rosenthal's wife?
3. In which series did Eamonn Walker play Winston the home help?
4. Which comedy features the occasionally self-styled El Barto?
5. Which character in *Absolutely Fabulous* is a fashion magazine executive?
6. Who was the accident prone deputy manager of Whitbury Leisure Centre?
7. Which show features Isaac Hayes as 'Chef'?
8. What was the sequel to *No Honestly* featuring Lisa Goddard?
9. Which channel produces *Beavis And Butthead*?
10. Which comedian and star of Jolson played an ex-con in *Time After Time*?
11. Which *Doctor Who* appeared in *The Two Of Us*?
12. Which sitcom starred Nicola MacAuliffe and Duncan Preston as surgeons?
13. Which sitcom was set in Maplin's Holiday Camp?
14. What was the sitcom starring Judy Loe and Roger Rees set around a singles bar?
15. Who played the butler in *Two's Company*?
16. *Home James* was a spin off from which sitcom starring Jim Davidson?
17. Who played Clarence the short sighted removal man?
18. Which series was a sequel to *The Growing Pains of P.C. Penrose*?
19. Which American actress starred in *Shirley's World*?
20. Did Gary get married in *Men Behaving Badly*?
21. What was Derek Fowlds recovering from in *Affairs of the Heart*?
22. What was the sequel to *Happy Ever After* starring June Whitfield and Terry Scott?
23. Which claymation featured cavemen?
24. Name the sequel to *In Bed With MeDinner*.
25. Which hapless, eccentric silent character always causes disaster?
26. Which *Heartbeat* actor was *The Gaffer*?
27. Which sitcom featured John Thaw and Reece Dinsdale?
28. From which sitcom was *Going Straight* the sequel?
29. Is Rab C Nesbit Irish or Scottish?
30. Who starred with Julia Mackenzie, as her husband, in *French Fields*?

Answers: see Quiz 53, page 61   LEVEL I

1. Who played Bobby Grant in *Brookside*?
2. What was Patsy Palmer's character in *Eastenders*?
3. In the children's series *Johnson and Friends* what animal is Johnson?
4. Who is the presenter of the Karaoke-style *Night Fever* on Channel 5?
5. Which annual event concludes with the playing of *Land of Hope And Glory*?
6. Who presents *Murray and Martin's F1 Special*?
7. Which U.S. series featured the character Potsie?
8. Which fantasy series stars Lucy Lawless?
9. How many zones are there in *The Crystal Maze*?
10. How did Anneka Rice fly in *Treasure Hunt*?
11. Which character does Kazia Pelka portray in *Heartbeat*?
12. Which Channel 4 series features two teams building a project from salvaged items?
13. Who presents Channel 5's *The Movie Chart Show*?
14. Who was the traveller in *Lonely Planet*?
15. Who presented her *Wine Course*?
16. Who has a son Leo in *Brookside*?
17. Who succeeded as chef on *Food And Drink*?
18. Who took over John Freeman's role in *Face To Face*?
19. Which S.F. novelist presented his *Mysterious World*?
20. Which comedy series featured the characters Brenda and boyfriend Malcolm?
21. What is Antonio Carluccio's occupation?
22. Who are the stars of *Chucklevision*?
23. Which lifestyle guide was presented by Paul Ross?
24. Which series featured the culinary arts of the nobility?
25. Which fly on the wall documentary followed the staff of Selly Oak Hospital, Birmingham?
26. Which programme presented by Ed Hall previewed the weeks television?
27. Which Channel 4 series was concerned with nightmares and dreams?
28. What is the twice-daily five times a week soap on Channel 5?
29. Which green creature was Frank Oz the voice of?
30. Which sitcom featured the Drs. Latimer?

Comedy 10 (see Quiz 53)

1. Mildred. 2. Maureen Lipman. 3. *In Sickness and in Health*. 4. *The Simpsons*. 5. Edina. 6. *South Park*. 7. Peter Cook. 8. *Yes, Honestly*. 9. Dibley. 10. Brian Conley. 11. Patrick Troughton. 12. *Surgical Spirit*. 13. *Hi-de-Hi!* 14. *Singles*. 15. Donald Sinden. 16. *Up The Elephant And Round The Castle*. 17. Ronnie Barker. 18. Rosie. 19. Shirley Maclaine. 20. *Grace and Favour*. 21. Heart attack. 22. *Terry And June*. 23. *Gogs*. 24. *Still In Bed With MeDinner*. 25. *Mr. Bean*. 26. Bill Maynard. 27. *Home To Roost*. 28. *Porridge*. 29. Scottish. 30. Anton Rodgers.

Answers: see Quiz 56, page 64   LEVEL 1

1. What was the name of the children's series about a seaside boarding house?
2. Which character aged 13 and three quarters was played by Gian Sammarco?
3. Which children's series featured Cut Throat Jake and Tom the Cabin Boy?
4. In which children's series was Mr. Cresswell the biscuit factory manager?
5. Which series featured Jim and Cindy Walsh and their two children?
6. In which children's series was Mr. Troop the Town Hall Clerk?
7. What was the name of Aaron Spelling's daughter who appeared in *Beverley Hills 90210*?
8. Which children's programme featured a canal boat owner?
9. In which children's cartoon series was the character Buggles Pigeon a flying ace?
10. What is the name of Wallace's dog?
11. Which character had Wish Wellingtons?
12. Which children's series features a boy genius who can make himself invisible?
13. Which S.F. series features Rembrandt Brown?
14. Which art show featured Morph?
15. Who presents *Fun House*?
16. What is the title of ITV's children's medieval comedy drama?
17. Whose *Excellent Adventures* are a cartoon series?
18. Who *Explains it All* on the children's series?
19. What is the children's series about a mystical board game?
20. Who is CITV's female witch?
21. Which children's programme featured Brian Cant and Humpty Dumpty?
22. Which animated character lived in a clock?
23. Who played Colin in the children's comedy drama *Microsoap*?
24. Which children's animated series features a polar bear and his chums?
25. Who presented *Live And Kicking* with Zoe Ball?
26. What was the name of the BBC's overnight service designed to be taped for children?
27. In which children's series did Richard Waites plays Cuthbert Lily?
28. If Bill was one, who was the other Flowerpot man?
29. Where did *The Borrowers* live?
30. Where would you find Florence and Dylan?

Answers: see Quiz 55, page 63 LEVEL I

1. Which BBC drama series was centred around the lives of three Edwardian nannies?
2. Who played Pascoe in *Dalziel and Pascoe*?
3. What was the subject of the two part drama *Seesaw*?
4. In which drama series did Robson Green portray Detective Dave Cregan?
5. Which Ex-*Grange Hill* actor appeared as Billy in *London's Burning*?
6. Who played Carol in *Band of Gold*?
7. Which series starred Derek Jacobi as a roman emperor?
8. Which future James Bond played Ivanhoe in the 1950s?
9. Who created *The Governor*?
10. Which story by Peter Mayle had John Thaw moving to France?
11. Which star of *The Golden Child* appeared in *Jewel In The Crown*?
12. Which Scottish singer appeared in *Band Of Gold*?
13. What have Blanco in *Porridge* and Scullion in *Porterhouse Blue* in common?
14. In which series was Janet McPherson a doctors housekeeper?
15. Which paramedic in *Casualty* lost his family in a house fire?
16. Which piece of furniture featured in the title of the Sunday night dramas of the sixties?
17. Which ex-*Eastender* appeared in the drama *Big Cat*?
18. Which actor appeared as a detective in both *Between The Lines* and *Liverpool One*?
19. What is the name of Peter Falk's rumpled detective?
20. In which series was No.2 played by Leo McKern?
21. Which series featured Special Agents Earle and Hardy?
22. Who played Rick in *Beverley Hills 90210*?
23. In which series is the character John McKeever?
24. In which series did Michael Kitchen play Richard Crane?
25. Who was the star of *Father Dowling Investigates*?
26. Who did Baz marry in *Casualty*?
27. Which Lynda la Plante series was set in the world of the Internet?
28. Who plays Sam Ryan in *Silent Witness*?
29. Which series featured the character Stringfellow Hawke?
30. Who starred in *The Beiderbecke Affair*?

Answers: see Quiz 58, page 66 LEVEL I

1. In which programme is Merlin a machine?
2. Who presents *Open House* on Channel 5?
3. Who presents *Strike It Rich*?
4. Which store was featured in *The Shop*?
5. Which adult animation series features Kyle, Kenny and Cartman?
6. What type of programme is Channel 5's *Sick as A Parrot*?
7. What nationality are comedians Roy and H.G.?
8. In which road do *The Simpsons* live?
9. Whose culinary series was *Far Eastern Cookery*?
10. What was the fly on the wall documentary about traffic wardens?
11. Which relation featured in the title of the commemoration of 75 years of the BBC?
12. Which black comedy series concerning gangland figures starred Mike Reid and James Fleet?
13. Who presents *X-Rated Ricki*?
14. Which chat show host was *All Talk*?
15. Which radio presenter hosted *Confessions*?
16. Who hosts *Masterchef*?
17. Which star of *Red Dwarf* was *A Prince Among Men*?
18. Which *Men Behaving Badly* actress appeared in *Kiss Me Kate*?
19. Which fly on the wall documentary featured Sunderland Football Club?
20. Who presented her Brunch on Channel 5?
21. Which behind the scenes documentary series featured a holiday centre?
22. Which ex-*Eastender* appeared in *Get Well Soon*?
23. Which comedian had a *Sunday Service*?
24. What was Wolfie's surname in the south London based sitcom?
25. From which country did *The Paul Hogan Show* originate?
26. In which series does Daphne Moon look after Martin Crane?
27. Which film actress went in search of orang-utans?
28. Which footballer's daughter presents *On The Ball*?
29. What was John Smith's nickname in *The A-Team*?
30. Where did Marshall Teller move to in Indiana?

Comedy 11 (see Quiz 58)

ANSWERS

1. Yorkshire. 2. Nigel Havers. 3. *Have I Got News For You*. 4. Alexi Sayle. 5. Prison. 6. Betty. 7. Adam Faith. 8. Lyndsey De Paul. 9. *The Navy Lark*. 10. The Dead Donkey. 11. Arthur Dent. 12. Spitting Image. 13. *You Rang M'Lord*. 14. Jimmy Mulville and Rory McGrath. 15. Margaret. 16. Major Charles Winchester. 17. Kirstie Alley. 18. Paul and Barry. 19. Philadelphia. 20. *The Vicar Of Dibley*. 21. *Third Rock from The Sun*. 22. Ben Porter. 23. Joey Boswell. 24. Yellow. 25. Gordon Sinclair. 26. Irish. 27. Morecambe and Wise. 28. The Liver Birds. 30. *Soap*.

Answers: see Quiz 57, page 65

1. In which county was Arkwright's corner shop?
2. Who played Tony Britton's son in *Don't Wait Up*?
3. Which show once featured a tub of lard instead of a guest?
4. Who played Mr Bolovski in *The Young Ones*?
5. Where were the characters based in Porridge?
6. What was Frank Spencer's wife called?
7. Who played *Budgie* in the program of the same name?
8. Who wrote and sang the theme for *No Honestly*?
9. The nautical TV series *HMS Paradise* was based on which comedy radio show?
10. What do you drop in the newsroom comedy?
11. Who was the very English hero of *The Hitchhikers Guide To The Galaxy*?
12. Which programme was famous for its latex puppets?
13. What was the sitcom about servants and masters written by Jimmy Perry and David Croft?
14. Who wrote and starred in *Chelmsford 123*?
15. Which character is Victor Meldrew's wife in *One Foot In The Grave*?
16. Who replaced Major Frank Burns in *M*A*S*H*?
17. Who is the female star of *Veronica's Closet*?
18. What are the names of *The Chuckle Brothers*?
19. Where did the *Fresh Prince Of Bel Air* originate from?
20. Which sitcom features the character Geraldine Grainger?
21. In which comedy series are the characters Dick Solomon and Dr. Mary Albright?
22. Which plumber has an aggressive assistant Christine in *2 point 4 Children*?
23. Which character did Peter Howitt portray in *Bread*?
24. What colour were the taxis in the US sitcom *Taxi*?
25. Which Gordon stars in the ITV comedy *Loved By You*?
26. What nationality is TV comedian Frank Carson?
27. Whose Christmas special was watched by 28 million people in 1977?
28. Which Birds were Liverpudlian flatmates?
29. Tim Brooke-Taylor was one third of which comic trio?
30. In which show did the butler Benson originally appear?

Answers: see Quiz 60, page 68

LEVEL 1

1. Julia Somerville was newsreader with which news service?
2. Sue Cook and Jill Dando have presented which crimebusting series?
3. Which Sophie is a TV cook?
4. Michael Fish provided what type of news service?
5. Which Anne presented *Watchdog*?
6. Who presents the BBC's *999*?
7. What is the name of BBC's motoring programme presented by Jeremy Clarkson?
8. At what time is the BBC's late evening news programme?
9. Which brothers presented the 1997 General Election coverage on BBC and ITV?
10. How many guests form the panel on *Question Time*?
11. Big Ben appears at the start of which national news programme?
12. The late Gordon Honeycomb read the news on which channel?
13. Where was the marriage of Prince Charles and Lady Diana Spencer broadcast from?
14. Which Grade became head of Channel 4 in the 1980s?
15. Which Ms Ford was a BBC newsreader?
16. Who sang about John Kettley and Michael Fish?
17. Which BBC2 news programme is broadcast each weekday night?
18. Which Martin switched from news reporting to government in 1997?
19. The trial of which ex-American footballer was followed extensively on TV?
20. Anne Robinson presented which viewers reply series?
21. On which night is *Question Time* broadcast?
22. BBC1's *Country File* is presented by which children's newsreader?
23. The ITV wildlife series, *Birdwatch*, is hosted by naturalist Chris who?
24. *Animal Rescuers* follows the work of which Royal society?
25. On which channel is Montel William's chat show?
26. Which former Goodie presents the animal series *Animal House* on Channel 5?
27. British historian Richard Holmes takes us on what kind of walks on BBC2?
28. The garden challenge series, *Ground Force*, is presented by which TV gardener?
29. Which ITV series about real-life disasters was presented by Richard Madeley?
30. *Ricki Lake* hosts a chat show on which channel?

Crime 3 (see Quiz 60)

ANSWERS

1. *The Professionals*. 2. *A Touch Of Frost*. 3. Channel 4. 4. *Columbo*. 5. Jaguar. 6. Haskins. 7. *The New Avengers*. 8. *Heartbeat*. 9. New York Police Department. 10. Inspector Morse's. 11. *Prime Suspect*. 12. *Quincy*. 13. Kavanagh QC. 14. *Heartbeat*. 15. Dempsey. 16. Edward Woodward. 17. Both. 18. Miami. 19. *Porridge*. 20. Agatha Christie. 21. Helen Mirren. 22. James Garner. 23. Pierce Brosnan. 24. Hoffman. 25. *Magnum PI*. 26. *Cracker*. 27. Hill Street. 28. Adam. 29. A chef. 30. Captain Haddock.

Answers: see Quiz 59, page 67   LEVEL 1

1. Bodie and Doyle featured in which series?
2. David Jason stars as Jack Frost in which series?
3. Which channel featured an evening of cop shows called *The Blue Light Zone*?
4. Which American crime-fighter has a shabby raincoat and no known first name?
5. Which make of car did Inspector Morse drive?
6. Who was Regan's boss in *The Sweeney*?
7. Did Joanna Lumley play the role of Purdey in *The Avengers* or *The New Avengers*?
8. Nick Berry starred as PC and later Sergeant Nick Rowan in which series?
9. What does the NYPD in *NYPD Blue* stand for?
10. Kevin Whateley stars as whose police assistant?
11. Superintendent Jane Tennison is the lead character in which series?
12. Which medical examiner was played by Jack Klugman?
13. John Thaw plays which QC?
14. Which ITV police drama is set in 1960s Yorkshire?
15. Who was the male half of *Dempsey And Makepiece*?
16. Which Edward played *Callan*?
17. Which of the TV cops *Cagney and Lacey* was female?
18. Don Johnson starred in which *Vice*?
19. Who created Hercules Poirot?
20. The character Fletcher was a jailbird in which comedy series?
21. The star of *Prime Suspect* was Helen who?
22. Who plays Jim in *The Rockford Files*?
23. Who played *Remington Steele*?
24. Which character Theodore was played by Daniel Benzali in *Murder One*?
25. Tom Selleck played which Private Investigator?
26. The character Eddie Fitzgerald appears in which series?
27. Captain Furillo ran the blues in which street?
28. What is detective Commander Dalgleish's first name?
29. In *Pie In The Sky*, Henry combined policing with which other profession?
30. What is the name of Tin-Tin's fishy sailor friend?

Answers: see Quiz 62, page 70   LEVEL 1

1. Which Llewellyn presents his *Indoor Garden*?
2. What was the subject of *Several Careful Owners*?
3. Who is the bartender in *The Simpsons*?
4. Which children's detective was a Koala Bear?
5. Who is Dorothy's mother in *The Golden Girls*?
6. What is Sheriff Buck's first name in *American Gothic*?
7. Which series features twins Brittany and Cynthia Daniel?
8. In which series was Nathan Bridger the captain of a submersible?
9. Which fly on the wall documentary concerned cabin crew staff?
10. In which series was Troy the family pet?
11. What was *Robin's Nest*?
12. Which character played by Bill Maynard had the christian name Selwyn?
13. What was the occupation of the workers in *Common As Muck*?
14. Which angling programme was presented by Nick Fisher?
15. What was the BBC's longest running observational documentary series?
16. Whose comedy series was *As Seen On TV*?
17. Which summer 98 music festival event was hosted by John Peel?
18. Which S.F. drama series featured the invasion of Scotland by UFOs?
19. Whose series of sketches and stand up comedy was titled *Merry Go Round*?
20. Which sitcom starred Emma Wray as a nurse?
21. Which country did the game show *Endurance* come from?
22. Which quiz is presented by Bradley Walsh and Jenny Powell?
23. Who was the star of *Worzel Gummidge Down Under*?
24. What was *George and Mildred*'s surname?
25. Who hosted *That's Showbusiness*?
26. Who was Lenny in *Lenny's Big Amazon Adventure*?
27. What is Donahue's first name?
28. Which Gaby was presenter of *The Real Holiday Show*?
29. Who was *The Man From Auntie*?
30. Which sitcom featured the characters Eric and Hattie?

A N S W E R S

Soaps 7 (see Quiz 62)

1. Derek Wilton. 2. *Eastenders*. 3. Kathy Mitchell. 4. *Prisoner Cell Block H*. 5. Duffy. 6. Jaqui Dixon.
7. Toyah. 8. Courtney. 9. Steven Carrington. 10. Louise Raymond. 11. *Dynasty*. 12. Janice.
13. Max. 14. Leanne Battersby. 15. Viv. 16. Ken Barlow. 17. Sonia Jackson. 18. Audrey Roberts.
19. Bianca. 20. Gary. 21. Gail Tilsley. 22. Don Brennan. 23. *Prisoner*. 24. Mandy (Lisa Riley).
25. Samir Raschid. 26. *Sweeney*. 27. Daniel. 28. Grant Mitchell. 29. Firman's Freezers. 30. Paul
Usher.

Answers: see Quiz 61, page 69

LEVEL 1

1. Who had his gnome kidnapped in *Coronation Street*?
2. Which soap has a Sunday lunchtime omnibus edition?
3. Which character in *Eastenders* was played by Gillian Taylforth?
4. What was the original title of *Prisoner*?
5. Which character does Cathy Shipton portray in *Casualty*?
6. Which Jacqui in *Brookside* carried a child for Max and Susannah?
7. Which of the Battersbys was held hostage in a wood in *Coronation Street*?
8. What is the name of Grant Mitchell's daughter in *Eastenders*?
9. Who was Ted Dinard's gay lover in *Dynasty*?
10. Who is Grant Mitchell's mother-in-law in *Eastenders*?
11. Which soap starred John Forsythe and Linda Evans?
12. Which character in *Coronation Street* is married to Les Battersby?
13. Who is Susannah Farnham's husband in *Brookside*?
14. Who married Nick Tilsley in *Coronation Street*?
15. Who is Vic Windsor's wife in *Emmerdale*?
16. Who gave French lessons to Raquel in *Coronation Street*?
17. Who plays a trumpet in *Eastenders*?
18. Who in *Coronation Street* succeeded her husband as a Weatherfield councillor?
19. Who is Frank Butcher's daughter-in-law in *Eastenders*?
20. Who in *Brookside* is Lindsay Corkhill's husband?
21. Who bought a share in Alma's cafe in *Coronation Street* for £9,000?
22. Who burnt down Mike Baldwin's factory in *Coronation Street*?
23. In which series does Val Lehman play Bea Smith?
24. Which Dingle from *Emmerdale* presents *You've Been Framed*?
25. What was the name of Dierdre's late husband in *Coronation Street*?
26. What is Sinbad's surname in *Brookside*?
27. What is the name of Ken and Denise's son in *Coronation Street*?
28. Who had a relationship in *Eastenders* with his wife's mother Louise?
29. Where was Hayley Patterson an assistant manager in *Coronation Street*?
30. Which *Brookside* actor starred in *Liverpool One*?

Answers: see Quiz 64, page 72   LEVEL 1

1. Which US sitcom featured Zack and Screech?
2. Who is *Cybil's* best friend?
3. Who played Elaine Nardo in *Taxi*?
4. Which sitcom featured the Huxtable family?
5. Which character did Gary Coleman play in *Diff'rent Strokes*?
6. Who played Alex Keaton in *Family Ties*?
7. Which character did John Laurie portray in *Dad's Army*?
8. In which series do Sue Johnston and Ricky Tomlinson play Mam and Dad?
9. What was the title of Lenny Henry's Saturday night series?
10. In which sitcom did James Bolam play Terry Collier?
11. Which comedy series featured the character Samantha Stevens?
12. In which series did Norman Beaton play a hairdresser?
13. Who presented *Canned Carrot*?
14. Which comedy series was the forerunner to *Whoops Baghdad*?
15. In which series did Jim Hacker become Prime Minister?
16. In which sitcom did Elaine Stritch co-star with Donald Sinden?
17. Which UK sitcom featured Joe McGann as a housekeeper?
18. What was the setting for *Waiting For God*?
19. Who played Angela Thorne's working class downstairs neighbour in *Three Up Two Down*?
20. Which service was featured in *Get Some In*?
21. What is Cliff's surname in *Cheers*?
22. Which character is the producer of *The Larry Sanders Show*?
23. What are D.J.'s first names in *Roseanne*?
24. Which character does Michael Richards play in *Seinfeld*?
25. In *Drop The Dead Donkey* which character replaced Alex in the office?
26. What was Mike Berry's role in *Are You Being Served*?
27. In which sitcom does Tia Leone play Nora Wilde?
28. In which sitcom did Jeff Conway play Bobby Wheeler, a cab driver?
29. Which retired priest lives with *Father Ted*?
30. Which sitcom featured Janet Dibley and Nicholas Lyndhurst?

1. Which sport is the subject of *Big Break*?
2. What was PC Penrose's nickname?
3. Which US series featured the lives and relationships of people on a cruise ship?
4. Who narrated *Classic Homes* on Channel 4?
5. Who presents the children's show *Get Your Own Back*?
6. Which interior design programme is presented by Mark Curry?
7. In which series is The Aidensfield Arms?
8. What was the name of the lovers in *The Glums*?
9. Which Howard in *Howard's Way* was played by Maurice Colbourne?
10. Who presented *That Was The Week That Was*?
11. Who was Darwin in *Seaquest DSV*?
12. What was Gerry Anderson's 90's S.F. space series?
13. Where did *Billy Liar* work?
14. Who was the transsexual in *Coronation Street*?
15. What was Cliff Huxtable's full christian name in *The Cosby Show*?
16. In which state was *Eerie* a weird town?
17. Which Irish comedian was famous for his cigarette and bar stool?
18. Which western series was about a cattle drive?
19. Which Saturday sports programme is presented by Steve Rider?
20. Which series chronicled the 20th Century?
21. On which motorway is *Motorway Life* filmed?
22. Who was the boss of Firman's Freezers in *Coronation Street*?
23. Which series was presented by Rhona Cameron and Richard Fairbrass?
24. Who links *Blind Date* to *The Moment Of Truth*?
25. Which company celebrated *30 Years Of Laughter With Denis Norden*?
26. On which day is *Fully Booked* transmitted?
27. Which antiques show is presented by Jilly Goolden?
28. What is the Sunday evening hymns programme on BBC1?
29. Which magicians presented their *Unpleasant World*?
30. Which makeover programme was presented by John Leslie?

Answers: see Quiz 64, page 74

LEVEL 1

1. What were the enemy in *Ultraviolet*?

2. In which fantasy series is MacLeod an immortal?

3. Which actor is newsreader John Suchet's brother?

4. Who wrote *Cold Lazarus*?

5. What was Nick Rowan's daughter's name in *Heartbeat*?

6. Which series starred Mr. T?

7. What was the name of the bar in *Ballykissangel*?

8. Which Scottish series featured Neil the Bus?

9. What is the christian name of Kavanagh QC?

10. Who did Eric Close play in *Dark Skies*?

11. Where was the wake for Assumpta in *Ballykissangel*?

12. In which series was Charlie Hume the Managing Editor of The Los Angeles Tribune?

13. Which series featured Detective Gina Calabrese?

14. In which series was there a Chief Superintendent Gordon Spikings?

15. What character in *The Waltons* was played by both Richard Thomas and Robert Wightman?

16. On which series was the writer of *Roughnecks* a presenter?

17. Which character is a barmaid at the Aidensfield Arms in *Heartbeat*?

18. Who recorded the music for *Robin Of Sherwood*?

19. Which Steven Poliakoff drama about a London cult starred Joely Richardson?

20. Who played Uncle Tom in *Rumpole Of The Bailey*?

21. Which ex-*Casualty* nurse plays a D.I. in *Dangerfield*?

22. In which series did David Duchovny play a special agent before *The X Files*?

23. In which series did Julia Sawalha play Lydia Bennett?

24. Which series about an antique dealer was set in East Anglia?

25. What was the subject of the drama *Threads*?

26. In which country was *Ballykissangel* set?

27. Which character is played by Jeff Stewart in *The Bill*?

28. In which series is Chris Stevens a DJ on KBHR?

29. Which series featured an angel named Jonathan?

30. Which Dennis Potter drama was recorded in 1976 but not broadcast until 1987?

Children's TV 6

LEVEL 1

Answers: see Quiz 65, page 73

1. Which DJ and Mr Fixit ran charity marathons?
2. What is *Grange Hill*?
3. Which surname links TV presenters Johnny and Zoe?
4. Which show originally featured Rod, Jane and Freddy?
5. Whose mother was played by both Lulu and Julie Waltes?
6. Whose programme did Mr. Blobby first appear on?
7. Who was the dog in *The Magic Roundabout*?
8. Which country does Ivor The Engine come from?
9. Which character was the leader of *The Tomorrow People*?
10. Who links Darth Vader and The Green Cross Code Man?
11. Barbara Euphan Todd wrote about which scarecrow, the stories of whom were adapted for TV?
12. What were *Pinky and Perky*?
13. Which cartoon series is about talking babies?
14. Shep the dog originally appeared with John Noakes on which TV programme?
15. Which comedian created the Diddy Men?
16. On which Island did the Fraggles live?
17. Which puppet's catchphrase is "Boom, boom!"?
18. The knowledgeable twins Ross and Norris McWhirter helped present which TV series?
19. Charlie Brown and Snoopy appear in which cartoon series?
20. What was the children's comedy series featuring The Meakers and a group of ghosts?
21. What creatures are *Tom and Jerry*?
22. Which show featured Uncle Bulgaria?
23. *Spiderman* had what kind of special blood?
24. What colour is *Batman*'s cape?
25. Which substance makes *Superman* lose his special powers?
26. What is Charlie Brown's favourite sport?
27. Which former *Blue Peter* presenter went on to host Duncan Dares?
28. Which Terry hosted *The Really Wild Show*?
29. What creature was the puppet Lennie?
30. What does Noddy have on the end of his hat?

Drama 8 (see Quiz 65)

1. Vampires. 2. *Highlander*. 3. David. 4. Dennis Potter. 5. Katie. 6. *The A Team*. 7. Fitzgerald's. 8. *Hamish MacBeth*. 9. James. 10. John Loengard. 11. On the hill above the lake where she and Peter walked. 12. *Lou Grant*. 13. *Miami Vice*. 14. *Dempsey And Makepiece*. 15. John Boy. 16. *Tomorrow's World*. 17. Gina Ward. 18. Clannad. 19. *The Tribe*. 20. Richard Murdoch. 21. Jane Gurnett. 22. *Twin Peaks*. 23. *Pride And Prejudice*. 24. *Lovejoy*. 25. Nuclear war. 26. Ireland. 27. PC Reg Hollis. 28. *Northern Exposure*. 29. *Highway To Heaven*. 30. *Brimstone And Treacle*.

ANSWERS

Answers: see Quiz 68, page 76

LEVEL I

1. Who presented his C4 programme *Real Food*?
2. Which Weekend programme is presented by Anne Robinson?
3. On the quiz, whose *Price Is Right*?
4. Which science series was presented by Richard Vranch?
5. Of which football club is the subject of *The Alex Ferguson Story* the manager?
6. Which star of *The Color Purple* has her own talk show?
7. Who presented ITV's *What Will They Think Of Next*?
8. What was *Clothes Show* presenter Franklyn's christian name?
9. Who was Mandy to marry in *Game On*?
10. Who is Butch's father in *Emmerdale*?
11. What was the BBC's first digital channel?
12. Which channel broadcasts live League Cup football?
13. What is Pauline McLynn's character in *Father Ted*?
14. Who does Victoria Smurfit portray in *Ballykissangel*?
15. On which game show does Melanie Stace assist Jim Davidson?
16. What was Sanjay's surname in *Eastenders*?
17. From where were the 1998 Commonwealth Games televised?
18. Who was the presenter of *Still In Bed With MeDinner*?
19. Who is David Baddiel's co-presenter on *Fantasy Football League*?
20. What is Mr. Bing's first name in *Friends*?
21. Which children's TV presenter took over the stage role of Joseph?
22. What does Brendan Foster commentate on?
23. What was Jason Donavon's character in *Neighbours*?
24. Who is the northern motorbike fan who co-presents *Top Gear*?
25. In which fantasy series did Granny Weatherwax appear?
26. Who is Sally Webster's youngest daughter?
27. Who is magician Penn's partner?
28. On which channel is *DOSH*?
29. Who shares a show with Ren?
30. Who places the letters on *Countdown*?

Answers: see Quiz 67, page 75

LEVEL 1

1. Which comedy series set in a POW camp starred Bob Crane?
2. In which series is the character Frank Doberman?
3. What was *Sanford and Son* an American version of?
4. What was Cliff's wife's name in *The Cosby Show*?
5. Who is Thelma's husband in *Whatever Happened to the Likely Lads*?
6. What is Bigfoot's name when he moves in with the Hendersons?
7. Which channel broadcasts *The Comedy Zone*?
8. In which sitcom do David and Hugo Horton appear?
9. Which comedienne *Does The Season*?
10. In which sitcom is the character Roz Doyle?
11. Who is Jack's driver in *On The Buses*?
12. Which comedy character has a son named Gash?
13. Who plays Louise in *Get Real*?
14. Who is the regular presenter of *Eurotrash*?
15. What relation is Arkwright to Granville in *Open All Hours*?
16. Who was Wendy Craig's character in *Butterflies*?
17. Which sitcom featured doctors Tom and Toby?
18. Which comedy series featured policemen Louie and Briggs?
19. Who starred in *The Thoughts Of Chairman Alf*?
20. What is the name of Brett Butler's sitcom?
21. What was that name of Gareth Blackstock's wife in *Chef*?
22. In which cartoon series is Principal Skinner a character?
23. Who was the senior saleslady of the ladies department of Grace Brothers?
24. Whose children were Serge and Saffron in *Absolutely Fabulous*?
25. What did *The Beverley Hillbillies* find on their land that made their fortune?
26. Which sitcom featured the character Gunner Lofty Sugden?
27. Which of the *Monty Python* team was an animator?
28. Who starred as *The New Statesman*?
29. Which S.F. series features Kochanski?
30. What was Boysie's occupation in *Only Fools And Horses*?

Answers: see Quiz 70, page 78

LEVEL I

1. *Lucky Numbers* was hosted by which Shane?
2. Who presents *Play Your Cards Right* on ITV?
3. What was *Strike It Rich* previously called?
4. On which show did Bruce ask Anthea for a twirl?
5. *The Golden Shot* featured what kind of weapon?
6. What colour is the book on *This Is Your Life*?
7. Which former Dr Who presented the TV whodunnit game *Cluedo*?
8. *Celebrity Squares* was based on which game?
9. Which quiz game was based on darts?
10. How many contestants in total sit with Cilla at the end of each episode of *Blind Date*?
11. Which Terry presented *Blankety-Blank*?
12. Which TV magician hosted *Every Second Counts*?
13. *The Great Garden Game* is broadcast on which channel?
14. Who is the current presenter of *Call my Bluff*?
15. Which Michael has presented *Blockbusters*?
16. *Today's The Day* hosted by Martyn Lewis is broadcast on which channel?
17. What type of plant did the leader appear as on *The Adventure Game*?
18. On which evening of the week was *It's A Knockout* broadcast?
19. Which Lesley preceded Bruce Forsyth as host of *The Price Is Right*?
20. Sue Barker chairs *A Question of ...* what?
21. Which show featured "the Phantom Raspberry Blower"?
22. How many male contestants are there in each episode of *Man-O-Man*?
23. What do the contestants do in *Stars In Their Eyes*?
24. What is the name of the show, hosted by Dale Winton, in which contestants guess the identity of other people's partners?
25. Which former *Krypton Factor* host presents *A Word In Your Ear*?
26. What percentage is the title of Channel 5's general knowledge quiz?
27. Chris Evans warned us *Don't Forget Your* ... what in his Channel 4 game show?
28. Nicky Campbell and Carol Smillie asked contestants to spin which wheel?
29. What kind of maze did Richard O'Brien ask contestants to navigate?
30. Who does quizmaster Angus Deayton have news for on BBC2?

Answers: see Quiz 69, page 77

LEVEL I

1. Who was Gita's husband in *Eastenders*?
2. Who presented *Euroballs*?
3. What kind of animal is *Babar*?
4. Who presented *The Private Life Of Plants*?
5. Which character in *Coronation Street* had only one leg?
6. What is HG of Roy And HG's surname?
7. Who wrote *Wyrd Sisters*?
8. Who presented *Hearts Of Gold*?
9. Who presented *Smillies' People*?
10. What is *Supermarket Sweep*'s Winton's first name?
11. What is the first name of presenter DeVine?
12. What type of programme is BBC2's *Just One Chance*?
13. Who hosted *The National Lottery Dreamworld*?
14. What is Max's surname in *Brookside*?
15. Who presented *She's Gotta Have It*?
16. Who presents *The Countryside Hour*?
17. Which ex-*Coronation Street* actor appears as Jack Gates in *Family Affairs*?
18. What is the name of BBC2's short series of 10 minute films by new directors?
19. What did Ivy run in *Last Of The Summer Wine*?
20. Who portrayed *Maximum Bob*?
21. Who narrated *Cold War*?
22. What was the subject of the documentary series *Glory of The Geeks*?
23. Which channel is dedicated to cookery?
24. Who is the father of presenter Samantha Norman?
25. Who created *Ballykissangel*?
26. Which game show is presented by Lily Savage?
27. Who was Roland Rat's sidekick?
28. Which series featured Gillian Taylforth as one of a family on their way to the 1998 World Cup?
29. Which terrestrial channel first broadcast *The X-Files*?
30. What kind of a programme is Channel 5's *100 Per cent*?

Answers: see Quiz 72, page 80

LEVEL 1

1. Which *Brookside* ex-con became a teacher?
2. Which soap featured the characters Fin and Angel?
3. During a horse robbery, who was run over in *Emmerdale*?
4. Whose gaoling in *Coronation Street* even caused comment from Tony Blair?
5. Which medical series was set in St. Angela's Hospital?
6. Who was Simon Wicks' half brother?
7. In which soap were Todd and Katie Landers?
8. Which di Marco in *Eastenders* had an affair with Tiffany?
9. Which character in *Coronation Street* cheated on his girlfriend Fiona to sleep with her best friend Max?
10. In which soap was there a pizza parlour named Pizza Parade?
11. What was the name of the hotel in *Neighbours*?
12. Who does Belinda Emmett portray in *Home and Away*?
13. What substance is Lucy Benson hooked on in *Hollyoaks*?
14. Who is Lachie's brother in *Home and Away*?
15. What is the name of Fiona's son in *Coronation Street*?
16. What number in Ramsey Street do the Bishops live?
17. Who was Betty Williams' second husband in *Coronation Street*?
18. Whose mother had Alzheimer's disease in *Eastenders*?
19. Who is Ruth Benson's husband in *Hollyoaks*?
20. Who replaced Barbara Bel Geddes as Miss Ellie in *Dallas*?
21. In which series is PC Alf Ventress?
22. Which early soap was set in wartime Australia?
23. Which soap features Harchester United Football Club?
24. Who in *Eastenders* has twins named Lucy and Peter?
25. In *Neighbours* who did Des get engaged to after Daphne's death?
26. What is Eleanor Kitson's profession in *Brookside*?
27. In which soap did Bronwyn Davies marry Henry Ramsey?
28. Which actor played Lachie in Home and Away and Sam Kratz in *Neighbours*?
29. Who is Ollie Simpson's life partner in *Brookside*?
30. What did Norris Cole bury in the allotment in *Coronation Street*?

Answers: see Quiz 71, page 79

LEVEL I

1. Which series featured the character Chief Inspector Cato?
2. Who did Dr. Philip Capra replace in *Northern Exposure*?
3. Who wrote *The Tribe*?
4. Who did Rachel have an affair with in *Casualty*?
5. Which Lady was the star of the drama *This Could Be The Last Time*?
6. Who is Sean Dillon's teenage daughter in *Ballykissangel*?
7. In which series is the character Nick Georgiadis a station officer?
8. Who played the title role in *The Amazing Howard Hughes*?
9. Who plays Edna in *Supply and Demand*?
10. Which U.S. police series is set in Baltimore?
11. Which Victorian detective is played by Eoin McCarthy?
12. What is Ally McBeal's occupation?
13. Who played Olive Martin in *The Sculptress*?
14. Which former sister returned to *Casualty* as an agency nurse?
15. Which priest replaced Peter Clifford in *Ballykissangel*?
16. Which character was played by both Tim Piggott-Smith and Martin Shaw?
17. Who wrote *Middlemarch*?
18. Who wrote and starred in *Stark*?
19. Who in *Rumpole Of The Bailey* is 'She you must be obeyed'?
20. Which policeman's beat is Lochdubh?
21. What is *Petrocelli's* occupation?
22. What is Duffy's full name in *Casualty*?
23. Who created *All Creatures Great And Small*?
24. Which drama charted the fortunes of a Liverpool shipping family?
25. Who is Niamh's father in *Ballykissangel*?
26. Who was Jock Ewing's wife in *Dallas*?
27. In which era are the *Inspector Pitt Mysteries* set?
28. Who wrote *The Tommyknockers*?
29. Who wrote *Black Eyes*?
30. In which series did Janet McTeer play Helen Hewitt?

Answers: see Quiz 74, page 82

LEVEL I

1. Who's 'Angels' were undercover detectives?
2. Who was the streetwise informant in *Starsky And Hutch*?
3. Who did Biff Fowler sleep with on her wedding night?
4. What was BBC2's sheepdog trials programme called?
5. In which series is Jack Klugman a pathologist?
6. On which children's programme did Nigel Planer succeed Eric Thompson as narrator?
7. Which was the football highlights show, *Match Of The Day* or *The Big Match*?
8. Which sitcom was set behind the bars of H.M.P. Slade?
9. Who is the senior officer of Sun Hill in *The Bill*?
10. Who played Snudge in *The Army Game*?
11. Who is Tea Leone's husband?
12. In which series is Dr. Sean Maddox the senior house officer?
13. What was Wallace and Gromit's first adventure?
14. What sort of animal was *Mr Ed*?
15. What job did Beth Saunders do in *Dangerfield*?
16. Who was Alan Jackson's grandmother in *Eastenders*?
17. On which ship is Lt. Tom Paris an officer?
18. What was the full name of the satirical programme abbreviated to *TW3*?
19. Who narrated *Roobarb & Custard*?
20. Which entertainer's catch-phrase is "Awright!"?
21. Who starred with Peter Cook in *Not Only... But Also*?
22. Which ex-*Eastender* appeared in *Real Women*?
23. What was Roy Scheider's character in *Seaquest DSV*?
24. What is amateur detective Mrs Wainthropp's first name?
25. In 1963, which Fab Four pop group were panellists on *Juke Box Jury*?
26. Which BBC current affairs programme began broadcasting in 1953?
27. Who played Uncle in *Only Fools And Horses*?
28. Which S.F. show began by announcing "Do not adjust your set"?
29. Which ex-Tiswas host presents *Man-o-Man* on ITV?
30. Who presented *Tip Top Challenge*?

Comedy 14 (see Quiz 74)

ANSWERS

1. *The Simpsons*. 2. Roy Clarke. 3. Joey. 4. Grace Bros. 5. *To The Manor Born*. 6. Cybill Shepherd. 7. *The Vicar Of Dibley*. 8. Lister. 9. *Bottom*. 10. Mark. 11. Karl Howman. 12. John Alderton. 13. James Bolam. 14. George Cole. 15. Patricia Brake. 16. Bruce Forsyth. 17. Peter Jones. 18. Patricia Hodge. 19. Kathy Burke and Paul Whitehouse. 20. *Chef*. 21. Howard. 22. Leonard. 23. *Only When I Laugh*. 24. Bouquet. 25. Richard Briers. 26. O'Reilly. 27. *Oh Brother*. 28. David Renwick. 29. Principal Victoria. 30. Ren.

Answers: see Quiz 73, page 81

1. Which cartoon series features Groundskeeper Willie?
2. Who wrote Last of The Summer Wine?
3. Whose surname in Friends is Tribiani?
4. In which store was Mr. Rumbold the manager?
5. In which series did Richard de Vere buy Grantleigh Manor?
6. Who is Cybill?
7. Which sitcom featured Trevor Peacock as Jim Trott?
8. What is Dave's surname in Red Dwarf?
9. In which comedy series does the character Spudgun appear?
10. Which character was David's brother in Roseanne?
11. Who played Mulberry in the sitcom of that name?
12. Who played Hannah Gordon's husband in My Wife Next Door?
13. Which Likely Lad starred in Second Thoughts?
14. Who portrayed Henry Root in Root Into Europe?
15. Who played Ingrid in Going Straight?
16. Whose catchphrase was 'Nice to see you – to see you nice'?
17. Who played Mr. Fenner in The Rag Trade?
18. Which actress played an army officer in Holding The Fort?
19. Who were Harry Enfield's Chums?
20. What was Terry's job in Fawlty Towers?
21. Who was Marina courting in Last Of The Summer Wine?
22. Who was Ria's secret admirer in Butterflies?
23. Which sitcom featured Figgis, Glover and Norman?
24. How did Patricia Routledge pronounce her name in Keeping Up Appearances?
25. Who played Martin in Ever Decreasing Circles?
26. Which builder from Fawlty Towers appeared in Ballykissangel?
27. What was Oh Father starring Derek Nimmo a sequel to?
28. Who created Victor Meldrew?
29. What is the headmistress in South Park called?
30. What is the name of Stimpy's cartoon partner?

QUIZ 75 Quiz & Games 3

Answers: see Quiz 76, page 84

LEVEL 1

1. *Blankety Blank* host Lily Savage hails from which northern city?
2. Which Bob chairs the comedy quiz *Not A Lot Of People Know That*?
3. How many celebrities contest the improvisation series *Whose Line Is It Anyway*?
4. What did *Strike It Lucky* change its name to?
5. Which *Watchdog* presenter, Alice, hosts the celebrity finance quiz, *Easy Money*?
6. Who is the presenter of *Countdown*?
7. Which boardgame inspired a whodunit show?
8. On which programme did Patrick Moore and Dominic Diamond both appear?
9. Which Bob is the comedy partner of Vic Reeves on *Shooting Stars*?
10. Which Derek Batey show tested how well couples knew each other?
11. On which game show is there a Yes/No interlude?
12. Which magician presented *Wipeout*?
13. Which Liverpudlian comedian hosted *Name That Tune*?
14. What is the first non-zero guaranteed minimum prize on *Who Wants To Be A Millionaire*?
15. Max Bygraves, Bob Monkhouse and Les Dennis all hosted which family game show?
16. Who presents both *Big Break* and *The Generation Game*?
17. Which former children's presenter hosts *Talking Telephone Numbers*?
18. What is the final event of *The Gladiators*?
19. What must you win to succeed at Richard O'Brien's Maze?
20. Which DJ Nicky is the presenter of *Wheel Of Fortune*?
21. Which quiz show featured opposing schools?
22. Which series trophy was won in 1998 by Magdalen College?
23. Which *Opportunity Knocks* host presented *Double Your Money*?
24. On which sports quiz show is Lee Hurst a panellist?
25. Which animal game show was presented by Dale Winton?
26. Which Shane hosts *Lucky Numbers*?
27. Who presented *Celebrity Ready Steady Cook*?
28. *Name That Tune* was originally part of which Wednesday Night variety show?
29. How many competitors were there in each episode of *Mastermind*?
30. BBC1's *Ask The Family* was hosted by which Robert?

Sport 4 (see Quiz 76)

1. Eric Bristow. 2. Snooker. 3. Boxing. 4. No. 5. *Grandstand.* 6. Three. 7. USA. 8. 1966 – England vs. West Germany. 9. Paul Elliott. 10. ITV. 11. Herbie Hide. 12. Royal Ascot. 13. Tennis. 14. Alan Shearer. 15. Channel 4. 16. Wembley. 17. Liverpool. 18. Ruud Gullit. 19. Liverpool and Arsenal. 20. *The Big Match.* 21. 1980s. 22. June. 23. Chas and Dave. 24. Brian Woolnough. 25. David Vine. 26. Freddie Mercury. 27. Torvill and Dean. 28. Eurosport. 29. Horse racing. 30. *They Think It's All Over.*

ANSWERS

Answers: see Quiz 75, page 83   LEVEL 1

1. Who is darts' "Crafty Cockney"?
2. The Crucible hosts which sporting events?
3. Harry Carpenter is a commentator on which sport?
4. Did England win the Ashes in 1998?
5. *Football Focus* is part of which sports programme?
6. On *A Question Of Sport* how many members are there in each team?
7. From which country were the 1996 Summer Olympics broadcast?
8. In which year did England win the World Cup?
9. Which former Chelsea footballer helps present *Football Italia* on Channel 4?
10. On which channel is Formula 1 motor racing currently broadcast – BBC1 or ITV?
11. Which Herbie retained the WBO Heavyweight Championship in a fight against Willie Fischer televised live on Sky Sports?
12. Coverage of which annual Royal race meeting is broadcast by the BBC?
13. Former Great Britain international Mark Cox commentates on which racquet sport?
14. Who scored a first half penalty for England against Argentina in the 98 World Cup?
15. The sports magazine show *Transworld Sport* can be viewed on which channel?
16. From which stadium is the F.A. Cup Final televised each year?
17. With which football club did commentator Alan Hansen end his playing career?
18. Which former Chelsea manager helped present the 1988 World Cup Finals?
19. Who was playing when Brian Moore famously said "It's up for grabs now" in 1989?
20. Clive Tyldesley appears on which programme – *The Big Match* or *Match Of The Day*?
21. In which decade was the London Marathon first screened on TV?
22. Coverage of Wimbledon is traditionally broadcast in which month?
23. Which cockney duo composed and sang *Snooker Loopy*?
24. Who hosts *Hold The Back Page*?
25. Which David hosted *Super Stars*?
26. Who joined Montserrat Caballe on the BBC's theme for the Barcelona Olympics?
27. Name the British ice skating duo televised being awarded maximum marks in the World Championships.
28. Which satellite channel broadcasts ten-pin bowling?
29. With which sport is TV personality Willie Carson associated?
30. On which sports game show do the panellists have to 'feel the celebrity'?

Answers: see Quiz 78, page 86 LEVEL 1

1. Which character was *Roseanne's* sister?

2. What was Norm's surname in *Cheers*?

3. Which Royal Prince appeared on *Des O'Connor Tonight* in 1998?

4. Who always told a long joke from a black chair on *The Two Ronnies*?

5. Who was "smarter than the average bear"?

6. What was Roobarb's feline companion called?

7. What kind of animated animal is Alvin?

8. What is the name of BBC1's early morning financial programme?

9. Which country's football league has a *Serie A*?

10. Which daytime show is presented by Richard Whiteley?

11. Which S.F. series featured the character Major Wilma Dearing?

12. In which series does Victor French play Mark?

13. Who were Brenda and Brandon Walsh's parents in *Beverley Hills 90210*?

14. What ex-Avenger appeared in *The Upper Hand*?

15. Which Bob assists Cilla Black in *Surprise, Surprise*?

16. Which programme became known as 'the antiques rogue show'?

17. Who presents *Through The Cake Hole*?

18. Which doctor in *Eastenders* had the christian name Harold?

19. What was the drama series set in Cornwall written by Winston Graham?

20. Which *Python* was a qualified doctor?

21. What is the christian name of the presenter of *Frostrup On Friday*?

22. Which series presented by Kate Sanderson features news items from the world of entertainment?

23. On which programme does Alice Beer appear?

24. On which series is Tiff Needell a presenter?

25. Which English actress played Dr. Tracey Clark in *Ally McBeal*?

26. In which U.S. series is there a policeman named Garner?

27. Which *Opportunity Knocks* presenter died in 1997?

28. What was Donna's surname in *The Jump*?

29. Who was *Desperately Seeking Something* on C4?

30. In which drama series were Milly and Anna lawyers?

Answers: see Quiz 77, page 85

LEVEL 1

1. Which of her relations did Denise have an affair with in *Coronation Street*?

2. Who was murdered outside a nightclub in *Coronation Street* in 1989?

3. Which character in *Eastenders* is played by Martine McCutcheon?

4. Which soap features Sol and Kate Patrick?

5. Which *Dallas* character died in 1982?

6. Who is Sally Webster's eldest daughter in *Coronation Street*?

7. Who in *Dynasty* had a son named Little Blake?

8. Who is Grant and Phil's sister in *Eastenders*?

9. Where did Curly and Raquel spend their honeymoon in *Coronation Street*?

10. On which soap did Robbie Williams play an extra?

11. What was Channel 4's first major UK soap?

12. Who was Melanie's husband in *Neighbours*?

13. Which character has been in *Coronation Street* since its inception?

14. Which *Big Breakfast* presenter played Joe Mangel in *Neighbours*?

15. What is Terry's surname in *Emmerdale*?

16. What is Liz Dawn's character in *Coronation Street*?

17. Which *Brookside* actress was also Gloria in *Coronation Street*?

18. What is Judith's surname in *Hollyoaks*?

19. Who is Lance's sister in *Neighbours*?

20. Which butcher owns the corner shop in *Coronation Street*?

21. What is Maud's surname in *Coronation Street*?

22. What was Jacqui Dixon's baby's name in *Brookside*?

23. In which soap did Lily Savage appear?

24. Which ex-*Coronation Street* actor played Barry Scripps in *Heartbeat*?

25. What was Julie Goodyear's character in *Coronation Street*?

26. Who not only appeared in but directed *Eastenders*?

27. Which Eastender starred in *Hugh and I*?

28. What was Polly Becker's occupation in *Eastenders*?

29. Who played Dr. John Forrest in *The Young Doctors*?

30. What was the name of Mike's dog in *Neighbours*?

Answers: see Quiz 80, page 88

1. What is comedian Sykes's first name?
2. Which Channel 4 comedy series is set in a TV Newsroom?
3. Who sang the theme song for the sitcom *On The Up*?
4. Which *Whose Line Is It Anyway* performer advertised a Canadian Airline?
5. Which actor appeared in both *One Foot In The Grave* and *KYTV*?
6. In which children's series did Tony Robinson play the Sheriff Of Nottingham?
7. Which company produced the *Tom and Jerry* cartoons?
8. Whose voice does Dan Castellaneta supply in *The Simpsons*?
9. What was the name of Dave Allen's first show?
10. What is the name of the pub in *Goodnight Sweetheart*?
11. Which US series featured the surgeons of the 4077th Mobile Army Surgical Hospital?
12. Which sitcom featured the workers of Fenner's Fashions?
13. What was Jessica's mum's name in *Some Mother's Do 'Ave 'Em*?
14. What was Saffy's proper name in *Absolutely Fabulous*?
15. Complete the comedy review title: *The Mary Whitehouse ...* ?
16. Who was Bertie Wooster if Dennis Price was Jeeves?
17. Which Street featured celebrity impressions by John Sessions?
18. Which class did Arthur Lowe try to keep under control as *AJ Wentworth B A*?
19. What was Bunter of Greyfriars first name?
20. What was the name of Eddie's wife in *Love Thy Neighbour*?
21. Who lived at Railway Cuttings, East Cheam?
22. Who was Miss Jones's landlord in *Rising Damp*?
23. Where did the *Happy Days* gang hang out?
24. What was Mr. Boswell's christian name in *Bread*?
25. Who played Timothy Lumsden in *Sorry*?
26. Who was 'The One with the Glasses' in the comedy duo Morecambe and Wise?
27. Alastair Sim played which litigious man in the sitcom about his *...Misleading Cases*?
28. Who connects Purdy with Patsy?
29. Who played Penny in *Just Good Friends*?
30. Which cricketing sitcom starred Timothy Spall and Josie Lawrence?

QUIZ 80 Pot Luck 25

Answers: see Quiz 79, page 87

LEVEL 1

1. Which US series featured the heroine seeing a dancing baby?
2. Who presented her chat show *Lowri*?
3. What was *Dangerfield*'s christian name?
4. Who played Auntie Wainwright in *Last Of The Summer Wine*?
5. Which cook presented a series on herbs?
6. Which sitcom starred and was written by Jack Docherty and Moray Hunter?
7. Where was the series *Out Of The Blue* located?
8. Which interviewing barrister was *All Talk*?
9. Which actress from *This Life* appeared in *Undercover Heart*?
10. Which journalist reported for the BBC from Tripoli in 1986 on the American bombing?
11. Which Team helped those in trouble in the 1980s?
12. Who played Tristan Farnon in *All Creatures Great And Small*?
13. What was the name of *The Family*?
14. What was the first name of McCoist in *McCoist And McCauley*?
15. Which sporting gameshow features a 'what happens next' board?
16. Who replaced Nick as Station Officer in *London's Burning*?
17. Who played Mossie Sheehan in *Falling For A Dancer*?
18. Which Australian presenter met *The Supermodels*?
19. Who presented *On The Record*?
20. Which American film actress appeared in Peugeot commercials?
21. Which bandleader had a son with the same name who became a BBC executive?
22. Where did *M*A*S*H* take place?
23. Who said 'And The Next Tonight Will Be Tomorrow Night'?
24. What was the name of broadcasters David and Jonathan's father?
25. Which quiz, hosted by Eamonn Andrews, featured Gilbert Harding as a panellist?
26. Which Joseph worked with a gopher?
27. Who is Spike's brother in *Peanuts*?
28. What was the name of *Roseanne*'s son?
29. Where did Vera and Jack Duckworth live in 1998?
30. In which children's series was there a rival school named Brookdale?

ANSWERS Comedy 15 (see Quiz 79)

1. Eric. 2. *Drop The Dead Donkey*. 3. Dennis Waterman. 4. Mike McShane. 5. Angus Deayton.
6. *Maid Marian and Her Merry Men*. 7. MGM. 8. Homer Simpson. 9. *Dave Allen At Large*. 10. The
Royal Oak. 11. *MASH*. 12. *The Rag Trade*. 13. Betty. 14. Saffron. 15. *Experience*. 16. Ian
Carmichael. 17. *Stella Street*. 18. Third Form. 19. Billy. 20. Joan. 21. Hancock. 22. Rigsby.
23. Arnolds. 24. Freddie. 25. Ronnie Corbett. 26. Eric Morecambe. 27. AP Herbert. 28. Joanna
Lumley. 29. Jan Francis. 30. *Outside Edge*.

Answers: see Quiz 82, page 90

1. Who was Lorcan Cranitch's character in *Ballykissangel*?
2. What was *The Jump* in the series of the same name?
3. Which drama series features the character Dr. Neil Bolton?
4. What is PC Quinnan's first name in *The Bill*?
5. Which Wonderwoman appeared in *Hawkeye*?
6. What was the name of Iain Banks's first drama series?
7. In which police series was John Kelly a detective?
8. Which adventure series starred Tony Curtis and Roger Moore?
9. What was Mrs. Peel's christian name in *The Avengers*?
10. Who played Charlie in *The Darling Buds Of May*?
11. Who created *Maximum Bob*?
12. Who played Caesar Augustus in *I, Claudius*?
13. Who portrayed Lillie in the story of *Lillie Langtrey*?
14. Who produced *Cathy Come Home*?
15. Who played Dr. Beth Glover in *Peak Practice*?
16. What was the name of ITV's children's drama showcase of the 1980s?
17. Which drama series featured Warren and Joe?
18. Draz and Kurt feature in which Australian series?
19. In which series does Ben Roberts play Chief Inspector Conway?
20. Who does Bill Cosby play in *The Cosby Mysteries*?
21. Which award winning film featured the life of Quentin Crisp?
22. How were Jimmy Nail's shoes described in his drama series title?
23. What was *Perry Mason*'s occupation?
24. Who played wheeler-dealer Frank Stubbs?
25. Who did Ruth Patchett become in Fay Weldon's novel and drama series?
26. Who was the Born Free actor who played John Ridd in *Lorna Doone*?
27. Which series was the sequel to *Public Eye*?
28. Which singer played Zoe Wanamaker's partner in *Love Hurts*?
29. Who was the Sheriff of Trinity in *American Gothic*?
30. In which surreal drama was Laura Palmer killed?

Children's TV 7 (see Quiz 82)

1. *The Muppet Show*. 2. A snail. 3. Mungo. 4. Batman. 5. *Thunderbirds*. 6. Grandpa Pickles.
7. *Animaniacs*. 8. Playschool. 9. Red. 10. *Rainbow*. 11. Ball. 12. Blue. 13. Maggie Philbin.
14. Pugwash. 15. Linford Christie. 16. Spinach. 17. *Sesame Street*. 18. *Animal Magic*. 19. *Worzel Gummidge*. 20. Saturday. 21. *The Herbs*. 22. Barbera. 23. Robinson Crusoe. 24. *The A-Team*.
25. Pizza. 26. *Bugs Bunny*. 27. Tin-Tin. 28. Huckleberry Hound. 29. *Speedy Gonzales*. 30. Mr Magoo.

ANSWERS

Answers: see Quiz 81, page 89 LEVEL I

1. In which series did the wild and impetuous Animal play the drums?
2. What kind of creature was Brian in *The Magic Roundabout*?
3. In *Mary, Mungo and Midge*, which character was the dog?
4. What is Bruce Wayne's alter ego?
5. International Rescue featured in which puppet adventure series?
6. Which old man regularly looks after the *Rugrats*?
7. Which cartoon is set in the Warner Brothers' studio?
8. Which children's series showed a house in its opening credits?
9. What colour is *Postman Pat's* van?
10. Which series featured Zippy?
11. Which Johnny presented *Think Of A Number*?
12. What colour is *Thomas The Tank Engine*?
13. The *Multi-Coloured Swap Shop* was co-presented by which Maggie?
14. The cartoon pirate was Captain what?
15. Who took over *Record Breakers* and changed its name?
16. What was Popeye famous for eating?
17. Which show featured Big Bird and The Count?
18. Johnny Morris hosted which animal series?
19. Which Worzel was a scarecrow?
20. *Live And Kicking* is broadcast on which day?
21. Dill the Dog featured in which series?
22. Who partnered Hanna to produce TV cartoons?
23. Who was marooned on a desert island with Man Friday?
24. In which series did BA, Face and Hannibal appear?
25. What is the favourite food of the *Teenage Mutant Turtles*?
26. 'What's Up Doc?' is the catchphrase of which cartoon character?
27. Whose adventures did Hergé chronicle?
28. Which cartoon hound's favourite song was *My Darling Clementine*?
29. Who was the "fastest mouse in all Mexico"?
30. What was the short-sighted cartoon character whose voice was provided by Jim Backus?

Answers: see Quiz 84, page 92

LEVEL 1

1. Which council workman was played by Bill Maynard?
2. Which star of Dallas appeared in *I Dream Of Jeannie*?
3. Which star of *The Rock Follies* had a No.1. hit with *Don't Cry For Me Argentina*?
4. Which Pamela appeared on *Not The Nine O' Clock News*?
5. Which demobbed RAF serviceman was played in a series by Kenneth Cranham?
6. Who was Christopher Timothy's character in *All Creatures Great And Small*?
7. Which northern lass famous for *She Knows You Know* starred in *Not On Your Nellie*?
8. In which series did Timothy West play Arkwright, a mill owner?
9. Who was Natasha's twin sister in *Grange Hill*?
10. Which TV cop recorded *Don't Give Up On Us Baby*?
11. Who was *Roseanne's* real life husband who appeared in the series?
12. In *Home Improvements* what was Tim's job?
13. Which collie had her own TV series?
14. What was Lister's first name in *Red Dwarf*?
15. How many *Goodies* were there?
16. What was Dirty Den's surname in *Eastenders*?
17. Which weekly series was often televised from the Hammersmith Palais or The Lyceum?
18. Which talent show was presented by Hughie Green?
19. What was Jeff's surname in *Dynasty*?
20. Who is Cheggers?
21. What was Richard Beckinsale's character in *Rising Damp*?
22. Which programme linked Cyril Fletcher to Esther Rantzen?
23. Whose Half Hour featured 'the lad himself'?
24. What was chat show host Harty's first name?
25. Which Australian had a puppet named Kojee Bear?
26. Which Kennedy was *Game For A Laugh*?
27. Where does ITV get its revenue from?
28. What was the subject of the variety show *The Good Old Days*?
29. *Antiques Roadshow* is broadcast on which day of the week?
30. Whose boyfriend Liam was killed in *Grange Hill* while cycling to a school fight?

ANSWERS

Comedy 16 (see Quiz 84)

1. Alan B'Stard. 2. Margaret Meldrew. 3. *Dad's Army*. 4. Derek Fowlds. 5. Alec Callender. 6. Tom And Barbara Good. 7. The Yellowcoats. 8. No. 9. Norman Stanley Fletcher. 10. Dawn French. 11. *Absolutely Fabulous*. 12. *Are You Being Served?* 13. Laos. 14. Nicholas Lyndhurst. 15. *Birds Of A Feather*. 16. The Fonz. 17. Russ Abbot. 18. Margaret. 19. American. 20. *It Ain't Half Hot Mum*. 21. *Bread*. 22. Ireland. 23. The Boswells. 24. Ian Lavender. 25. Kenneth Williams. 26. Chris Barrie. 27. Dave Allen. 28. Craig. 29. Bob. 30. The piano.

Comedy 16

Answers: see Quiz 83, page 91   LEVEL I

1. Which MP was *The New Statesman*?

2. What is Annette Crosbie's character in *One Foot In The Grave*?

3. Which sitcom concerned the antics of a Home Guard platoon in the Second World War?

4. Who played Bernard in *Yes Minister*?

5. Who was Anton Rodgers' character in *May To December*?

6. Who practised self-sufficiency in Surbiton in a sitcom?

7. How were the camp entertainers known in *Hi De Hi*?

8. Does Maggie Simpson ever talk?

9. Which Ronnie Barker character was sent to Slade Prison?

10. Who is Lenny Henry's wife?

11. Edina, Saffron and Patsy appear in which comedy?

12. Mrs Slocombe and Captain Peacock featured in which series?

13. Where is Hank Hill's oriental neighbour from?

14. Which actor stars in *Goodnight Sweetheart*?

15. Sharon and Tracy are the lead characters in which BBC comedy?

16. The actor Henry Winkler played which character in *Happy Days*?

17. Which TV comedian formerly led the pop group the Black Abbots?

18. What is the name of Victor Meldrew's wife in *One Foot In The Grave*?

19. Is *South Park* American or British?

20. Melvyn Hayes played Gloria in which series?

21. Nellie Boswell was the mother in which BBC sitcom?

22. *Ballykissangel* is set in which country?

23. Jean Boht starred as the mother of which TV family?

24. Who played Private Pike in *Dad's Army*?

25. Which Carry On star narrated *Will-O-The-Wisp*?

26. Which Chris starred in *The Brittas Empire* and *Red Dwarf*?

27. Which Irish comedian would say "may your God go with you"?

28. Which Wendy starred in *Butterflies*?

29. What is the first name of Mr. Fleming, the coughing 'country ways' presenter on the *Fast Show*?

30. With which musical instrument do you associate Dudley Moore?

Pot Luck 26 (see Quiz 83)
1. Selwyn Froggitt. 2. Larry Hagman. 3. Julie Covington. 4. Stephenson. 5. Harvey Moon. 6. James Herriot. 7. Hylda Baker. 8. Brass. 9. Natalie. 10. David Soul. 11. Tom Arnold. 12. TV Presenter of *Tooltime*. 13. *Lassie*. 14. Dave. 15. Three. 16. Watts. 17. Come Dancing. 18. Opportunity Knocks. 19. Colby. 20. Keith Chegwin. 21. Alan Moore. 22. *That's Life*. 23. Tony Hancock's. 24. Russell. 25. Rolf Harris. 26. Sarah. 27. Advertising. 28. *The Old Time Music Hall*. 29. Sunday. 30. Justine's.

Answers: see Quiz 86, page 94

LEVEL I

1. What was the name of Hercule Poirot's friend and assistant?
2. Which Lynda wrote *Prime Suspect*?
3. Which London policeman said "Good evening all"?
4. Which Conan Doyle detective fought the arch villain Moriarty?
5. Pierce Brosnan starred as Remington who?
6. Private detective Jim Rockford appeared in which popular series?
7. Did Regan and Carter both smoke in *The Sweeney*?
8. Which Hamish was the title character in a Scottish police drama?
9. Who had a sidekick called Tonto?
10. Jan Hammer wrote the theme music for which US police series?
11. Whose sidekick was called Rocky?
12. What was unusual about *Ironside*?
13. Who drives a red Jaguar?
14. Joan Hickson played which Agatha Christie sleuth?
15. Which TV company broadcast *Z Cars*?
16. Who starred as *Spender*?
17. What colour was Starsky And Hutch's car?
18. What does *Jonathan Creek* design for a living?
19. Which *A-Team* actor George played detective *Banacek*?
20. *Pacific* what was a US police series on Channel 5?
21. What was the name of Gordon Jackson's character in *The Professionals*?
22. Who is Dalziel's police partner?
23. Richard Wilson and Samantha Beckinsale star in which police series set on a river?
24. Which Raymond stars as Perry Mason?
25. Martyn Lewis presents which crime series on BBC1?
26. Which *Birds Of A Feather* star plays detective *Maisie Raine*?
27. What was Burnside's first name in *The Bill*?
28. Which Hetty, played by Patricia Routledge, Investigates?
29. In *The Wimbledon Poisoner*, which actor Robert attempted to kill his wife, played by Alison Steadman?
30. Was Kojak played by Raymond Burr?

Pot Luck 27 (see Quiz 86)

1. Mr. Robson. 2. Hanna-Barbera. 3. Julie Kavner. 4. *Fairly Secret Army*. 5. William Hartnell. 6. David Essex. 7. The Gnomes Of Dulwich. 8. *Man About The House*. 9. Caresse. 10. *The Rag Trade*. 11. Bebe Daniels. 12. Jeff Rawle. 13. Judy Loe. 14. Jaguar. 15. *Auf Weidersehen Pet*. 16. Priscilla White. 17. Juke Box Jury. 18. Liverpool. 19. Roger Moore. 20. Dudley Moore and Peter Cook. 21. Fairclough. 22. Amsterdam. 23. Glenda Jackson. 24. Farrah Fawcett. 25. Jack Duckworth. 26. Lady Jane Felsham. 27. BBC 2. 28. Titchmarsh. 29. Charlie Dimmock. 30. Wine.

ANSWERS

Answers: see Quiz 85, page 93

LEVEL I

1. Which character did Stuart Organ play in *Grange Hill*?
2. Who directed *Tom and Jerry* cartoons?
3. Who is the voice of Marge Simpson?
4. In which series was Major Harry Truscott played by Geoffrey Palmer?
5. Who introduces *The Clothes Show*?
6. Which pop star starred in *The River*?
7. Where did Terry Scott and Hugh Lloyd portray garden ornaments?
8. Which series featured a trainee chef sharing a flat with two girls?
9. Who was writing a book about Alexis in *Dynasty*?
10. In which comedy series did Gillian Taylforth appear as a machinist before *Eastenders*?
11. Who was Ben Lyons's wife?
12. Which actor from *Drop The Dead Donkey* played *Billy Liar*?
13. Who was the late Richard Beckinsale's actress wife?
14. What car did Joey drive in *Bread*?
15. Which series about building workers in Germany was written by Dick Clement and Ian La Frenais?
16. What is Cilla Black's real name?
17. On which pop show did a 'Hooter' signify a miss?
18. With which English football team did Alan Hanson win cup honours?
19. Who first played Simon Templar on TV?
20. Who were Dud and Pete?
21. What was Rita Sullivan's former surname?
22. Where was *Van Der Valk* set?
23. Which MP played *Elizabeth R*?
24. Which Charlie's Angel married Lee Majors?
25. Who kept pigeons in *Coronation Street*?
26. What was Phyllis Logan's character in *Lovejoy*?
27. On which channel was *Not The Nine O'Clock News* shown?
28. Who is Alan presenter of *Gardeners World*?
29. Who is the redhead in *Ground Force*?
30. What is Jilly Goolden an expert on?

Crime 4 (see Quiz 85)

1. Captain Hastings. 2. Lynda La Plante. 3. *Dixon Of Dock Green*. 4. Sherlock Holmes. 5. *Remington Steele*. 6. *The Rockford Files*. 7. Yes. 8. *Hamish Macbeth*. 9. The Lone Ranger. 10. *Miami Vice*. 11. *Boon*. 12. He was confined to a wheelchair. 13. *Inspector Morse*. 14. *Miss Marple*. 15. BBC. 16. Jimmy Nail. 17. Red. 18. Magic tricks. 19. George Peppard. 20. *Pacific Blue*. 21. Cowley. 22. Pascoe. 23. *Duck Patrol*. 24. Raymond Burr. 25. *Crime Beat*. 26. Pauline Quirke. 27. Frank. 28. Wainthropp. 29. Robert Lindsay. 30. No (it was Telly Savalas).

ANSWERS

Answers: see Quiz 88, page 96

1. Steed and Gambit were the male stars in which TV adventure series?
2. In which BBC series did Tinker and Lady Jane appear?
3. Which Richardson starred in the Steven Poliakoff teleplay *The Tribe*?
4. What is the occupation of the lead character in *Bramwell*?
5. Who played *The Chancer*?
6. In *Silent Witness* what is Sam Ryan's profession?
7. In what type of building is *ER* set?
8. Which Sean stars as *Sharpe*?
9. Which Pam starred in *The Darling Buds Of May*?
10. In *Sapphire & Steel*, which title character did Joanna Lumley play?
11. *Poldark* was set in which century?
12. In which Western series did the Cartwrights reside at the Ponderosa?
13. In *A Family At War* in which northern city did the Ashtons live?
14. Which medical drama was set in Oxbridge General Hospital?
15. Which king was played by Keith Mitchell in 1970?
16. In which ITV series did the characters Dave Tucker and Paddy Garvey appear?
17. Amanda Burton appeared in which series about a doctors practice in Derbyshire?
18. The character Yosser Hughes featured in which drama series?
19. Which comedy duo played *Jeeves and Wooster*?
20. What was the name of James Herriott's wife in *All Creatures Great And Small*?
21. Which series is based at the fictitious Holby General Hospital?
22. Who was Reginald Perrin's boss?
23. *Harry's Game* was set in which part of the UK?
24. *The House Of Cards* was set in which governmental establishment?
25. The butler Hudson featured in which period drama?
26. In *This Life* was Ferdy or Miles gay?
27. Peter and Anna Mayle spent a year where?
28. *Tenko* was set during which war?
29. Which *Men Behaving Badly* star is also *The Vanishing Man*?
30. Which Royal was played by Amy Clare Seccombe in Channel 5's *The People's Princess: A Tribute*?

Soaps 10 (see Quiz 88)

1. Paul Robinson. 2. Betty Turpin. 3. Bill Gregory. 4. In a motorway crash. 5. Alf Roberts. 6. Todd. 7. Harris. 8. Annie Walker. 9. Cousin. 10. A lorry crashed into the Rovers Return near where Alf was sitting. 11. Den and Angie Watts. 12. Noele Gordon. 13. *Emergency Ward*. 14. Brookside Close. 15. Angie. 16. A rose. 17. *The Colbys*. 18. Australia. 19. Ramsey Street. 20. Mike Baldwin. 21. The Kabin. 22. Bet Gilroy. 23. Bobby. 24. Sugden. 25. *Brookside*. 26. The Snug. 27. Katie. 28. Jim Robinson. 29. *Coronation Street*. 30. Mavis Riley.

Answers: see Quiz 87, page 95

LEVEL I

1. Who did Gail Lewis marry in *Neighbours?*
2. Who was Gordon Clegg's real mother in *Coronation Street?*
3. Who did Elsie Tanner go to Portugal with in 1983?
4. How did Len Fairclough die in *Coronation Street?*
5. Who was the last Mayor of Weatherfield in *Coronation Street?*
6. Who was Katie Landers' brother in *Neighbours?*
7. What was Jane's surname in *Neighbours?*
8. Who was the last Mayoress of Weatherfield in *Coronation Street?*
9. What relation was Shane to Henry in *Neighbours?*
10. How did Alf Roberts end up in a coma in *Coronation Street?*
11. When *Eastenders* began who were in charge at The Queen Victoria?
12. Which *Crossroads* actress worked with John Logie Baird?
13. What was ITV's first hospital soap?
14. Where did Sinbad Sweeney live in 1998?
15. What was Sharon Watts mother's name in *Eastenders?*
16. What kind of flower is Ena Sharples?
17. In which series did Rock Hudson play Heather Locklear's father?
18. In which country is Cell block H in *Prisoner?*
19. Where do Susan and Karl Kennedy live?
20. Who fired Hayley in *Coronation Street* when he found out she was a transsexual?
21. Where do the *Coronation Street* characters buy their newspapers?
22. Who preceded The Duckworths as licensee of The Rovers Return?
23. Which Simpson was Sam's mother in *Home and Away?*
24. Which surname links Percy in one soap to Jack in another?
25. In which soap was Trevor Jordache buried under a patio?
26. Where in The Rovers Return would you have found Ena and Minnie having a drink?
27. Who was Todd Landers sister in *Neighbours?*
28. Who did Dr. Beverley Marshall marry in *Neighbours?*
29. Which soap moved from two to three transmissions a week in 1989?
30. Who did Victor Pendlebury go on a walking holiday with in *Coronation Street?*

Drama 11 (see Quiz 87)

1. *New Avengers.* 2. *Lovejoy.* 3. Joely. 4. Doctor. 5. Clive Owen. 6. A pathologist. 7. A hospital. 8. Sean Bean. 9. Pam Ferris. 10. Sapphire. 11. The 18th Century. 12. *Bonanza.* 13. Liverpool. 14. *Emergency – Ward 10.* 15. Henry VIII. 16. *Soldier, Soldier.* 17. *Peak Practice.* 18. *Boys From The Blackstuff.* 19. Fry and Laurie. 20. Helen. 21. *Casualty.* 22. C.J. 23. Northern Ireland. 24. The House Of Commons. 25. *Upstairs, Downstairs.* 26. Ferdy. 27. *A Year In Provence.* 28. World War Two. 29. Neil Morrissey. 30. Princess Diana.

Answers: see Quiz 90, page 98

LEVEL I

1. What is Mr Clarke from *Food And Drink's* christian name?
2. Which P.I. drove his employer's red Ferrari?
3. Where did a sum on a blackboard recurr often on television screens?
4. Which cookery competition is hosted by Lloyd Grossman?
5. On which talent show was Pam Ayres a winner?
6. In which series did Yosser Hughes first appear?
7. Which chat show host did The Bee Gees walk out on?
8. What liquid refreshment was advertised by Pete and Dud?
9. Who was Bernie Winters' brother?
10. Who plays Onslow in *Keeping Up Appearances*?
11. Who was the snail on *The Magic Roundabout*?
12. Who was the youngest Boswell boy in *Bread*?
13. In which series were Mrs Bridges and Mr Hudson?
14. What was featured in *Thank Your Lucky Stars*?
15. What is the christian name of actor McKern of *Rumpole* fame?
16. What is TV cook Grigson's first name?
17. In which comedy series was Penelope Wilton married to Richard Briers?
18. What was Hyacinth's husband's name in *Keeping Up Appearances*?
19. In which series was Geoffrey Palmer a collector of a variety of flying creature?
20. Who was Rita's father in *Till Death Do Us Part*?
21. Which saga was the last to be broadcast in black and white on the BBC?
22. Who created Hercule Poirot?
23. The Ministry of Funny Walks appeared in which series?
24. Which Ruth Rendell character is played by George Baker?
25. Which medieval monk is a crime solver?
26. Who ran the Neighbourhood Watch Scheme in *Coronation Street*?
27. Which 1960s western series was about a cattle drive and the drovers?
28. What is Rick Stein's gastronomic speciality?
29. Which actor in *Happy Days*, apart from Ron Howard, has directed feature films?
30. What was Bridget's surname in *Grange Hill*?

LEVEL I

1. Which Clive starred as Corporal Jones in *Dad's Army*?

2. In which BBC series did the Yellow Coats feature?

3. Nerys Hughes and Polly James starred together in which 1970s BBC comedy?

4. Who stars as the *Chef*?

5. Anton Rodgers starred in which series named after months of the year?

6. Fenn Street school featured in which comedy?

7. Which comedy cartoon superhero, named after an insect, often shouted "Spoon!"?

8. What were the first names of the duo Scott and Whitfield?

9. Who presented his *Half Hour*?

10. Which Hattie starred opposite Eric Sykes?

11. How many seats did the Goodies' bike have?

12. Which Harry starred in *Men Behaving Badly*?

13. Does Bart visit the Moon in *The Simpsons*?

14. Lesley Joseph plays which character in *Birds Of A Feather*?

15. Which baby wore glasses in *Rugrats*?

16. On which show would you find the fictitious chaotic Spanish TV station Channel 9?

17. What creature appears in the opening and closing credits of *One Foot In The Grave*?

18. Who was the creator and presenter of Channel 4's irreverent satire *Brass Eye*?

19. Who played Granville in *Open All Hours*?

20. *Monty Python's Flying Circus* often changed sketch with the words "And now for something completely..." what?

21. Which comedy featured Vivien Bastard?

22. Which magazine created the Fat Slags?

23. Which Scottish singer portrayed Adrian Mole's mother?

24. Which spoof wartime series featured a painting by Van Clomp?

25. Which show features Eddie and Richie?

26. Who introduced *TV Nation*?

27. Who starred as Tom Good?

28. Miss Gatsby, Miss Tibbs and the Major were all guests at which hotel?

29. Who daydreamed of his mother-in-law as a hippo?

30. Which *Eastender* played Miss Brahms in *Are You Being Served*?

Answers: see Quiz 92, page 100

LEVEL 1

1. On which channel is the science documentary series *Equinox* broadcast?
2. Which Jack hosts a late night chat show on Channel 5?
3. What is the name of ITV's breakfast channel?
4. *Watchdog: Value For Money* is presented by chatshow host Vanessa who?
5. What was the name of *Top Gear*'s boating series?
6. US presenter Jerry Springer hosts what kind of show?
7. Which British 1960s Supermodel hosts a chat show on ITV?
8. Which US comedienne presented the series *Ruby Does The Season*?
9. Which popular BBC1 science and technology programme first went on air in 1965?
10. Who was the regular astrologer on *Breakfast Time*?
11. The holiday programme *Wish You Were Here* was presented by which Judith?
12. Which *Mona Lisa* actor Bob rode an elephant in search of tigers?
13. Which university offers courses on BBC TV?
14. *What The Papers Say* is broadcast on which channel?
15. The viewers access programme on Channel 4 is called *Right To...* what?
16. BBC TV's book series *Bookworm* was introduced by which comedian, Griff?
17. What was the name of the BBC fashion show originally presented by Jeff Banks?
18. Patrick Moore hosts which long-running astronomy series?
19. Which Rat revived *TV-AM*'s ratings?
20. BBC2's *The Money Programme* was hosted by which ex-Blue Peter presenter Valerie?
21. Dr Ian Dunbar offers advice on training which animals?
22. Melvyn Bragg introduces which Sunday evening arts show?
23. Archaeology enthusiast Tony Robinson goes digging at sites with which Team?
24. Who presented *That's Life* in the 1970s?
25. Robert Kilroy-Silk hosts which talk show on BBC1?
26. Which series, started in 1956, looks at the week's newspapers?
27. Which John presented the talk show *The Time ... The Place* on ITV?
28. *Chrystal Rose* hosts what kind of show?
29. Is the science documentary series *Horizon* broadcast on BBC2 or Channel 4?
30. Which Angus presented *The Temptation Game*?

LEVEL 1

Answers: see Quiz 91, page 99

1. What kind of Leap does actor Scott Bakula take in his time-travel drama?
2. To which century was *Buck Rogers* transported?
3. Which Gerry produced the Sci-Fi series *Space 1999*?
4. In *Dr. Who*, what was Sarah-Jane's surname?
5. In the comedy series *Weird Science* what do the two friends produce using their computer?
6. Who had a computer called TIM?
7. Lex Luther is the arch-enemy of which Superhero?
8. David Duchovny and Gillian Anderson play the lead characters in which US drama?
9. What is the name of *Xena: Warrior Princess'* scribely side-kick?
10. Who was Mr. Vandemar's murderous brother in *Neverwhere*?
11. In which city do the *Sliders* slide?
12. What colour is Beverley Crusher's hair in *Star Trek: Next Generation*?
13. What type of vehicle was *Blue Thunder*?
14. In *Space Above & Beyond*, what insulting term was used for clones?
15. Which planet in the *Hitch-Hiker's Guide to the Galaxy* was the home of Slartibartfast?
16. What was Lorne Greene's character in *Battlestar Galactica*?
17. How do you kill an immortal in *Highlander: The Gathering*?
18. Which cartoon series featured a space age family?
19. Which sci-fi series had one letter as its title?
20. Which time-fighting duo were assisted variously by Lead and Silver, amongst others?
21. From what did *Mandrake* draw his powers?
22. Lou Ferrigno played the part of which angry green transformation?
23. In which series did the characters G'kar, Morden and Delenn appear?
24. Which character was an Amazon princess turned superhero?
25. How many million dollars was the Bionic Man worth?
26. On which mining ship would you find robot janitors called Scutters?
27. Which Susannah helped Jack Davenport hunt vampires in *Ultraviolet*?
28. Who played the shape-shifting *Manimal*?
29. Avon and Gan were members of which sci-fi team?
30. Which character was a revolutionary on the planet Mongo?

Answers: see Quiz 94, page 102

LEVEL 1

1. Which Daily Mirror character was played on TV by James Bolam?
2. Whose *Audience With* ... featured singing with the *Spice Girls*?
3. Who plays a wobble board?
4. Who was Charlie Hungerford's son-in-law?
5. What are Cobra and Hunter?
6. What colour costumes do the lifeguards in *Baywatch* wear?
7. Who is John Mortimer's legal hero?
8. In which advert do Prunella Scales and Jane Horrocks appear?
9. Who played Endora in *Bewitched*?
10. Which member of Bucks Fizz became a TV presenter?
11. Which Simon left a 1960s pop group to present his own chat show?
12. Who presents *Surprise, Surprise*?
13. Which chocolate bar promised to help you "work, rest and play"?
14. What was Channel 4's film channel called, launched in November 1998?
15. Which Superheroic figure helped children to cross the road?
16. Which Meg appeared on *National Lottery Live*?
17. Who is credited with inventing TV?
18. Which independent TV company covers the London area?
19. Who is Sir David Attenborough's famous film director brother?
20. What kind of programmes did the late Geoff Hamilton present on BBC TV?
21. The TV fitness instructor Diana Moran is known as 'The Green...' what?
22. The Sunday evening programme *Highway* was hosted by which former Goon and singer?
23. Who hosted *Challenge Anneka*?
24. Who hosts *Blind Date*?
25. *The Big Breakfast* is broadcast on which channel?
26. Who presented *Film 97*?
27. What does BBC stand for?
28. Christopher Timothy starred in which acclaimed BBC vet drama?
29. Which BBC antiques series hosts weekly shows in venues around the country?
30. Is *Songs Of Praise* broadcast on BBC or ITV?

ANSWERS Children's TV 8 (see Quiz 94)
1. Fred Flintstone. 2. A Killer Whale. 3. BBC1. 4. Bill and Ted. 5. *Art Attack*. 6. *Pet Detective*.
7. Newcastle. 8. Children's Independent Television. 9. Zag. 10. A dog. 11. A penguin.
12. Spiderman. 13. Superman. 14. Emma Forbes. 15. *Power Rangers*. 16. Yvette Fielding.
17. BBC1. 18. KITT. 19. A cat. 20. *Fingermouse*. 21. Noddy. 22. *Captain Scarlet*. 23. Xena.
24. Mars. 25. Sooty. 26. Four. 27. A bear. 28. A cat. 29. *CHiPs*. 30. *Live And Kicking*.

Answers: see Quiz 93, page 101

LEVEL 1

1. Which stone-age cartoon character was played by John Goodman in the 1990s film?
2. What kind of creature features in the animated *Free Willy*?
3. The Saturday morning show *The Pop Zone* is broadcast on which channel?
4. Who have *Excellent Adventures* on Channel 4?
5. Neil Buchanan introduces which ITV children's art show?
6. What kind of detective is *Ace Ventura*?
7. In which north-eastern city is *Byker Grove* set?
8. What does CITV stand for?
9. Who is Zig the puppet's partner?
10. What kind of animal is *Lassie*?
11. *Pingu* is what type of creature?
12. Who was bitten by a radioactive spider and gained super powers?
13. Lois Laine is associated with which Superhero?
14. *Live and Kicking* was presented by Andi Peters and which Emma?
15. Which Rangers are teenage superheroes?
16. Which Yvette is a former *Blue Peter* presenter?
17. Andy Crane hosted children's evening TV with Ed The Duck on which channel?
18. What was the name of David Hasslehoff's talking car?
19. Heathcliff is what kind of cartoon animal?
20. Which children's series featured finger puppet animals?
21. Which Enid Blyton creation lives in toyland?
22. Which puppet Captain battles with the Mysterons?
23. Lucy Lawless stars as which Channel 5 Warrior Princess?
24. The *Biker Mice* are from which planet?
25. Which puppet bear celebrated his 50th birthday in 1998?
26. How many *Teletubbies* are there?
27. What kind of creature is *Paddington*?
28. *Garfield* is what kind of cartoon animal?
29. Which show was about US motorcycle cops?
30. Zoe Ball and Jamie Theakston present which Saturday morning show for children?

QUIZ 95 Comedy 18

Answers: see Quiz 96, page 104

LEVEL 1

1. Jasper Carrott is Bob Louis in which BBC comedy?
2. In *Don't Wait Up* what did father and son, Tom and Toby, do for a living?
3. Dorothy, Blanche, Rose and Sophie were collectively known as what?
4. Does MTV make any comedy programmes?
5. Which blond actress plays Deborah in *Men Behaving Badly*?
6. Alec and Zoe Callender were the lead characters in which BBC1 sitcom?
7. What was the profession of *Steptoe And Son*?
8. In which comedy did Paul Shane appear as a holiday park comedian?
9. Michael Crawford played Frank Spencer in which sitcom?
10. Alan Alda was a US army surgeon in which long-running series?
11. Which comic cartoon series is set in the US town of Springfield?
12. Which Nigel starred in *Don't Wait Up*?
13. Audrey Fforbes-Hamilton was played by which Penelope?
14. Alf and Rita Garnett were leading characters in which comedy?
15. Complete the title: ... *Goes Forth*.
16. The character Charlie Burrows is a footballer-turned-housekeeper in which sitcom?
17. Which Jim was the lead character in *Yes, Prime Minister*?
18. Which former Minder was *On The Up*?
19. Rick, Neil, Vyvyan and Mike were known collectively as what?
20. Who played Patsy Stone in *Absolutely Fabulous*?
21. Terry who starred with June Whitfield in *Happy Ever After*?
22. Who played Alan B'Stard?
23. What is Rab Nesbitt's middle initial?
24. Oz, Neville and Denis were characters in which series set on building sites?
25. Where might you see Mariah Carey & Jim Carrey locked in a duel to the death?
26. Arnold Rimmer was a hologram on board which ship?
27. In which country was the sitcom *Duty Free* mostly set?
28. Which father and son lived in Oil Drum Lane, Shepherd's Bush?
29. Jerry, Elaine, Kramer and George are the four characters in which successful US sitcom?
30. The BBC comedy *Roger, Roger* concerns which public service?

Pot Luck 30 (see Quiz 96)

1. Hugh Scully. 2. Husband and wife. 3. Nick Owen. 4. Craddock. 5. Delia Smith. 6. Rolf Harris. 7. Alan Titchmarsh. 8. Gary Lineker. 9. John Logie Baird. 10. Gaby Roslin. 11. Carol Smillie. 12. Access card. 13. Westerns. 14. *Songs Of Praise*. 15. *Colditz*. 16. Channel 4. 17. *What's My Line?* 18. Eamonn Andrews. 19. Adam Faith. 20. March 1997. 21. Central. 22. BBC2. 23. *On The Night*. 24. *Happy Days*. 25. Mr Hooperman. 26. Anneka Rice. 27. *Minder*. 28. Bruce Willis. 29. A cigar. 30. A hospital.

A N S W E R S

QUIZ 96 Pot Luck 30

Answers: see Quiz 95, page 103

LEVEL I

1. Which Hugh presents *Antiques Roadshow*?
2. How are ITV presenters Richard Madeley and Judy Finnigan related?
3. Who was Anne Diamond's co-presenter in the daytime show *Anne And Nick*?
4. What was the surname of the husband and wife TV cooks, Fanny and Johnny?
5. Which Delia is a TV cook?
6. Who presents *Animal Hospital* on BBC1?
7. Which Alan is a TV gardener?
8. Which former England football captain advertises crisps?
9. Which TV inventor had the middle name Logie?
10. Which Gaby presented *The Big Breakfast*?
11. *The Midweek Lottery* was first presented by which Carol?
12. What was advertised on TV as "your flexible friend"?
13. *Laramie* and *Maverick* were what sort of programmes?
14. What is the name of BBC1's Sunday evening religious service programme?
15. Which programme took place in a POW castle?
16. Which TV channel was involved in the making of the hit film *Four Weddings And A Funeral*?
17. In which show did people try to guess others' occupations?
18. Which Irish presenter hosted *This Is Your Life*?
19. Which pop singer starred as *Budgie*?
20. In which month of 1997 did Channel 5 start broadcasting?
21. Which TV company serves the Midlands?
22. Which channel was the UK's third terrestrial channel?
23. When will it be Alright with Dennis Norden?
24. Which show featured Richie Cunningham?
25. Who was Miles' boss in *This Life*?
26. The TV presenter Annie Rice is better known as who?
27. George Cole starred with Denis Waterman in which TV series?
28. Which Bruce starred in *Moonlighting*?
29. What did Jimmy Savile always hold in *Jim'll Fix It*?
30. The documentary Jimmy's was about what kind of establishment?

ANSWERS

Comedy 18 (see Quiz 95)

1. *The Detectives*. 2. *Doctors*. 3. *The Golden Girls*. 4. Yes. 5. Leslie Ash. 6. *May To December*. 7. Rag and bone men. 8. *Some Mothers Do Ave Em*. 9. *M*A*S*H*. 10. *The Simpsons*. 11. Nigel Havers. 12. Penelope Keith. 13. *Til Death Us Do Part*. 14. Peter Bowles. 15. *Blackadder*. 16. *The Upper Hand*. 17. Jim Hacker. 18. Denis Waterman. 19. *The Young Ones*. 20. Joanna Lumley. 21. Terry Scott. 22. Rick Mayall. 23. C. 24. *Auf Wiedersehn Pet*. 25. Celebrity Deathmatch. 26. *Red Dwarf*. 27. Spain. 28. *Steptoe And Son*. 29. *Seinfeld*. 30. A Minicab service.

Answers: see Quiz 98, page 107

LEVEL 1

1. What was Kylie Minogue's character in *Neighbours*?
2. Which Liverpool Close is the title of a Soap?
3. What is "Curly" Watts' real name in *Coronation Street*?
4. Which soap character who was a Riley became a Wilton?
5. What colour is Bianca's hair in *Eastenders*?
6. Who is the mechanic who lives in *Coronation Street*?
7. What nationality is Ruth Fowler in *Eastenders*?
8. In which soap does Maud Grimes appear?
9. What was the name of Rita Sullivan's business in *Coronation Street*?
10. Where does Huw Edwards come from in *Eastenders*?
11. Cindy Beale appeared in which soap?
12. In *Coronation Street* who was Maureen's wheelchair-bound mother?
13. What was the scheming Fred Elliott's profession in *Coronation Street*?
14. Which of the MacDonald twins went to prison in *Coronation Street*?
15. How did Dave Glover die in *Emmerdale*?
16. The character Sinbad appears in which Channel 4 soap?
17. Tiffany and her daughter Courtney can be seen in which BBC series?
18. What was the profession of Ivy Brennan's husband in *Coronation Street*?
19. In 1997 for which national service did ex-*Eastenders* stars appear in a TV ad?
20. In *Neighbours* what did the following characters have in common – Scott, Lucy, Paul?
21. In *Coronation Street* which couple have a villainous son called Terry?
22. To which country did David Wicks move on leaving Albert Square?
23. What is the name of Bianca's mother in *Eastenders*?
24. In which soap does Barbara Windsor star?
25. Shane and Angel married in which Australian soap?
26. In *Coronation Street* who is Curly's estranged wife?
27. Near which Australian city is *Home and Away* set?
28. What is the name of Phil and Kathy Mitchell's son?
29. Tinhead appeared in which soap?
30. Betty Williams is a barmaid in which soap?

Answers: see Quiz 99, page 107   LEVEL I

1. Angel Jonathan and his companion Mark are travelling the Highway to where?
2. On Channel 4, Armistead Maupin offers More *Tales Of...* what?
3. Which mythical hero offered *The Legendary Journeys* on Channel 5?
4. What kind of princess is Xena according to the title of her series?
5. To which US family does Jim Bob belong?
6. The BBC1 medical drama is *Chicago* what?
7. Kevin Whateley plays what kind of investigator in *The Broker's Man*?
8. DJ Jack Killian answers what kind of caller?
9. Charisma, Sicknote, and Bayleaf have all been fire-fighters in which series?
10. Who wrote *Pennies From Heaven*?
11. Robson Green starred in which ITV army series?
12. Derek Thompson and Patrick Robinson played nurses in which BBC hospital drama?
13. According to the title of the spy series, who was from U.N.C.L.E.?
14. Vintage Western series, *Rawhide*, featured which Hollywood star?
15. In The BBC adaptation of Dickens's classic which Martin was portrayed by Paul Schofield?
16. Which actor/singer played Jed Sheppard in *Crocodile Shoes*?
17. *The Flying Doctors* was set in which country?
18. Which ITV series revolved around customs and excise?
19. Whose children included Primrose & Petunia?
20. *Maximum Bob* stars which US actor Beau as Judge Gibbs?
21. Who played Rocky in *Boone*?
22. Whose boss was Dr. Gillespie?
23. Where was *Poldark* set?
24. If Lord Bellamy was Upstairs, where were his servants?
25. What was *Revisited* in the classic series?
26. What was Rumpole's first name?
27. Which series was about a Yorkshire vet?
28. Who had an affair with Ken Masters in *Howards Way*?
29. Which series featured Mr. Shirovski as a music teacher?
30. What was detective Mrs. Wainthropp's first name?

Soaps 11 (see Quiz 97)

1. Charlene Robinson. 2. *Brookside*. 3. Norman. 4. Mavis. 5. Red. 6. Kevin Webster. 7. Scottish.
8. *Coronation Street*. 9. The Kabin. 10. Wales. 11. *Eastenders*. 12. Maud Grimes. 13. A butcher.
14. Steve. 15. In a fire. 16. *Brookside*. 17. *Eastenders*. 18. A taxi driver. 19. BT. 20. All were
members of the Robinson family. 21. Jack and Vera Duckworth. 22. Italy. 23. Carol.
24. *Eastenders*. 25. *Home And Away*. 26. Raquel. 27. Sydney. 28. Ben. 29. *Brookside*.
30. *Coronation Street*.

Answers: see Quiz 97, page 105   LEVEL 1

1. What nationality is Ulrika Jonsson?
2. Rick Stein presented programmes about which type of food?
3. What is *Dangermouse's* nemesis called?
4. On which channel is the National Lottery televised live?
5. C J Parker was a character in which US series?
6. To which magician is Debbie McGee married?
7. Which BBC1 antiques show is broadcast on Sunday evenings?
8. In which series would you meet the Lone Gunmen?
9. Who is Richard Madeley's co-presenter on *This Morning*?
10. Which Shane advertises washing powder?
11. What is the name of the series presented by undercover reporter Roger Cook?
12. Clive Owen starred as which 1980s risk-taking businessman?
13. Which series showing compilations of TV clips is presented by Chris Tarrant?
14. *Morning Worship* is screened on which channel on Sunday Mornings?
15. What kind of shows do Penn and Teller present?
16. BBC1's *The Rankin Challenge* is what kind of series?
17. Who presents *Television's Greatest Hits* on BBC1?
18. What is the name of Esther Rantzen's chat show?
19. Dorinda Hafner presented *The Tastes of* which country on Channel 4?
20. Which cheese are Wallace and Gromit forever in search of?
21. Which Zone is BBC2's educational service?
22. Who hosted *Schofield's Quest* on ITV?
23. On what mountain do *The Waltons* live?
24. Hilary Jones has what role on TV?
25. Terry Christian co-presented which Channel 4 youth magazine programme?
26. Denise Van Outen and Johnny Vaughan co-presented which morning programme?
27. Name BBC1's long-running nature series, presented by Sir David Attenborough.
28. The BBC 2 series *The Beechgrove Garden* concerns which subject?
29. BBC2's *Watch This Or The Dog Dies* was subtitled *The History of...* what type of TV?
30. Handy Andy is the wizard with wood in which BBC interior design show?

📺📺 Medium Questions

For the majority of quiz situations, these questions are going to be your primary line of attack. They're tricky enough to make people think about the answer, but they're not so mind-straining that your audience is going to walk off feeling humiliated. And that's important. Where people fall down totally will be in program areas that they know nothing about. If you're setting a quiz for lone contestants, make good use of these questions.

If you're working with teams, you may find that this section is a little on the simple side. Pick any four or five people from the bar, and you'll find that between them, they watch quite a range of different shows, so they know most of the answers to this level of question. That means that scores for teams on this sort of material should be around the 75% mark, which leaves plenty of room for doing well or doing badly, but still lets everyone feel good about themselves.

So, either way, use these questions wisely. Rely on their power to help you out of a sticky situation (although that might just be beer on the pub carpet), and you won't go far wrong. They will provide the backbone of your quiz.

Answers: see Quiz 2, page 110

LEVEL 2

1. Which Anne presented *Watchdog*?
2. What type of programs does Sophie Grigson present?
3. What was the ocupaton of Dorothy McNabb in *Two's Company*?
4. Who punched her future husband in *Neighbours*, the first time they met?
5. Who went from *Doomwatch* to *The Detectives*?
6. What is the first name of *Kavanagh QC*?
7. What does *The Great Antiques Hunt* have as a mascot?
8. Which BBC TV commentator described the Queen's Coronation service?
9. What transport do the Two Fat Ladies favour?
10. In *Life And Loves Of a She Devil*, the cenral character Ruth was played by whom?
11. On top of what building was *Gardening Club* filmed?
12. What instrument does astronomer Patrick Moore play?
13. *Where The Heart Is* was set in which county?
14. What is the name of *Rab C Nesbitt's* wife?
15. In *Whoops Apocalypse* which comedian played Commissar Solzhenitsyn?
16. Jamiroquai's lead singer, Jay Kay, composed the theme for which sporting ITV feature?
17. Who played the leading female role in *Triangle*?
18. Which actor links *The A-Team* to *Battlestar Galactica*?
19. Which *Emmerdale* couple renewed their wedding vows in Ripon Cathedral?
20. In *Bramwell*, what is the name of the infirmary?
21. Which astrologer has worked on both the BBC's *Breakfast Time* and GMTV?
22. Who was the Radio Times' Sexiest Woman on TV in 1997?
23. Who starred as *Lovejoy*?
24. Which descendent of the Bounty mutineer Fletcher Christian appeared as the cook on *Breakfast-Time*?
25. Whose characters included Marcel Wave and Gizzard Puke?
26. In *Peak Practice*, which female doctor replaced Beth Glover?
27. Which role was played by Harry Enfield in *Men Behaving Badly*?
28. Who is the presenter of *Blind Date*?
29. In which English county was the soap *Howard's Way* set?
30. Which US actor accompanied Martin Bell on his election campaign?

Answers: see Quiz 1, page 109

1. Who was Starsky and Hutch's Chief?
2. Which character does Robbie Coltrane play in *Cracker*?
3. In which district of London was *The Chinese Detective* set?
4. Who did Lonely pass information to?
5. What was the profession of David Gradley's partner in *Zodiac*?
6. Which actor played *Cribb*?
7. Which actor links *Dangerfield* to *Casualty*?
8. What was Dangerfield's occupation?
9. Who did Eddie Shoestring work for?
10. What was the subject of *The Defenders*?
11. Which American drama series starred, amongst others, Jimmy Smitz and Susan Dey?
12. Which make of car does Morse drive?
13. Micky Spillane's 'Mike Hammer' was played by which actor?
14. Which detective was played by William Conrad?
15. Who portrayed Rumpole of the Bailey?
16. What was the subject of *The Knock*?
17. Which agent did Robert Stack play in *The Untouchables*?
18. Who did Paul Drake work for?
19. Who preceded Tim Piggott-Smith as *The Chief*?
20. Which TV series took its title from the cockney rhyming slang for Flying Squad?
21. Al Waxman played which character in *Cagney and Lacey*?
22. Which Frank was a DI in *The Bill*?
23. Which series starred Cybil Shepherd and Bruce Willis?
24. In which European city is *Cadfael* filmed?
25. Rupert Davies and Richard Harris both played which TV character?
26. Which series starred Daniel Benzali as a defence lawyer?
27. In *NYPD Blue*, which character's son had joined the police before being killed in a bar?
28. Edward Hardwicke and David Burke have both played which character?
29. Which court drama is an updated version of *Crown Court*?
30. Nick Ross presents which real-life crime programme?

Answers: see Quiz 4, page 112

LEVEL 2

1. What race does bar-owner Quark belong to?
2. Which spaceship was powered by the Infinite Improbability Drive?
3. Where was *Quatermass II* set?
4. Who was the creator of *TekWar*?
5. Which star of *The Color Purple* is a regular in *Star Trek-Next Generation*?
6. In The *X-Files* what is Mulder's first name?
7. In *Babylon 5*, Londo Molari is the Ambassador for which race?
8. Who played Frank Bach in *Dark Skies*?
9. What was the name of Michael Knight's robot car?
10. In which series did Lori Singer play an on-line crime-buster?
11. Who on Red Dwarf is Holly?
12. Which creature did Dr. David Banner become when stressed?
13. Who did Lorne Greene play in *Battlestar Galactica*?
14. Which series featured Tweaky?
15. Which series written by Ray Bradbury starred Rock Hudson?
16. Where do the *Sliders* slide to?
17. What was the sixties SF series starring James Darren?
18. What, speaking chemically, were *Sapphire and Steel* supposed to be?
19. Where would you have found Old Bailey selling Rook stew at the Floating Market?
20. Which futuristic organisation featured in the science fiction drama *UFO*?
21. Who created *Space Precinct*?
22. Which character did Sally Knyvette play in *Blake's Seven*?
23. Which hero was aided by the Destiny Angels?
24. In which series did you meet the character Duncan Macleod?
25. What number was Patrick McGoohan?
26. In which series did Roddy McDowall play a chimpanzee?
27. Which electronic hero was aided by Desi Arnaz Jr?
28. Which character did George Takei play in *Star Trek*?
29. How were Homo Superior more commonly known?
30. Who is Data's brother?

Answers: see Quiz 3, page 111

1. Who was the computer-created character who developed out of a science fiction TV film starring Matt Frewer?
2. What was the name of Tony Robinson's *Blackadder* character?
3. Which series starred Geoffrey Palmer and Dame Judy Dench as a middle-aged couple?
4. Who went from *Solo* to become *The Mistress*?
5. In *For the Love of Ada*, who were in love?
6. Who was Bilko's commanding officer, played by Paul Ford?
7. Who play the *Babes In The Wood*?
8. How old was Adrian Mole when he wrote his Secret Diary?
9. In *Sykes*, how were Eric and Hatty related?
10. Who plays a Trotter brother and Gary Sparrow?
11. Which Dame starred in *A Fine Romance*?
12. What national motoring organisation was portrayed in *The Last Salute*?
13. Who in the series *Sitting Pretty* was described as "the Jackie Onassis of Bethnal Green"?
14. What was the setting for *The Brittas Empire*?
15. Which rap singer plays the title role in *The Fresh Prince of Bel-Air*?
16. In which comedy series did a giant cat terrorise London?
17. Who played the respective children of the rivals in *Never The Twain*?
18. What ministry did Jim Hacker run before becoming PM?
19. What was the name of Franklin Howerd's first TV series in 1952?
20. Who are *The Detectives*?
21. Who were "Just Good Friends"?
22. Which Likely Lad ended up a patient in *Only When I Laugh*?
23. In *Goodnight Sweetheart* which year is the hero transported back to?
24. What was the sequel to *Up Pompeii!*?
25. In *The Growing Pains of PC Penrose*, which actor played the title role?
26. What was the name of Lucille Ball's husband who starred with her in *I Love Lucy*?
27. Which army sergeant turned antiques dealer?
28. Who starred as Reginald Perrin?
29. Which *Fifteen-to-One* presenter produced *Bless This House*?
30. What are Father Ted's equally odd colleagues called?

Answers: see Quiz 4, page 114

LEVEL 2

1. Who first said 'Come on down' in the UK?
2. On what show would you find contestants playing with Lightning?
3. Who preceded Des O'Connor as host of *Take Your Pick*?
4. Who presented *Bullseye*?
5. Who hosted *The Krypton Factor*?
6. Who co-hosted the first season of *Robot Wars* with Phillippa Forrester?
7. Who hosted *Punchlines*?
8. Who was the host of *Going for Gold*?
9. What was the children's version of *Criss Cross Quiz*?
10. How many celebrity guests appear each week on *Blankety Blank*?
11. What was the top prize on *Turner Round The World*?
12. Who originally presented *Dotto*?
13. Name the quiz featured on *Sunday Night at the London Palladium*?
14. Who was Larry Grayson's co-host on *The Generation Game*?
15. Who presented *Family Fortunes* after Bob Monkhouse?
16. Which game show has been chaired by both Robert Robinson and Bob Holness?
17. Which programme has been chaired by Max Robertson and Michael Parkinson?
18. Which trophy has been won by both an underground train driver and a cabbie?
19. Which show hosted by Bob Monkhouse required phone contestants to direct the shooting of an arrow at a target?
20. Glyn Daniel chaired which popular quiz in which an expert panel had to identify unusual objects?
21. Who had charge of the gong in the yes/no interlude on *Take Your Pick*?
22. Who was the first woman to present *Busman's Holiday*?
23. Which Channel 4 show was both presented and devised by Tim Vine?
24. Name the team captains on *Shooting Stars*.
25. What is Channel 5's gardening quiz called?
26. Who resides over the Channel 4 quiz *Fifteen-to-One*?
27. On *Countdown*, how many points are awarded for correctly solving the conundrum?
28. Who hosted *Wheel of Fortune* after Nicky Campbell and before John Leslie?
29. Who hosted *The $64,000 Question*?
30. What shape are the cells that hold the letters on the *Blockbusters* board?

QUIZ 6 — Current Affairs 1

LEVEL 2

Answers: see Quiz 5, page 113

1. Which series boasted: 'A window on the world behind the headlines'?
2. Which female newscaster hosted *Pebble Mill*?
3. *Roving Report* was produced by which news team?
4. Which chat show host clashed with singer Grace Jones?
5. *DEF II* was produced by whom?
6. Which comic impersonates Trevor Macdonald's news reading on Channel 4?
7. Who presented *In The Footsteps of Alexander the Great*?
8. Who replaced the late Geoff Hamilton on *Gardener's World*?
9. Who is Richard Madeley's partner?
10. Who was Nick of Anne and Nick?
11. Who formed the original panel of experts on *Don't Ask Me*?
12. Who is the presenter of *Working Lunch*?
13. In which studios was *Tonight* produced?
14. Name the presenter of *Face to Face*.
15. Who presents *Right to Reply*?
16. Which award-winning television programme featured life on the paediatric wards?
17. Who walked out on Sir Robin Day during an interview in 1983?
18. Name the presenter of *Eye of the Storm*.
19. Who presents *The Sky at Night*?
20. Which chat show host recently returned after many years away?
21. Jon Snow presents which Channel's evening news service?
22. The documentary *A Prince For Our Time* was about which modern Royal?
23. Which singer found fame on *The Cruise*?
24. Which TV weathergirl is the daughter of a famous footballer?
25. Who presented *The Island of the Colour Blind*?
26. Which silver-haired presenter hosts a weekday morning debate show?
27. What was the name of the Liverpool Hotel in the fly-on-the-wall series of the same name?
28. Who interviewed Princess Diana on *Panorama* in 1995?
29. Who was ITN's Mike in the Falklands?
30. Who travelled from *Pole to Pole*?

Quiz & Games Shows 1 (See Quiz 5)

1. Leslie Crowther. 2. *The Gladiators*. 3. Michael Miles. 4. Jim Bowen. 5. Gordon Burns. 6. Jeremy Clarkeson. 7. Lenny Bennet. 8. Henry Kelly. 9. *Junior Criss-Cross Quiz*. 10. Six. 11. Two round the world air tickets. 12. Robert Gladwell. 13. *Beat the Clock*. 14. Isla St.Clair. 15. Les Dennis. 16. *Call My Bluff*. 17. *Going for a Song*. 18. The Mastermind Trophy. 19. *The Golden Shot*. 20. *Animal, Vegetable, Mineral*. 21. Alec Dane. 22. Sarah Kennedy. 23. *Fluke*. 24. Mark Lamarr and Ulrika Johnson. 25. *The Great Garden Game*. 26. William G. Stewart. 27. Ten points. 28. Bradley Walsh. 29. Bob Monkhouse. 30. Hexagonal.

Answers: see Quiz 8, page 116

LEVEL 2

1. Which superheroes had a robot janitor called Mo and a computer named Sentinel 1?
2. Who lives in Bedrock?
3. Who said 'Time for Bed' on *The Magic Roundabout*?
4. What tubby schoolboy was played by Gerald Campion?
5. Who grew between *The Flowerpot Men*?
6. What is the name of *Captain Simian's* band?
7. What was Supergran's real name?
8. Which singer co-presented *Record Breakers* with both Roy Castle and Kris Akabusi?
9. What were Orinoco and Uncle Bulgaria?
10. Which magician did Basil Brush first appear with?
11. What were Flicka and Fury?
12. Which hero rode the mighty Battle Cat?
13. Who was the creator of *The Snowman*?
14. Who provided the voice for Father Christmas?
15. Who was the leader of the *Thundercats*?
16. Who did Ted Cassidy play in *The Addams Family*?
17. Which twins presented *Record Breakers*?
18. What colour was Lady Penelope's Rolls Royce?
19. Where was the Thunderbirds' base?
20. Which actor/singer played Teggs in *Grange Hill*?
21. Who played Grandpa in *The Munsters*?
22. Which entertainer made Gordon the Gopher a hit on childrens' television?
23. Jay North portrayed which trouble-making comic character?
24. Name the *Trumpton* firemen.
25. Who played Circus Boy?
26. In *Battle of the Planets*, 7-Zark-7 watched over G-Force from Center Neptune. What was the full name of his robot dog, Rover?
27. Who was the creator of *Morph*?
28. Which cowboy said, 'Hi ho Silver'?
29. Which substance is harmful to Superman's powers?
30. Who rode Trigger?

Answers: see Quiz 7, page 115

LEVEL 2

1. *Russ Abbott's Madhouse* regular Jeffrey Holland also played the part of an entertainer in which comedy series?

2. Who ran the Tea Shop in *Blackadder The Third*?

3. What was *Boon* before he became a despatch rider?

4. Who starred as Edna the *Inebriate Woman*?

5. Who played the title role in *Dear John: USA*?

6. Which larger than life actor played Danny McGlone in *Tutti Frutti*?

7. Name the original title of *The Phil Silvers Show* starring the character Bilko?

8. Which female comic duo formed part of the *Comic Strip* team?

9. Honor Blackman plays whose passionate mother in *The Upper Hand*?

10. Which series told of the misadventures of young Dr Stephen Daker?

11. Which retirement home features in *Waiting For God*?

12. Who played the head porter, Scullion, in *Porterhouse Blue*?

13. Which singer/actress played Adrian Mole's mother in *The Growing Pains of Adrian Mole*?

14. Who are Elizabeth and Emmeline better known as?

15. How many arms did Zaphod Beeblebrox have in the *Hitchhiker's Guide to the Galaxy*?

16. What is the name of Martin Crane's dog in *Frasier*?

17. Which *To the Manor Born* actor starred in *Lytton's Diary*?

18. Which duo link *Blackadder* to *Jeeves and Wooster*?

19. In which district of South London was *Only Fools and Horses* set?

20. Name the DIY show in *Home Improvement*.

21. Alexei Sayle played which forger in *Selling Hitler*?

22. Which *Are you Being Served* actress played Nerys Hughes' mum in the *Liver Birds*?

23. In which comedy would you find the character Bubbles?

24. Name *The Goodies*.

25. Peter Howitt played which Boswell in *Bread*?

26. Sgt Flagg was played by which actor in *The Growing Pains of PC Penrose*?

27. What were the names of Lucille Ball's neighbours in *I Love Lucy*?

28. Which *Good Life* actress went it alone in *Solo*?

29. Complete the title of this series starring Sid James: *Bless This...*?

30. Who played Barry in *Auf Wiedersehen Pet*?

Answers: see Quiz 10, page 118

LEVEL 2

1. Who ran the Rovers Return before the Duckworths?
2. Which soap was made in Esholt until 1997?
3. In *Eastenders*, what was Carol Jackson's sister called?
4. In *Dallas* what relation was Cliff Barnes to Pamela Ewing?
5. Which *Coronation Street* actress achieved *Rapid Results* when she donned a leotard?
6. What kind of establishment was *Crossroads*?
7. Which *Brookside* baddie was buried under a patio?
8. How many episodes in total of *Albion Market* were recorded?
9. What is "Curly" Watts first name?
10. The soap opera *United!* was about what?
11. Which soap was a spin-off from *Dynasty*?
12. What was the first major UK soap on Channel 5?
13. Who left *Dallas* and became *The Man From Atlantis*?
14. Who had a brief affair with Ricky Butcher in *EastEnders*?
15. Who left *Eastenders* to become a policeman in *Heartbeat*?
16. Who shot J.R.?
17. Who is Sarah's brother in *EastEnders*?
18. Who was kidnapped by a UFO in the *Colbys*?
19. In *Brookside*, who did the Farnhams pay to act as a surrogate mother?
20. What was ITV's first long running twice-weekly soap?
21. What connects *Eastenders* and *Are You Being Served*?
22. Who in *Coronation Street* decided to have blue and white cladding on the front of their house?
23. Which English actress played Alexis in *Dynasty*?
24. What role did Bill Treacher play in *Eastenders*?
25. In which district of Melbourne is *Neighbours* set?
26. What kind of market stall did Pete Beale own in *Eastenders*?
27. *Home and Away* is set in which fictitious bay?
28. Who is the longest serving member of *Coronation Street*?
29. Where did Alexis marry Cecil Colby?
30. Which actress, better known for her comic roles, plays the Mitchell brothers' mum?

Answers: see Quiz 9, page 117

LEVEL 2

1. On which Island would you find Mr Rorke?
2. David Carradine starred in which Western series?
3. Who was *The Undercover Agent*?
4. Richard Rogers played which relation to William Tell in *The Adventures of William Tell*?
5. Who played Dan Tempest in *The Buccaneers*?
6. What was the name of Maverick's English cousin?
7. Which actor starred in the TV version of *Pennies from Heaven*?
8. Who starred as *The Singing Detective*?
9. What is the longest running police series on British TV?
10. Which 1998 vampire series starred Jack Davenport?
11. On which ranch was *The Virginian* set?
12. Who wrote the book on which the seventies mini series *Roots* was based?
13. The series *The Adventures of Long John Silver* was based on which book?
14. Which TV series contained the line, 'I am not a number, I am a free man'?
15. In which town is *The Little House on the Prairie*?
16. For whose household did Mr Hudson and Mrs Bridges work?
17. In which series did ex-investment banker Steven Crane help save a midlands car firm?
18. The 1979 mini-series *From Here to Eternity* was set in which US state at the time of Pearl Harbour?
19. Who wrote *Middlemarch*?
20. Which prison is *Prisoner Cell Block H* set in?
21. Who played the title role in *Smiley's People*?
22. Who was *The Texan*?
23. Who played the owner of *The Royalty Hotel*, Mrs Mollie Miller?
24. Which actress starred in *Tenko* and was later seen *Waiting for God*?
25. Who plays *Casualty*'s Little John?
26. At which real-life airport was the setting for *Garry Halliday*?
27. Which Dame starred in *Jewel in the Crown*?
28. How was *Jungle Boy* orphaned?
29. Who, early in his career, played Ivanhoe and Beau Maverick?
30. Which former publican ran *The Paradise Club*?

Answers: see Quiz 12, page 120

1. Who presented *Son Of The Incredibly Strange Film Show*?

2. Peter Capaldi played The Angel Islington in which surreal BBC 2 series?

3. Who hosted drama workshops as the spoof "Professional Personality", Nicholas Craig?

4. Who or what was Orac?

5. In *Drop the Dead Donkey*, whose catchphrase was "I'm not here"?

6. What was Reggie Perrin's boss called?

7. Who plays *Dr. Quinn, Medicine Woman*?

8. Where did Paula Yates hold interviews on *The Big Breakfast*?

9. Which character's son had an affair with Sandy Merrick in *Emmerdale*?

10. Who was the presenter of the 1940's series *Television Garden*?

11. Which Geoff Hamilton series was first shown after his death?

12. The series *Lovejoy* was based on whose novels?

13. Where was Dot living before returning to Walford in 1997?

14. When did John Logie Baird first experiment in colour TV?

15. Who played the title role in the series *Kate*?

16. Which UK river featured in *Howard's Way*?

17. Where does *Master Chef* presenter Loyd Grossman originate from?

18. In *Brothers In Law*, Richard Briers played which up and coming barrister?

19. Who took a break from *Dr Finlay's Casebook* to be 'Mr Justice Duncannon'?

20. In *The Cheaters*, which insurance company did John Hunter work for?

21. Who first presented *Gardening Club* in 1955?

22. Who hosted *Jim'll Fix It*?

23. In what year was the first televised church service?

24. Which antiques expert starred in the original series of *Antiques Roadshow*?

25. In which program were three children sent through time hunting the Nidus, with which they could free the magician Rothgo from the trap of his evil enemy, Belor?

26. In which year was the *Radio Times* first published?

27. What was the name of the adult version of *Tiswas*?

28. Who presented *Saturday Stayback*?

29. In which series would you find Benton Frazer?

30. Who is Suzy Aitchison's comedienne mother?

TV Comedy 3 (See Quiz 12)

1. Ted Danson (*Cheers & Gulliver's Travels*). 2. Bob was a girl. 3. Rodney Trotter. 4. Tom Selleck. 5. Hywell Bennett. 6. Dermot. 7. Sir Harry Secombe. 8. Army Motor Pool. 9. A padlock. 10. Dave Lister. 11. Grace Brothers. 12. A University Campus. 13. Jacko. 14. All starred Richard Beckinsale. 15. Students. 16. *Watching*. 17. *All In Good Faith*. 18. Alf Garnett. 19. Depressed / Paranoid. 20. The Nag's Head. 21. Marty Feldman's. 22. *The Two Ronnies*. 23. Paul McCartney. 24. 5, Sandra, Denise, Theo, Vanessa, Rudy. 25. Catherine Zeta-Jones. 26. Ben. 27. New York. 28. In a bank. 29. Grace Allen. 30. Cannon and Ball.

Answers: see Quiz 11, page 119

LEVEL 2

1. Which barman went on to become a Swift creation?

2. What was unusual about Bob in *Blackadder II*?

3. In *Only Fools and Horses*, who was studying computing?

4. Which former private investigator appeared as Monica's boyfriend in *Friends*?

5. Who starred as *Shelley*?

6. What was Harry Enfield's character called in *Men Behaving Badly*?

7. This Welsh singer and comedian provided voices for the telly Goons. Who is he?

8. What was the function of the army platoon to which Bilko was attached?

9. How did Mr Bean lock his car?

10. Who played the guitar on *Red Dwarf*?

11. What was the name of the store in *Are You Being Served*?

12. Where was the Practice based in the series *A Very Peculiar Practice*?

13. In *Brush Strokes*, what was the name of the lead character?

14. What is the connection between *Porridge, Bloomers* and *Rising Damp*?

15. What was the occupation of *The Young Ones*?

16. In which show did Brenda and Malcolm enjoy ornithology?

17. Which late '80s sitcom starred Richard Briers as a struggling inner-city vicar?

18. Whose son in law was a randy scouse git?

19. What was Marvin the Android's mental problem in the *Hitchhiker's Guide to the Galaxy*?

20. What is the name of the pub in *Only Fools and Horses*?

21. Whose first comedy series was called simply *Marty*?

22. If you heard, "So it's goodnight from me, and it's goodnight from him," which programme would you be watching?

23. Which former Beatles songwriter made a guest appearance in *Bread*?

24. How many children do Cliff and Claire Huxtable have in *The Cosby Show*?

25. Which actress played the role of Ma and Pa Larkin's eldest daughter, Marietta?

26. In *Two Point Four Children* what is the name of Bill's husband?

27. In which city is the sitcom *Spin City* set?

28. In *The Lucy Show*, Lucille Ball worked where?

29. George Burns appeared on TV with one of his wives. Whom?

30. Which duo starred in *Plaza Patrol*?

Answers: see Quiz 14, page 122

1. Who is the surrogate father in *NYPD Blue*?
2. What rank were Henry and Ray in *Hill Street Blues*?
3. Which role was played by both Loretta Swit and Sharon Gless?
4. Which police officer is central to the series *Heartbeat*?
5. What character did Robert Lee play in *The Chinese Detective*?
6. Which actor played Dodie and Boyle's boss?
7. In *Cribb*, name the famous elephant at London Zoo that was central to the plot in the episode called 'The Lost Trumpet'.
8. Who played the title role in *Jemima Shore Investigates*?
9. What department did George Carter work for?
10. Which actor played Quincy?
11. What is Skinner's FBI title in the *X-Files*?
12. Who is the creator of *Cracker*?
13. Which orchestra played the theme from *Van Der Valk*?
14. Who does *Columbo* frequently cite as his inspiration?
15. Who played Dan Tanner?
16. Name the female detective in *Cracker*.
17. Where was the setting for *Bergerac*?
18. Which two actresses originally made up the team with Jill Gascoine in *C.A.T.S Eyes*?
19. In *Knight Rider*, Michael Knight worked for the Foundation for what?
20. What was the name of Kojak's brother?
21. Jeremy Brett played which detective?
22. Name the central character in the series *Juliet Bravo*.
23. What did TV detective Jim Rockford live in?
24. Who sang the theme song from *Moonlighting*?
25. Who frequently said the words, 'Evening all'?
26. Who played Elliot Ness in the TV version of *The Untouchables*?
27. Whose catchphrase was, 'Book him, Danno'?
28. Name the actress who plays Sgt. June Ackland in *The Bill*.
29. What was the name of the twisted tycoon played by Stanley Tucci in *Murder One*?
30. Name Perry Mason's female assistant.

Answers: see Quiz 13, page 121

LEVEL 2

1. Which dark, shielding 'Element' assisted *Sapphire & Steel* in their first adventure?
2. Who played Oscar in *The Six Million Dollar Man*?
3. Which series features Roy Schneider in underwater adventures?
4. Who played the third incarnation of *Doctor Who*?
5. What was the Liberator's computer called?
6. What was Professor Quatermass' first name?
7. Simon McCorkindale starred as a shape-shifter in which series?
8. What is the name of *Voyager's* half-Klingon crew-member?
9. In *A For Andromeda*, what did an alien radio signal instruct scientists to build?
10. Who was the captain of the *Stingray*?
11. Which actor played The Cat in *Red Dwarf*?
12. Who played Dr. David Banner in *The Incredible Hulk*?
13. Who played Buck Roger's partner Wilma Deering?
14. Which character does Rene Auberjonois play in *Star Trek: Deep Space Nine*?
15. What was special about the spider that bit Peter Parker and gave him special powers?
16. Who created *Star Trek*?
17. Who was the narrator of *The Hitchikers Guide to the Galaxy*?
18. Which programme starts with the words 'do not adjust your sets'?
19. In which series would you find Moonbase Apha?
20. What pet species did Alf most like eating?
21. Which series is a spinoff from a fim starring Kurt Russell and James Spader?
22. In which mini-series would you have seen Diana swallow a rat?
23. Who played the last Number 2?
24. In which future decade was *UFO* set?
25. In the *X-Files* who killed the Red-headed Man?
26. Which planet was the home of the Shadows in *Babylon 5*?
27. What was KITT's evil twin called?
28. Which 60s SF series did Roy Thinnes play David Vincent?
29. Which series was based on the US Air Force Project Blue Book UFO investigations?
30. Who was *The Invisible Man* in the 1970s?

ANSWERS

Crime 2 (See Quiz 13)

1. Greg Medavoy. 2. Lieutenant. 3. Chris Cagney. 4. PC Nick Rowan. 5. Joe Ho, John's father. 6. Gordon Jackson. 7. Jumbo. 8. Patricia Hodge. 9. The Flying Squad. 10. Jack Klugman. 11. Assistant Director. 12. Jimmy McGovern. 13. The Simon May Orchestra. 14. His wife. 15. Robert Urich. 16. Penhaligon. 17. Jersey. 18. Leslie Ash and Rosalyn Landor. 19. Law & Government. 20. Stavros. 21. Sherlock Holmes. 22. Insp. Jean Darblay. 23. A Trailer. 24. Al Jarreau. 25. George Dixon (*Dixon of Dock Green*). 26. Robert Stark. 27. Steve McGarrett (*Hawaii Five-O*). 28. Trudie Goodwin. 29. Richard Cross. 30. Della Street.

Answers: see Quiz 16, page 124

LEVEL 2

1. Who plays Eddie in *Frasier*?
2. What was *The Littlest Hobo*?
3. What did the series of *Creature Comforts* animations advertise?
4. What product is associated with labrador puppies?
5. What was the name of the first award-winning documentary about Meercats?
6. Which childrens' show was presented by Terry Nutkin and Chris Packham?
7. Asta the dog featured in which series?
8. Who presented *Animal Magic*?
9. Vet David Grant appears in which RSPCA based series?
10. Who produced a television series named *Zoo Quest* in the 1950's?
11. In which series does Anton Rodgers play a vet?
12. Which breed of dog was Tricky Woo in *All Creatures Great and Small*?
13. Henry is a cartoon what?
14. What type of terrain is the land surround The Skeleton Coast?
15. What was the name of the Harts' dog in *Hart to Hart*?
16. Which city zoo sponsored the 1950's wildlife series *Zoo Quest*?
17. Which naturalist presented *Look* and *Faraway Look* in the 1950's and 1960's?
18. What is unusual about the Sundew?
19. Who was the posthumous presenter of *Paradise Gardens*?
20. What is the name of the cartoon dog in *Garfield & Friends*?
21. Where do you find the Giant Tortoise?
22. What type of creature does Rex Hunt work most closely with?
23. *Life in the Freezer* featured the natural history of which place?
24. Author and presenter Gerald Durrell had a zoo where?
25. In the title of the show, what was ... *Flicka*?
26. Who presented *Gardener's World* in 1998?
27. What was the name of David Bellamy's first TV series in 1972?
28. Do penguins live at the North or South pole?
29. The naturalist Aubrey Buxton was the original presenter of which long-running ITV nature series?
30. What word commonly describes people who follow tornados?

QUIZ 16 TV Comedy 4

LEVEL 2

1. How many *Fawlty Towers* episodes were made?
2. Who is Caroline Aherne's alter-ego?
3. Who plays Dr Dick Solomon, the alien professor in *Third Rock from the Sun*?
4. Who played Queen Elizabeth I in the second series of *Blackadder*?
5. Who in real life is Cherie's dad and, on TV, was Alf's son-in-law?
6. Which *Prime Minister* appeared in *The Good Life*?
7. Why did Dermot leave *Men Behaving Badly*?
8. Which brothers link *Drop the Dead Donkey* and *Keeping up Appearances*?
9. What rank was Ernie Bilko in *The Phil Silvers Show*?
10. Who is Gary's wartime wife in *Goodnight Sweetheart*?
11. Who played Hancock's sidekick Sid?
12. What is *The Vicar of Dibley* called?
13. What was the name of Adrian Mole's girlfriend?
14. Who employed Bubbles as an incompetent PA?
15. Which sitcom was set in Lord Meldrum's stately home?
16. Which actress played Daker's Polish distraction Grete Grotowska in *A Very Peculiar Practice*?
17. Which comedy show in the 80s was named after a Little Richard hit?
18. Who was the main 'Smeg-Head'?
19. Neil from *The Young Ones* had a chart-topper with which song?
20. What was the cab firm called in *Taxi*?
21. The comedy *Whack-O!* starred who as the headmaster?
22. What was the name of the charlady in *Acorn Antiques*?
23. In which city did the Boswell family reside in *Bread*?
24. Which comedy featured Dr Sheila Sabatini?
25. What was the name of the horse owned by the Steptoes?
26. The ex-wrestler Pat Roach played which *Auf Wiedersehen Pet* character?
27. In *Two Point Four Children* what are the names of the children?
28. What was Private Bisley's nickname in *The Army Game*?
29. Who played Sir Humphrey Appleby in *Yes, Minister*?
30. What was the name of Ronnie Corbett's character in *Sorry!*?

LEVEL 2

Answers: see Quiz 18, page 126

1. What was Ian Beale's catering business called?
2. Which Army captain played Mr Swindley in *Coronation Street*?
3. What did Raquel train to become?
4. In *Crossroads*, whose fiancee died on their wedding day?
5. Which tennis player's former father-in-law appeared in *Peyton Place*?
6. What was the name of the cook in *Dynasty*?
7. What was Tracy Corkhill's occupation in *Brookside*?
8. In *Crossroads*, who shot David Hunter?
9. Which actor played the market superintendent Derek in *Albion Market*?
10. Who are the feuding families in *Dallas*?
11. What is the name of the local football club in *EastEnders*?
12. What was Gail's maiden name in *Coronation Street*?
13. What was Lorna Cartwright's addiction in *EastEnders*?
14. Which soap role had Barbara Bel Geddes and Donna Reed shared?
15. Who was the Sheriff in *Flamingo Road*?
16. What domestic situation is Ken Barlow's claim to fame in *Coronation Street*?
17. After his character died in *Coronation Street*, actor Alan Rothwell appeared as a drug addict in which other soap?
18. Who played Constance McKenzie in *Peyton Place*?
19. What was the name of Jimmy Corkhill's son in *Brookside*?
20. Which Dallas star was in *I Dream of Jeannie* in the 1960s?
21. What was the name of the hospital that featured in *Emergency-Ward 10*?
22. How is Spider Nugent related to Emily Bishop in *Coronation Street*?
23. In *Coronation Street*, what does Mike Baldwin's company Underworld produce?
24. Which comedian lost his sense of humour as Frank in *EastEnders*?
25. What placed Kylie Corkhill's life in danger whilst she was in Sinbad's shop?
26. Which *Coronation Street* star went on to become a district nurse?
27. What role did Bill Treacher play in *EastEnders*?
28. Who ran The Kool for Kutz hairdressers in *EastEnders*?
29. What is the name of Grant and Tiffany's daughter in *EastEnders*?
30. In *Brookside*, whom did the Farnhams pay to act as a surrogate mother?

A N S W E R S
Childrens' TV 2 (See Quiz 18)
1. Oliver Tobias. 2. Paddington. 3. *Jackanory*. 4. Snowy. 5. The Teletubbies. 6. Wimpey. 7. Brown. 8. Michael Rodd. 9. Peter Glaze. 10. Chihuahua. 11. Woodstock. 12. The Childrens' Television Workshop. 13. Rag Dolly Anna. 14. Huey, Louie & Dewey. 15. Burt Ward. 16. Basil Brush. 17. Leila Williams. 18. Anna Sewell. 19. Daktari. 20. Emma Forbes. 21. Angelo. 22. The Penguin. 23. Mrs Goggins. 24. Dave Prowse. 25. Bamm-Bamm & Pebbles. 26. Mr Benn. 27. Bug Juice. 28. Peter Sallis. 29. Hanna-Barbara. 30. John Gorman.

QUIZ 18   Children's TV 2

Answers: see Quiz 17, page 125

LEVEL 2

1. Who played Arthur of the Britons?
2. Sir Michael Hordern was the voice of which popular bear?
3. Which storytelling programme had guest narrators?
4. What was the name of TinTin's dog?
5. Who lives in Home Hill?
6. Who was Popeye's hamburger-eating friend?
7. What was the surname of Just William?
8. Who presented *Screen Test*?
9. In *Crackerjack*, who played the comic stooge?
10. What type of dog is Ren?
11. What is the name of Snoopy's feathered friend?
12. Who produces *Sesame Street*?
13. Pat Coombs appeared with which doll?
14. Name Donald Duck's nephews.
15. Who played Robin in *Batman*?
16. With which puppet did Rodney Bewes appear?
17. Name the first female presenter of *Blue Peter*.
18. Who was the author of Black Beauty?
19. Which animal series starred Marshall Thompson?
20. Who co-presented the first series of *Live & Kicking* with Andi Peters?
21. What was the alien that Mike discovered in a wardrobe called?
22. Burgess Meredith played which character in *Batman*?
23. Who is the postmistress in Greendale?
24. Who was the Green Cross Code man?
25. Name the children in *The Flintstones*.
26. Who visited a costume shop before embarking on various adventures?
27. What is the daytime series about American children at summer camp called?
28. Who is the voice of Wallace from the duo Wallace and Gromit?
29. Which company produced *Huckleberry Hound* and *Yogi Bear*?
30. Which member of *Scaffold* appeared in *Tiswas*?

ANSWERS

Soaps 2 (See Quiz 17)

1. The Meal Machine. 2. Arthur Lowe. 3. A Beautician. 4. Benny. 5. John McEnroe (Ryan O'Neal). 6. Mrs Gunnerson. 7. Hairdresser. 8. Rosemary. 9. David Hargreaves. 10. The Ewings and the Barnes. 11. Walford Town. 12. Potter. 13. Alcohol. 14. Miss Ellie in *Dallas*. 15. Titus Sample. 16. He was the first to have an inside toilet. 17. Brookside. 18. Dorothy Malone. 19. Jimmy Junior. 20. Larry Hagman. 21. Oxbridge General Hospital. 22. Nephew. 23. Underwear. 24. Mike Reid. 25. A gas-explosion. 26. Sarah Lancashire. 27. Arthur Fowler. 28. Steve & Della. 29. Courtney. 30. Jacqui Dixon.

Answers: see Quiz 20, page 128

1. Who played John Wilder in *The Power Game*?
2. The original presenters of the BBC'S *Breakfast Time* were Frank Bough, Selena Scott, and one other. Who?
3. Who introduces *It'll be Alright on the Night*?
4. Which artist played a digeridoo?
5. *The Simpsons* became the longest-running cartoon family in 1997, replacing whom?
6. Who was the original weatherman on BBC's *Breakfast Time*?
7. Which character in *EastEnders* is Mark's wife?
8. In which year did the BBC TV schools service begin?
9. Which actress had to survive on her own on a desert isle?
10. Who is Jennifer Paterson's cooking partner?
11. What was the name of the first space ship used by *Blake's 7*?
12. Which fictional village is *Heartbeat* set in?
13. Which rodent starred on *TVAM*?
14. What was an Admag, banned by Parliament in 1963?
15. Who presented *The Human Body*?
16. What is the profession of the major characters in *This Life*?
17. What did the ARP Warden call Captain Mainwaring?
18. In which decade was *Hi-De-Hi!* first set?
19. Which early evening programme do Mel and Sue introduce?
20. Who is the current host of *Going for a Song*?
21. Which actress played *The Sculptress*?
22. Who was *Lovejoy's* original love interest?
23. Which actor was Maxwell Smart?
24. Who played Tom Howard's wife in *Howard's Way*?
25. In which city was PI Daniel Pike based?
26. Who moved from *Blue Peter* in 1996 to *Songs of Praise*?
27. What TV first occurred during the 1953 Naval Review at Spithead?
28. Who played Adam Cartwright in *Bonanza*?
29. Which satellite was used for the first Transatlantic broadcast?
30. In what year did *The Sky at Night* begin?

---

1. Name the actor who played Rowan Atkinson's *Blackadder* sidekick.

2. What was Bernard Breslaw's catchphrase in *The Army Game*?

3. Which US character has children called Becky, Darlene and DJ?

4. David Jason played Skullion in which series?

5. What is the name of Dorien's husband in *Birds of a Feather*?

6. What is the name of *Drop The Dead Donkey*'s TV news company?

7. When Granada revived *Bootsie and Snudge* in 1974, who had become a millionnaire?

8. Who plays Tony in *Men Behaving Badly*?

9. Who played Bilko's accomplices Corporals Barbarella and Henshaw?

10. Which actor played Adrian Mole?

11. In *The River*, the part played by David Essex was originally intended for which other well known singer?

12. Which comedienne presented *Can We Talk*?

13. At the end of which series of *Hancock's Half Hour* did Sid James leave the show?

14. In *A Very Peculiar Practice*, which doctor, played by David Troughton, didn't like his patients?

15. Which famous ancient site did Edina rearrange for a fashion show in *Ab Fab*?

16. Who played Blanco in *Porridge*?

17. Who was the American Python?

18. Which character does Thora Hird play in *Last of the Summer Wine*?

19. Who was the presenter of *Zoo Time*?

20. Whose catchphrase is "It's the way I tell 'em"?

21. Who played the 'dragon' in *George and The Dragon*?

22. Which comedy duo have the first names Tommy and Bobby?

23. Which Channel 4 sitcom led to the spin off *Frasier*?

24. What is the name of Father Ted's doting housekeeper?

25. What was the name of the central character in *Solo*?

26. What was the name of Sir Humphrey's over-zealous assistant in *Yes, Minister*?

27. What was Lady Lavender's pet, 'Captain', in *You Rang M'Lord*?

28. Who had a landlord called Jerzy Balowski?

29. In *Bread*, which actor played Grandad?

30. Which actress played the dreaded mother in *Sorry!*?

Answers: see Quiz 22, page 130

LEVEL 2

1. Who played Lady Chatterley?
2. Who was the star of *Lou Grant* and *Rich Man, Poor Man*?
3. Who was the creator of *ER*?
4. In the 1950's, Conrad Philips was famous for playing which role?
5. Who played Bart in *Maverick*?
6. In which city was *Gunsmoke* set?
7. Keith Michell starred as which King Henry?
8. What was Zoë's job in *May to December*?
9. In *Blade on the Feather*, who starred as the retired Soviet spy?
10. Who sang the theme from *Rawhide*?
11. What was McCallum?
12. In which year was Dixon promoted from Police Constable to Sergeant in *Dixon of Dock Green*?
13. Jon Finch played which Australian outlaw?
14. In the serial *Cathy Come Home* which actor played Cathy's husband?
15. What was Tinker's surname in *Lovejoy*?
16. Who played the sheriff in *American Gothic*?
17. Which Canadian actor later seen in *Bonanza* starred in *Sailor of Fortune*?
18. What happens to the message tape in *Mission Impossible*?
19. Who took over from David Caruso in *NYPD Blue*?
20. What did Yozzer famously want?
21. What was the name of the evil organisation in *The Man From UNCLE*?
22. Which actress played the fiercely critical character Maud in *Flickers*?
23. Who was promoter Frank Stubbs?
24. What was the name of the cook in *Rawhide*?
25. Who played *The Virginian*?
26. What was the name of Big John's brother-in-law in *The High Chapparel*?
27. Margaret Lockwood played which character in *The Flying Swan*?
28. Hari Kumar in *Jewel In The Crown* was played by which actor?
29. In which city is *Hill Street Blues* set?
30. Who starred as an obnoxious gossip columnist named Lytton?

1. Which former *Blue Peter* presenter starred as *Dangerfield's* son?
2. In which year was the first TV broadcast of an Agatha Christie mystery?
3. Who played the female surveillance expert in the first series of *Bugs*?
4. What was the name of the feature-length one-off *Inspector Morse* film in 1995?
5. The 1939 dramatisation *The Anatomist* was about which pair of bodysnatchers?
6. The series *Jemima Shore Investigates* was based on whose novels?
7. Which newspaper critic adapted the stories for the first British Sherlock Holmes series in 1951?
8. What is 'Pie in the Sky' in the name of the series?
9. The crime series *Dragnet* was set in which US city?
10. In which European city was much of *Cadfael* filmed?
11. Which detective's 'love interest' was Agatha Troy?
12. *A Touch of Frost* is based on the books by which author?
13. Which series was a spin off from *Canned Carrott*?
14. What was Fitz's wife, played by Barbara Flynn, called in *Cracker*?
15. Which series was inspired by Nicholas Rhea's 'Constable' novels?
16. In *The Beiderbecke Affair*, what was the name of the amateur detective?
17. In *Boyd QC*, who played Boyd's clerk and narrator?
18. Who played Bodie and Doyle in *The Professionals*?
19. In which fictional area of London is *The Bill* set?
20. In which series did Neil Pearson star as ambitious Tony Clark?
21. Where was the police drama *Highway Patrol* set?
22. Which police detective is famous for his old mac?
23. In which series about a Geordie investigator did Denise Welch play Jimmy Nail's wife?
24. Which writer created *Prime Suspect*?
25. Which actress took over the role of Insp. Jean Darblay in *Juliet Bravo* in 1983?
26. Which Geordie actor plays Spender?
27. Which actor played Barry Chan in *The New Adventures of Charlie Chan*?
28. The character Wycliffe first appeared in which 1993 TV film?
29. Which comic crime show was Dawn French 's first major solo series?
30. *Dial 999* starred which Canadian as Det. Insp. Mike Maguire?

Answers: see Quiz 24, page 132　　　　　　　　　　LEVEL 2

1. Name the presenter of *Cosmos*.
2. Who presented *Connections*?
3. Who interviewed J. Paul Getty and The Sultan of Brunei?
4. The ceiling of the Sistine Chapel features in which programme titles?
5. Who was the author and presenter of *Pebble Mill At One*?
6. From the top of which US building was *Roving Report* first broadcast?
7. Who famously "counted them all out, and counted them all back"?
8. What do Fyfe Robinson, Alan Wicker and Trevor Philpot have in common?
9. Who interviewed Prince Charles on the programme which marked the 25th anniversary of his investiture as Prince of Wales?
10. What was the name of the David Attenborough's series about Antarctica?
11. Which two Peters were among the first presenters of *Newsnight*?
12. Jeremy Spake found fame working for which airline?
13. What was Britain's first breakfast TV programme called?
14. What was the year in which *Picture Page* was finally broadcast?
15. Who hosted a satellite talk show called *Surviving Life*?
16. In which year was the BBC TV *Newsreel* introduced?
17. What does ITN stand for?
18. Which French explorer presented *Under The Sea*?
19. What is the longest running TV current affairs programme?
20. Who first presented *Panorama*?
21. Where was *Jimmy's* set?
22. Who was the BBC's royal correspondent at the time of Princess Diana's death?
23. In which year was *BBC TV News* first broadcast?
24. Which co founder of TV am was married to a future Leader of the House of Lords?
25. Whose reporting of the Ethiopian famine in 1984 inspired Bob Geldof's Band Aid?
26. Who launched a singing career after telling her story on *Lakesiders*?
27. Which science show was first transmitted six months before the first satellite launch?
28. What was the follow-up series to *Diving to Adventure*?
29. Who was the original producer of *Frontiers of Science*?
30. Who first introduced *This Week* in 1956?

Answers: see Quiz 23, page 131

1. Who played Miss Brahms in *Are You Being Served*?
2. What is the name of Rene's wife in *'Allo 'Allo*?
3. Who first said "bloody" 78 times in half an hour in a sitcom?
4. Which comedian is quoted as saying, 'The mother in law thinks I'm effeminate; not that I mind that because beside her, I am'?
5. Which football team did Eddie Large play for before becoming a comedian?
6. Who played Fletcher in *Porridge*?
7. E. Blackadder Esq was butler to whom?
8. Which series had words from an Abba song in its title?
9. What was the colour of *Monty Python's* Big Red Book?
10. Harry Worth played the father in which comedy?
11. Which sitcom, starring Rodney Bewes, was the sequel to *Dear Mother... Love Albert*?
12. Who played Jim Hacker in *Yes Minister*?
13. In which war is *M*A*S*H* set?
14. Which actors played the bickering grandparents in *Three Up, Two Down*?
15. What was the name of Manuel's Andalucian hamster?
16. How many children does *Absolutely Fabulous* character Edina have?
17. Who played the daughter in *Bless This House*?
18. What was the name of the sequel to *A Very Peculiar Practice* which was set in Poland in 1992?
19. Where did Fonzie live?
20. Who played Chachie in *Joanie Loves Chachie*?
21. Who was the male star of *Evening Shade*?
22. Who played Rev. Jim in *Taxi*?
23. Who was the diminutive star of *Sorry!*?
24. Carleton was whose doorman?
25. What nationality were the men of *The Airbase*?
26. Who was the object of Ronnie Barker's affections in *Open All Hours*?
27. What kind of car did Mr Bean drive?
28. How many episodes were in the first series of *Auf Wiedersehen Pet*?
29. She played Frasier's wife in *Cheers*. Who is she?
30. Which brew did Paul Hogan advertise?

Answers: see Quiz 26, page 134

LEVEL 2

1. Who played the author Ian Fleming on televsion?
2. Which breakfast presenter hosted *Moviewatch*?
3. Which TV companies merged to form BSkyB?
4. Who played Jake Hanson in *Melrose Place*?
5. In 1957 how much did a colour TV cost?
6. What is *The X Files'* David Duchovny's masters degree in?
7. Who has produced *Kavanagh QC* and presented *Food & Drink*?
8. Who was the first male presenter of *Gladiators*?
9. Who was the first Director General of the BBC?
10. Which soap revolved around a West End department store?
11. Which pop star's production company launched *The Big Breakfast*?
12. Which company replaced Thames TV in the early 90s?
13. Which drink did Rutger Hauer advertise?
14. What does GMTV stand for?
15. How much did the first TV licence cost?
16. Which actor played Frank Marker?
17. Who played Hereward the Wake?
18. Which Kennedy was in love with Ann Wilkinson in *Neighbours*?
19. Who was the very first presenter of *This Is Your Life*?
20. Where was *Hadleigh* set?
21. Which role did Lane Smith play in *Superman*?
22. Which actor was *The Charmer*?
23. Who originally presented the sports summaries on *Breakfast Time*?
24. Which actress played Beryl in *The Loners*?
25. Who was the first Prime Minister to install a TV at home?
26. Roddy McMillan played which Scottish PI?
27. Which actor portrays Andy Dalziel?
28. Who presented *In Bed with MeDinner*?
29. Who gave the first direct TV broadcast by a Prime Minister in 1948?
30. Name the narrator of *The Valiant Years*.

Answers: see Quiz 25, page 133

1. Which *Coronation Street* former dustman is now *Keeping up Appearances*?
2. Who was Sam's mum in *Home and Away*?
3. Which impresario played Betty Turpin's Gordon in *Coronation Street*?
4. What was the name of the first minicab company in *EastEnders*?
5. What was the name of Robbie's dog in *EastEnders*?
6. Which soap was set on the Scottish Glendarroch Estate?
7. In which soap did Amanda Burton play Heather Huntington?
8. What was the name of Elsie Tanner's daughter?
9. Who played Hilda Ogden's daughter in *Coronation Street*?
10. What was the Christian name of Ken Barlow's father?
11. In which city was *Albion Market* set?
12. Which late producer was dubbed 'The Godmother of Soap'?
13. Who originally played Mark Fowler before Todd Carty?
14. Which Ewing moved to *Knotts Landing*?
15. What was the name of Max Farnham's first wife?
16. Which soap was launched in 1992 with the promise of 'sun, sand, sangria and sex'?
17. What is the postcode of the London Borough of Walford?
18. Where did Gary Stanlow hide drugs when Lindsey, Kylie and Mike left the country?
19. How did Sue, Terry Sullivan's wife, die?
20. What was the name of Sue and Terry's son?
21. What was the name of Jimmy Corkhill's dog?
22. Who was the creator of *Emergency-Ward 10*?
23. What number house did the Jordache family live at?
24. Which US soap starred the widow of a rock star and the daughter of an American singing and acting legend?
25. What was the name of Ron Dixon and Bev's house?
26. What was Mick Johnson's first shop in *Brookside* called?
27. What is the nickname of Carmel's son in *Brookside*?
28. What is Sinbad's real name?
29. How did Gladys Charlton die?
30. What was Ron Dixon's lorry called?

Pot Luck 4 (See Quiz 25)

1. Jason Connery. 2. Johnny Vaughn. 3. Sky Television and BSB. 4. Grant Show. 5. £175. 6. English Literature. 7. Chris Kelly. 8. John Fashanu. 9. Lord Reith. 10. *Harper's, West One*. 11. Bob Geldof. 12. Carlton. 13. Guinness. 14. Good Morning Television. 15. Ten shillings (50p). 16. Alfred Burke. 17. Alfred Lynch. 18. Billy. 19. Eamon Andrews. 20. Yorkshire. 21. Perry King. 22. Nigel Havers. 23. David Icke. 24. Paula Wilcox. 25. Ramsay MacDonald. 26. Daniel Pike. 27. Warren Clarke. 28. Bob Mills. 29. Clement Attlee. 30. Richard Burton.

Answers: see Quiz 28, page 136

LEVEL 2

1. Who used to say, 'We thank you - we really do'?
2. The entrance to the studios of which TV company gave *The Tube* its name?
3. What is the connection between Peter Dimmock, Sylvia Peters, Brian Johnston, Terry Wogan, Angela Rippon and Rosemarie Ford?
4. Which song did the BBC release for *Children in Need* in 1997?
5. In which year was *The Good Old Days* first televised?
6. Which member of a famous singing family appeared in *Fame*?
7. Which pianist who had a hit with "*Side Saddle*" was a regular on *Billy Cotton's Band Show*?
8. Who were Legs and Co?
9. What was Britain's first *Eurovision Song Contest* entry?
10. This singer and one-time TV host changed his name from Nick Perido. Who was he?
11. Vince Hill presented which popular music series?
12. Which TV host sang 'Swinging in the Rain'?
13. Who starred in *Set 'Em Up Joe*?
14. Where is *TFI Friday* broadcast from?
15. Which large pink spotty character was introduced on *Noel's House Party*?
16. Whose name appeared 'Later' in the music shows of the early 1990s?
17. Which girlfriend of soccer's Ryan Giggs presented *The Word*?
18. Which *Men Behaving Badly* star briefly presented *The Tube*?
19. Which dancers appeared on *Sunday Night at The London Palladium*?
20. Whose catchphrase was 'You lucky people'?
21. In the first *Celebrity Stars in their Eyes*, who said "Tonight Matthew I'm going to be Cher"?
22. Which comedy duo's theme song, composed by one of them, was 'Goodbye-ee'?
23. Which opera star hosted a Saturday Night show in the autumn of 1998?
24. Which *Magpie* presenter was a regular *Juke Box Jury* panellist as "a typical teenager"?
25. What was the first full length musical play shown on TV in 1939?
26. Who replaced Richard Baker hosting the *Proms* on TV?
27. Which pop star hosted the 1998 *Miss World Contest* for Channel 5?
28. Which long-standing dance programme was first shown in 1949?
29. Which *Top of the Pops* presenter was voted Britain's best dressed man in 1998?
30. Where was the 1998 *Three Tenors Concert* televised from?

ANSWERS TV Comedy 7 (See Quiz 28)

1. Simon Callow. 2. Rosie (PC Penrose). 3. Sid. 4. Lee Whitlock. 5. Vienna. 6. Gizzard Puke.
7. Benny Hill. 8. Anna Karen. 9. Helen Atkinson Wood. 10. Fred MacMurray. 11. Hercules.
12. Shelley Long. 13. Hannah Gordon. 14. *Whoops Baghdad*. 15. *Saturday Night Armistice*. 16. 3.
17. TV repair man. 18. Mathilda Ziegler. 19. Valerie Harper. 20. BJ Hunnicut. 21. Nora Batty.
22. Timothy Spall. 23. Edina. 24. 4. 25. Hyacinth. 26. *Ever Decreasing Circles*. 27. *Outside Edge*.
28. Sharon and Tracey. 29. Dick Clement & Ian la Frenais. 30. Lenny Godber.

Answers: see Quiz 27, page 135

1. Who played Tom Chance in *Chance in a Million*?
2. Paul Greenwood played which comic policeman?
3. What is the name of Ivy's husband in *Last Of The Summer Wine*?
4. Who played Harvey Moon's son?
5. In *Rising Damp*, Rigsby's cat shares its name with a capital city. What is it?
6. What was the name of Kenny Everett's punk caricature?
7. Fred Scuttle was an comic charcter created by which comedian?
8. Which actress played Reg Varney's sister, Olive, in *On The Buses*?
9. In *Blackadder The Third*, Mrs Miggins was played by which comic actress?
10. Who starrred in *My Three Sons*?
11. What was the name of Steptoe and Son's horse?
12. Which *The Money Pit* actress played Diane Chambers in *Cheers*?
13. Who played *My Wife Next Door*?
14. What was the follow up to *Up Pompeii!*?
15. Which 1995 Saturday Night series was presented by Armando Iannucci?
16. How many sons does Tim have in *Home Improvement*?
17. What was Gary's job in the first series of *Goodnight Sweetheart*?
18. Who played Mr Bean's long suffering girlfriend?
19. Who starred as Rhoda?
20. Who was Trapper John's replacement in *M*A*S*H*?
21. Who was Wally's wife in *Last Of The Summer Wine*?
22. Who played Frank Stubbs?
23. Who is Saffron's mother in *Absolutely Fabulous*?
24. How many sons did Mrs Boswell have in *Bread*?
25. What was Mrs Bucket's first name in *Keeping Up Appearances*?
26. Penelope Wilton and Peter Egan appeared together as neighbours in which sitcom?
27. Which sitcom about a local cricket club starred Timothy Spall and Josie Lawrence as married couple?
28. Who were Dorien's neighbours in *Birds Of A Feather*?
29. Who wrote *Auf Wiedersehen Pet*?
30. Who was Fletcher's cellmate in *Porridge*?

QUIZ 29 Children's TV 3

Answers: see Quiz 30, page 138   LEVEL 2

1. In which children's series did Sally James appear?
2. Where did Fred Flintstone work?
3. Who made *Worzel Gummidge*?
4. Geoffrey Bayldon played which children's character?
5. What is the number plate on the postman's van in Greendale?
6. Who was the first *Blue Peter* presenter to be sacked, for taking cocaine?
7. Name the snail in *The Magic Roundabout*.
8. Who was the star of *Dick Turpin*?
9. Which series was a role reversal version of Robin Hood?
10. Where do *the Munsters* live?
11. What colour are the Smurfs?
12. Who was Superted's friend?
13. Which series featured a pantomime horse?
14. Spike the Dog features in which cartoon?
15. Who first played Long John Silver in a television series?
16. What was the name of the lion in *The Lion, The Witch and The Wardrobe*?
17. Who hosted *Runaround*?
18. What is the name of Kermit the frog's nephew?
19. Which ventriloquist worked with Lenny the Lion?
20. Who was Ray Alan's inebriated dummy?
21. Which green duck wore a nappy?
22. Who 'rode' an ostrich?
23. What was the name of the cow in *The Magic Roundabout*?
24. Where was *Crackerjack* first produced?
25. Which E Nesbitt dramatisation featured a legendary bird?
26. What was Lamb Chop?
27. Where did the *Teenage Mutant Ninja Turtles* live?
28. From which century did *Catweazle* come?
29. For which character is Jay Silverheels remembered?
30. Whose language included the word "Flobalob"?

QUIZ 30   Crime 4

Answers: see Quiz 29, page 137

LEVEL 2

1. In *Martin Kane, Private Investigator*, which actor played the title role?
2. In *Heartbeat*, what was Nick's first wife called?
3. Which character does Helen Mirren play in *Prime Suspect*?
4. What rank was *Cribb* in the programme of the same name?
5. In which series did Alan Cade replace John Stafford in the top job?
6. Which actor plays the title role in *Dangerfield*?
7. Which city was *Petrocelli* set?
8. In which series did Jimmy Smits play Bobby Simone?
9. In which series did Det. Sgt. John Ho appear in the early 80s?
10. Which character had a partner called Penfold?
11. Who played Det. Chief Insp. Nick Lewis in *The Enigma Files*?
12. What disability is Columbo actor Peter Falk afflicted with?
13. Which actor plays D.I. Frost?
14. Which actor from *The Bill* died shortly after being sacked from the show because of his drinking?
15. Who did Jill Dando replace on *Crimewatch UK*?
16. What is *Cadfael's* profession?
17. What did C.A.T.S. stand for in the series *CATS Eyes*?
18. Who created *Hazell*?
19. Name the lead character in *Highway Patrol*.
20. Which Glasgow-based series developed from a three part thriller called *Killers*?
21. *Wolf to the Slaughter* was the first programme to feature which famous Ruth Rendell detective?
22. Which former Doctor Who played private detective Albert Campion?
23. In which police station was *Juliet Bravo* set?
24. Who partnered *Crime Traveller* Chloe Annett?
25. Which actor played Charlie Chan?
26. After leaving *EastEnders* which crime series did Paul Nicholls star in?
27. Who introduced the series *Lady Killers*?
28. Name the author of *Inspector Morse*.
29. Which Eurovision Song Contest entrant starred in *Liverpool One*?
30. What relation was Charlie Hungerford to Jim Bergerac?

Childrens' TV 3 (See Quiz 29)

1. *Tiswas*. 2. Bedrock Quarry. 3. The Crow Man. 4. Catweazle. 5. PAT1. 6. Richard Bacon.
7. Brian. 8. Richard O'Sullivan. 9. *Maid Marian and Her Merry Men*. 10. Mockingbird Lane.
11. Blue. 12. Spottyman. 13. *Rentaghost*. 14. Tom & Jerry. 15. Robert Newton. 16. Aslan.
17. Mike Read. 18. Robin. 19. Terry Hall. 20. Lord Charles. 21. Orville. 22. Bernie Clifton.
23. Ermintrude. 24. Television Theatre, Shepherds Bush. 25. *The Phoenix and The Carpet*.
26. A puppet. 27. In the sewers. 28. 11th. 29. Tonto. 30. Bill & Ben (*The Flowerpot Men*).

ANSWERS

Answers: see Quiz 32, page 140

LEVEL 2

1. Who wrote *Widows*?
2. Who starred in the role of James Onedin?
3. Which Dennis Potter drama was banned in 1976 and shown in 1987?
4. She played *The Duchess of Duke Street*. Who was she?
5. Name the main protagonist in *The Adventures of William Tell*.
6. Who was the female star of *The Champions*?
7. What was the name of the series starring Jesse Birdsall and filmed on the Isle of Wight?
8. Which character did David Longton play in *Upstairs Downstairs*?
9. Where is the series that starred Kevin Whately and Sam Shepherd set?
10. In which steamy serial did Sean Bean star alongside Joely Richardson?
11. Which series used 'Cry Me a River' as the theme?
12. Which Estate was the subject for the filming of *Brideshead Revisited*?
13. Which son of a famous soap star starred in *Seaforth*?
14. Which Avenger appeared in *Upstairs Downstairs*?
15. What was Peter Graves' character called in *Mission Impossible*?
16. In which American State was *The Ponderosa*?
17. Who played the title role in *Hunter*?
18. What was the subject of the series *Flickers*?
19. Who was William Tell's enemy?
20. In which series did Geraldine James play Sarah Layton?
21. Who played Cpt. Grant Mitchell's shipmates Alfonso and Sean?
22. Who was Sarah in *Thomas and Sarah*?
23. Which rag-trade series featured Stephanie Beacham?
24. Which actor was Matt Houston?
25. Which drama series starred Bob Peck and Joe Don Baker?
26. In which century was *The Buccaneers* set?
27. Which actor pursued Dr Richard Kimble?
28. Who did Ed Byrnes play in *77 Sunset Strip*?
29. Which company made *Cheyenne*, *Bronco* and *Tenderfoot*?
30. Who was the ramrod in *Rawhide*?

ANSWERS

TV Comedy 8 (See Quiz 32)

1. *The Mary Whitehouse Experience*. 2. Gregor Fisher. 3. *Fawlty Towers*. 4. Dustin Gee. 5. Yetta Feldman. 6. Betty Spencer. 7. *Rising Damp*. 8. Julia McKenzie. 9. *Police Squad*. 10. Paul Calf. 11. *Rowan & Martins' Laugh-In*. 12. *Magpie's* Jenny Handley is daughter to *Don't Wait Up's* Dinah Sheridan. 13. Captain. 14. Dervla Kirwan. 15. Lance Percival. 16. Dermot. 17. Johnny Speight. 18. Gunther. 19. Latimer. 20. *Dick & the Duchess*. 21. Blamire. 22. Reece Dinsdale. 23. She has never been seen. 24. Roadsweeper. 25. Nick Frisbee. 26. 'Radar' O'Reilly. 27. F Troop. 28. Sgt. Bilko. 29. Lanford. 30. Grace Brothers (*Are You Being Served?*).

Answers: see Quiz 31, page 139

1. Which Radio 1 comedy show spawned *Newman and Baddiel in Pieces*?
2. Who created the character Rab C Nesbit?
3. In classic comedy do Polly and the Major both appear?
4. Who was Les Dennis' late comedy partner?
5. Whose was the female ghost in *So Haunt Me*?
6. Who was married to Frank in *Some Mothers Do Ave Em*?
7. In which series did Richard Beckinsale and Frances de la Tour play harassed lodgers?
8. Who played Hester in *Fresh Fields*?
9. Which spoof cop series featured Leslie Neilson?
10. Which offensive drunk was created by Steve Coogan on Channel 4's *Saturday Zoo*?
11. Which comedy show did Dick and Dan compere?
12. What is the link between *Magpie* and the comedy *Don't Wait Up*?
13. In *Blackadder Goes Forth*, what rank was Blackadder?
14. Who was the star of both *Goodnight Sweetheart* and *Ballykissangel*?
15. Who created calypsos on *That Was The Week That Was*?
16. Which character was played by Harry Enfield in *Men Behaving Badly*?
17. Who wrote *'Til Us Do Part*?
18. In *Friends*, who in Central Perk is a secret admirer of Rachel?
19. What is the surname of father and son in *Don't Wait Up*?
20. The character Dick Starrett was a troubled American insurance investigator in which 50's comedy?
21. Who did Michael Bates play in *Last of the Summer Wine*?
22. Who played John Thaw's son in *Home to Roost*?
23. From the viewer's point of view, what is unusual about Niles' wife Maris in *Frasier*?
24. What was the occupation of Mr Boswell in *Bread*?
25. Which Brian Conley character has a puppet assistant called Larry the Loafer?
26. What was the nickname of Gary Burghoff's character in *MASH*?
27. What was the name of the US comedy about the cavalry?
28. Colonel Hall was which Master Sergeant's superior officer?
29. In which town does Roseanne live?
30. In which store did the actors Larry Martin and Arthur English appear?

1. Which sixties soap centred on the editorial office of a woman's magazine?
2. At the start of WWII how much notice did the government give the BBC to close their service?
3. Which form of art do you associate Nancy Kaminsky?
4. Which television region produced *Houseparty*?
5. Who is Emma Forbes' actress mother?
6. Who was the BBC's first director of TV?
7. Who is Mel Giedroyc's partner on *Late Lunch*?
8. What was the name of the head porter in *Porterhouse Blue* played by David Jason?
9. In *Tutti Frutti* how long had the rock band The Majestics been together?
10. Which firestation features in *London's Burning*?
11. *Soldier, Soldier* follows the activities of the fictitious "A" Company of which infantry regiment?
12. Which budding singer-songwriter did Jimmy Nail play in *Crocodile Shoes*?
13. Who was the host of *Lunchbox*?
14. Who supplied the BBC commentary for the Coronation of King George VI?
15. Which disc jockey married Anthea Turner?
16. Which gardener leads the *Ground Force* team?
17. What are the Christian names of the Hurt twins in *Family Affairs*?
18. What is the title of BBC 2's early morning educational programmes?
19. What forced daytime shutdown of TV transmissions in Feb-March 1947?
20. Which newsreader presents *I-Spy*?
21. How many lines are broadcast on UHF on British Television?
22. Which larger-than-life actor advertised sherry?
23. Which female television personality has a daughter named Trixie-Belle?
24. How long did the 1953 Coronation broadcast last?
25. Which impresario was the brother of Lou Grade?
26. Which channel broadcast *The Girlie Show*?
27. Who was the BBC's first DIY expert?
28. Which actor was 'Walker, Texas Ranger'?
29. *Sharpe* is set during which war?
30. Who does Roger Griffith play in *Pie In The Sky*?

Answers: see Quiz 33, page 141

1. Which football presenter is a former Spurs and England captain?
2. Where is the starting point of the University Boat Race?
3. Which 400 metre runner presents *Record Breakers*?
4. Who was the first presenter of *Grandstand*?
5. Which female presenter joined Barry Venison presenting *On The Ball* in 1998?
6. Who are *Saint and Greavsie*?
7. Where is the 'hot' setting for snooker on television?
8. Who is cricket's 'Jonners'?
9. Who are captains of England and *They Think It's all Over*?
10. Which diminutive jockey was a team captain on *A Question of Sport*?
11. Which TV chef cooked on TV for his favourite team Manchester United?
12. Who first hosted the late evening sports chat show *On Side*?
13. Which sport were Eddie Waring and Ray French associated with?
14. Which tennis player was BBC Sports Personality of 1997?
15. Who presented *Football Focus* before leaving for ITV in 1994?
16. The first Olympics to be televised were held where?
17. Which BBC show transmits outtakes from sporting events gone wrong?
18. Which early 1950's sports programme was introduced by Max Robertson and screened on Wednesday evening?
19. With which TV sport do you associated Jimmy White?
20. Dan Maskell commentated on which sport?
21. Aintree is the location for which televised sporting event?
22. Footballer and manager Jack Charlton is often seen on TV in which other sport?
23. Which channel did cricket move to from the BBC in 1999?
24. Who presents *Ski Sunday*?
25. Which Raymond provides BBC's showjumping commentaries?
26. What was cricketer Gary Sobers TV claim to fame?
27. Which sport has been televised being played on the moon?
28. Which Formula One world champion commentated on Grand Prix races?
29. Which former Fulham player and Coventry chairman presented *Match of The Day*?
30. Which football team does Des Lynam support?

Answers: see Quiz 36, page 144

LEVEL 2

1. In *EastEnders* what are Ian Beale's twins called?
2. What did DD Dixon's shop sell?
3. Who was the best man at the marriage of Alf and Audrey Roberts?
4. Which *Brookside* character worked in a bar in order to buy a ticket to Rome?
5. What is Gerard Rebecchi's nickname in *Neighbours*?
6. What is the name of Kim Tate's son in *Emmerdale*?
7. Who was Annie Walker's husband in *Coronation Street*?
8. Who created *Brookside*?
9. In which country was *Eldorado* set?
10. Which soap was the first American one on British television?
11. In *Emmerdale*, who is the vet?
12. Name the three Kennedy children in *Neighbours*?
13. What is Curly Watt's Christian name?
14. Jason Donovan appeared as which character in *Neighbours*?
15. Which sixties soap was set in the offices of a magazine?
16. What is the name of the second pub in *Emmerdale*?
17. What was Pauline Fowler's mother's name?
18. In *Crossroads*, who did Paul Henry play?
19. Who played Blake Carrington in *Dynasty*?
20. Where is Ramsay Street?
21. Who played Joe Sugden in *Emmerdale*?
22. Which character left Albert Square for a job in the USA?
23. Which character in *Coronation Street* was played by Jean Alexander?
24. What job was Seth Armstrong offered by NY Estates?
25. Who was Dr Roger Moon in *Emergency-Ward 10*?
26. Who is Lachie's girlfriend in *Home and Away*?
27. What was the spin-off feature film made from *Emergency-Ward 10* in 1958?
28. Who opened "Deals on Wheels" in *EastEnders*?
29. What was the name of Derek Riley's wife in *Coronation Street*?
30. Which role did Clive Hornby play in *Emmerdale*?

Answers: see Quiz 35, page 143

1. Who wrote the original book upon which *Blott on the Landscape* was based?
2. In which series did Maureen Lipman take on student boarders, including Martin Clunes?
3. What was Private Fraser's occupation in *Dad's Army*?
4. *Selling Hitler* was a black comedy about what affair?
5. In which series did Philip Franks become David Jason's son in law?
6. Whose catchphrase was, 'Shut that door'?
7. Who is known as The Big Yin?
8. Who wrote *The Odd Couple*?
9. Who is Eddie Large's sidekick?
10. Which of the *Goodies* is a qualified doctor?
11. Which male comedian created the flirtatious character Mandy?
12. Which ex Bond girl played Caroline's mother in *The Upper Hand*?
13. What was the name of Jed Clampitt's daughter in the *Beverley Hillbillies*?
14. Who played Lukewarm in *Porridge*?
15. Why was the Earth destroyed in *A Hitchhiker's Guide to The Galaxy*?
16. Who played Mrs Roper in *George and Mildred*?
17. Which stand-up comedian starred in *Up The Elephant and Round The Castle*?
18. Who on *Red Dwarf* had the alter-ego Dwayne Dibley?
19. Who did Alf Garnett nickname Marigold?
20. Who plays Dr Toby Latimer?
21. Which *Faith* actress advertises stock cubes?
22. Which series was a spin-off from *American Graffiti*?
23. Who played the wife of Dick Starrett in *Dick And The Duchess*?
24. Of which football team was Eric Morecambe a director?
25. What was the name of the *Vicar of Dibley*'s curate?
26. Who played Mork's Mindy?
27. Who was the creator of the series *Oh Boy*?
28. Which ex Python wrote and performed the theme to *One Foot in the Grave*?
29. What was Hyacinth Bucket's brother in law called?
30. Which English actor appeared as Rebecca's boyfriend in *Cheers*?

Answers: see Quiz 38, page 146

LEVEL 2

1. Which TV playwright wrote the *Quatermass* serials?
2. Which sci-fi series began the day after President Kennedy's death?
3. Who starred as *Kolchak: The Nightstalker*?
4. What were the names of the computers in *Blake's Seven*?
5. Name the author of *The Hitch-Hiker's Guide to The Galaxy*.
6. What was the name of the first episode – and heroine – of *Neverwhere*?
7. Which comic hero was played by Dean Cain?
8. Which Edwardian adventurer had been trapped in ice and thawed out in the Sixties?
9. What kind of spacecraft was *Red Dwarf*?
10. Who was the star of *Darling* who appeared in *A For Andromeda*?
11. Who does Patrick Stewart play in *Star Trek: The Next Generation*?
12. In *The Avengers*, what was Peter Peel's widow called?
13. What was the revamped version of *Battlestar Galactica* called?
14. Which squad was Don Quick a member of in *The Adventures of Don Quick*?
15. How was Jaime Sommers better known?
16. In which BBC programme would you find the character of Dr Spencer Quist?
17. What name was given to the three superhumans whose job it was to maintain world peace, in the series first seen in the 60s and re-run in the 90s?
18. Which Rock featured in *The Martian Chronicles* mini-series?
19. Which programme starred Scott Bakula as Sam Beckett?
20. In *The X-Files* which character is a medic?
21. Dominick Hyde travelled into which 20th century decade?
22. How was David McCallum's character Daniel Westin also known?
23. In *UFO*, why had SHADO been set up?
24. Which star of *Baywatch* starred in *Knight Rider* in the 1980s?
25. In *The Stone Tapes*, what did the scientific team try to extract from the walls of a Victorian mansion?
26. Which 11th century wizard became trapped in the 20th century?
27. What was the profession of the *Six Million Dollar Man*?
28. *The Survivors* survived which global disaster?
29. In *Space: 1999*, part of which heavenly body is cast into space after a nuclear explosion?
30. Which character did Joanna Lumley play in *The New Avengers*?

Answers: see Quiz 37, page 145

LEVEL 2

1. What is the link between *Fraggle Rock* and *Porridge*?
2. Which cartoon character has an anchor tattooed on his arm?
3. Who was the first male presenter of *Blue Peter*?
4. Name the creator of *Wallace and Gromit*.
5. Who was Captain Scarlet's superior?
6. Which member of *The Monkees* wore a woolly hat?
7. Name the lion in *The Herbs*.
8. Who preceded Andy Crane as presenter of *Children's BBC*?
9. Which badge features a sailing ship?
10. Which Monkee's father was The Count of Monte Cristo?
11. Who is Dick Dastardly's pet dog?
12. In *Lost in Space*, which character was played by Mark Goddard?
13. On which show might you visit the Roundabout Stop?
14. Who narrated the first series of *Thomas the Tank Engine and Friends*?
15. Which country recording artists appeared in *The Beverley Hillbillies*?
16. Which Hanna-Barbera cartoon featured Penelope Pitstop?
17. Which character lived in Scatterbrook?
18. What do Archie Duncan and Clive Mantle have in common?
19. Eartha Kitt and Julie Newmar both played which character?
20. Who wore glasses in *Thunderbirds*?
21. What sort of creatures were Tobermory and Orinoco?
22. What colour is Teletubby Laa Laa?
23. '*Walking in the Air*' was the theme for which cartoon film?
24. Rod, Jane and Freddy featured in which childrens' TV programme?
25. What is the name of the school holiday morning series for children on Channel 4?
26. On what would you find the words 'Jim Fixed It For Me'?
27. Who is Snoopy's owner?
28. What is the name of Keith Harris's talking monkey?
29. Complete the following, 'It's Friday, it's five o'clock, and it's…'
30. In the cartoon version of *Batman*, who provided the voice for Robin?

Answers: see Quiz 40, page 148

LEVEL 2

1. Whose nickname is Woz?

2. Loyd Grossman presents which cookery programme?

3. Which cook's husband wore a monocle?

4. Which TV chef is a director of Norwich City football club?

5. Which Susan cooks on *This Morning*?

6. Who is chef Ross from *Light Lunch*?

7. Which form of transport is popular with the *Two Fat Ladies*?

8. Which chef also advertises Tate & Lyle and his own ready meals?

9. Name the former presenter of *Food and Drink*.

10. Which actress is host of the morning show *Good Living*?

11. What does the runner up receive on *Celebrity Ready Steady Cook*?

12. Who presented *Tastes of Britain*?

13. Which Indian actress is also a well-known food expert?

14. Which country does Glen Christian originate from?

15. Which chef uses a '*Hot Wok*'?

16. Which *Bird of a Feather* ran a café?

17. Name the larger than life West Indian lady TV cook.

18. What was the name of Keith Floyd's first TV series?

19. Who is Paul Rankin's Canadian wife who is also an expert chef?

20. In *Ready Steady Cook*, what are the symbols used to identify each team?

21. Who presents *Real Food* on Channel Four?

22. Who was *The Galloping Gourmet*?

23. Name Jilly Goolden's wine-tasting partner.

24. Philip Harben presented which type of programme on post-war TV?

25. Which TV cook is the daughter of late cookery expert Jane?

26. Valentina Harris specialises on food from which country?

27. In what did Rachel lose her engagement ring in *Friends*?

28. On which magazine programme did Keith Floyd show his skills in the early 1980s?

29. Name Keith Floyd's series which explored cooking in the Far East?

30. What would be the main ingredient if your meal was being prepared by Rick Stein?

1. In which year was Jim Hacker elected Prime Minister?
2. Which actress played Roseanne's grandmother?
3. Which family had 'Two Point Four Children'?
4. Who wrote *Clochemerle*?
5. Which character does Brett Butler play in her TV series?
6. What is the name of the book shop in *Ellen*?
7. What is Ross's professional passion in *Friends*?
8. Which series took the viewer behind the scenes at Globelink News?
9. Who plays John in *Ally McBeal*?
10. Who did Wendy Richard play in *Are You Being Served*?
11. Who played Jeffrey Fairbrother, the original manager of the holiday camp in *Hi-De-Hi!*?
12. Who played Timothy Lumsden in *Sorry!*?
13. What did Citizen Smith's girlfriend's mother mistakenly call him?
14. Which 80's comedy series featured two feuding antiques dealers?
15. What is Sarge's hobby in *Duck Patrol*?
16. Who is Billy Connolly's wife?
17. On which show did Bernard Manning, Mike Reid and Jim Bowen come to prominence?
18. On which programme do Steven Frost, Greg Proops and Josie Lawrence regularly improvise?
19. Which show featured 'The Ministry For Silly Walks'?
20. What was the name of Lenny Henry's rastafarian character?
21. Who was Hattie Jacques husband?
22. Which car ad features Nicole running away from her marriage to Vic Reeves?
23. Which female comedian satirised Hannibal Lecter?
24. Who is the used car salesman in *Only Fools and Horses*?
25. Who plays Tom Latimer's mother in *Don't Wait Up*?
26. Which actor played Blott in *Blott on the Landscape*?
27. What is the name of the hotel in *Heartbreak Hotel*?
28. How many *Girls on Top* were there?
29. Which *Game For A Laugh* presenters shared a surname?
30. What was the name of Dorothy's ex-husband in *The Golden Girls*?

1. Which science programme have Maggie Philbin and William Woolhand presented?
2. Which *This Week* reporter reported on the Queen's 1977 visit to Northern Ireland which was banned from transmission?
3. What does Sister Wendy review?
4. Who founded *Roving Report*?
5. Trude Mostue found fame in a documentary training for which profession?
6. Jack Hargreaves presented which show?
7. Which presenter interviewed Charles and Diana two days before their wedding?
8. Which store featured in *The Shop*?
9. What was the name of the 1970 junior version of *The Sky at Night*?
10. Who was the first presenter of *Tonight*?
11. *City Hospital* with Gaby Roslin was broadcast live daily from where?
12. Which news magazine programme featured Magnus Magnusson as a reporter?
13. Name the presenter of the documentary series *This Wonderful World*.
14. Who was the Consultant Physician in the early programmes of *Your Life in Their Hands*?
15. Who was *Driving School's* most famous pupil?
16. Who founded CNN?
17. How did *Face to Face* open and close?
18. Who hosted the TV review programme *Did You See...?*
19. Which drama documentary caused a rift between Britain and Saudi Arabia?
20. Who took the first of the *Great Railway Journeys of the World*?
21. Who was the narrator of the series *Hollywood*?
22. Name the presenter and writer of the series *Ireland: A Television History*.
23. Which pun-like title was used for the docu soap about chalet girls in a ski resort?
24. When was *Newsnight* first aired?
25. Which women's prison featured in a four-night 1982 Granada TV documentary?
26. Who was the subject of the documentary *American Caesar*?
27. What was the follow up to David Attenborough's *Life on Earth* called?
28. Who was the first female presenter of the BBC's *Breakfast Time*?
29. What was the subject of the series *Crime Inc*?
30. In what year was *Crimewatch* UK first aired?

Answers: see Quiz 39, page 149

LEVEL 2

1. Milburn Stone played which character in *Gunsmoke*?
2. Who had a limp in *Gun Law*?
3. Which actor was the star of *Kung Fu*?
4. Which *Morse* actor is also *The Broker's Man*?
5. In which hospital is *Casualty* based?
6. Where was *The Adventures of William Tell* filmed on location?
7. In *Upstairs, Downstairs*, Mrs Bridges was played by which actress?
8. Where is Blue Watch's fire station in *London's Burning*?
9. Who is the star of *Spencer: For Hire*?
10. What was the name of James Onedin's ship?
11. Which Victorian doctor does Jemma Redgrave play?
12. Name the series about the Suffragette movement.
13. Who was the writer of the series *Black Eyes*?
14. In which series about an all-girl group did Rula Lenska star?
15. Name the girl-next-door in *The Larkins*.
16. What's the name of the costume drama which featured the characters Ross and Demelza?
17. In which series did Noel Harrison partner Stephanie Powers?
18. Which character replaced Emma Peel in *The Avengers*?
19. Who created *Trial and Retribution*?
20. What was the name of Arnie Cole's theatre in *Flickers*?
21. Which literary hero has been played on TV by Peter Cushing, Alan Badel and Colin Firth?
22. Which late actor played an angel in *Highway to Heaven*?
23. In *Imogen's Face*, who played the title role?
24. Bryan Marshall starred as a naval captain in which series?
25. John Thaw portrayed this writer in *A Year in Provence*.
26. Which *Soldier, Soldier* actor also appeared in *Touching Evil*?
27. Who played the two lead roles in *Staying On*, set in India?
28. Which English doctor had an affair with Peter Benton in *ER*?
29. In which drama series did the McGann brothers play the Phelan brothers?
30. Who originally played Blackbeard in *The Buccaneers*?

QUIZ 43 Pot Luck 6

LEVEL 2

1. Who was the last presenter of *Rugby Special* on BBC2?
2. Whose catchphrase was 'Walkies!'?
3. Where would you find Zippy, Bungle and George?
4. Which former Ulster TV presenter introduced the magazine programme *Sunday Sunday* for eight years?
5. Which keep fit expert was dubbed 'The Green Goddess'?
6. Who was the first female member of the *Ground Force* team?
7. Who journeyed *Around The Pacific Rim*?
8. Brian Glover played which private detective's man servant?
9. Which pop singer played a game show host in *Miami Vice*?
10. Who played Q in *Star Trek: The Next Generation*?
11. What was Peter Parker's alterego?
12. What was the subject of *Tour of Duty*?
13. In *Emmerdale*, what's the real life connection between Chris and Kim Tate?
14. Helen Baxendale played which character in *An Unsuitable Job for a Woman*?
15. What did the first televised Church service commemorate?
16. Name the presenter of *Through the Keyhole*.
17. Who played characters in *Fame* and *VR5*?
18. What was the estimated number of UK viewers of the 1953 Coronation?
19. Who was Marty Feldman's writing partner?
20. Jean Harvey, Nicholas Selby, and Gareth Davies played editors of which fictional magazine?
21. Who ended his programme with the words "The next *Tonight* is tomorrow night"?
22. On election nights who wields his Swingometer?
23. What was David Bellamy's chat show called?
24. Who presented *Mad Movies*?
25. Which actress played *The Very Merry Widow*?
26. Which cereal is advertised as the one that goes, 'Snap, Crackle and Pop'?
27. Which post did Alastair Milne hold finally at the BBC?
28. Who made the controversial *The War Game*?
29. Which organisation did Mary Whitehouse represent?
30. What is the BBC's house magazine?

ANSWERS

TV Comedy 11 (See Quiz 44)

1. Sir Humphrey Appleby. 2. Armed Robbery. 3. Lisa Riley. 4. *You Rang M'Lord?* 5. Pvt. Godfrey.
6. Jerzy Balowski. 7. Liz Estensen. 8. Lurcio. 9. *The Bishop Rides Again.* 10. Jaguar. 11. Antiques.
12. *Five Go Mad in Dorset.* 13. Corky. 14. Wendy Craig. 15. Patsy Rowland. 16. Sally Thomsett.
17. Pearl. 18. Artois. 19. *Friends.* 20. All-night bakery. 21. *M*A*S*H.* 22. Yellow. 23. Paris.
24. *After Henry.* 25. *Alas Smith and Jones.* 26. Roy Barraclough. 27. Hot Gossip. 28. Jerry.
29. Steve Punt. 30. *Last of the Summer Wine.*

Answers: see Quiz 43, page 152

1. Who was Jim Hacker's Cabinet Secretary?
2. What crime did Chris and Daryl commit in *Birds of a Feather*?
3. Who replaced Jeremy Beadle on *You've Been Framed*?
4. Which Croft & Perry sitcom was set in an Edwardian household?
5. Which character in *Dad's Army* had sisters named Dolly and Cissy?
6. What was the name of the landlord in *The Young Ones*?
7. Who, apart from Polly James, Pauline Collins and Nerys Hughes, has starred as a *Liver Bird*?
8. What was Frankie Howerd's character called in *Up Pompeii*?
9. Which late 60s sitcom starred Derek Nimmo as a bishop?
10. Which car did Joey drive in *Bread*?
11. In *Never The Twain* Windsor Davies and Donald Sinden were feuding member of which trade?
12. Which Enid Blyton spoof was made by the Comic Strip team in 1982?
13. Which policeman did Derek Guyler play in *Sykes*?
14. Who starred with Ronald Hines in *Not in Front of the Children*?
15. Who played Trevor's wife in *Bless This House*?
16. Who played Jo in *Man About the House*?
17. Who was Jethro's mother in *The Beverley Hillbillies*?
18. What was Rene's surname in *'Allo 'Allo*?
19. *'I'll Be There For You,'* was the theme music for which Channel 4 series?
20. What was the venue of the Keith Barron comedy *All Night Long*?
21. In which comedy series did David Ogden Stiers replace Larry Linville?
22. What colour was Del Boy's van?
23. In *Just Good Friends*, where did Vince and Penny finally marry?
24. In which comedy series did Joan Sanderson play the mother of Prunella Scales?
25. *Alas Sage and Onion* was a Christmas version of which comedy series?
26. Who partnered Les Dawson in the roles of Cissy and Ada?
27. Who were the dance troupe on *The Kenny Everett Video Show*?
28. What is Seinfeld's first name?
29. Who is Hugh Dennis' comic partner?
30. In which comedy series are Pearl and Marina rivals for the same man?

Answers: see Quiz 46, page 154

LEVEL 2

1. What was Joan Collins character in *Dynasty*?
2. Where did Kathy Mitchell go when she left Albert Square?
3. Which star of *Goodnight Sweetheart* pulled the pints at the Woolpack?
4. Who was taken hostage in a Post Office raid in *Emmerdale*?
5. Which character was played by Leslie Grantham in *EastEnders*?
6. Who returned to *Neighbours* as a member of the Salvation Army?
7. Which character did Sarah Lancashire play in *Coronation Street*?
8. Who played Frank Tate in *Emmerdale*?
9. What was Anita Dobson's character in *EastEnders*?
10. Which real life father and son appeared in *Neighbours*?
11. Who did Victoria Principal play in *Dallas*?
12. What was the name of Minnie Caldwell's lodger in *Coronation Street*?
13. Who was Danni's mother in *Neighbours*?
14. Which character in *Crossroads* wore a woolly hat?
15. What was Dr Dawson's nickname in *Emergency Ward 10*?
16. Who has a husband in *EastEnders* named Ricki?
17. What was the name of the Ewing ranch?
18. Who did Nick Bates accidentally kill?
19. In which series did we meet the Tates and the Campbells?
20. Which of the *Neighbours* ran a chauffeuring service?
21. Who first ran the café in *EastEnders*?
22. Which company produces *Emmerdale*?
23. In which soap spoof would you find Mrs Overall?
24. In which hospital did Dr Baz Samuels work?
25. What was the name of Gita and Sanjay's daughter in *Eastenders*?
26. This character in *Neighbours* married Bronwen. Who is he?
27. Who was Caress's sister in *Dynasty*?
28. Which soap was originally to be called *The Midland Road*?
29. Which Mrs Frank Sinatra found fame in *Peyton Place*?
30. Who married Charlene in *Neighbours*?

QUIZ 46   Crime 5

Answers: see Quiz 45, page 153

LEVEL 2

1. Who played Charlie Hungerford in *Bergerac*?

2. Who wrote *Ultraviolet*?

3. Who played Lois in *Undercover Heart*?

4. In *The Chinese Detective*, Ho's superior, Det. Chief Insp. Berwick, was played by which actor?

5. Joan Hickson played which Agatha Christie character?

6. What was the occupation of Nick Rowan's wife Kate in *Heartbeat*?

7. In which 1998 Tony Garnett series were officers Mel and Natalie?

8. Name the creator of Adam Dalgleish.

9. Jemima Shore had first appeared in *Quiet as A Nun*, in 1978. Who played Jemima?

10. What was Sam Ryan's occupation in *Silent Witness*?

11. Which was the last of the Jeremy Brett Sherlock Holmes productions in 1994?

12. In *The Bill*, which police officer was the target of an assassin?

13. Who played *Mitch* in the series of the same name?

14. Who is Inspector Wexford's DI assistant?

15. Who is Jack Frost's superior?

16. Which actor played Boyd QC?

17. Cowley in *The Professionals* was portrayed by which actor?

18. Warren Clarke and Colin Buchanan played which detective duo?

19. Which actress played Trevor's girlfriend Jill Swinburne in *The Beiderbecke Affair*?

20. In *Charters and Caldicott*, who played the two sleuths?

21. Who was EW Hornung's famous gentleman thief?

22. *Operation Julie* was based on facts about what?

23. Which TV impressarion created and produced *Knight Rider*?

24. Which of Cagney and Lacey was single?

25. Which 70s detective campaigned with Martin Bell in Tatton in 1997?

26. Name the first *Taggart* story shown without Mark McManus in 1995.

27. What was Crockett's pet in *Miami Vice*?

28. In which abbey is *Cadfael* based?

29. Inspector Marlowe was played by which actor in *The New Adventures of Charlie Chan*?

30. Which character did Dennis Waterman play to John Thaw's Regan?

Soaps 5 (See Quiz 45)

1. Alexis. 2. South Africa. 3. Michelle Holmes. 4. Viv Windsor. 5. Den Watts. 6. Harold Bishop.
7. Raquel Wolstenhume. 8. Norman Bowler. 9. Angie Watts. 10. Jason & Terence Donovan.
11. Pamela Ewing. 12. Sonny Jim. 13. Cheryl Stark. 14. Benny. 15. Digger. 16. Bianca Butcher.
17. Southfork. 18. Jed Cornell. 19. *Soap*. 20. Helen Daniels. 21. Sue Osman. 22. Yorkshire
Television. 23. *Acorn Antiques*. 24. Holby (*Casualty*). 25. Shamilah. 26. Henry Ramsay. 27. Alexis.
28. *Crossroads*. 29. Mia Farrow. 30. Scott Robinson.

ANSWERS

Answers: see Quiz 48, page 156   LEVEL 2

1. Which newsreader presented *Treasure Hunt*?
2. How many 'lives' do *15 - 1* contestants start with?
3. Who was the first host of *University Challenge*?
4. In which show would you watch 'Mr Trick Shot'?
5. Which TV quiz had contestants bid for prizes, Nicholas Parsons presenting?
6. Who was Hughie Green's co-presenter on *Double Your Money*?
7. Who took over from Bob Monkhouse on *The Golden Shot*?
8. What was the booby prize on *3-2-1*?
9. What was ITV's mid-90s lunchtime culinary quiz?
10. Who replaced John Fashanu as a presenter on the *Gladiators*?
11. Who was replaced by Edward Tudor-Pole of Ten Pole Tudor fame on *The Crystal Maze*?
12. What was Britain's first daily game show, in which 16-18 year olds took part?
13. Who presented *Junior Criss Cross Quiz*?
14. Who was the host of *Play Your Cards Right*?
15. Which series required a panel to guess the profession of a contestant?
16. What is Channel 5's regular quiz for older contestants called?
17. On *The Sky's The Limit*, what could contestants win a voucher to do?
18. What was the very first Channel 4 programme to be televised?
19. How frequently was the quiz *Animal, Vegetable, Mineral* broadcast?
20. Who is the host of ITV's *Who Wants To Be A Millionaire*?
21. Which former radio programme moved to BBC TV in 1955?
22. Who was the original question master on *The Brains Trust*?
23. Who was the first blonde to present *Blankety Blank*?
24. How many *Celebrity Squares* were there?
25. Which winner of *New Faces* went on the present the show in the late 80s?
26. Who was the original question master of *Take Your Pick*?
27. Which show aimed to find the "Super-Person Of Great Britain"?
28. In *Treasure Hunt* how did Anneka Rice get from location to location?
29. Which Gaby Roslin show has its theme song sung by Status Quo?
30. Which Cilla Black show gave contestants a week to master a task with the hope of a £20,000 win?

Answers: see Quiz 47, page 155

1. Name John Sullivan's comedy with Tim Healy and Clive Russell as Falklands veterans.
2. What was Geoffrey Palmer's occupation in *Butterflies*?
3. Adrian Edmondson is the husband of one of his co-stars in *Comic Strip*. Who?
4. Where did Mork originate in *Mork and Mindy*?
5. Who sings in Bar Rene in *'Allo, 'Allo*?
6. Where was *Only When I Laugh* set?
7. Who did Bubbles work for in *Absolutely Fabulous*?
8. Robert Morley starred as an upper-class version of Alf Garnett in which comedy?
9. Who play the old gits?
10. In *Only Fools and Horses* who does Trigger refer to as Dave?
11. Who played Tom in Chance in a Million?
12. Who team sang 'I'm a Lumberjack'?
13. Which educational sitcom was set in Galfest High School?
14. Richard Griffiths was importing wine and skirting bankruptcy in which comedy?
15. Which sitcom featured Thord Hird running a funeral home?
16. Which Eddie was a character in *Tutti Frutti*?
17. Who wrote *Doctor In The House*?
18. Who starred as J Pinwright in the 1940's comedy series *Pinwright's Progress*?
19. In *Bewitched*, what was the name of Samantha's daughter?
20. Who wrote the scripts for the comedy series *The Howerd Crowd*?
21. Arthur Askey, Dickie Henderson and Diana Decker joined in which fortnightly BBC comedy series in the 1950s?
22. Who starred in the ITV sitcom *Love and Kisses*?
23. *The Benny Hill Show* first appeared in 1955 on which channel?
24. Which comedian wrote and starred in the silent TV film *Eddie In August*?
25. Which TV channel created *Celebrity Deathmatch*?
26. Which family featured in *Bless This House*?
27. Where do the *Birds of a Feather* live?
28. What was PC Penrose's nickname in *The Growing Pains of PC Penrose*?
29. Who played Lucille Ball's frustrated employer in *The Lucy Show*?
30. Who is Paul Whitehouse's writing partner for *The Fast Show*?

Answers: see Quiz 50, page 158

LEVEL 2

1. What was the title of Roy Rogers' TV theme music?

2. Who loves Scooby snacks?

3. What nationality is Asterix?

4. Which series was translated into Irish and transmitted as *Tomas an Traien*?

5. Where does Yogi Bear live?

6. What instrument does Bart Simpson's sister, Lisa, play?

7. Which animated film from a Raymond Briggs story had Peter Auty singing to a famous flying sequence?

8. Who was Perky's partner?

9. Joe Inglis became resident vet on which show in 1998?

10. In which show might you meet Dump Pea?

11. How many windows featured in *Play School*?

12. Complete the following, taken from *Mr Ed*'s theme song, 'A horse is a horse...'

13. Who presented *Record Breakers* and got his name in the title?

14. Who might be accompanied by Snowy and Captain Haddock?

15. Which family lived under the floorboards?

16. What was the name of the dog in *The Woodentops*?

17. Who was the voice of the cartoon series *Willo the Wisp*?

18. What were *Roobarb and Custard*?

19. Where does *Paddington Bear* keep his marmalade sandwiches?

20. What was the name of *Captain Pugwash*'s ship?

21. Who narrated *Ivor the Engine* and *Noggin the Nog*?

22. What series featured Hammy the Hamster?

23. Jenny Hanley presented which ITV rival to *Blue Peter*?

24. What was the British name of *Top Cat*?

25. In which program would you have met Pootle, Posie and Perkin?

26. What is the name of the large yellow bird residing in *Sesame Street*?

27. Name the Teletubbies.

28. In which part of the country was *Byker Grove* set?

29. *Garfield* is what type of animal?

30. In which children's series could actress Sue Nicholls be seen playing Miss Popoff?

Answers: see Quiz 49, page 157

1. Who was the creator of *Edge of Darkness*?
2. Where was the location of the first live *Gardener's World* show?
3. *This Is Your Life* was first shown on which channel?
4. Who was the host of *The White Heather Club*?
5. What in TV production history was a VERA?
6. Dominic Diamond presented which computer programme?
7. Which Neighbour later appeared in *The Flying Doctors*?
8. Which product did Nanette Newman advertise?
9. Who played Frank Buck in *Dark Skies*?
10. Which star of *The Newcomers* appeared in *Manhunt*?
11. Kyle MacLachlan appeared in which unusual series?
12. Were Alexandra Palace TV studios in north or south London?
13. Which gardening programme came from Scotland?
14. Which fictitious TV station taught viewers to 'Ski in Your Home'?
15. Who was the sixth Dr Who?
16. Which footballer and Northern Ireland manager refused to be the subject of a *This Is Your Life* programme?
17. Name the annual gardening event screened from the Royal Hospital.
18. Who played 'Mrs Thursday'?
19. Which former Arsenal star hosted his own Friday Night chat show?
20. Which TV chef hosted *Party of a Lifetime*?
21. In which year were the first BBC TV studios formed?
22. What was Joe Loss's signature tune?
23. Which political commentator is brother of Jonathan and the son of Richard?
24. Who is the survival expert on *Wildtracks*?
25. Who was the Royal presenter of *Crown And Country*?
26. Which former newsreader hosted the *Clothes Show*?
27. Who is the screenwriting husband of Maureen Lipman?
28. What are Dame Edna Everage's favourite blooms?
29. In the post-war magazine programme *Kaleidoscope* who was the Memory Man?
30. What is Bruce Forsythe's real name?

Answers: see Quiz 52, page 160

1. Who was Crockett's right hand man in *Miami Vice*?
2. Which newspaper crossword does Morse frequently complete?
3. Where was the setting for *Heartbeat*?
4. Who was the male star in *The Wasp's Nest*, the first Agatha Christie play to be televised in 1937?
5. Which 60 year old Lancashire detective has a sidekick called Geoffrey?
6. Which fictitious actor (played by Roy Clarke) is Pulaski?
7. Which sport did Lord Peter Wimsey play?
8. Who played 18 different roles in the first three series of *Murder Most Horrid*?
9. What was the name of the spin-off series from *Rockcliffe's Babies*?
10. What type of literature does Inspector Adam Dalgliesh write?
11. What was billed as 'The Ruth Rendell Christmas Mystery' in 1988?
12. Who plays Inspector Wexford?
13. Carl Galton (played by Iain Glen) led a violent north London gang in which serial?
14. Who played *Poirot* in the series of the same name?
15. What breed of dog did Columbo have?
16. What is the name of Sherlock Holmes' brother?
17. Who called people 'pussycat'?
18. Which actor played Campion's valet?
19. Who solved all his cases without even standing up?
20. Which legal champion frequently adjourned to Pomeroy's Wine Bar?
21. What was the 90s equivalent of the 60s series Crown Court called?
22. Which Government body did The Chief frequently clash with?
23. Where is *Cadfael* set?
24. Which series about a Highland policeman starred Robert Carlyle?
25. Where was *Waterfront Beat* based?
26. Who was Charlie Chan's 'Number One Son'?
27. Which supreme defence counsel was played for ten years by Raymond Burr?
28. In *The French Collection*, Spender went to which city?
29. What was the subject of *Between the Lines*?
30. Who left *EastEnders* to play D.I. Mick Raynor in 1994?

QUIZ 52 TV Comedy 13

Answers: see Quiz 51, page 159

LEVEL 2

1. Who starred with Charlie Drake in *Drake's Progress*?
2. Which *Sale Of The Century Show* host first tasted fame in The Arthur Haynes Show?
3. In which crime drama did Hale and Pace make their straight acting debut in 1994?
4. To which army camp was Bilko transferred after leaving Fort Baxter?
5. Which sitcom was a spoof of *Secret Army*?
6. How many *Friends* are there?
7. Name the two lead characters in *The Two of Us*.
8. Which disaster-prone comedy character drove a mini?
9. In which year was *Hancock's Half Hour* first screened?
10. In *Absolutely Fabulous*, what is Edina's surname?
11. Who was the owner of the store in *Are You Being Served*?
12. Who made the puppets in *Spitting Image*?
13. Which of the *Girls on Top* was not British?
14. What is the BBC's outtakes show hosted by Terry Wogan called?
15. In which comedy series did sisters Brenda and Pamela live together?
16. Maureen Lipman played the part of what in *Agony*?
17. What was the name of Queen Elizabeth's female companion in *Blackadder*?
18. Who played Adrian's mother in *The Growing Pains of Adrian Mole*?
19. What a was Victoria Wood's first sitcom called?
20. Who used to say 'Get that bus out'?
21. Who played insurance investigator Dick Starrett?
22. Which show featured Alan Beresford B'Stard?
23. Which series featuring two girls was a spin-off from *Happy Days*?
24. In *Blott on the Landscape*, Sir Giles Lynchwood was played by which actor?
25. Who starred as Mr Nesbitt in *The Nesbitts Are Coming*?
26. What battered car does Mrs Bucket's son-in-law, Onslo, drive?
27. Minister James Hacker was played by which actor?
28. Who played Inspector Fowler in *The Thin Blue Line*?
29. Who played Private Bisley in *The Army Game*?
30. In which series did Nichola McAuliffe play the acerbic Sheila Sabatini?

ANSWERS

Crime 6 (See Quiz 51)

1. Tubbs. 2. The Times. 3. North Yorkshire. 4. Francis L. Sullivan. 5. Hetty Wainthropp. 6. Larry Summers. 7. Cricket. 8. Dawn French. 9. *Rockcliffe's Folly*. 10. Poetry. 11. *No Crying He Makes*. 12. George Baker. 13. *The Fear*. 14. David Suchet. 15. Bassett Hound. 16. Mycroft. 17. Kojak. 18. Brian Glover. 19. Ironside. 20. Rumpole. 21. *The Verdict*. 22. The Home Office. 23. Shrewsbury. 24. *Hamish Macbeth*. 25. London's Docklands. 26. Barry Chan. 27. Perry Mason. 28. Marseilles. 29. Police Internal Investigations. 30. Leslie Grantham.

Answers: see Quiz 53, page 162

LEVEL 2

1. Who was the headmaster in *Home and Away*?
2. Who was Natalie Horrocks' son in *Coronation Street*?
3. Who was Walford's doctor in the early days of *EastEnders*?
4. Who links Bugs to *Neighbours*?
5. What happened to Emily Bishop's husband, Ernest?
6. Which *Neighbours* actor presented *The Big Breakfast*?
7. Who seduced Dave Glover in the stables in *Emmerdale*?
8. In *Brookside* where was Trevor Jordache buried?
9. Who played the part of Brad Willis in *Neighbours*?
10. How did Cindy leave the country when she left Ian in *EastEnders*?
11. Which soap had the working title *One Way Street*?
12. Who used to be a stripper in Ramsay Street?
13. Who played Sheila Grant in *Brookside*?
14. Who was Rod the Plod?
15. In *Emmerdale*, who was passed over in his father Jacob's will?
16. In *Dallas*, Lucy was the daughter of which of the Ewing clan?
17. At which number *Coronation Street* did the Ogdens live?
18. Which TV company was set up to make *Brookside*?
19. Which character did Sheila Mercier play in *Emmerdale*?
20. Which actress left Albert Square and returned to direct the soap?
21. In *Coronation Street* what was the job of the father of Fiona's baby?
22. Which soap had a restaurant called The Diner?
23. In 1980, who did Joe Sugden go to work for?
24. Which was the first soap to be shown on Channel 5?
25. Where did Liz move to when she left *Coronation Street* with Michael?
26. Which soap was set in Los Barcos?
27. How did Pat Sugden die?
28. Who left *EastEnders* and turned up in *The Hello Girls*?
29. In which US city was *The Colbys* set?
30. What is *Coronation Street*'s newsagent's called?

Drama 5 (See Quiz 54)
1. Sir Francis Drake. 2. Peter Strauss. 3. Lily Langtree. 4. The *Jewel in the Crown*. 5. Algy Hernes.
6. Marcia Blaines. 7. Moll Flanders. 8. *How Green Was My Valley*. 9. Mrs Bridges. 10. Children played by adults. 11. Charles Ryder. 12. Orson Welles. 13. Alan Bennet. 14. Prison Commandant.
15. Chicken George. 16. *Inn for Trouble*. 17. *The Monocled Mutineer*. 18. CS Lewis. 19. A baby.
20. John Duttine. 21. Flint McCulloch. 22. *Cardiac Arrest*. 23. Ben Elton. 24. Wellinton's. 25. Dr Jack Kerruish. 26. 1950s. 27. *Pygmalion*. 28. *Love Hurts*. 29. *The Camomile Lawn* 30. Imperial Crescent.

ANSWERS

1. Which Elizabethan seafarer and adventurer was played by Terence Morgan?
2. Which actor starred with Nick Nolte in *Rich Man, Poor Man*?
3. Francesca Annis played which actress acquaintance of Edward VII?
4. Which period drama set in India was based on *The Raj Quartet* novels?
5. Who played the headmaster in *To Serve Them All My Days*?
6. Miss Jean Brodie taught at which school for girls?
7. Julie Foster played which fun-seeking 17th century character?
8. Stanley Baker starred in which 1976 classic drama set in Wales and chronicled the lives of the Morgan family?
9. What was the name of the cook in *Upstairs, Downstairs*?
10. In what way was the TV play *Blue Remembered Hills* unusual?
11. Jeremy Irons played which character in *Brideshead Revisited*?
12. Which actor and director narrated *Shogun*?
13. *Fortunes of War* featured which Yorkshire playwright?
14. Bernard Hepton played which role in *Colditz*?
15. Complete the name of this character from *Roots*, 'Chicken ...' ?
16. What was the title of the feature film spin-off of *The Larkins*?
17. Paul McGann played Percy Topliss as what kind of mutineer?
18. *Shadowlands* was about which author?
19. In *Upstairs, Downstairs* Mrs Bridges appeared in court after stealing what?
20. *To Serve Them All My Days* starred actor John who?
21. What was the name of the trail scout, played by Robert Horton in *Wagon Train*?
22. In which series did Helen Baxendale star as Claire Maitland?
23. Who starred in his own TV adaptation of his novel *Stark*?
24. Sharpe was a cavalry officer in whose army in the first series of the drama?
25. In *Peak Practice* who joined the Cardale medics after working in Africa?
26. In which decade was Dennis Potter's *Lipstick on Your Collar* set?
27. Margaret Lockwood made her TV debut in which GB Shaw play in 1948?
28. In which series did Adam Faith play plumber Frank Carver?
29. Which adaptation of a Mary Wesley novel was Peter Hall's TV directorial debut?
30. Which London hotel featured in *The Inch Man*?

Answers: see Quiz 56, page 164

1. Which pop band helped to launch Channel 5?
2. When were the inter-regional competitions in *Come Dancing* introduced?
3. Who succeeded Bob Monkhouse as presenter of *Opportunity Knocks*?
4. Which presenter of *The Tube* was previously a member of the band *Squeeze*?
5. Where did The Three Tenors first perform together?
6. Who performed with Lord Lloyd Webber on *Top of the Pops* in 1998?
7. Which character in *The Young Ones* had a hit with 'Hole in My Shoe'?
8. Who sang "Life is the name of the game" in introducing his show?
9. What was the precursor of *The Good Old Days*?
10. What placing did the UK's first entry in the *Eurovision Song Contest* get?
11. In 1998 which Royal appeared on *Des O'Connor Tonight*?
12. Who played Marie Lloyd in *Our Marie*?
13. Which talent show had the theme song "You're A Star"?
14. Who was the illusionist who accompanied David Nixon on *It's Magic*?
15. Which 007 has presented Sunday Night at the London Palladium?
16. Who was the resident host of *Showtime*?
17. Which star of *Common as Muck* is President of the British Music Hall Society and a regular on radio?
18. Who first hosted *Whose Line Is It Anyway*?
19. Who first hosted *Sunday Night At The Palladium*?
20. Who added 'Who Else?' to his show when he moved to Channel 4?
21. Who kicked her way through *Let's Face The Music and Dance* in '78?
22. Who produced *The Billy Cotton Band Show*?
23. On which show would you have seen Zoo and Ruby Flipper?
24. Whose music career took off after she appeared on *The Cruise*?
25. How many panellists were there on *Juke Box Jury*?
26. What days was *Cool For Cats* broadcast?
27. When was *Opportunity Knocks* first shown?
28. Which magician had a fan club called Secrets?
29. Who was in the first televised *Royal Variety Show* and celebrated 40 years in showbusiness in 1998?
30. 'Anyone Can Fall in Love' was a song from which soap's theme tune?

Answers: see Quiz 55, page 163

LEVEL 2

1. Which Friend is notoriously houseproud?
2. What was the name of the punk with studs in *The Young Ones*?
3. In *Yes, Prime Minister*, who played the Private Secretary Bernard Woolley?
4. Who was the female in *Three Of A Kind*?
5. Who is Judi Dench's real-life husband who starred with her in *A Fine Romance*?
6. Who is the man-hungry neighbour in *Birds of a Feather*?
7. Name the female presenter of *Game For A Laugh*.
8. Who hosted *You've Been Framed*?
9. Which former *PlaySchool* presenter played Shirley in *Desmond's*?
10. In *Blackadder II*, the Elizabethan period, what was Blackadder's first name?
11. What was Mrs Slocombe's pet?
12. Who replaced Simon Cadell as manager of the holiday camp in *Hi-De-Hi!*?
13. Who wrote *Last of the Summer Wine*?
14. What is Garth's occupation in *Birds of A Feather*?
15. Who created the villainous Two Rons?
16. In *Never The Twain*, what event brought together the lead characters?
17. Who kept a secret diary on ITV?
18. Who famously said "Nice hat" in a much hyped episode of *Friends*?
19. What is the name of Mrs Bucket's son?
20. What was Norman Wisdom's first TV sitcom?
21. What was the sequel to *Are You Being Served?* called?
22. Who starred in *All Good Things*?
23. Why were plans for a 1993 series of *Only Fools and Horses* put on hold?
24. In the second series of *Auf Wiedersehen Pet*, which country did they all travel to?
25. Which comic priest on *Father Ted* went on to host his own chat show?
26. Who played Gemma Palmer in *Solo*?
27. What was Frank and Betty Spencer's daughter called in *Some Mothers Do 'Ave 'Em*?
28. In which series did Harry Enfield play the Rev Tony Blair?
29. How old was Ronnie Corbett's character in *Sorry!*?
30. Name the character played by Jamie Farr in *M*A*S*H*.

Answers: see Quiz 58, page 166   LEVEL 2

1. What is Mr Motivator's real name?
2. Whose wife, Debbie, was killed in an accident in *EastEnders*?
3. In which year did Granada TV start covering the North-West of England?
4. Which was the first truly local independent TV station?
5. On which UK TV programme did Clive James first appear?
6. Who presented the first *Gardener's World Live* show on BBC1 in 1993?
7. Which role did Robert play in *Two's Company*?
8. Which series of plays starred John Alderton and Pauline Collins in various guises?
9. Who played the lead role in *The Fall and Rise of Reginald Perrin*?
10. Name the Canadian born TV presenter and actor married to Barbara Kelly.
11. Who was the first Chief Executive of Channel 4?
12. On which show did Laurence Llewelyn find fame?
13. Which Python created *The Rutles*?
14. Who replaced Vanessa on ITV's daytime discussion show?
15. What is Roy Vasey's stage name?
16. When TV was interrupted in 1939 by WWII what programme was on?
17. How is Anthony Robert McMillan better known?
18. Whose catchphrase is 'I wanna tell you a story'?
19. Which of the *Two Fat Ladies* travels in the sidecar?
20. Who hosts a late night chat show on Channel 5?
21. Who first presented *Holiday*?
22. Who interviewed the male members of *Friends* on Channel 4?
23. Who played Marian to Michael Praed's Robin?
24. What was Joan Ferguson's nickname in *Prisoner Cell Block H*?
25. Who is Sting's actress wife?
26. The father is Johnny, the daughter is Zoe. What is their surname?
27. Which TV gardener wrote a steamy novel called *Mr MacGregor*?
28. Who was the star of *And Mother Makes Three*?
29. Name the presenter of *I, Camcorder*.
30. Who presents *The Antiques Roadshow*?

QUIZ 58 Current Affairs 4

Answers: see Quiz 57, page 165

LEVEL 2

1. Who were the original presenters of *Crimewatch UK*?
2. Name the presenter of *The Living Planet*.
3. Who came prominence reporting the siege at the Iranian Embassy in 1980?
4. *Jimmy's* is a real life medical drama series set in which hospital?
5. Which programme featured a spoof spaghetti harvest?
6. Apart from *DEF II*, which C4 programme was produced by Janet Street-Porter?
7. Who were the presenters of *Rough Guide to Europe*?
8. Who presented *Rapido* on BBC 2?
9. Who presented *Dance Energy* on BBC 2?
10. At what longitude did Michael Palin trek from the North to the South Pole?
11. What does ENG stand for?
12. Who replaced Anthea Turner on the GMTV sofa?
13. Which doctor is a regular contributor to *Newsnight*?
14. Who presented *The Trials of Life*?
15. Which documentary examined America's Central Intelligence Agency?
16. *In The Company of Men* featured which army regiment?
17. Who did David Dimbleby replace on *Question Time*?
18. What was *Charles: Private Man, The Public Role* commemorating?
19. Which *Monty Python* member presented *The Last Machine*?
20. *Rock Family Trees* was based on the diagrams drawn by which music journalist?
21. Which 1995 documentary charted the development of the submarine?
22. Which BBC project aims to chronicle twentieth century historical events through the eyes of ordinary people who lived through them?
23. Who presented *The Private Life Of Plants*?
24. Who conducted the famous *Panorama* interview with Diana, Princess of Wales?
25. Who was the original presenter of the arts programme *Aquarius*?
26. What was the name of Diana Dors' afternoon talk show?
27. Which 1970 documentary searched for the Amazonian tribe, The Kreen-Akrore?
28. Who was Parkinson's very first guest on TV?
29. Which short-lasting film review series was presented by Michael Wood?
30. Who first presented *Newsround*?

ANSWERS

Pot Luck 8 (See Quiz 57)

1. Derrick Evans. 2. Nigel Bates. 3. 1956. 4. Southern Television, Southampton. 5. *University Challenge*. 6. Geoff Hamilton. 7. Dorothy McNab's Butler. 8. *Wodehouse Playhouse*. 9. Leonard Rossiter. 10. Bernard Bradan. 11. Jeremy Isaacs. 12. *Changing Rooms*. 13. Eric Idle. 14. *Trisha*. 15. Roy 'Chubby' Brown. 16. A Mickey Mouse cartoon. 17. Robbie Coltrane. 18. Max Bygraves. 19. Clarissa Dickson Wright. 20. Jack Docherty. 21. Cliff Mitchelmore. 22. Gaby Roslyn. 23. Judi Trott. 24. The Freak. 25. Trudie Styler. 26. Ball. 27. Alan Titchmarsh. 28. Wendy Craig. 29. Robert Llewelyn. 30. Hugh Scully.

Answers: see Quiz 60, page 168   LEVEL 2

1. Name Dangermouse's sidekick.
2. Who was the original voice of the *Wombles*?
3. What animal was Flipper?
4. Who did Zoe Ball replace on *Live and Kicking*?
5. What type of bird was the Big Bird on *Sesame Street*?
6. How many *Monkees* were there?
7. What are the names of Fred and Barney's wives in *The Flintstones*?
8. Who was the TV artist in *Vision On*?
9. When *Bagpuss*' friend Professor Yaffle was asleep, what function did he serve?
10. One of the Addams Family's children is named after a day of the week. Which one?
11. What creature is Casper?
12. Which puppet was sad because it 'can't fly, right up to the sky'?
13. What was the name of Ken Dodd's puppet pals?
14. What was the name of Gloria Hunniford's daughter who was a *Blue Peter* presenter?
15. Which family lived at Mockingbird Heights, 1313 Mockingbird Lane?
16. In *The Flowerpot Men*, what was Slowcoach?
17. In which television series did Ray Winstone play Will Scarlett?
18. Who moved from Children's BBC front man to *Saturday Superstore* and *Going Live!*?
19. Who was television's first *Robin Hood*?
20. Whose catchphrase was 'Boom, Boom'?
21. What was the name of the Australian series about a kangaroo?
22. In which cartoon series would you find Muskie?
23. Who first hosted TV am's *Wide Awake Club*?
24. What was the nickname of Stebson in *Grange Hill*?
25. What type of creature is CBBC's Otis?
26. What is the name of the company which produces *Wallace and Gromit*?
27. Who presented *Zoo Time*?
28. Name Popeye's enemy.
29. Where did Wallace and Gromit go for *A Grand Day Out*?
30. Who sung 'Champion the Wonder Horse'?

Answers: see Quiz 59, page 167

1. Which was the first *Comic Strip*?
2. Who played the landlord in *The Young Ones*?
3. What was the name of the comedy about a Victorian family starring Alfred Marks?
4. Who played *The Bounder*?
5. Which *Last of the Summer Wine* actor narrates *Wallace & Gromit*?
6. Which *Friends* star is the god daughter of the late Telly Savalas?
7. Which actor played Martin Bryce in *Ever Decreasing Circles*?
8. Which unusual instrument did Sykes' policeman friend, Derek Guyler play?
9. Which comedy performer was the male 'Rear of the Year' in 1998?
10. In which Channel 4 comedy did Porkpie appear?
11. What was the name of the bar manager played by Kirstie Alley in *Cheers*?
12. Anton Rodgers and Julia McKenzie played the primary roles in which comedy?
13. Who was the woman behind Mrs Merton?
14. What was the follow-up series to *Jane*?
15. In what building were *Dad's Army* based?
16. Who were the original three pals in *Last of the Summer Wine*?
17. Which series told the tale of three priests on an island?
18. Which sitcom used the music from Casablanca as its theme tune?
19. How many TV series did Norman Wisdom star in?
20. Which potty actor was the star of *All Square*?
21. Who asks the questions in *Have I Got News For You*?
22. In which building was the Trotter's flat in *Only Fools and Horses*?
23. Who wrote *Just Good Friends* and *Dear John*?
24. What were the gossipy women called played by Les Dawson and Roy Barraclough?
25. Paul Haigh and Colin Buchanan starred in which TA sitcom?
26. *Whack-O!* was turned into a feature film in 1960. What was the name of the film?
27. Which actor died before completion of the first series of *Auf Wiedersehen Pet*?
28. Who is the British-born male co-star of *Frasier*?
29. What was the name of the retirement home in *Waiting For God*?
30. What does the 'sit' of sitcom stand for?

ANSWERS

Children's TV 6 (See Quiz 59)

1. Penfold. 2. Bernard Cribbens. 3. A dolphin. 4. Emma Forbes. 5. Canary. 6. 3. 7. Wilma & Betty. 8. Tony Hart. 9. Bookend. 10. Wednesday. 11. A ghost. 12. Orville. 13. The Diddy Men. 14. Caron Keating. 15. *The Munsters*. 16. A tortoise. 17. *Robin of Sherwood*. 18. Phillip Schofield. 19. Richard Greene. 20. Basil Brush. 21. Skippy. 22. Deputy Dawg. 23. Timmy Mallett. 24. Gripper. 25. Aardvark. 26. Aardman Animations. 27. Desmond Morris. 28. Bluto. 29. The Moon. 30. Frankie Lane.

Answers: see Quiz 62, page 170

1. Who had an affair with Kim Tate in 1992?
2. Who took over Glendarroch estate after Elizabeth Cunningham was killed?
3. How did Leonard Kempinski die?
4. Who played Rodney Harrington in *Peyton Place*?
5. Who was Zoe Tate's girlfriend and moved into The Smithy with her?
6. What occupation was Mavis going to take up in the Lake District after she left *Coronation Street*?
7. What was the name of the hotel complex in *Neighbours*?
8. Who played the character Rachel Tate in *Emmerdale*?
9. Which actor played Dirty Den in *EastEnders*?
10. Who plays Butch Dingle?
11. Who owned a burger van in *Emmerdale*?
12. In *EastEnders* what was Phil and Kathy's son called?
13. Which soap mounted a 'Free George Jackson' campaign?
14. In *Dallas*, who did Miss Ellie marry after Jock died?
15. What major event occurred in *Emmerdale* on the 30th December, 1993?
16. Who went from *No Hiding Place* to *Coronation Street*?
17. Who plays Jack Sugden?
18. Which character does Alyson Spiro portray in *Emmerdale*?
19. How much did Frank offer Kim to move back to Home Farm?
20. Who was Zak Dingle's crooked brother?
21. Who is Tiffany's mother in *EastEnders*?
22. Who had dancing lessons with Terry Woods?
23. Who did Nick Bates kill?
24. Who did Sally Webster go into personal and business partnership with when she left Kevin?
25. How did Dave Glover die?
26. Why was *Emmerdale Farm* demolished?
27. Which soap was one of the BBC's first daytime scheduled serials?
28. Which two brothers did Cindy have affairs with in *EastEnders*?
29. What was Alma's surname before she married the Street's Mike Baldwin?
30. How did Shirley Turner die?

Pot Luck 9 (See Quiz 62)

1. *Grass Roots*. 2. Judy Carne. 3. Anthony Newly. 4. *Floyd Uncorked*. 5. Carroll O'Connor. 6. Pauline Yates. 7. Cot Death Syndrome. 8. Antoine de Caunes. 9. Clive Anderson. 10. Barbara Feldon. 11. Ray Walston. 12. British Academy of Film and Televsion Arts. 13. *Nighthawks*. 14. Citroen. 15. 30-line. 16. Charles Hill. 17. White City. 18. Mack McKenzie. 19. *The Real Life Holiday Show*. 20. Monty Don. 21. Angela Rippon. 22. *World in Action*. 23. Nixon. 24. Gerald Seymour. 25. The Earl of Listowel, Postmaster General. 26. Dirk, Nasty, Stig & Barry. 27. Rolf Harris (*Anilmal Hospital*). 28. Andy. 29. David Frost. 30. *Points of View* (Robinson).

ANSWERS

Answers: see Quiz 61, page 169

LEVEL 2

1. Richard Jackson presents which programme?
2. Which Judy was the *Laugh-In* girl?
3. Which actor played Gurney Slade?
4. What was Keith Floyd's series touring vineyards called?
5. Who played Archie Bunker?
6. Reggie Perrin's wife, Elizabeth was played by which actress?
7. Which cause does Ann Diamond campaign for?
8. Who introduces *Eurotrash*?
9. Who has a show called *All Talk*?
10. Who played 'Agent 99' in *Get Smart*?
11. Who was the star of *My Favourite Martian*?
12. What does BAFTA stand for?
13. Name the series which featured three nightwatchmen.
14. Which make of car did Bryan Brown advertise?
15. Was the original 1930's TV definition system 30-line, 50-line or 70-line?
16. Which TV doctor became chairman of the BBC?
17. Where is BBC TV Centre?
18. Which character did Kevin Dobson play in *Knotts Landing*?
19. Which holiday programme did Gaby Roslin introduce?
20. He presented *Real Gardens*. Who is he?
21. Which female newsreader danced with Morecambe and Wise?
22. What is the name of Granada TV's weekly current affairs programme?
23. Which president spoke live to the first man on the moon?
24. Name the writer of *Harry's Game*.
25. Who formally declared TV services open after its WWII closure?
26. Who were the 'pre-fab four' in *The Rutles*?
27. Which Australian presents programmes from the Harmsworth?
28. Which resident DIY expert on *Changing Rooms* is 'handy'?
29. Who created the company Paradine Productions?
30. Which programme has been presented by both Anne and Robert who share the same surname?

Soaps 7 (See Quiz 61)

1. Neil Kincaid. 2. Lady Margaret & Sir John Ross-Gifford. 3. A car struck him. 4. Ryan O'Neal.
5. Emma Nightingale. 6. Running a guest house. 7. Lassiters. 8. Glenda McKay. 9. Leslie
Grantham. 10. Paul Laughran. 11. Mandy Dingle. 12. Ben. 13. *Brookside*. 14. Clayton Barlow.
15. The air disaster. 16. Johnny Briggs. 17. Clive Hornby. 18. Sarah Sugden. 19. £1 Million.
20. Albert. 21. Louise Raymond. 22. Viv Windsor. 23. Jed Cornell. 24. Greg Kelly. 25. Trying to
save James Francis from a fire. 26. To make way for Demdyke Quarry Access Road.
27. *Neighbours*. 28. Simon and David Wicks. 29. Sedgewick. 30. Shot in a Post-Office raid.

Answers: see Quiz 64, page 172

LEVEL 2

1. The 1950's series *Fabian of Scotland Yard* was based whose career?
2. Who played Winston Smith in the 1954 adaptation of George Orwell's *1984*?
3. In the 1960s adaptation of *The Three Musketeers*, who played D'Artagnan?
4. In ITV's 1950's series, *The Adventures of Robin Hood*, who played the title role?
5. What was Robson Green's character called in *Soldier Soldier*?
6. *The Children of the New Forest* was serialised in three times. Who wrote the original?
7. Who was the lead in the detective series *Colonel March of Scotland Yard*?
8. In which series did Jimmy Nail play factory worker Jed Shepherd?
9. Which actress played Miss Kitty in *Gunsmoke*?
10. What were the first names of the two sisters in *The House of Eliott*?
11. Which drama series title meant 'roll call' in Japanese?
12. *Buccaneer* was concerned with which small air freight company?
13. As which character was Bernard Hill looking for a job?
14. *A Voyage Round My Father* was an autobiographical drama about which writer and barrister?
15. Which actress and model was CJ in *Baywatch*?
16. What have *Operation Diplomat* (1952), *Portrait of Alison* (1955), *The Scarf* (1959), *Paul Temple* (1970–1) in common?
17. *The Fall Guy* starred which actor?
18. Which traitor's meeting with Coral Browne was dramatised in *An Englishman Abroad*?
19. How long was each episode of *Sailor of Fortune*?
20. Which helicopter did Jan Michael Vincent pilot?
21. In which city is *ER* based?
22. What was the name of the cook in *Wagon Train*?
23. Who wrote *The Count of Monte Cristo*?
24. In *Widows*, what had been the women's husbands occupation before their deaths?
25. *The Buccaneers* was set in which Islands?
26. Who was the Range Rider?
27. Who replaced Michael Praed's *Robin of Sherwood* and became Robert of Huntingdon?
28. In which series did Ian Richardson first play MP Francis Urquhart?
29. In which series were the experiences of Major Pat Reid based?
30. Name *Jungle Boy*'s companion lion cub.

Answers: see Quiz 63, page 171

LEVEL 2

1. The 'arts programme' *La Dame Axe Gladiolas* featured who?
2. Which comedy performer was managed by his wife Cheryl?
3. Which sitcom was set in a house called Dalentrace?
4. Who links *Dear John* to *2 Point 4 Children*?
5. What was the spin-off from *The Army Game*?
6. Tim McInnerny played which character in the second series of *Blackadder*?
7. In *Three of a Kind*, who was the female comedian?
8. Whose stand up comedy and sketch show was called *Through the Cakehole*?
9. Who played *The Gaffer*?
10. What was the setting for *The Brittas Empire*?
11. Which *New Faces* winner was born Lynne Shepherd in Sheffield?
12. In *Desmond's* what was Porkpie's former job?
13. Which city does Daphne Moon in *Frasier* originate from?
14. What was the name of the restaurant in *Chef!*?
15. Who performed as The Joan Collins Fan Club until Miss Collins' lawyers started to raise objections?
16. Who played the factory boss in *Making Out*?
17. Which one of the Goodies did NOT help write the sitcom *Astronauts*?
18. In *Last of the Summer Wine* what was Seymour's hobby, which often had disastrous results?
19. What was The Fonz's full name?
20. What's the name of Wayne and Waynetta Slob's daughter?
21. Which harassed young GP does Nigel Havers play in *Don't Wait Up*?
22. Who is the landlord in *Man About The House*?
23. Gordon Kennedy starred in which football-related sitcom?
24. Who plays Mrs Bucket's hen-pecked husband Richard?
25. What is the name of Boysie's wife in *Only Fools and Horses*?
26. Which Glaswegian was a member of the Humblebums?
27. Who starred as Robin Tripp?
28. In which capital city did Vince and Penny finally get married in *Just Good Friends*?
29. Which siblings appeared in Steve Coogan's *Three Fights, Two Weddings and a Funeral*?
30. Who specially wrote the script of *The Lady Is A Tramp* for Patricia Hayes?

Answers: see Quiz 66, page 174

LEVEL 2

1. Who played the ambitious detective Tony Clark in *Between the Lines*?
2. *Heartbeat* was set in the middle of which decade?
3. Which actor links *Rumpole* to *The Prisoner*?
4. Which 70s US detective was played by William Conrad?
5. Where did Nick Rowan originally arrive from in *Heartbeat*?
6. In the drama, *The Two Mrs Carrolls*, how did Geoffrey Carroll plan to murder his wife?
7. Which offbeat sleuth was played by Alan Davies opposite Caroline Quentin?
8. In which magazine did the *Addams Family* first appear?
9. Who partnered Det. Insp. Sam Sterne in *Sam Saturday*?
10. Whose refusal to make further series of *Shoestring* led to the creation of new sleuth Bergerac?
11. Which specialist squad featured in the first series of *Liverpool One*?
12. In *Dragnet*, who played officer Frank Smith?
13. Det. Chief Insp. Nick Lewis was consigned to the PPO in the *Enigma Files*. What was the PPO?
14. What award did David Jason win in 1993?
15. Who wrote *The Beiderbecke Affair*?
16. What is the name of Poirot's companion?
17. With which female detective did Fitz have a volatile relationship in *Cracker*?
18. Which drama, starting in 1984 was originally called *Woodentop*?
19. Who played Chief Inspector Roderick Alleyn in the 1993 BBC series?
20. *The Chief* was head of which fictitious constabulary?
21. Which New York duo did Victor Isbecki work with?
22. Which actor plays *Cadfael*?
23. Who wrote *Waterfront Beat*?
24. Who is the star of *Murder, She Wrote*?
25. Who was assisted by Magersfontein Lugg?
26. In *99-1*, what did DI Mick Raynor specialise in?
27. *Underworld* was a series about Britain's notorious criminals. Which actor narrated it?
28. Rupert Davies played which character in *The New Adventures of Charlie Chan*?
29. Who plays the title character in *Wycliffe*?
30. Who starred with Robert Powell in *The Detectives*?

Answers: see Quiz 65, page 173

LEVEL 2

1. Which *EastEnders* character released her Secret Diary in 1999?
2. How did Peggy Skilbeck die?
3. In *Coronation Street* what was Alec Gilroy's grand daughter called?
4. Which character in *The Colbys* shared her name with a type of fur?
5. What was the name of the detention centre in *Prisoner Cell Block H*?
6. Who played Nellie Dingle?
7. Who was Bobby married to in *Dallas*?
8. Which Prime Minister's wife sent a letter of complaint when the London region decided not to transmit *Crossroads*?
9. In *EastEnders* what were Irene Hills' children called?
10. Which *Emmerdale* star had a hit with the song, 'Just This Side of Love'?
11. In which pub would you have bought Churchill Strong?
12. Which Albert Square character had a pug called Willie?
13. What is the name of *Coronation Street's* repetitive butcher?
14. What was the name of the 'Woolpacker's' album?
15. Which Hollywood superstar played Jason in The *Colbys*?
16. Who was Ricky Butcher's first mother in law in *EastEnders*?
17. Which medical series did Edwina Currie describe as left wing propaganda?
18. Which character did Anna Friel play in *Brookside*?
19. Who was buried under the patio in *Brookside*?
20. What is the name of the local brewery in *Coronation Street*?
21. Who were the original landlord and landlady of the Queen Vic?
22. How did Beth Jordache die?
23. On what days of the week was *Emergency-Ward 10* screened?
24. Who played Nurse Carole Young?
25. What was the BBC soap about student nurses called?
26. What was the 1961 spin-off from *Emergency-Ward 10*?
27. In *Neighbours*, what was the name of Jim Robinson's youngest daughter?
28. Which *Coronation Street* character had twins at Christmas 1998?
29. In *EastEnders* what was Alex Healy's profession?
30. Who played Dougal Lachlan in *Take the High Road*?

ANSWERS

Crime 7 (See Quiz 65)

1. Neil Pearson. 2. Mid-Sixties. 3. Leo McKern. 4. Cannon. 5. London. 6. Slow poisoning.
7. *Jonathan Creek*. 8. The New Yorker. 9. Det. Sgt. Jim Butler. 10. Trevor Eve. 11. Drugs squad.
12. Ben Alexander. 13. The Prisoners' Property Office. 14. Royal Television Society's Male Performer of the Year (*A Touch of Frost*). 15. Alan Plater. 16. Capt. Hastings. 17. DS Jane Penhaligon. 18. *The Bill*. 19. Patrick Malahide. 20. Eastland Constabulary. 21. *Cagney and Lacey*. 22. Derek Jacobi. 23. Phil Redmond. 24. Angela Lansbury. 25. Campion. 26. Undercover Operations. 27. Bob Hoskins. 28. Inspector Duff. 29. Jack Shepherd. 30. Jasper Carrott.

Answers: see Quiz 68, page 176

LEVEL 2

1. In the first series of *Blockbusters*, what was the maximum number of contestants competing at any one time?

2. Who was the first 'runner' in the helicopter in *Treasure Hunt*?

3. Who hosts *Have I Got News For You*?

4. What is the association between Ken Platt, Ted Ray and Jackie Rae?

5. On what fictional dragon planet was BBC 2's *The Adventure Game* set?

6. Who succeeded Tom O'Connor as host of *Name That Tune*?

7. In which quiz do contestants team up with a professional snooker player?

8. How many times per week was *Criss Cross Quiz* televised?

9. Name the host of *Supermarket Sweep*.

10. Which *Changing Rooms* presenter was voted '98 'Rear of the Year'?

11. Which show has a round called 'Feel the Sportsman'?

12. Name the host of *Blockbusters*.

13. Which crimebuster presented *Dotto*?

14. During *Sunday Night at the Palladium*, how much was the Beat the Clock jackpot prize?

15. How long after *Play Your Cards Right* was first transmitted was it renamed *Bruce Forsyth's Play Your Cards Right*?

16. Who presented the 90s version of *Going For A Song*?

17. *Bullseye* combined a quiz with which game?

18. Which former newsreader presented *What's My Line*?

19. Who is the presenter of *Countdown*?

20. Who asked *Who Wants To Be A Millionaire?* and offered the largest cash prize on TV?

21. The family game show *We Love TV* was presented by which TV personality?

22. Which TV company produced *Blockbusters*?

23. Who went from *Food and Drink* to *The Great Antiques Hunt*?

24. What was the fate of the famous black chair when *Mastermind* finished?

25. Who is Jim Davidson's longest serving *Generation Game* assistant?

26. How many clues how to be solved in 45 minutes in *Treasure Hunt*?

27. Who has presented *Blue Peter* and *Wheel of Fortune*?

28. Who was the announcer on *Take Your Pick*?

29. Name the original host of *Celebrity Squares*?

30. Which cult play was created by the first presenter of *The Crystal Maze*?

QUIZ 68 TV Comedy 17

Answers: see Quiz 67, page 175

LEVEL 2

1. Which comic duo present *Alas Smith And Jones*?
2. *'Allo, 'Allo* was a spoof of which drama series?
3. Which two of the three current old men were in the first *Last of the Summer Wine*?
4. What was the name of Tom Chance's partner in *Chance in a Million*?
5. Which Portuguese megastar did Steve Coogan create for *Comic Relief* 1997?
6. Who played Keith Barron's wife in *Duty Free*?
7. Which *Dad's Army* character often announced "We're doomed!"?
8. What was the first comedy serial to top the ratings with all six of its first series shows in 1991?
9. Peter Egan played the threat next door in *Ever Decreasing Circles*. What was his name?
10. *The Fainthearted Feminist* was based on the column in which newspaper?
11. Who created the character Cosmo Smallpiece?
12. Which cartoon character was dubbed "Darling of the Forces"?
13. Who played the busybody neighbour Sonia in *Fresh Fields*?
14. Which comedian made commercials for John Smith's beer in the early 90s?
15. What was the dog called in *Frasier*?
16. How were Dilly Keane, Adele Anderson and Denise Wharmby known collectively?
17. Which sitcom centred on life at Sunshine Desserts run by CJ?
18. Name the disc jockey portrayed by Lenny Henry.
19. Whose sister was played by Thora Hird in *Last of the Summer Wine*?
20. Who played the unscrupulous landlord in *The Young Ones*?
21. Which wacky DJ and comedy performer started out on *Nice Time* in 1968?
22. What was the name of the *Spitting Image* 1995 New Year special?
23. Which *Fast Show* character likens most things to "beautiful women"?
24. Which Liverpool comedian appeared in the *Dr Who* story *Delta And The Bannermen*?
25. What are the names of Hyacinth Bucket's two sisters?
26. Who wrote the script for *Only Fools and Horses*?
27. What was the name of the stately home in *Blott on the Landscape*?
28. Which show featured the celebrated Dead Parrot sketch?
29. What is the name of Victor Meldrew's long-suffering wife, played by Annette Crosby?
30. The *Girls on Top* were played by Dawn French, Jennifer Saunders, Tracey Ullman and who else?

QUIZ 69 Children's TV 7

Answers: see Quiz 70, page 178

LEVEL 2

1. Who presented *Live and Kicking* with Zoe Ball?
2. What were Ruff 'n' Ready?
3. In which year was *Rocket Robin Hood* set?
4. What kind of craft is Jimbo?
5. What did Rocky Jones do for a living?
6. What was the cartoon character *Dudley Do-Right*?
7. Dr Marsh Tracy was a leading character in which series set in Africa?
8. Who hosted the *Multi-Coloured Swap Shop*?
9. Who gave the voice to *Ollie Beak* the owl?
10. What was the school attended by Billy Bunter?
11. Which presenter of *Crackerjack* hosted a daily afternoon show on Radio 2?
12. What on *Teletubbies* is the Noo Noo?
13. Who was the voice of *Dangermouse*?
14. What was the canine cartoon version of the Three Musketeers called?
15. What was Fred and Wilma Flintstone's baby called?
16. Who alerted Bill and Ben to signs of danger?
17. *Follyfoot* was about what types of animals?
18. Who created *Magic Roundabout*?
19. In *Grange Hill* what was Samuel McGuire's nickname?
20. Bonnie Langford played whom in *Just William*?
21. In which series was the schoolteacher called Mr Onion?
22. Which Scottish actor was The Skunner Campbell, adversary of Supergran?
23. What does B.A. in BA Baracus stand for?
24. Who created *The Moomins*?
25. What was the name of the witch in the *Emu* children's series?
26. Who was the female presenter on *How 2*?
27. Who hosted *Fun House* on ITV?
28. Which locomotive was driven by Jones the Steam?
29. What was *Casey Jones*?
30. Who is the youngest of *The Simpsons*?

Soaps 9 (See Quiz 70)

1. 1987. 2. Vic & Viv Windsor. 3. *High Road*. 4. Liverpool. 5. *Brookside*. 6. Manchester. 7. Maxine.
8. Edna. 9. Gardener. 10. Peggy and Louise 11. E20. 12. The Beales & the Fowlers. 13. Kylie
Minogue. 14. The Queen Vic. 15. *Civvy Street*. 16. Emily and Matthew. 17. Los Barcos.
18. *Eldorado*. 19. Beckindale. 20. Max Wall. 21. St. Angela's. 22. Annie. 23. Thirteen. 24. Hotten.
25. His garden gnome. 26. The Kabin. 27. Wicksy. 28. *Eastenders*. 29. Ashley. 30. *Eastenders*.

Answers: see Quiz 69, page 177

LEVEL 2

1. In which year was Elizabeth Cunningham killed in *Take the High Road*?
2. Who took over Emmerdale's local Post Office in 1993?
3. In 1994, *Take the High Road*'s name was shortened to what?
4. *Brookside* is located in which city?
5. *Damon and Debbie* was a spin-off from which soap?
6. *Albion Market* was a covered market set in which city?
7. What was Fiona's assistant called at *Coronation Street*'s hair salon?
8. What was Harry Cross's wife's name in *Brookside*?
9. In *Crossroads*, what did Carney do for a living?
10. What are Courtney Mitchell's grannies called in *EastEnders*?
11. What is the postal code for *EastEnders*?
12. Who were the two central families featured in *EastEnders*?
13. Who played Charlene in *Neighbours*?
14. What is the name of the local pub in *EastEnders*?
15. What was the name of the 1988 *EastEnders* special, set in Christmas 1942?
16. What were the name's of Max and Susannah Farnham's children?
17. *Eldorado* was set in which fictitious village in Spain?
18. Patricia Brake and Jesse Birdsall appeared together in which soap?
19. Which fictitious village features in *Emmerdale*?
20. Which comedian in 1979 appeared as the grumpy Arthur Braithwaite?
21. Which hospital featured in *Angels*?
22. In *EastEnders* what was George Palmer's club owning daughter called?
23. How many episodes of *Coronation Street* were originally made?
24. What is the nearest market town to *Emmerdale*?
25. In *Coronation Street*, who did Derek suddenly lose and then start to receive holiday postcards from?
26. What's the name of Rita Sullivan's newsagents?
27. Which part was played by Nick Berry?
28. Before presenting *Daytime Live*, Ross Davidson could be seen in which soap?
29. In *Coronation Street* what was the name of Fred Elliott's nephew?
30. Which soap is associated with a laundrette owned by Mr Papadopoulos?

Answers: see Quiz 72, page 180

LEVEL 2

1. Barry Davies commentates on which sport?

2. Superstars champion Brian Hooper participated in which athletic sport?

3. In which year was a football home international first televised?

4. Who presented *Superstars*?

5. Football from which country is broadcast on Channel 4 on Sundays?

6. Other than football *Match of the Day* has been regularly used as a programme title for which sport?

7. On BBC's *Sportsnight*, which presenter succeeded David Coleman?

8. *The Superbowl* is screened on which TV channel?

9. Which cricketer has been a team captain on *A Question of Sport*?

10. Who was the ITV wrestling commentator?

11. Before becoming a sports presenter, Sue Barker was a player of which sport?

12. Who was the first woman presenter of *Grandstand*?

13. In which year was *Match of the Day* first televised?

14. Former *Grandstand* presenter Frank Bough joined who after leaving the BBC?

15. Murray Walker is associated with which sport?

16. Which former Blue Peter star presented darts?

17. Who was the presenter of *Sportsview*?

18. Which newspaper reporter presented *Star Spangled Soccer*, about football in the US?

19. Murphy's Mob featured which sport?

20. *Holiday Show* presenter Kathy Taylor competed in which athletic discipline?

21. On the BBC, it's *Match of the Day*. What is it's equivalent on ITV?

22. *It's a Knockout* star Eddy Waring was the regular BBC commentator on which sport?

23. TV presenter Suzanne Dando was captain of which British Olympics team?

24. Which sport is featured in *Playing for Real*?

25. On *A Question of Sport*, how many points are awarded for a home question?

26. Saint and who are TV sports pundits?

27. Cricket presenter Richie Benaud was captain of which nation's cricket side?

28. Who was the first host of the ITV outtakes show *Oddballs*?

29. Which racing commentator recently retired after commentating on The Grand National in 1998?

30. Whose last commentary before retiring was the 1998 World Cup Final?

1. In *Dad's Army*, what rank was Wilson played by John le Mesurier?
2. Who made a banned spoof record about *The Magic Roundabout*?
3. Who produced *The Max Headroom Show*?
4. In which comedy series was Rab C Nesbitt first seen?
5. Who was Felicity Kendall the mistress to?
6. Who was Geraldine's verger in *The Vicar of Dibley*?
7. Which year did Fitz have a one night stand with his son's mother in *Relative Strangers*?
8. What are the names of the two children in *The Upper Hand*?
9. Which sitcom featured 'Spare Cheeks' magazine?
10. Which town lay near the camp at which Bilko and his platoon were based?
11. *The Brighton Belles* was an adaptation of which US sitcom?
12. Who played Adrian Mole's slobbish father?
13. How did Scullion in *Porterhouse Blue* travel around the college?
14. In *The Good Life* what did Jerry Leadbetter's company make?
15. Whose fictional characters included Slack Alice and Apricot Lil?
16. Whose middle names were Aloysius St John?
17. What was Vince Tulley's trade in *Side by Side*?
18. Which 16 year old winner of *New Faces* starred in *The Fosters*?
19. Which comedian famous for his sitcoms and sketches starred with Michael Caine in *The Italian Job*?
20. On TV, how were George Logan and Patrick Fyffe better known?
21. Who owned Acorn Antiques?
22. What was Bombardier Beaumont's nickname in *It Ain't Half Hot Mum*?
23. Who was Jimmy Edward's assistant headmaster in *Whack-O!*?
24. What does Denis Norden always hold in *It'll Be Alright on the Night*?
25. Where did Bill Porter work in *Two Point four Children*?
26. Whose catchphrase was 'nick nick'?
27. Where did Vince and Penny first meet in *Just Good Friends*?
28. Tessa Wyatt played whom in *Robin's Nest*?
29. TV's funnyman Rowan Atkinson appeared in which Bond film?
30. Who is the Meldrew's naïve female friend?

Answers: see Quiz 74, page 182

LEVEL 2

1. Who was the creator of *Star Trek*?

2. Who played the Bionic Man?

3. Who was Richard and Judy's first guest when their programme moved to London?

4. Which arts show replaced *Aquarius* in 1977?

5. For what were Mary Malcolm and Sylvia Peters known?

6. On which show do you hear advice from Bunny Campione and Henry Sandon?

7. Who plays Michael Hayes?

8. Which actor has actress daughters named Michelle and Karen?

9. Who left *The Big Breakfast* on New Year's Day 1999?

10. Who played Samuel and Pearl Foster in the comedy *The Fosters*?

11. Which film buff left the BBC for Sky in 1998?

12. Which celebrity chased around in a beach buggy answering challenges?

13. Which spin-off from *Holiday* features celebrities working in holiday resorts?

14. What was the first British TV soap?

15. Where did The Robinsons get lost?

16. From where on the moon did Neil Armstrong broadcast?

17. What is the name of Magnus's presenter daughter?

18. Which fictitious group sang 'All You Need is Lunch' and 'WC Fields Forever'?

19. Who starred in *My Three Sons*?

20. Who was the opposing team captain to John Parrott on *A Question of Sport*?

21. *Every Loser Wins* was a hit sung by which former soap star?

22. Who played the Professor in *Sliders*?

23. Who was *Man-O-Man*'s first presenter?

24. Who played Ben Casey?

25. *The Squirrels* was set in an accounts department of what kind of business?

26. Whose nickname is "Parky"?

27. Who presented *Motorworld*?

28. Who was *Our man In Goa*?

29. Who presented *The Good Sex Guide*?

30. Name the original host of *Going for a Song*.

Answers: see Quiz 73, page 181

1. Who succeeded George Margo as Blackbeard?
2. Which writer created *Soldier, Soldier*?
3. Peter Hammond played which character in *The Buccaneers*?
4. Which drama series about a fashion house was written by actresses Eileen Atkins and Jean Marsh?
5. In which series did the hero's girlfriend, Jo Franklin, run off with his enemy, Piers?
6. Which troubleshooter later played Churchill?
7. Which show would feature Blue Watch B25 Blackwall?
8. In *Gunsmoke*, what was the name of the Long Branch saloon keeper?
9. Derek Jacobi played the title role in which series about a Roman Emperor?
10. What did *The Manageress* manage?
11. *Grafters* was about brothers in which trade?
12. Patrick Troughton played which character in *The White Falcon*?
13. Who wrote *Big Women*, about a feminist publishing house, shown on Channel 4?
14. Rachel from *This Life* went on to star as the heroine of which Andrew Davis adaptation of a classic novel?
15. Who played the 'older woman' opposite Robson Green in *Reckless*?
16. Who was *Waiting For the Telegram* in *Talking Heads 2*?
17. Which bowler hatted comic was portrayed on TV by Joe Geary?
18. Who played the title role in *John Silver's Return to Treasure Island*, screened in 1986?
19. Who replaced Father Peter in *Ballykissangel*?
20. Who wrote about life at *Skeldale House*?
21. Which actor played O.S.S. Agent, Major Frank Hawthorne?
22. Which drama series told of forty something single girl Tessa Piggott?
23. What is unusual about the members of the jury in the courtroom drama *Verdict*?
24. Which actress played the receptionist in *The Royalty*?
25. What was Lovejoy's car called?
26. In which controversial WWI drama did Paul McGann play Percy Toplis?
27. Who played Tatum O'Neil's film role in the TV version of *Paper Moon*?
28. What was the occupation of Molly Manning's daughter in *The Flying Swan*?
29. Who was the subject of *The Naked Civil Servant*?
30. Which actor played Cheyenne Bodie?

Answers: see Quiz 76, page 184   LEVEL 2

1. Who was obsessed with his 'little grey cells'?
2. Which comedy duo first played Reginald Hill's detectives *Dalziel and Pascoe* on TV?
3. What was the nationality of the creator of French detective *Maigret*?
4. In which drama was there a global crime syndicate called THRUSH?
5. What is *Dangerfield's* occupation?
6. Eric Richards plays which character in *The Bill*?
7. Which actor plays *Kavanagh QC*?
8. Which 1995 drama set in South Yorkshire followed the hectic duties of a CID unit headed by DI Eric Temple?
9. Which pop star played Crockett's girl friend in *Miami Vice*?
10. What was the name of the novelist in *Murder She Wrote*?
11. The President of the Court was played by which actor in *Crime of Passion*?
12. *Rumpole of the Bailey* made it's first appearance in which 1970's BBC series?
13. Which 60s classic was about Chief Supt Lockhart and also starred Johnny Briggs?
14. Who played Hugh Ryan in *Ryan International*?
15. Which nephew joined Arthur Daley in later series of *Minder*?
16. Which actor played *Shoestring*?
17. *Barlow at Large* was a spin-off from which police drama series?
18. Which lady barrister featured in the series *Justice*?
19. Which crime writer created Paul Temple?
20. Who portrayed Lord Peter Wimsey in the 1970's series?
21. Which comedy by Ben Elton was set in Gasforth police station?
22. Which actor played *Maigret*?
23. Name the creator of *Van Der Valk*.
24. Which lawyer's secretary was Della Street?
25. Who conducted an investigation of the facts regarding Jack the Ripper?
26. *Hunter's Walk* was set in which fictitious Midland's town?
27. Who was the parking lot attendant in *77 Sunset Strip*?
28. What was the occupation of John Sutherland in *Sutherland's Law*?
29. Which women's prison featured in *Within These Walls*?
30. Which police drama had a recipe or cookery tip in every episode?

Answers: see Quiz 75, page 183 LEVEL 2

1. What was Jacko's occupation in *Brush Strokes*?
2. Whose catchphrases included "Titter ye not!"?
3. In *Just Good Friends* what were Penny's parents called?
4. Kate Robbins is a cousin of which ex Beatle?
5. What is the name of the character played by Leslie Ash in *Men Behaving Badly*?
6. Where did John live after his divorce in *Dear John*?
7. Which road did Sykes live in?
8. Who had neighbours called Elizabeth and Emmet?
9. Who played Elaine in *The Two of Us*?
10. Which comic actor wrote *East of Ipswich* which was adapted for television?
11. How were Ian and Janette Tough better known?
12. Who plays Waynetta Slob?
13. KYTV developed from which anarchic radio show?
14. In *The Likely Lads*, who did Bob eventually marry?
15. Which star of *Butterflies* and *And Mother Makes Five* wrote scripts as Jonathan Marr?
16. In *Hancock's*, Tony Hancock was the owner of what kind of establishment?
17. What was the name of the university in *A Very Peculiar Practice*?
18. Who provided the voice of Eccles in *The Tele Goons*?
19. At the end of *The Likely Lads* both Bob and Terry enlisted for the army but why was Bob rejected?
20. Michael Troughton played Alan B'Stard's assistant. What was his name?
21. Who played Sandra's over-bearing mother in *The Liver Birds*?
22. Who were the two main members of the cast of *The Long Johns*?
23. Which male character in *M*A*S*H* dressed in women's clothing?
24. Fletcher's daughter Ingrid in *Porridge* was played by which actress?
25. How many episodes of *Andy Capp* were shown on television?
26. In which series did Anton Rogers play solicitor Alec Callender?
27. Which comic played Colin in *Colin's Sandwich*?
28. Which comedy series shot Robin Williams to superstardom?
29. Which duo were originally formed with the encouragement of one of their mothers, Sadie Bartholomew?
30. What was the primary occupation of the villainous Two Rons in *Hale and Pace*?

Answers: see Quiz 78, page 186

LEVEL 2

1. Who led the BBC's news programme when Princess Diana's death was announced?
2. Who presented *The Human Zoo*?
3. Who left *Newsnight* for *Tomorrow's World* in 1997?
4. What is the subject of *One Foot in The Past*?
5. Where did Harty Go To in 1984?
6. The documentary *The Ascent of Man* was presented by whom?
7. *The World At War* documented which war?
8. Who has presented *Newsround* and *Here and Now*?
9. Where did Michael Palin travel after *Around the World in 80 Days*?
10. Which satellite channel had the slogan 'Make the voyage'?
11. Who hosted *Police Five* for nearly 30 years?
12. What was the sequel to the series *Don't Ask Me*?
13. Who added her name to the *Mysteries* series?
14. Where did the Wilkins, the subject of the documentary *The Family*, live?
15. What was the follow-up to *The Family*, 10 years after the original?
16. Which BBC 2 programme won a series of BAFTA awards for "Best Programme Without a Category"?
17. What 1975 documentary was about two runaway children in London?
18. Which news programme launched the two-presenter format in the UK?
19. What has ITN traditionally called its newsreaders?
20. The *HMS Brilliant* patrolled waters off the coast of where in 1995?
21. The history of what subject was explored in *All You Need Is Love*?
22. Which 1978 documentary saw the British Colonial Force policing Hong Kong?
23. *A Detective's Tale; A Villain's Tale; A Brief's Tale;* and *A Prisoner's Tale* were the four plays in which 1978 series?
24. Which newsreader was an original presenter of *Top Gear*?
25. Which two women have presented main news bulletins for BBC and ITV?
26. Which steeplejack appeared in his own show?
27. *Life On Earth* was presented by which naturalist?
28. Who chaired *Question Time* for the first ten years of its existence?
29. Who took over the chair of *Question Time* in 1989?
30. Which Newmarket trainer featured in the 1992 documentary *The Racing Game*?

1. Who failed an audition for *Opportunity Knocks* as Gerry Dorsey but found superstardom later on?
2. Who would have asked you to "name that tune in one"?
3. Who was the male compere of *Ready Steady Go?*
4. Who was called British TV's first lady of popular music in the late 1950s/early 60s?
5. In *Chelsea At Nine* who were the resident song and dance troupe?
6. Which ventriloquist had a dummy called Lord Charles?
7. Which Channel 5 show highlighted the best hit singles?
8. The 1998 *Royal Variety Show* was a tribute to which singer who died that year?
9. Who interrupted Michael Jackson's stage performance at the *Brit Awards?*
10. Who presented *The City Varieties?*
11. Which British lady presented the *Eurovision Song Contest* for many years?
12. Which resident band backed solo artists on *Six-Five Special?*
13. Who has presented *Highway* and *Songs of Praise?*
14. A special New Year's Eve show called *Twelve-Five Special* was presented from where?
15. *The Val Doonican Show* provided a regular comedy spot for which Irish comedian?
16. Who was the creator and producer of *Oh Boy!?*
17. Bob Harris introduced which weekly Rock programme from 1972?
18. Who was the compere of *The Good Old Days?*
19. Whose *Saturday Night Out* was followed by a series with only his surname in the title?
20. Who was the first presenter of *Drumbeat?*
21. 'Living Doll' by Cliff Richard and the Young Ones raised money for which charity?
22. Which entertainer's Saturday night show included his 'Car Boot Quiz'?
23. What connects Victoria Wood, Marti Caine, Lenny Henry and Jim Davidson?
24. In which variety programme did Gracie Fields make her first TV appearance?
25. In which show was 'The Funky Gibbon' first heard?
26. What was the compilation of *Songs of Praise* clips presented by Thora Hird called?
27. A special variety show from the London Palladium was screened in 1998 to celebrate whose 70th birthday?
28. Who hosted the 1979 version of *Juke Box Jury?*
29. Name the 80's daytime magazine show about the London entertainment scene.
30. Who hosted *Hit, Miss or Maybe* in 1998?

Answers: see Quiz 80, page 188

1. A novel by Grace Metalious was the basis for which sixties US soap?
2. Which *Eastenders* actor played Graham Lodsworth in *Emmerdale*?
3. What is unusual about Hayley Patterson in *Coronation Street*?
4. In which soap did comedian Larry Grayson once appear?
5. Australian soap, *Sons and Daughters*, featured which two families?
6. Which *Coronation Street* actor could be seen stripping off in *The Full Monty*?
7. Who did Deirdre have an affair with while still married to Ken Barlow?
8. Who played the Geordie porter Jimmy Powell in *Casualty*?
9. Which character does Chris Chittell play?
10. In *Home and Away* Craig McLachlan played a character with which name also famous for a character in a British soap?
11. Which soap featured the fictional Moldavia in one of its plots?
12. In which valley is *A Country Practice* set?
13. Who played Carol in *The Rag Trade*?
14. Which character in *Coronation Street* was fatally injured in a dispute outside a nightclub?
15. Which newspaper did Tony work for in *Eastenders*?
16. Who was Lorraine's son in *Eastenders*?
17. What was the name of Jason Donovan's character in *Neighbours*?
18. In *Dallas* where was JR when he was shot?
19. Who is Claire's guardian in *Eastenders*?
20. Which star of *Kiss Me Kate* moved to *Dallas*?
21. Who played Meg Mortimer in *Crossroads*?
22. Who played Krystal Carrington in *Dynasty*?
23. Which 60s pop star played hairdresser Viv in *Albion Market*?
24. Which 80s soap was popular in its home country France but failed over here?
25. Curly Watts is the manager of which supermarket?
26. What is the name of Mark Fowler's younger brother?
27. Which *Dynasty* star's autobiography was called *Past Imperfect*?
28. In which soap did President Reagan's ex wife star?
29. What was Rita's maiden name in *Coronation Street*?
30. What is the name of Grant and Phil Mitchell's mother in *Eastenders*?

1. What is Dorothy's profession in *Men Behaving Badly*?
2. The Two Rons featured in their own series. What was it called?
3. Name the original army camp at which Sgt. Bilko was stationed?
4. Name the actresses who are *Birds of a Feather*.
5. Who stars with Geoffrey Palmer in *As Time Goes By*?
6. Who played Mike and Laura's daughter in *A Fine Romance*?
7. In which London borough was *Desmond's* barber shop?
8. Which star of the small screen went on to make *The Ultimate Disaster Movie*?
9. Which actor was frequently to be seen with *The Babes In The Wood*?
10. In *On the Buses* whose catchphrase was "I 'ate you Butler"?
11. Where abroad were a trio of Mrs Merton shows screened from in 1997?
12. What was the rat called on the *Muppet Show*?
13. Where was the series *Naked Video* first made?
14. Which fictional MP was treasurer of the 'Keep Britain Nuclear' pressure group?
15. Who played Queenie in *Making Out*?
16. What was Tom O'Connor's profession before he found fame on *The Comedians*?
17. Name Grace's daughter in *Grace Under Fire*.
18. *Surgical Spirit* was set in what kind of establishment?
19. The role of female surgeon Sheila Sabatini was played by which actress?
20. Who wrote the theme music to the comedy *Yes-Honestly*?
21. Which comedian played Fletcher in *Porridge*?
22. *Keeping Up Appearances* was written by whom?
23. Where was cockney wide boy stranded in *Bad Boys*?
24. In *Don't Wait Up*, who does Tom have to pay rent to for his doctor's surgery?
25. Who did Robin Tripp live with in *Robin's Nest*?
26. Which 90s sitcom created highlighted the decline of the railways in the 60s?
27. Whose comic roles included Brother Dominic in *Oh Brother* and Noote in *All Gas and Gaiters*?
28. What was Victor Meldrew before retiring?
29. Name the oddball landlady in *Girls on Top*.
30. How many sons did Nellie Boswell have in *Bread*?

Answers: see Quiz 82, page 190

LEVEL 2

1. Timmy Mallett, Michaela Strachan and Tommy Boyd presented which TV-AM children's programme?
2. What was Keith Chegwin's pop music programme?
3. *Saturday Superstore* was presented by which DJ?
4. Where do the Ewoks live?
5. What was Dougal's favourite food on the *Magic Roundabout*?
6. What was it that Tweety Pie "taut" he "taw"?
7. Fraser Hines wore a kilt in *Dr Who*. True or False?
8. In which geological feature were *The Space Sentinels* based?
9. Richard O'Sullivan played which highwayman in the 1980s?
10. On which channel did Pob appear?
11. Who is Bod's aunt?
12. Who hosted *The Quack Chat Show*?
13. On which afternoon in the week was *Playaway* shown on TV?
14. In *The Flintstones*, what was the Rubble baby called?
15. Who presented *Jim'll Fix It*?
16. Diana Dors played which character in the 1976 adaptation of *Just William*?
17. In Britain it was called *Just Dennis*. How was it known in the USA?
18. The fifties series *Whirlybirds* was about what?
19. Who played the little girl in *Skippy The Bush Kangaroo*?
20. Which alien organisation were G-Force opposing in *Battle of the Planets*?
21. Who played Maid Marion in the 1977 BBC version of *Robin Hood*?
22. How many times a week was *Magpie* screened on children's TV?
23. On what days is *Blue Peter* screened?
24. Which redhead played Violet Elizabeth Bott in the 70s series of *Just William*?
25. What was *Mandrake*?
26. Who was the talkative woodpecker in *Bagpuss*?
27. Who was *Muffin The Mule*'s human companion?
28. Who was Mr Pastry?
29. What was the name of Larry The Lamb's canine chum?
30. Who were *Andy Pandy*'s two friends?

1. Which soccer pundits' show was started with a spot on *World of Sport*?
2. In *Only Fools and Horses* what does Trigger always call Del Boy?
3. Name the late presenter of *Gardener's World*.
4. During the BBCs experimental period in 1936 live transmissions were sent to which show at Olympia?
5. What is the BBC's rolling news service called?
6. Who founded Verity Productions?
7. Which US comedienne bought the US rights to *Absolutely Fabulous*?
8. Where were kittens playing with wool and the potter's wheel featured?
9. Which former Dr Kildare played John Blackthorne in the 80s *Shogun*?
10. Where was *Tenko* set?
11. Who first introduced *Stars on Sunday*?
12. Name the long-time host of *The Tonite Show*.
13. Who wrote *Up the Junction*?
14. In which series did Helen Baxendale play doctor?
15. Which planet does *Dr Who* come from?
16. Who is the presenter of *Time Team*?
17. Who was the Oscar-winning actor who appeared in *Playaway*?
18. Name the *This is Your Life* former newsreader?
19. In *The Fosters*, who played their busybody neighbour, Vilma?
20. In *Open All Hours*, what was the name of the corner-shop keeper?
21. Which 'brother and sister' lived at 28 Sebastopol Terrace during the 70s sitcom?
22. In which year was the soap *The Grove Family* first transmitted?
23. Who sang the theme from *Minder*?
24. Which singer do you associate with sweaters and a rocking chair?
25. Who was the regular female performer on *The Frost Report*?
26. Which Irish redhead co presents *Animal Hospital*?
27. Who presented his *Italian Feast*?
28. Which chat show host has interviewed Tony Blair and William Hague on his TV show?
29. Which group of renegades were played by George Peppard, Dirk Benedict, Dwight Schultz and Mr T?
30. Who sang the theme to *That was the Week that Was*?

Answers: see Quiz 84, page 192

1. What kind of dog does Hamish Macbeth own?
2. What animal appears in the opening sequences of *Northern Exposure*?
3. What non-human primate formed part of the experiment in *First Born*?
4. What was the name of Bernie Winter's St Bernard?
5. Cheetah was the chimpanzee companion of which jungle dweller?
6. Which animal is seen on the opening sequence of *Coronation Street*?
7. *One By One* featured which zoo vet?
8. Wally Whyton, the voice of *Ollie Beak* the owl, sang of Willum. Who was Willum?
9. Who was the puppeteer behind Basil Brush?
10. What was the name of *Blue Peter's* first pet dog?
11. Which horse created by Mary O'Hara featured in a fifties children's saga?
12. What kind of cartoon animal is *Snagglepuss*?
13. Which naturalist was made controller of BBC 2 in 1965?
14. Who was Roland Rat's sidekick?
15. Which husband and wife team presented *The Amateur Naturalist*?
16. Which Australian celebrity presented *Animal Hospital*?
17. Which comic pretended to kill himself in despair over global warming before going looking for lemurs in Madagascar?
18. Which famous animal impersonator appeared with Morecambe and Wise?
19. Which brand of dog food claimed it "prolongs active life" according to its TV commercial?
20. A series of adverts links Billy Connolly to which type of fish?
21. What was the name of Jed Clampett's pet dog in the *Beverly Hillbillies*?
22. Which well-known environmentalist and botanist is impersonated by Lenny Henry?
23. Who is the vet in *Emmerdale*?
24. Which BBC comedy series character mistook a Dachshund for a telephone?
25. Whose veterinary surgery was located in the fictional town of Darrowby?
26. In which series do we meet real-life vet Trude Mostue?
27. Which canine hero's home was Fort Apache?
28. On whose programme did the Cookie Bear appear?
29. Who are *Chip 'n' Dale*?
30. What kind of animal was Fury?

Answers: see Quiz 83, page 191

LEVEL 2

1. In *One Foot In The Grave*, what happens to Victor Meldrew's house while he is on holiday in Spain?
2. Who was the driver in *On The Buses*?
3. Who played Tony Carpenter in *On the Up*?
4. Which bar does Sam Malone run?
5. In *Only Fools and Horses* what is Boycie's wife called?
6. What was the setting of *Only When I Laugh*?
7. What is the occupation of the object of Granville's affections in *Open All Hours*?
8. Which *Back To The Future* star is deputy mayor in Channel 4's *Spin City*?
9. Which Australian comedian played Pat Cleary in *Anzacs*?
10. Who played Joe McGann's equivalent in the US version of The *Upper Hand*?
11. Who wrote the book on which the TV series, *Porterhouse Blue* was based?
12. What was Sgt. Bilko's first name?
13. In *Please Sir* what was Bernard Hedges' nickname?
14. What sentence was given to Norman Stanley Fletcher at the beginning of *Porridge*?
15. Who links *One Foot In The Grave* and *Waiting For God*?
16. Which comic's real name is Jim Moir?
17. What was the follow-up to comedy series *Murder Most Horrid*?
18. Who changed her surname from Barr to Arnold and then dropped her surname?
19. Liza Goddard played Matt's secretary in *Yes Honestly*. What was her character's name?
20. Who was the British female on Rowan and Martin's *Laugh In*?
21. What was Gunner Sugden's nickname in *It Ain't Half Hot Mum*?
22. In *Selling Hitler* who played the role of Goering's daughter, Edda?
23. Which half of the Marshall-Renwick writing team created *Two Point Four Children*?
24. Which sitcom had a Manhattan deli called Monk's?
25. What was the name of Julie Walter's character in *Acorn Antiques*?
26. What was Ma and Pa Larkin's eldest son called?
27. Which comedy series was based at Hut 29 the surplus ordnance depot at Nether Hopping?
28. How is Paul O'Grady better known?
29. Which show was about 'Britain's smallest TV network'?
30. Who revived Galton and Simpson scripts for a rerun of Hancock sketches in the 90s?

Answers: see Quiz 86, page 194

LEVEL 2

1. In *Bronco*, which actor played the title role?

2. Who played the title role in *The Adventures of William Tell*?

3. Who played Anna in *This Life*?

4. Which daughter of Rosemary Harris starred in the 1995 *Pride and Prejudice*?

5. In which steamy series did Harriet Walter play Charity Walton?

6. Who played Dr Kildare's mentor?

7. Which seedy dance hall did Danny and Frank Kane run, played by Leslie Grantham and Don Henderson?

8. In which drama did Dennis Potter create Arthur Parker?

9. Which playwright is married to actress Maureen Lipman?

10. What does Rumpole always call the judges?

11. Where was *St Elsewhere* based?

12. Squire Gurth, companion of *Ivanhoe* was played by which actor?

13. Who played henpecked husband, Alf, in *The Larkins*?

14. Which DJ wrote the theme song for *Trainer*, sung by Cliff Richard?

15. Tim Piggott-Smith played which character in *Jewel in the Crown*?

16. Which actor was the Japanese POW Commandant in *Tenko*?

17. Which actress, famous as a wife in a 90s sitcom, played Henry's first wife in *The Six Wives of Henry VIII*?

18. What was the occupation of Mike Nelson in *Sea Hunt*?

19. Which regiment featured in *Soldier Soldier*?

20. Which spy drama with Alec Guinness focused on the agency known as 'the circus'?

21. Robert Mitchum played which character in the WWII drama *The Winds Of War*?

22. Between which years did *Sunday Night Theatre* run on BBC TV?

23. Which famous cowboy guest starred in 'The Colter Craven Story' taken from *Wagon Train*?

24. Which Philadelphia based drama featured the Westons and Steadmans?

25. Who played the title role in *Garry Halliday*?

26. Richard Chamberlain was the star of which drama set in mediaeval Japan?

27. Which actor played the *Jungle Boy*?

28. Which *ER* actor appeared in *Roseanne*?

29. Which saga about a black American family starred OJ Simpson?

30. Which brothers were Bo and Luke?

ANSWERS

Crime 9 (See Quiz 86)

1. Helen Forrester. 2. Horace Rumpole. 3. GK Chesterton. 4. Crockett (*Miami Vice*). 5. Kate Jackson. 6. Anouska Hempel. 7. Safe Deposit Boxes. 8. Alan Wheatley. 9. MG. 10. Stacey Keach. 11. Garfield Morgan. 12. Miss Marple. 13. Stratford Johns & Frank Windsor. 14. Dave. 15. Tony Curtis. 16. *Magnum PI*. 17. James Bolam. 18. Jack Roffey. 19. Hercule Poirot. 20. Policeman. 21. Into those who played cricket and those who did not. 22. *Thames Valley*. 23. Colin Blakely. 24. Christopher Strauli. 25. Det. Supt. Steve Hackett. 26. Pepper. 27. Leslie Nielsen. 28. Terry Venables. 29. A Bank Robber. 30. Jane Tennison.

QUIZ 86　Crime 9

Answers: see Quiz 85, page 193

LEVEL 2

1. Who replaced the actress Googie Withers in the prison series *Within These Walls*?
2. Leo McKern played which well-known Old Bailey lawyer?
3. *Father Brown* was based on which author's famous amateur detective?
4. Which US cop lived on a boat called St Vitus Dance?
5. Who played Mrs King in *The Scarecrow and Mrs King*?
6. Which actress played the astrologer Esther Jones in *Zodiac*?
7. What did the two small-time crooks steal in the series *Turtle's Progress*?
8. Who played the first TV Sherlock Holmes in 1951?
9. What car did Nick restore in *Heartbeat*?
10. Who played detective Mike Hammer but spent time in Reading jail for real life drug offences?
11. Who played the Flying Squad boss, Det. Chief Insp. Haskins in *The Sweeney*?
12. Who always got the better of Inspector Slack?
13. Which two actors appeared in the lead roles in *Second Verdict*?
14. In *Minder*, who owned the Winchester club?
15. Who played the US half of the duo in *The Persuaders*?
16. Which PI was bossed around by Higgins, his employer's representative?
17. Which actor played Trevor Chapman in *The Beiderbecke Affair*?
18. Who was the main author in *Boyd QC*?
19. Which detective lived at Whitehaven Mansions?
20. What was Doyle's occupation before joining *The Professionals*?
21. How did Charters and Caldicott divide the world?
22. The 1982 controversial fly on the wall police documentary filmed which police force?
23. Who played Det. Insp. Richard Lee in *Operation Julie*?
24. Which actor played Bunny Manners in the series *Raffles - The Amateur Cracksman*?
25. Which police detective played by Patrick Mower was featured in the series *Target*?
26. In *Police Woman* what was Sgt. Suzanne Anderson known as?
27. Which star of the *Naked Gun* films starred in the zany *Police Squad* in the 80s?
28. *Hazell* was based on the crime novels by Gordon Williams and who else?
29. What was Frank Ross in *Out*?
30. Who did Helen Mirren play in *Prime Suspect*?

1. The coronation of which monarch was the first to be broadcast?
2. The Director General, Hugh Carleton Greene, was the brother of which novelist?
3. What is the spending limit for each team on *Changing Rooms*?
4. In *To the Manor Born*, what was the name of the Manor?
5. What was Dudley Moore always searching for in the series of Tesco ads?
6. How were PJ and Duncan also known?
7. What was the name of the company in *The Squirrels*?
8. Which gardening programme developed from *Gardening Club* in 1968?
9. In which show would you meet Ludicrus Sextus and Stovus Primus?
10. Why does Carol Hershey hold the record as the most seen face on British TV?
11. What was the name of the character played by David Jason in *Open All Hours*?
12. Which Esther Rantzen series was a follow up to *Braden's Week*?
13. What are the first names of scriptwriters Galton and Simpson?
14. Who asked, 'so who would live in a house like this...'?
15. Which royal relative was the subject of *This Is Your Life* in jubilee year, 1977?
16. Which *Top Gear* presenter was given his own chat show in 1998?
17. Who hosted the pop programme *America's Top Ten*?
18. Who played Mr Grove in *The Grove Family*?
19. What is the name of the spiky-haired TV chef?
20. Queen Elizabeth II is the only British sovereign to have ever visited a TV studio. True or false?
21. What do The Osmonds, The Jackson Five and The Beatles have in common?
22. Dickens and Fenster had the same trade. What was it?
23. What was Boon before he was forced into retirement?
24. Name the original presenter of *Gardening Club*.
25. Which tennis star took over from Anneka Rice in *Treasure Hunt*?
26. Which series asked the question "Who killed Laura Palmer?"
27. Who wrote *Barmitzvah Boy*?
28. In *Dr Who*, who played Romana and was also married to Tom Baker?
29. Which sister channel to UK Gold used the slogan 'You can't help getting involved'?
30. Whose TV career took off after the highly publicised breakdown of her marriage to a rugby player?

Answers: see Quiz 87, page 195

LEVEL 2

1. Which Scottish comedian and actor was born John Marshall in 1953?
2. Who played Arthur's wife in *The Arthur Askey Show*?
3. Who played Sgt Major Bullimore in *The Army Game*?
4. Which Bird of a Feather played Maggie in *Shine On Harvey Moon*?
5. In which comedy did Lenny Henry play a DJ on the run?
6. In *On the Up*, starring Dennis Waterman, which Joan played his cook?
7. Who was the *Batchelor Father*?
8. What was Snudge in the second series of *Bootsie and Snudge*?
9. Which duo from *Not The Nine O'Clock News* formed their own company Talk Back Productions?
10. Martin Clunes plays which character in *Men Behaving Badly*?
11. Which sitcom star was famous for doing his own stunts including roller skating under a lorry?
12. What does Frank Stubbs do for a living?
13. In *Beryl's Lot*, what did Beryl's husband do for a living?
14. In *Spitting Image* which of Thatcher's cabinet was portrayed as a skinhead bully?
15. Who lived at Mews Cottage, Oil Drum Lane?
16. Whose catchline was "Phenomenal" in *Sitting Pretty*?
17. Which comic became resident compere on *Sunday Night at the London Palladium*?
18. In *Yes Honestly*, what was Matt's occupation?
19. In which Jasper Carrott series did *The Detectives* make their debut?
20. What was the setting for the action in *Big Jim and the Figaro Club*?
21. Who was a *Big Boy Now!*?
22. What nickname did Alf Garnett give his son in law?
23. In *Russ Abbot's Madhouse*, who was Russ's female sidekick?
24. What was Penelope Keith's character in *To The Manor Born*?
25. What is Gary Sparrow's job in *Goodnight Sweetheart*?
26. Newman, Baddiel, Dennis and who else formed *The Mary Whitehouse Experience*?
27. Which comedy featured the Scottish kings of rock *The Majestics*?
28. How was Gerald Wiley, who wrote scripts for The Two Ronnies, otherwise known?
29. In The Rag Trade which actress's catchphrase was "Everybody out"?
30. What was the name of Paul Calf's own show?

Answers: see Quiz 90, page 198

LEVEL 2

1. In *Eastenders*, who is Beppe's brother?

2. Who was Hattie's granddad in *Eastenders*?

3. Who is the landlady of the Rovers Return?

4. Which soap pub sells a pint of Churchills?

5. Where did Caress appear?

6. Who did Peter Dean play in *EastEnders*?

7. Who went from *Emergency-Ward 10* to the Woolpack?

8. How many actresses have played Lucy in *Neighbours*?

9. Who was Des's first wife in *Neighbours*?

10. What is the name of the local newspaper in *Emmerdale*?

11. What was the business of *Falcon Crest*?

12. What is the family link between *Eastenders* and *Faith in the Future*?

13. Which *Last of the Summer Wine* actress played Doris Luke in *Crossroads*?

14. What is Betty Turpin's famous dish?

15. Which actor played Sir Lancelot before moving into *Coronation Street*?

16. Who in *Emmerdale* does Billy Hartman portray?

17. Which actress star of *The Bitch* ran the *Crossroads* motel?

18. Who was Ivy Brennan's son?

19. Who was confined to a wheelchair in *Crossroads*?

20. Who created *Emmerdale*?

21. In what year was *Emmerdale Farm* first broadcast?

22. Which character in *Knotts Landing* did Ted Shackleford play?

23. In *EastEnders*, which of the Jackson family witnessed a bank robbery causing them to leave the Square?

24. Who was the creator of *Coronation Street*?

25. In *Coronation Street* what was Des Barnes brother called?

26. Who appeared in the very first scene in *Emmerdale Farm*?

27. Which *EastEnders* star is a regular panellist on radio's *Just A Minute*?

28. Who plays Kathy Glover?

29. Which celebrity opened the refurbished Woolpack in *Emmerdale*?

30. Who recorded *Hillbilly Rock, Hillbilly Roll*?

Sci-Fi 4 (See Quiz 90)

1. Martin Landau. 2. *Red Dwarf*. 3. *Lost in Space*. 4. Tracy. 5. Gerry and Sylvia Anderson. 6. Gareth Thomas. 7. The Moon. 8. Astronomer Fred Hoyle. 9. Gary. 10. Time travel project. 11. Three. 12. An earthquake. 13. Mr Spock. 14. James Garner. 15. Submarine. 16. *Supercar*. 17. Gor. 18. Environmental Harm. 19. Nathan Spring. 20. *Survivors*. 21. Windsor Davies. 22. Lou Ferigno. 23. Lorne Green. 24. *The Outer Limits*. 25. Boris Karloff. 26. Roddy McDowell. 27. *The Six Million Dollar Man*. 28. Jellybabies. 29. *Doomwatch*. 30. Mayhew.

Answers: see Quiz 89, page 198

1. Who played the Moonbase Commander in *Space: 1999*?
2. Which series was originally called *Dave Hollins-Space Cadet*?
3. In which TV series was the character Dr. Zachary Smith?
4. Which family feature in *Thunderbirds*?
5. Whose first attempt at real life Sci-Fi was in *UFO*?
6. In *Blake's Seven*, who played Blake?
7. *Target Luna* featured a trip around what?
8. Who created *A For Andromeda*?
9. Which Ewing starred in *Space Precinct*?
10. What was the *Quantum Leap* in the sci show of the same name?
11. Of the first four Quatermass series how many were released on the cinema circuit?
12. In 'The Stranger' episode from the series *One Step Beyond*, Harold Kaskett saved three children from what natural disaster?
13. In *Star Trek* who relaxes by playing 3-D chess?
14. Who, famous as Jim Rockford, starred in the mini series *Space*?
15. What sort of vehicle was Stingray?
16. Which children's series had Mike Mercury and Professor Popkiss?
17. What was the nickname of the baby in *First Born*?
18. What did the *Doomwatch* team investigate?
19. Who was *Starcop*?
20. Which 70s series, rerun on satellite, told of people who remained after a killer plague struck the world?
21. Which star of *It Ain't Half Hot Mum* provided the voice of Major Zero in *Terrahawks*?
22. Who played the *Incredible Hulk*?
23. Which Western star captained the *Battlestar Gallactica*?
24. Which 60s series was an anthology of frightening Sci-Fi stories?
25. Which actor famous for his horror roles narrated *Out of This World*?
26. Which Hollywood actor played Galen in *The Planet of the Apes*?
27. Which Man was bionic?
28. Which type of sweet did Tom Baker's *Dr Who* enjoy?
29. Which 70s series starred Robert Powell as Toby Wren?
30. What was Richard's surname in *Neverwhere*?

Answers: see Quiz 92, page 200   LEVEL 2

1. On which programme would you find Humpty and Jemima?

2. Harry Corbett is associated with which puppet?

3. Where did *Larry The Lamb* live?

4. Which fox have both David Nixon and Roy North worked with?

5. Which school did Billy Bunter attend?

6. What did Bill and Ben live in?

7. What animals were Rag, Tag and Bobtail respectively?

8. What did prizewinners on *Crackerjack* receive?

9. Who was *He-Man's* arch-enemy?

10. Who was the "Wonder Horse"?

11. Who cried "Hi, Ho, Silver, and away!" at the end of each episode of his show?

12. What was the name of *Blue Peter* presenter John Noakes' dog?

13. What was Archie Andrews in *Educating Archie*?

14. What was *Metal Mickey*?

15. Who played the Sheriff of Nottingham in *Maid Marian and Her Merry Men*?

16. What did Mr. Benn's shopkeeper wear on his head?

17. What was the name of the punk dog on *Tiswas*?

18. In *Teletubbies* the baby's face is in the middle of what?

19. What was the name of *Rainbow's* pink hippo?

20. In which town does Postman Pat do his rounds?

21. On which day does *The Snowman* come alive?

22. Who was the voice of Toad in the 1983 animated serialisation of *Wind In The Willows*?

23. What was Aunt Sally in *Worzel Gummidge*?

24. Who narrated the 1980's animated series *Thomas The Tank Engine*?

25. Name the 4 children who feature in *The Chronicles Of Narnia*?

26. Who played *The Storyteller* on Channel 4?

27. Who played the editor, schoolgirl Lynda Day, in *Press Gang*?

28. Who led *The Smurfs*?

29. Who played the gawky schoolboy Peter Payne in *Teenage Health Freak*?

30. Which comedy series featured an intergalactic TV station and earthbound reporters?

LEVEL 2

Answers: see Quiz 91, page 199

1. In *Outside Edge*, who was the captain of the village cricket team?
2. How is Caroline Hook now known once again?
3. What is the surname of the family in *Bread*?
4. In *Albert and Victoria*, what were the names of the two gentlemen who Albert Hackett would not have mentioned in his home?
5. What tie linked rich June Whitfield and poor Pat Coombs in *Beggar My Neighbour*?
6. What was the name of Harry Corbett's character in *The Best Things In Life*?
7. How did Ada and Walter meet in *For The Love of Ada*?
8. Which sitcom featured The Royal Artillery Concert Party?
9. Which of the *Girls on Top* spent five years with the RSC?
10. Who played the female lead roles in *Girls About Town*?
11. Which half of a comedy duo had a St Bernard called Schnorbitz?
12. What was the name of Kenny Everett's whacky space captain?
13. Who wrote the Screen One TV film *Pat and Margaret*?
14. Which husband and wife team starred in *No-Honestly*?
15. Why was there a seven month delay before the last episode of *Fawlty Towers*?
16. Whose career blossomed with his impersonations of Harold Wilson and Ted Heath?
17. *The Misfit* had returned to London after having lived the good life for many years where?
18. Who played the barking-dog Corporal in *Get Some In!*?
19. Which programme was the first to win the BAFTA Best Comedy series three years in succession, in the 1980s?
20. Which *Madhouse* host has also played Fagin in *Oliver!* at the Palladium?
21. Which Maureen Lipman series did Anna Raeburn advise on?
22. In *'Allo, 'Allo* who painted 'The Fallen Madonna with the Big Boobies'?
23. Which duo played the detectives Charley Farley and Piggy Malone?
24. What was the name of the Goods' goat in *The Good Life*?
25. Which character did Frankie Howerd play in *Whoops Baghdad!*?
26. Who played the title role in *I'm Alan Partridge*?
27. In *Are You Being Served?* who showed a constant concern for her pussy?
28. Who was head of the Abbott household?
29. Which *Auntie's Bloomers* show showed outtakes from wildlife programmes?
30. Mike McShane was Sandi Toksvig's large lodger in which series?

Answers: see Quiz 94, page 202   LEVEL 2

1. Who succeeded Farrah Fawcett-Majors in *Charlie's Angels*?
2. Name the presenter of *Changing Rooms*.
3. Which comedian's father appears on *WatchDog*?
4. Who founded Verity Productions?
5. Who presented *The Great Egg Race*?
6. Name the female presenter of *Robot Wars*.
7. Which Knight advertised eggs?
8. Who played Charlie Endell in *Budgie*?
9. On what days of the week was the soap *Triangle* broadcast?
10. Which five times Wimbledon doubles title winner with Martina Navratilova commentates for the BBC at the championships?
11. Who played Elizabeth in *Blackadder II*?
12. Which Channel 4 artistic competition is associated with Hannah Gordon?
13. What is the name of Oprah Winfrey's production company?
14. Who is the actor father of Emily Lloyd?
15. What was the occupation of Bradley Walsh before he became a TV star?
16. Who undertook the task to circumnavigate the world 115 years after Phileas Fogg?
17. Which duo present *Late Lunch* on Channel Four?
18. Which Pan's People dancer married Robert Powell?
19. Which late night Channel 4 chat show was hosted by Jonathan Ross?
20. What ingredient did Gary Rhodes advertise on TV?
21. What was the name of the regular band on *The Last Resort*?
22. Which two actors played the lead roles in *Two's Company*?
23. Which person on TV was famous for his Odd odes?
24. Which show first screened in 1963 featured resident singer Kathy Kirby?
25. Where did *Billy Liar* work?
26. Which actor played *The History Man*?
27. What company featured in the BBC soap, *Triangle*?
28. Who was Cilla Black's male accomplice in the early episodes of *Surprise, Surprise*?
29. In which year did John Logie Baird commence experiments in TV?
30. Which film and TV star was born Daniel Kaminski?

---

1. Which top security hospital was featured in *The Secret Hospital*?
2. Who was given a major TV interview with Earl Spencer after Diana's death?
3. Who was the first presenter of *Question Time*?
4. How much money was raised in relief funds in response to the documentary *Year Zero - The Silent Death Of Cambodia*?
5. Which actor narrated *The World At War*?
6. Who presented News Swap on *Multi Coloured Swap Shop*?
7. Who presented *All Our Yesterdays* between 1987 and 1989?
8. Which couple had a *Journey Of A Lifetime* through the Holy Land in the 1960s?
9. Who was the first host of *Points Of View*?
10. Which arts programme was hosted by Lord Harewood?
11. *The Valiant Years* was based on which Prime Minister's memoirs?
12. *America* was whose personal history of the USA?
13. David Jessel presented which news programme?
14. Sir Alistair Burnett read which news?
15. Presenter Kirsty Wark appears on which BBC2 daily news series?
16. In 1976 Robert Kee read news commemorating the 50th anniversary of what?
17. Jasper Carrott's satirical news series was "*Carrot...*" what?
18. Who was the first female newsreader on British TV?
19. What is the name of Lenny Henry's comic newsreader?
20. Which late newsreader's autobiography was *Let's Get Through Wednesday*?
21. Which former newsreader hosts *Desert Island Discs*?
22. Nicholas Witchell read the news on which channel?
23. Which ITN newscaster reported back from the Afghanistan war?
24. Which African country did Diana visit in the landmines documentary?
25. Jan Leeming was "Newsreader of the Year" in which two consecutive years?
26. Who first interviewed George Michael about his arrest in the USA?
27. Who presented the 1978 BBC documentary *Americans*?
28. Which UK airport was featured in the 1978 BBC documentary *Airport*?
29. Which former MP has a morning talk show?
30. Who presented the documentary series *Civilisation*?

Answers: see Quiz 96, page 204 LEVEL 2

1. What was *Jungle Boy*'s zebra companion called?
2. Which handy US action man has been described as 'the ultimate boy scout'?
3. What is the real-life name of *The Prisoner*'s Village?
4. What are the names of the Maverick brothers?
5. Which actor played Danger Man?
6. Who played Edward in *Edward and Mrs Simpson*?
7. Who played Beau in *Maverick*?
8. Name the two Stephanies who co-starred in *Tenko*.
9. Which film star appeared in the lead role in *The Winds of War*?
10. In which children's drama did Ant and Dec find fame?
11. In *Blade on the Feather*, who played the mysterious visitor sent to kill the old man?
12. What was the name of the Russian-speaking male celebrity in *Airport*?
13. Which Beethoven Symphony was the haunting theme music to the 70s drama *Manhunt*?
14. Who played Tony Blair in *Buccaneer*?
15. What name was given to the mini series of half hour plays for TV in early 70s?
16. Who played the title role in *Drake's Venture*?
17. *The Chancer*'s greatest enemy, Jimmy Blake, was played by whom?
18. Which actor played Remington Steele?
19. Who played Casanova in the series scripted by Dennis Potter?
20. In which production did Kenneth Branagh play *Guy Pringle*?
21. In *Flickers*, what was Arnie Cole's personal ambition?
22. Who played the Sherrif of Nottingham in *Robin of Sherwood*?
23. What was the sequel series to *Hammer House of Horror* in 1984/85?
24. Who proved to be a traitor in *Neverwhere*?
25. In which fictitious town was *The Spoils Of War* Set?
26. In *Staying On* which two characters remained in India after the British Raj?
27. What is the occupation which Neeley, Cody and Donna have in common?
28. Who wrote *Brideshead Revisited*?
29. Which 1981 drama was the first to be set in a psychiatric unit?
30. Who was the writer and star of *Nanny*?

1. In *To The Manor Born* what was Audrey's butler called?
2. Which Ronnie was famous for spoonerisms?
3. Which TV film won an Oscar in 1994 for best animation?
4. Which *Sale of the Century* presenter was Arthur Haines' straight man?
5. Who provided the voice-overs for the comedy *Clochemerle*?
6. Eddie and Joan Booth lived next door to Gill and Barabara Reynolds in which comedy?
7. George and Suzy Bassett were a couple getting divorced in which comedy?
8. Who played the irritatingly well-off friend Gavin in *The Cuckoo Waltz*?
9. Who said, 'Woe, woe and thrice woe' in *Up Pompeii!*?
10. Which Diana starred with Sid James in *Bless This House*?
11. Who wrote the song used as the theme music for *Absolutely Fabulous*?
12. Which stand up series from 1971 introduced Mike Reid, Bernard Manning and Frank Carson to our screens?
13. *Hi-De-Hi!* was created by which famous writing partnership?
14. Who with Peter Goodwright was the resident impressionist on *Who Do You Do?*
15. Which sitcom centred on Mrs Stubbs and her sister?
16. Rick in *The Young Ones* was a fan of which pop star?
17. Which character did Micheal Bates play in *Last of the Summer Wine*?
18. What profession do father and son share in *Don't Wait Up*?
19. In which series were Clive Mantle and Sarah Lancashire expecting a baby?
20. Who is worried about the size of her bum in the fast show?
21. Which *Eldorado* actor was also in the sitcom *Blind Men*?
22. What is the name of Dr Tom Latimer's ex-wife?
23. Which couple were played by Brian Murphy and Yootha Joyce?
24. Who played the self styled leader of the Tooting Popular Front in *Citizen Smith*?
25. Sir Giles Lynchwood was MP for which area in *Blott on the Landscape*?
26. In *Robin's Nest* who played the father of Robin's girlfriend, Vicky?
27. Which two actors are *Just Good Friends*?
28. Where did the Grandad Boswell live in *Bread*?
29. Which two ex Pythons starred in *Ripping Yarns*?
30. Which actress played the long-suffering Betty in *Some Mother's Do 'Ave 'Em*?

Answers: see Quiz 99, page 207   LEVEL 2

1. Which comedian played Zak Dingle's brother?
2. Which 60s soap centred on the activities within a struggling soccer club?
3. Which 70s medical saga began in a twice weekly afternoon slot?
4. What was the title of *Coronation Street* creator Tony Warren's autobiography?
5. In which soap was the Cattleman's Club?
6. What is Vera Duckworth's son called?
7. Which character did Mia Farrow play in *Peyton Place*?
8. Which actors, later chart-topping singers, played Scott and Charlene in *Neighbours*?
9. Which Corkhill became a policeman in *Brookside*?
10. Where did Jonathan Gordon-Davis's girlfriend Cherie live before she came to England?
11. Who did Val Lehman play in *Prisoner Cell Block H*?
12. Which singer/actress played Ros Thorne in *Eastenders*?
13. Ken Barlow was a reporter with which newspaper?
14. Who plays Jude Cunningham in *Hollyoaks*?
15. Who does Diane Burke play in *Brookside*?
16. What was Anne Malone's job in *Coronation Street*?
17. Which character does Anna Brecon play in *Emmerdale*?
18. Who was the loving foster mum in *Home and Away*?
19. Which couple have a daughters named Leanne and Toyah in *Coronation Street*?
20. Who is Lady Tara Oakwell's chauffeur?
21. What was Mandy's burger van called in *Emmerdale*?
22. Who plays Kevin Webster in *Coronation Street*?
23. Which nasty character is played by Chris Chittell in *Emmerdale*?
24. Who is Lindsay Corkhill's husband?
25. Who played Sam in *Neighbours* and Dr Lachlan Fraser in *Home and Away*?
26. Where did the Carrington's live in *Dynasty*?
27. What is Chloe's daughter's name in *Home and Away*?
28. Which soap was a spin off of *Dallas*?
29. Who eloped to Gretna Green to get married in *Coronation Street*?
30. Who lied to Deirdre about being an airline pilot?

Answers: see Quiz 97, page 205 LEVEL 2

1. In *Out*, what was Frank Ross obsessed with discovering after being released from prison?
2. In *Father Brown*, who played the sleuth?
3. Who was the barrister-playwright creator of *Rumpole*?
4. Which series began as an *Armchair Theatre* one off called Regan?
5. In which fictitious town was Juliet Bravo set?
6. Freelance detective Bulman also ran what kind of shop?
7. Which detective was the son in law of Charlie Hungerford?
8. What was the name of Daniel Benzali's character in *Murder One*?
9. Which famous sleuth did Ellis Peters create?
10. In which crime drama series created by Jimmy McGovern did DS Jane Penhaligon appear?
11. Who is the town of Denton's most famous offbeat detective?
12. In *Second Verdict*, who investigated famous crimes from the past?
13. Which actor played the character Det. Sgt Chisholm in *Minder*?
14. *The Professionals* worked for which organisation?
15. Which Inspector appeared in *Something to Hide* in 1968?
16. In *Barlow at Large*, which actor played Det. Chief Supt. Barlow?
17. Who sang the theme music to early editions of *Heartbeat*?
18. In *Inspector Morse* what was the profession of Max?
19. Who played *Shoestring's* radio station boss?
20. *International Detective* was which PI?
21. Who was assisted by Eric and Tinker?
22. Which actor portrayed *Van Der Valk*?
23. What was the name of Maigret's assistant?
24. Which 'man behaving badly' became *Boon's* sidekick Rocky?
25. Who narrated *On Trial*?
26. Whose novels were adapted for *The Inspector Alleyn Mysteries*?
27. In *Sutherland's Law*, which actor played John Sutherland?
28. In *77 Sunset Strip*, which actor played Kookie?
29. Who walked "the lonely streets of London with his police dog, 'Ivan'"?
30. Who played his first leading role in the series *Brothers In Law*?

ANSWERS

Quiz & Game Shows 4 (See Quiz 99)

1. *The Crystal Maze*. 2. Ian Hislop and Paul Merton. 3. *Small Talk*. 4. *Big Break*. 5. Bob Monkhouse. 6. Sandi Toksvig. 7. Jeremy Hawk. 8. Jenny Powell. 9. Tom O'Connor. 10. Jilly Goolden. 11. *Strike It Rich* and *Strike It Lucky*. 12. George Daws. 13. Loyd Grossman. 14. Fred Dineage. 15. *100 Per Cent*. 16. Monica Rose. 17. David Jacobs. 18. Magnus Magnusson. 19. *Mr and Mrs*. 20. Nicholas Parsons. 21. Hamper. 22. *The Krypton Factor*. 23. Cilla Black. 24. £1,000. 25. Each correct answer. 26. Kenny Everett. 27. Contestants had to answer questions without saying 'yes' or 'no'. 28. *Can't Cook, Won't Cook*. 29. *Fifteen to One*. 30. 3.

1. In which show did contestants have to collect time crystals?

2. Name the two team captains on *Have I Got News For You*?

3. Ronnie Corbett presented which quiz show based on children's perceptions?

4. In which quiz show did Jim Davidson make his BBC TV debut?

5. Who replaced Paul Daniels as questioner on *Wipeout*?

6. Who was the first female team captain on *Call My Bluff*?

7. Name the original quiz master of *Criss Cross Quiz*?

8. Nicky Campbell and who host *Wheel of Fortune*?

9. Who presented the crossword based quiz *Crosswits*?

10. Who presents *The Great Antiques Hunt*?

11. Which two successful quiz shows were hosted by Michael Barrymore?

12. Name the big baby who keeps the score in *Shooting Stars*?

13. Who is the American presenter of *Through the Keyhole*?

14. Who hosted the weekday elimination quiz *Pass The Buck*?

15. On the first anniversary of her death which quiz show's questions were all on the subject of the late Princess of Wales?

16. Who was the female assistant on *The Sky's The Limit*?

17. Who succeeded Eamonn Andrews as chair of *What's My Line* in the 1970's?

18. Who was the question master on *Mastermind*?

19. Alan Taylor was the original quizmaster on which quiz in which couples answered questions about each other?

20. *Sale of the Century* was hosted by whom?

21. What does the runner up receive on *Ready Steady Cook*?

22. Which game show aimed to find 'the Super Person of Great Britain'?

23. Who hosted the first series of *The Moment of Truth*?

24. In *Double Your Money*, how much was the treasure trail prize?

25. *I Love Lucy* starred which comedienne?

26. Which comic and former DJ provided the voice over for *Celebrity Squares*?

27. What happened during the sixty second spot in *Take Your Pick*?

28. What was the name of the daytime culinary game show for reluctant chefs?

29. Which general knowledge quiz is a regular show before Countdown?

30. On *The Krypton Factor*, how many contestants were there each week?

📺📺📺 Hard Questions

Ah yes, the hard questions. Cackle fiendishly, and take just a moment to stroke your white, diamond-collared cat before rubbing your hands together gleefully, because these questions are the real McCoy. The posers in this selection will sort the men out from the boys, and no mistake. If you do find any boys in the public bar by the way, be sure to let the landlord know, so he can give them a packet of crisps and a bottle of coke and send them outside. The quizzes in this section will make even the most dedicated TV addict or couch potato quake with fear. No-one is going to get loads of them correct, so if someone turns out an incredible score on these questions, search their coat for a copy of this book.

When you're setting a quiz, use these questions sparingly, like hot chilli powder. Even for teams, they're going to be tricky. You'll need to allow some time for people to think about each question, too. What you don't want to do is make an entire night's TV quizzing out of these, because you'll only make people feel stupid, and everyone hates a smart alec who makes them look dumb. A few of these questions, strategically placed, can go a long way.

Answers: see Quiz 2, page 210

1. Which pop show was the title of a Squeeze hit?
2. Who had success with the song *Hi-Fidelity*?
3. Who was the entertainment committee chairman at *The Wheeltappers and Shunters Social Club*?
4. What was Clannad's first TV theme hit?
5. Who sang *Nappy Love*?
6. On which show did the Rolling Stones make their national TV debut?
7. Which TV group sang the song *OK*?
8. With which all-female group did *Hi-De-Hi!*'s Su Pollard start her entertainment career?
9. Who sang the theme song of the comedy *Going Straight*?
10. Jackie Lee sang the theme tune for which children's favourite?
11. *The Maigret Theme* brought success for which band leader?
12. Which duo were the stars of the musical drama *Ain't Misbehavin'*?
13. The BBC record charts are compiled by who?
14. In *Tutti Frutti*, who was bass player with The Majestics?
15. On which show did pianist Bobby Crush make his TV debut?
16. *Thank You For Being A Friend* was whose theme?
17. Who was the choreographer of Pan's People?
18. How were the singing brothers Tony, Mike and Denis better known?
19. Who accompanied Lesley Garret in a memorable 'Three Little Maids form School' in her 1998 TV show?
20. Who sang the *Auf Wiedersehn Pet* theme song?
21. What was the name of the Salvation Army group which regularly sang on TV?
22. Which record producer changed his name from Michael Haues?
23. Why was the Byrds song *Eight Miles High* banned by BBC TV?
24. Which soap theme was composed by Eric Spear?
25. Why did *Rock Follies'* Charlotte Cornwell sue the Sunday People?
26. The series *Off The Record* concerned what?
27. Which type of instruments did Bruno play in *Fame*?
28. What type of music was played on *Honky Tonk Heroes*?
29. Name the *Opportunity Knocks* winner who went on to star in *Gypsy on Broadway*.
30. What was the name of the 60's heavy rock programme broadcast on BBC1?

Answers: see Quiz 1, page 209

LEVEL 3

1. In *Blake's 7*, Gan could not commit violent acts. Why?
2. What were the last words of the bowl of petunias in *Hitch-Hiker's Guide to the Galaxy*?
3. Who organised the murder of Door's family in *Neverwhere*?
4. What alien discovery was made in *Quatermass And The Pit*?
5. What is the correct name of *Xena: Warrior Princess's* 'round killing thing'?
6. According to *Sapphire & Steel*, which "Heavy Elements may not be used where there is life"?
7. Who plays Autolycus, King of Thieves, in *Hercules: The Legendary Journeys*?
8. Which actor accompanies Sam Beckett on his *Quantum Leaps*?
9. The Knight Industries Two Thousand had an evil counterpart. What was its full name?
10. What firm did Ernest Borgnine run in *Airwolf*?
11. Who was the Sandman an evil enemy of?
12. *Automan* created solid objects out of thin air with the aid of what/who?
13. *Manimal* had two preferred non-human shapes, a hawk and which other?
14. Which race is Lt. Tuvak a representative of in *Star Trek: Voyager*?
15. Who played Jake Cardigan in *TekWar*?
16. What rank was Don West in *Lost In Space*?
17. In *VR5*, Lori Singer starred as which computer expert?
18. In which city was *Space Precinct* set?
19. Which group opposed the Fathers in *Wild Palms*?
20. Which race is led by The Great Nagus in *Deep Space Nine*?
21. What colour is Klingon blood?
22. Which of *Dr. Who's* enemies posed as shop dummies, sofas and other artificial items?
23. After the Treaty of Algeron which zone was created in *Star Trek: Next Generation*?
24. How did *The Tomorrow People* refer to teleportation?
25. What was the name of the device looking like a weather baloon that guarded The Village?
26. What are the janitorial robot 'helping hands' on the *Red Dwarf* called?
27. Which star of *Alien* played a trailer park owner in *Twin Peaks*?
28. In *Babylon 5*, who gave up his life so that Ivanova could live?
29. Which Sci-fi writer served as creative consultant to the 80s *Twilight Zone*?
30. Which Switzerland-based group was the goal of the young heroes fighting *The Tripods*?

Answers: see Quiz 4, page 212

1. What was the first sport shown on ITV, in 1955?

2. Which sports event had the most viewers in 1994?

3. Who replaced Peter Dimmock as presenter of the pioneering *Sportsview*?

4. Which boxing commentator won the American Sportscasters' Association International Award in 1989?

5. Who was the first BBC Sports Personality of the Year of the 1990s?

6. Which two sports presenters have separately hosted *How Do They Do That*?

7. Who became LWT's Deputy Controller after a career in football management?

8. On which channel is *Sunday Grandstand* broadcast?

9. Jack Solomon's *Scrapbook* concerned which sport?

10. Who aspires to become a professional boxer in the comedy *Taxi*?

11. Which programme covered the International Sheepdog Trials?

12. What BBC sport competition was first won by Ray Reardon?

13. Which sportsman recorded *We Shall Not Be Moved*?

14. On which sport does Dorian Williams commentate?

15. Which sport was featured in *Cudmore's Call*?

16. Which Royal organised the *Grand Knockout Tournament*?

17. Who was the UK's very first American football commentator?

18. Who replaced Bob Wilson as presenter of *Football Focus*?

19. Which pop star featured in the closing ceremony of the 1984 Summer Olympics?

20. Who went from editor of the Cheshire County Press to TV sports reporter?

21. Who did Stuart Hall replace as host of *It's A Knockout*?

22. *The Sporting Triangles* teams wore what colours?

23. Who presented *Pro Celebrity Golf*?

24. For how many years did Dickie Davis present *World of Sport*?

25. The theme from *Chariots Of Fire* was used by the BBC for which Olympics?

26. Why in 1975 did Michael Angelow receive big publicity after visiting Lords?

27. For the coverage of which sporting event did the BBC launch its colour service?

28. What sport featured in *The Winning Streak*?

29. Who refereed the TV football match between the Rovers Return and Maurice Jones Building on *Coronation Street*?

30. Which breakfast food was advertised by Ian Botham and Henry and George Cooper?

Answers: see Quiz 3, page 211

1. Who was the very first Director General of The BBC?
2. In which year did Independent Television first hit the screens?
3. In which year did BBC2 commence broadcasting?
4. In which year was the *Radio Times* first published?
5. In which year was the *TV Times* first published?
6. In which year was the first BBC TV broadcast service commenced?
7. From where did the BBC TV service transmit?
8. Who was famous for his 50s cookery shows, *Cookery Lesson* and *What's Cooking?*
9. The first programme broadcast from France featured which town?
10. Who was the first Prime Minister to install TV in his home in the 1930s?
11. In which year were the first BBC TV studios founded?
12. Who chaired the first broadcasts of *What's My Line?*
13. Who was the BBC's first Director of TV?
14. Who was the BBC's first TV announcer?
15. Who presented *The Good Old Days* before Leonard Sachs?
16. In 1939 an estimated how many TV's were in regular use – 15,000, 13,000 or 11,000?
17. Which Dr Who was the first TV Robin Hood for children?
18. Which character played by Bruce Seton was one of the first TV detectives?
19. Who supplied the BBC commentary for the Coronation of King George VI?
20. What was the name of the quiz show on *Crackerjack?*
21. On which part of *Double Your Money* could you win the £1,000?
22. Who played George Dixon's daughter in the early years of *Dixon of Dock Green?*
23. Which comedienne was the neighbour of Fred and Ethel Mertz in a popular 50s sitcom?
24. What did the first ever TV church service celebrate?
25. Who was the presenter of the 1940's series Television Garden?
26. What forced the daytime shutdown of transmissions in Feb-March 1947?
27. Which Royal wedding was televised during November 1947?
28. Who gave the first direct TV broadcast by a Prime Minister?
29. In the post-war magazine programme *Kaleidoscope*, who was the "Memory Man"?
30. In which year did the BBC TV schools service begin?

ANSWERS

Sport 1 (see Quiz 3)
1. Boxing. 2. Torvill and Dean's Olympic Dance. 3. Brian Johnston. 4. Harry Carpenter. 5. Liz McColgan. 6. Desmond Lynam and Eamonn Homes. 7. Jimmy Hill. 8. BBC2. 9. Boxing. 10. Tony. 11. *One Man And His Dog.* 12. *Pot Black.* 13. Big Daddy. 14. Showjumping. 15. Sailing. 16. Prince Edward. 17. Nicky Horne. 18. Sam Leitch. 19. Lionel Richie. 20. David Coleman. 21. David Vine. 22. Yellow, green, red. 23. Peter Allis. 24. 16 years. 25. The 1984 Olympics. 26. He streaked on the pitch. 27. Wimbledon. 28. Rally driving. 29. Derek Wilton. 30. Shredded Wheat.

Answers: see Quiz 6, page 214

1. Which character did Brigit Forsyth portray in *Whatever Happened To The Likely Lads*?
2. In *M*A*S*H* what number was the medical unit?
3. Which composer conducted Eric Morecambe on the piano?
4. Which comedian played Al Johnson?
5. Who owned a dog called Fanny?
6. Who was the animator in the *Monty Python* team?
7. Who played a female driver in *Taxi*?
8. What are Lily Savage's 'children' called?
9. Which star of *Seinfeld* was the voice of Hugo in Disney's *The Hunchback of Notre Dame*?
10. What is Cliff's job in *Cheers*?
11. Which sport did Sam Malone play as a professional?
12. What was the nickname of the Inspector in *On The Buses*?
13. Which Carla created the *Liver Birds*?
14. Who created *Curry And Chips*?
15. Who was the star of *Ripping Yarns*?
16. In *No Place Like Home*, who starred as Arthur Crabtree?
17. Which actress appeared as Sid's wife in *Bless This House*?
18. What was Arthur Askey's catchphrase?
19. Where was *Get Well Soon* set?
20. Who used to say "She knows you know"?
21. Who played Bill in *Love Thy Neighbour*?
22. Who created the show *The Comedians*?
23. Patrick Cargill played the father in which family sitcom?
24. What was Arkwright's affliction?
25. Which comic trio dodged the traffic on a three-seater bike?
26. Who played Mrs Cravat opposite Tony Hancock?
27. What was Joe McGann's character in *The Upper Hand*?
28. Which comedian appeared in the TV play *An Evening With Gary Lineker*?
29. Who played Thora Hird's husband in *Meet The Wife*?
30. Which actor played Spike in *Hi-De-Hi!*?

ANSWERS

Drama 1 (see Quiz 6)
1. Greer Garson. 2. Michelle Collins. 3. Slavery. 4. Whitstanton Iron Works. 5. Luberon.
7. Barbara Gray. 8. Jenny Seagrove and Deborah Kerr. 9. HMP Stone Park. 10. Jack Ford. 11. PC David Graham. 12. Billie Whitelaw. 13. Mrs Murray. 14. *Tenko Reunion*. 15. Nigel Havers. 16. On the Titanic. 17. London. 18. Toy Marsden. 19. In a disused sandpit near Wareham, Dorset. 20. Dale Cooper. 21. *The Troubleshooters*. 22. Michael Angelis. 23. Nigel Davenport (father of Jack). 24. Denholm Elliot. 25. Editor of a newspaper. 26. Three. 27. Ray Lonnen. 28. David Addison. 29. Jack Frost. 30. Original broadcast date was also the start of the Falklands Crisis.

QUIZ 6   Drama 1

Answers: see Quiz 5, page 213

LEVEL 3

1. Which *Mrs Minerva* film star featured in *How He Lied To Her Husband* on TV?
2. Which ex EastEnder starred in the raunchy drama *Real Women*?
3. What was the trade in the drama series *A Respectable Trade*?
4. What was the name of the iron works which featured in *The Spoils Of War*?
5. Where in Provence did Peter Mayle recount his *Year*?
6. Who played Dr Edward Roebuck, head of a psychiatric unit, in the 80's drama *Maybury*?
7. What was the name of the lead character in *Nanny*, played by Wendy Craig?
8. Which two actresses played Emma Harte in Barbara Taylor Bradford's mini series *A Woman of Substance*?
9. Which prison featured in *Within These Walls*?
10. Which character was the hero of *When the Boat Comes In*?
11. Which role did Oscar winner Colin Welland play in *Z Cars*?
12. Who played the Dietrich-like character Bertha Freyer in the comic drama, *Private Schulz*?
13. What was the name of Robert Lindsay's pensioner mum in *GBH*?
14. What was the title of the 110-minute conclusion of the series *Tenko*?
15. Which actor played Randolph Churchill in *Winston Churchill – The Wilderness Years*?
16. In *Upstairs Downstairs* how did Lady Marjorie die?
17. In which city was the serial *World's End* set?
18. Which Roy played Jack Ruskin in the drama *Airline*?
19. Where was the BBC1 drama *Beau Geste* actually shot?
20. Who tried to solve the Laura Palmer mystery in *Twin Peaks*?
21. What were subsequent series of *Mogul* called?
22. Who played Chrissy in *Boys From The Blackstuff*?
23. Which father of a *This Life* star played James Brant in *Trainer*?
24. Who played the Smiley role in the ITV's *A Murder of Quality* in 1991?
25. In *Foxy Lady*, what was Daisy Jackson's job?
26. How many singles were there in the first series of *Thirtysomething*?
27. Who played the character Brown in the political thriller *Harry's Game*?
28. Who did Bruce Willis play on TV opposite Cybill Shepherd?
29. Which TV detective was a reluctant George Cross recipient?
30. Why was the final episode of *I Remember Nelson* held over for six months before being broadcast?

Comedy 1 (see Quiz 5)

ANSWERS

1. Thelma. 2. The 4077th. 3. Andre Previn. 4. Brian Conley. 5. Julian Clary. 6. Terry Gilliam. 7. Marilu Henner. 8. Bunty and Jason. 9. Jason Alexander. 10. Postman. 11. Baseball. 12. Blakey. 13. Carla Lane. 14. Johnny Speight. 15. Michael Palin. 16. William Gaunt. 17. Diana Coupland. 18. "Hello Playmates". 19. 1940s TB sanatorium. 20. Hylda Baker. 21. Rudolf Walker. 22. Jonny Hamp. 23. *Father, Dear Father*. 24. A stammer. 25. *The Goodies*. 26. Patricia Hayes. 27. Charlie. 28. Paul Merton. 29. Freddie Finton. 30. Jeffrey Holland.

LEVEL 3

Answers: see Quiz 8, page 216

1. Which ex soap star played Roy Osborne's mother in the sitcom *Get Well Soon*?
2. What was ITV's first 'soap' in 1955 called?
3. Which breakfast TV presenter starred as himself on *Brookside*?
4. Which three North Sea ports were visited by the ferry in *Triangle*?
5. What was the name of the ferry company in *Triangle*?
6. Which soccer expert was a consultant on the 60s soap *United!*?
7. Whose sister did Paula Wilcox play in *Coronation Street*?
8. Who was the narrator in *The Waltons*?
9. Which 60s soap followed the goings on at a large West End department store?
10. Jean Harvey, Nicholas Selby and Gareth Davies were editors of which fictional magazine?
11. Which soap shared its theme music with *The Upper Hand*?
12. Who played Gregory Sumner in *Knot's Landing*?
13. Which former soap star hosted *The Saturday Banana* in her teens?
14. Who as well as Grant claimed to be Courtney's father in *EastEnders*?
15. Who in *Home and Away* owned a car called 'The Bambino'?
16. Which *Coronation Street* actor's real name is William Piddington?
17. In *Heartbeat*, what is Sergeant Blaketon's first name?
18. Which twins from *Neighbours* were Des O'Connor's assistants on *Take Your Pick*?
19. In which year did the story of *The Sullivans* begin?
20. Which musical star appeared as a dodgy car dealer in *EastEnders* in 1998?
21. Luke Perry portrayed which character in *Beverley Hills 90210*?
22. In *Home and Away*, where did Joey live before moving in with Irene?
23. Which former *Coronation Street* actor played Jack Gates in *Family Affairs*?
24. Who has starred in *Emmerdale Farm*, *Coronation Street* and *Crossroads* but is most famous for her role in a long running sitcom?
25. What was the subtitle of the 1998 Albert Square video The Mitchells?
26. How were Justine and Aaron related in *Home and Away*?
27. In *The Bill* what was Tosh Lines' real first name?
28. In which Valley was *Falcon Crest* first filmed?
29. Which EastEnders star was Mrs Dale's milkman in the days of the classic radio soap?
30. With which family did *Home and Away*'s Aaron live?

Answers: see Quiz 7, page 215

LEVEL 3

1. Frankie Howerd hosted which game show?
2. Which Dani Behr show was fast action, laser lit and on skates?
3. Which game show started with the words "My name is..."?
4. Which 80s arts quiz was hosted by Bamber Gascoigne?
5. Who originally hosted *Password*?
6. In *The $64,000 Question*, how were the questions secured?
7. George Layton hosted which game show?
8. Which quiz was hosted by Paul Daniel's son?
9. What object was given to winning guests on *Through The Keyhole*?
10. Who was the original host of *Chain Letters*?
11. Which Bob Monkhouse game show was based on bingo?
12. Who hosted *The Man Who Got Away*?
13. On which channel was *Cyberzone* broadcast?
14. What is British TV's longest running quiz show?
15. What giant object featured on *All Clued Up*?
16. Who replaced Eamonn Andrews as chairman of *What's My Line?* in 1970?
17. Which show required guests to sign in?
18. On *Bullseye* what score was required to win the star prize?
19. Angela Rippon hosted which master quiz?
20. Which soap character appeared in the fictional quiz show *Cat And Mouse*?
21. Which comic hosted *Whose Baby*?
22. What couples game show was presented by Gloria Hunniford?
23. How many children appeared in each episode of *Ask The Family*?
24. Which *Good Life* star presented *What's My Line*?
25. On which show were questions asked by Sue Robbie?
26. Which game show assistant won a Miss Longest Legs contest judged by her future husband?
27. Who were the original captains on *A Question Of Sport*?
28. Who announced the prizes in the early years of *Take Your Pick*?
29. Chris Kelly chaired which kids TV quiz?
30. Princess Anne was a contestant in which TV quiz?

Answers: see Quiz 10, page 218

1. What was Britain's first half hour animation series?
2. Who was resident chef on *Good Morning* With Anne & Nick?
3. Who investigates *The Big Story*?
4. What is Caprice's surname?
5. Who was the manager who caused a stir in the doc soap *Hotel*?
6. What are the surnames of Mel & Sue?
7. In 1957 how much did a colour TV cost?
8. What was Channel 4's series of animations and animation-related programmes?
9. Sophie Anderton hosted which fashion magazine show?
10. The results of which General Election were the first to be televised?
11. Who was *The Mind Traveller*?
12. Which was the first British channel transmitted exclusively on the 625 line system?
13. Who spoke the first words on GMTV?
14. Which TV presenter was Bob Geldof's father in law?
15. Which gardening programme developed from *Gardening Club* in 1968?
16. Which conqueror of Everest has presented *Tomorrow's World*?
17. Which husband and wife team have presented *Watchdog*?
18. Who was the first woman weather presenter on BBC TV?
19. Who is *Top Gear's* primary motorbike correspondent?
20. Which husband and wife team went *On Safari*?
21. Alexei Sayle played the part of Commissar Solzhenitsyn in which 1982 series?
22. Which doctors hosted *Where There's Life*?
23. Which musical star played Berel Jastrow in *The Winds of War*?
24. What was Francis William's role on *Breakfast Time*?
25. On which show do Anna Ryder Richardson, Graham Wynn and Carol Smillie appear?
26. Which programme has Alan Hanson and Mark Laurenson as football analysts?
27. Who organised the annual *Miss World* event?
28. In *Coronation Street* what was Annie Walker's daughter's name?
29. Who was the female in *Three of a Kind* when Mike Yarwood was one of the three?
30. What was the film programme presented by Dave Lee Travis?

Answers: see Quiz 9, page 217

1. Who designed the *Blue Peter* badge?
2. Which children's show was BBC2's first transmission?
3. Which two footballers presented *Junior Sportsview*?
4. What was the catchphrase of Yogi Bear's girlfriend?
5. Who played Dolly Clothes-Peg to Jon Pertwee's Worzel Gummidge?
6. What were the Woodentop twins called?
7. Which *Dr Who* played the Judge in the 1946 adaptation of *Toad Of Toad Hall*?
8. Who was Toad in the 80s animation *The Wind in the Willows*?
9. *Larry The Lamb* first appeared on TV in which year?
10. Which song was the closing theme to *Stingray*?
11. Which animated characters have a family TV guide in Radio Times?
12. Which coin had magical powers in *The Queen's Nose*?
13. What was the subject of *Wham Bam Strawberry Jam!*?
14. Which former Gladiator presented *Finders Keepers*?
15. Who hosted *All Your Own*, a series of children's interests demonstrated by children?
16. Charlie Drake and Jack Edwards appeared as which children's TV duo in the 1950s?
17. Who was the voice of the computer SID in *Galloping Galaxies*?
18. Which Doctor Who was a presenter of *Vision On*?
19. Which Maid Marion presented the children's TV's *Picture Book*?
20. The name of which producer appeared at the end of the early *Tom and Jerry* cartoons?
21. Who designed *Blue Peter's* Italian sunken garden?
22. Who replaced Ringo Starr narrating *Thomas the Tank Engine and Friends*?
23. Whose magic ray had transformed Granny Smith into Supergran?
24. In *Supercar*, what was Jimmy's talking monkey called?
25. What was the name of the special Christmas reunion episode of *The Appleyards* in 1960?
26. What was the name of Billy Bunter's frustrated school master?
27. Which came first – *Andy Pandy* or *The Flowerpot Men*?
28. Who provided the voices for *Bill and Ben*?
29. *Rag, Tag and Bobtail* were glove puppets operated by which duo?
30. Whose Busy World has featured on BBC?

LEVEL 3

Answers: see Quiz 12, page 220

1. Which comedy double act appeared with Jasper Carrott?

2. What business did Nellie Pledge run?

3. Who wrote *An Evening With Gary Lineker*?

4. Which important character does Barry Bostwick play in *Spin City*?

5. For which role is Ardal O'Hanlon best known?

6. What was the first comedy shown on Channel 4?

7. Who links Rhoda with *The Simpsons*?

8. What was the name of Robert Guillaume's butler?

9. Who kidnapped Burt Campbell in *Soap*?

10. Name Jimmy Nail's character in *Auf Weidersehn Pet*?

11. Who married Alice Tinker in the *Vicar Of Dibley*?

12. Who appeared in *Men Behaving Badly* but was not recognised by Gary and Tony?

13. Who starred in *Stand Up for Nigel Barton*?

14. In 1979, the last episode of which sitcom netted 24 million viewers, the highest of that year?

15. What was the BBC equivalent of *You've Been Framed*, hosted by Shane Richie?

16. Who had a pet hamster called SPG?

17. How is the sometime comic actor Michael Smith better known?

18. Which magician married comedienne Victoria Wood?

19. In which comic series did Joe Lynch play a tailor?

20. Which David starred in *A Sharp Intake Of Breath*?

21. Which Goodie turned Twitcher?

22. Who starred in the title role in *I Dream Of Jeannie*?

23. Which former PM's secretary was a consultant on the first two series of *Yes Minister*?

24. In which series did Harry Worth play himself as a brass band conductor?

25. Who was played by Jamie Farr in *M*A*S*H*?

26. In which comedy did Ted Bovis appear as an entertainer?

27. Whose son was called Spud-U-Like?

28. Which part did Liza Tarbuck play in *Watching*?

29. What career did Jo Brand follow before being a successful comedy performer?

30. What is Ben's trade in *Two Point Four Children*?

Drama 2 (see Quiz 12)

1. Joanne Whalley. 2. Mel Smith. 3. James Fox. 4. John Mortimer. 5. Eric Porter. 6. *Washington – Behind Closed Doors*. 7. John Thaw. 8. WWII. 9. *St Elsewhere*. 10. Laura and Kate. 11. David Hemmings. 12. David Soul. 13. Thamesford. 14. Alan Bates. 15. The Sherpa Tensing Ward. 16. Jane Seymour. 17. *Give Us A Break*. 18. Julia Sawalha. 19. The British Army. 20. Martin Shaw. 21. Jeremy Sandford. 22. Russia. 23. John Gielgud and Laurence Olivier. 24. Their deceased husbands. 25. *Big Deal*. 26. Bounty Hunter. 27. White Ghost. 28. Gestapo. 29. Richard Belzer. 30. Maurice.

ANSWERS

LEVEL 3

Answers: see Quiz 11, page 219

1. Who appeared in her first major role in *A Kind Of Loving*?
2. Which comedian played the straight part of Tom Craig in BBC1's *Muck And Brass*?
3. Who played Nancy Astor's husband, Waldorf, in the drama *Nancy Astor*?
4. *A Voyage Round My Father* was the story of which writer?
5. Who played Chamberlain in *Winston Churchill, The Wilderness Years*?
6. Which 70s drama was based on the novel *The Company* by John Ehrlichman?
7. Who played Bomber Harris in the controversial drama?
8. *We'll Meet Again* was set during which war?
9. Which 80s medical drama was produced by the same company as *Hill Street Blues*?
10. In *Spender*, what were Spender's daughters called?
11. Who played secret agent *Charlie Muffin*?
12. Who played Rick Blaine in the 1980s TV remake of *Casablanca*?
13. Which Constabulary did Barlow and Watt work for in *Softly Softly Task Force*?
14. In the 1980s which actor played the traitor Guy Burgess?
15. In *The Singing Detective*, Philip E Marlow was confined to which hospital ward?
16. Which Bond girl played Mrs Simpson in *The Woman He Loved*?
17. Which 1983 drama showed actors Paul McGann and Robert Lindsay taking on the best in the snooker halls of London?
18. Which sitcom star took on a classic role as Mercy Pecksniff in *Martin Chuzzlewit*?
19. *The Irish RM*, played by Peter Bowles, had previously retired from which army?
20. Which US actor portrayed JFK in the TV drama *Kennedy*?
21. Who scripted the controversial *Cathy Come Home* in the mid 60s?
22. Where had *Reilly-Ace Of Spies* been born?
23. In *Brideshead Revisited* Jeremy Irons and Anthony Andrews played the central characters but who played their fathers?
24. In *Widows* the four women stage a robbery based on the previous plans of whom?
25. Ray Brooks played the habitual gambler Robby Box in which BBC drama?
26. What did *The Fall Guy* do to earn money in addition to being a stunt man?
27. In which episode of *Cracker* did Fitz travel to Hong Kong?
28. Which organisation did Helene Moskiewicz infiltrate, as shown in *A Woman At War*?
29. Who plays John Munch in *Homicide: Life On The Streets*?
30. Who does Barry Corbin play in *Northern Exposure*?

Answers: see Quiz 14, page 222

1. What were the christian names of The Smother Brothers?
2. What was the name of the BBC's 60s forerunner of *Whose Line Is It Anyway*?
3. What was the hit record in 1956 recorded by Eamonn Andrews?
4. Which JB was allegedly called 'The Thinking Man's Crumpet'?
5. Who co-presented *Notes and Queries* With Clive Anderson?
6. Who should have been *This Is Your Life's* first victim, but he found out?
7. Which award did *That's Life* bestow on shoddy goods?
8. Which afternoon series was presented by Mrs. Leigh Lawson?
9. On which television programme did Victoria Wood make her debut?
10. What dance series was presented by Wayne Sleep?
11. Which song did Marti Webb record to help a child shown on *That's Life* with liver disease?
12. Which two companies merged to create Thames TV?
13. Charles, the score reader in *Telly Addicts,* is a regular in which radio programme?
14. Which former Butlin's redcoat was born Michael Parker?
15. Which programme was presented by Peter McCann and Kate Bellingham?
16. Who kept the scores on *Bullseye*?
17. Who played Laura la Plaz, a trick shot artiste, in *Dad's Army*?
18. Who did Renee Bradshaw marry in *Coronation Street*?
19. Which Australian was 'Late' and is now *On TV*?
20. Which variety show was hosted by Kenneth Williams?
21. In which year did *Eastenders* begin on British Television?
22. Which satirist and broadcaster was co-founder of *TV-AM*?
23. Which former Ambassador to Washington presented *A Week In Politics*?
24. What did Teletext Ltd replace in 1993?
25. What was the name of the clothes shop that Emily Nugent ran in *Coronation Street*?
26. Where was Ricardo Montalban the host?
27. Which crime solving show presenter hosted the quiz show *Dotto* in the 50s?
28. In 1979, who performed St. Mark's Gospel on TV?
29. Which former presenter of *World In Action* was made a lord in 1998?
30. Which actor links *M*A*S*H* to House Calls?

Answers: see Quiz 13, page 221

1. Which member of the Fisher family did Travis marry in *Home and Away*?
2. What is Maggie Bolton's profession in *Heartbeat*?
3. Alex Dimitriades played Nick in which soap?
4. In *Knot's Landing* which character had the surname Clements?
5. Which *Coronation Street* actress played Marsha Stubbs in *Soldier, Soldier*?
6. Which soap manufacturer set up their own studio in the US to produce their own soaps?
7. Which was the first UK soap to be seen five days a week?
8. Which soap had the original title *Calling Nurse Roberts*?
9. Which comedy actress played Camilla Hope in the 60s soap *Compact*?
10. Which brother of Travis moved back to *Summer Bay*?
11. Who in *Neighbours* had a sister named Danni?
12. What is the real name of the ranch called South Fork in *Dallas*?
13. Where was *The Newcomers* set?
14. Who in *Brookside* was beaten up on his wedding day?
15. In *Dynasty* what was Alexis's dog called?
16. Who married Roy Evans in *Eastenders*?
17. Who in *Eastenders* was reunited with her daughter Donna after many years apart?
18. Which role did the one time father in law of John McEnroe play in *Peyton Place*?
19. Which short lived soap was set in in the inner suburb of Castlehulme?
20. Who is Simon and Tiffany's father in *Eastenders*?
21. Which Polly was a Walford Gazette reporter?
22. Who has had affairs with both Maxine and Sally in the Street?
23. What is Sinbad's surname in *Brookside*?
24. Name the teen soap which feature twin sisters.
25. What was Rod's profession in *Eastenders*?
26. Which character was once editor of the Weatherfield Gazette?
27. What was the area of *Brookside* destroyed in an explosion?
28. Who was forced to sell his wine bar to Cathy Glover in *Emmerdale*?
29. When *Coronation Street* went on air four times per week, on which extra day was it broadcast?
30. What was the name of the used car lot in *Eastenders*?

LEVEL 3

Answers: see Quiz 16, page 224

1. The launch of which evening programme in 1980 was the first time the BBC had combined news and current affairs at a regular time?
2. Which fellow GMTV reporter is Fiona Phillips married to?
3. Who in 1982 took over the reins of *Omnibus* for a short time?
4. Michael Woods went in search of which wars?
5. Who was the first face of Channel 5 News?
6. Which presenter has the middle name Paradine?
7. Who replaced Brian Walden on LWT's *Weekend World*?
8. In which year did Gordon Honeycombe retire from news-reading?
9. Which John grilled his guests on *Face To face*?
10. What nationality was explorer Hans Hass?
11. How did Wogan embarrass himself during the very first episode of his chat show?
12. Which Royal was the very first to be interviewed on TV?
13. Which late night current affairs series replacing *Tonight*?
14. Who hosted the Daybreak section in the first days of TV am?
15. Which award winning current affairs series began with the slogan 'A window on the world behind the headlines'?
16. Who was the first presenter of *Cinema*?
17. What is the most expensive war documentary ever made?
18. Who continued to read the news while Nicholas Witchell sat on a demonstrator?
19. Who presented *One To One*?
20. How many years had *The Sky At Night* been televised in 1998?
21. Cliff Richard, Cilla Black and Lulu accompanied which ITV broadcast in July 1969?
22. Which two of the first *News At Ten* presenters had first names beginning with A?
23. Who took over presentation of *Panorama* in 1967?
24. A documentary about which prison was hosted by Jimmy Saville?
25. Who was the first sports presenter on *Newsnight*?
26. What nationality was political commentator Robert McKenzie?
27. For which event were satellite pictures used for news broadcasts in Britain?
28. Who finished shows with the words "Goodnight and sleep well"?
29. Which documentary series examined the life of astronaut Buzz Aldrin?
30. Which BBC newsreader was the first actually to be seen?

LEVEL 3

Answers: see Quiz 15, page 223

1. Which programme featured Fred Savage as a boy growing up?
2. Name the teenage doctor?
3. What unusual present did Tony bring back from holiday for Gary in *Men Behaving Badly*?
4. Dana Garvey co-starred in whose World?
5. Which Australian duo hosted the show *The Big House*?
6. Who played Bloody Delilah in *The Dustbinmen*?
7. Who was the pianist in the first series of *Whose Line Is It Anyway*?
8. In which university was *A Very Peculiar Practice* set?
9. In *Absolutely Fabulous* who has a son called Serge?
10. Who played Uncle Mort in *I Didn't Know You Cared*?
11. Which stage show was *Up Pompeii!* based on?
12. Name Jack Douglas' comedy partner.
13. Who played Eleanor in *After Henry*?
14. Which 60s series starred Richard Briers and Prunella Scales?
15. Who played Mike in *The Young Ones*?
16. In which series do Judi Dench and Geoffrey Palmer play a married couple?
17. Who stars as *Caroline In The City*?
18. In whose show would you have met Private Paparrelli?
19. Which family were neighbours to the stuffy Drysdales?
20. Who starred as the dim-witted bartender in *Cheers*?
21. Who created *Rising Damp*?
22. Which comedy writer was a presenter of *Points of View* for many years?
23. Barbara Lott starred as an overbearing mother in which BBC comedy?
24. Which character did Maria Charles play in *Agony*?
25. Peter Denyer appeared as Dennis in which 60s/70s comedy?
26. Who became Audrey's mother in law in *To the Manor Born*?
27. What was the late night adult version of *Tiswas* called?
28. Peri Gilpin plays which radio producer?
29. Which duo starred in the series *Not Only ... But Also*?
30. Name the comedian who played Bottom in the 1964 TV adaptation of *A Midsummer Night's Dream*?

QUIZ 17 Music & Variety 2

Answers: see Quiz 18, page 226

1. Who composed the theme music for the documentary series *The Cosmos*?
2. On which Saturday night show were the Television Toppers a regular feature?
3. Which holiday company used *Step Into A Dream* to help promote its business?
4. Was *Hold Me Now* Johnny Logan's first or second Eurovision winning song?
5. What was highly unusual about the group The Archies who reached No 1 with *Sugar Sugar*?
6. As a boy *Duran Duran's* Simon le Bon made his TV debut in an ad for what product?
7. Who sang about a funky gibbon?
8. Which TV presenter was part of the girl band Faith, Hope and Charity?
9. Which pop star appeared in *How to be Cool*?
10. Which TV dance group released the song *Lover Please*?
11. *The Monkees* TV show was produced by which US television company?
12. Who won *The Eurovision Song Contest* when it was held in Brighton?
13. What was *Six-Five Special* presenter Don Lang's real name?
14. How was chart topper Ivor Biggun known to watchers of *That's Life*?
15. Who presented *No Limits* on BBC2?
16. Which song did Gloria Hunniford release with little success in the charts?
17. Which Hollywood dancer starred in the BBC's *Carissima* in the late 50's?
18. Which pop show has been hosted by Stevi Merike, David Jensen and Mike Reid?
19. Which *Clash* song was used to advertise jeans?
20. Who hosted the children's pop show *Razzamatazz*?
21. Who hosted a TV *Sketch Pad*?
22. Soap star Sophie Lawrence released *Love's Unkind* in 1991. Who had originally sung it in the 1970's?
23. Who sang *Something Tells Me* as a theme song to a Saturday night show?
24. Anne Nightingale presented which BBC2 pop show?
25. On whose show did Tom Jones make a comeback in the 1980s?
26. What was the *Van Der Valk* theme music called?
27. Which Sex Pistols song was banned by the BBC because of its anti-Royal theme?
28. Which comic released the song *Didn't You Kill my Brother*?
29. TV scientist Magnus Pike featured in which Thomas Dolby song?
30. About what did Patrick MacNee and Honor Blackman sing together?

QUIZ 18 Pot Luck 4

LEVEL 3

Answers: see Quiz 17, page 225

1. Which pop show was *Dig This* a successor to?
2. In what year was *Neighbours* first shown twice a day?
3. What was Tony Palmer's series on pop music called?
4. Which bearded interviewer had his own series of programmes in the 1970s?
5. Who was the chairman of *My Music*?
6. What was the Anglian series on Victoriana?
7. What was Clement's cookery series called?
8. Which entertainer had a 'Magic Box'?
9. Which *Coronation Street* star starred in the sitcom *Girls About Town*?
10. Who presented *Toolbox*?
11. Which soap actress presented *Songs That Matter*?
12. In which series did Roy from *Eastenders* appear with Diana Dors?
13. Which character's father did Rock Hudson play in *Dynasty*?
14. In which comedy series revival did Gillian Taylforth appear before *Eastenders*?
15. Who played Kelly in *Charlie's Angels*?
16. Whose role was Corkie in *Sykes*?
17. Max Bygraves, Bob Monkhouse and Les Dennis all hosted which game show?
18. Which character's middle name was Iolanthe?
19. Who played the widow next door in *The Bounder*?
20. Which company in Japan established the VHS video format?
21. Which family appeared in the fly-on-the-wall *Sylvania Waters*?
22. On which game show did Bruce Forsyth succeed Leslie Crowther?
23. Who hosted Searchline on *Surprise Surprise* for five years?
24. Which SF character has the first name Geordi?
25. What is Moe's occupation in *The Simpsons*?
26. What are the real names of the stars of *Chucklevision*?
27. Was Timothy West in *Bread*?
28. What was the name of Chandler's annoying roommate in *Friends*?
29. Who had to look on *The Bright Side*?
30. Which series featured the Ex-agent McGill?

ANSWERS

Music & Variety 2 (see Quiz 17)

1. Vangelis. 2. *The Black and White Minstrel Show*. 3. Butlins. 4. Second. 5. They were a cartoon band and didn't exist in real life. 6. Pepsi. 7. *The Goodies*. 8. Dani Behr. 9. Roger Daltry. 10. The Vernons Girls. 11. NBC. 12. Abba. 13. Gordon Langhorn. 14. Doc Cox. 15. Jonathan King. 16. A cover version of *True Love*. 17. Ginger Rogers. 18. *Pop Quest*. 19. *Should I Stay Or Should I Go*. 20. Alistair Pirie. 21. Bobby Davro. 22. Donna Summer. 23. Cilla Black. 24. *The Old Grey Whistle Test*. 25. Jonathan Ross'. 26. *Eye Level*. 27. *God Save The Queen*. 28. Alexei Sayle. 29. *She Blinded Me With Science*. 30. *Kinky Boots*.

Answers: see Quiz 20, page 228

LEVEL 3

1. Who wrote the scripts for *Rag, Tag and Bobtail*?
2. Who was the original compere of *Crackerjack*?
3. Which children's programme did Emma Thompson's mother present?
4. The 1950s comedy *Mick and Montmorency* was originally called what?
5. Which soccer side does Children's TV's Zoe Ball support?
6. What was the name of the junior version of *The Sky At Night* first screened in 1970?
7. Which former *Blue Peter* presenters hosted the programme *Next* in 1994?
8. Which non profit making organisation funded the early programmes of *Sesame Street*?
9. Eileen Brown, Josephina Ray and Peter Hawkins provided the voices for which children's puppet family?
10. Who created Morph?
11. Who retired as series editor of *Blue Peter* in 1988?
12. Who narrated *Roobarb and Custard*?
13. Which book was read on *Jackanory* to celebrate the programme's 3000th edition?
14. Which US president's son has co-presented *Record Breakers*?
15. Who was the female vocalist on *Rainbow*?
16. What was Sooty's friend the snake called?
17. Who sang the theme tune of *The Adventures Of Champion*?
18. Which ventriloquist operated *Lenny The Lion*?
19. What was *Noggin the Nog*'s son called?
20. When was *Play Away* screened?
21. Which programme has been sponsored by a company which makes a glue stick?
22. Who wrote the *Pink Panther* theme?
23. Who wrote the original *Lone Ranger* stories for radio?
24. Jan and Vlasta Dalibor were the operators of which famous puppet duo?
25. Which role did future pop star Michelle Gayle play in *Grange Hill*?
26. Who was the voice of Basil Brush?
27. Which puppet dog appeared with Wally Whyton on *Tuesday Rendezvous*?
28. Who replaced Phillip Schofield as CBBC presenter?
29. Who presented the rough travel guide on *DEF II*?
30. Who replaced Christopher Trace as presenter of *Blue Peter* in 1967?

Answers: see Quiz 19, page 227

1. Which drama was set at 165 Eaton Place?
2. What car did Emma Peel drive in *The Avengers*?
3. Who was the subject of *Paradise Restored*?
4. Sir John Wilder was a character in which drama?
5. Which 60's ITV play was spoken entirely in Greek?
6. *Selling Hitler* featured which playwright in an acting role?
7. Which comic went straight in *Amongst Barbarians*?
8. The spy character Captain Robert Virgin featured in which 60's series?
9. Which 1971 drama series appropriately had ten episodes?
10. What was the name of *Dr Kildare's* boss?
11. John Hart and Lon Chanry Jnr starred together in which Western series?
12. Who starred in *Sea Hunt*?
13. *The Big Deal* starred who?
14. Which character was played by Joan Collins in *Monte Carlo*?
15. The US series *Beacon Hill* was based on which successful British drama?
16. *A Family At War* consisted of how many episodes?
17. Who played Helene Moskiewitz in *A Woman At War*?
18. Who was the foreman at the Shiloh Ranch?
19. Kessler was a spin-off of which series?
20. Who stars in *Midnight Caller*?
21. Novelist Edna O'Brien guested in which drama?
22. *The Houseman's Tales* was set in which country?
23. Which part was played by Harold Pinter himself in the 1987 adaptation of his play *The Birthday Party*?
24. The character Hannibal Hayes had an alias in which Western series?
25. Coral Browne played who in Alan Bennett's *An Englishman Abroad*?
26. Where was *Raid On Entebbe* set?
27. *The Quiet Man* was set during which war?
28. What is the link between *Angels* and Simon MacCorkingdale?
29. Which 70's series had episodes entitled *Lion's Club* and *Sweet England's Pride*?
30. Who was the Welsh pirate in *The Buccaneers*?

Answers: see Quiz 22, page 230

1. Who owned the Dagmar pub in *Eastenders*?
2. Who was the mysterious head of the sect which Zoe joined in *Coronation Street*?
3. What was BBC Wales' soap, seen on BBC2 as *People of the Valley*?
4. How were Carol and April related in *Eastenders*?
5. Which three surnames did Jane Rossington have in *Crossroads*?
6. What was the job of *Home and Away's* Grant Mitchell?
7. Who had a pizza round in *Eastenders*?
8. In *Coronation Street* how did Ken's first wife die?
9. What character did Rebecca Ritters play in *Neighbours*?
10. Anne Charleston portrayed which *Neighbour*?
11. What was the first name of Jack Duckworth's mother in law?
12. Who wrote the lyrics of the theme for *Neighbours*?
13. Which soap star's mother starred in South Pacific at Drury Lane in the 1950s?
14. Who was the first husband in real life of the actress who played Allison Mackenzie in a US soap?
15. Which beer is the Woolpack famous for serving?
16. Which actor played Len Fairclough's partner in a *Coronation Street* building business?
17. How did Cheryl Starke die in *Neighbours*?
18. What was the name of Jim Robinson's youngest daughter?
19. What do Benny in *Crossroads* and Compo in *Last Of The Summer Wine* have in common?
20. Where did *Howard's Way* take place?
21. Which soap did Ronald Allan appear in before *Crossroads*?
22. Who were the original owners of the café in *Eastenders*?
23. What was the first US daytime series to be shown in the UK?
24. What nationality was Elsie Tanner's son-in-law?
25. Which Aussie soap featured the Palmers and Hamiltons?
26. What was Karl Kennedy's profession in *Neighbours*?
27. Which soap had a cafe called the Hot Biscuit?
28. Which actor links *Bugs* and *Neighbours*?
29. Which female *On The Buses* star joined *Eastenders*?
30. To which south coast city did Bill Webster move to the first time he left *Coronation Street*?

Answers: see Quiz 21, page 229

1. Who was the Chairman of *Jokers Wild*?
2. Which George wrote the scripts for *Don't Wait Up*?
3. Who played Mildred in *George and Mildred*?
4. Name the husband of Pamela Stephenson.
5. What was Alf Garnett originally to have been called?
6. What was the name of the zoo keeper in *Three Up Two Down*?
7. Where did Laverne and Shirley work?
8. Penelope Keith played which character in *To the Manor Born*?
9. Who was the female star of *Hallelujah*?
10. Name the character who runs the café in *Last of the Summer Wine*.
11. In *The Rag Trade*, whose catchphrase was, 'Everybody out'?
12. Name the cab company in *Taxi*.
13. Richard Pearson played Victor Meldrew's relation in *One Foot in the Grave*. How were they related?
14. Which Oscar winner's first TV comedy series was called *Alfresco*?
15. In *Cheers*, Woody replaced which character behind the bar?
16. Who played Polly Sherman in *Fawlty Towers*?
17. Who played the one-armed help in *Robin's Nest*?
18. What was the Fonz's trade in *Happy Days*?
19. Where was *Both Ends Meet* set?
20. Which Tim was one of *The Boys From The Bush*?
21. Where did Hinge and Bracket live?
22. What was the original *Comedy Playhouse* called that became the series *Steptoe & Son*?
23. Which actor and actress played husband and wife in *A Kind of Living*?
24. Which John played the star of *Father's Day*?
25. Which character was just starting his legal career in *Brothers In Law*?
26. Name the author of *A Bit of a Do*.
27. Who was Terry and June's surname in *Terry and June*?
28. Who played Sharon's boyfriend in *Please Sir*?
29. What was the name of the Scottish series following the comic adventures of a fishing boat crew?
30. Who was the co-writer of *The Fast Show* with Paul Whitehouse?

Answers: see Quiz 24, page 232

LEVEL 3

1. Which star of *Ben Hur* guested on *Friends*?
2. Which 'Mrs Thatcher' plays Valerie in *Noah's Ark*?
3. In which sitcom is Miss Wilkins a lodger?
4. Which presenter of *Gardeners World* died in 1996?
5. What was the name of Brian Benben's character in *Dream On*?
6. What was the name of Larry Sanders' wife?
7. Who alternated with Lecy Goranson the role of Becky in *Roseanne*?
8. Who was the first person to win the BBC *Sports Personality of the Year* twice?
9. Which actor links Jed Stone to Marty Hopkirk?
10. In 1998 what rank had Jacqui Reed achieved in *Taggart*?
11. Jonathan Maitland is an investigator on which *Weekend* programme?
12. Who played Miss Fozzard in *Talking Heads II*?
13. Who is the mother of actresses Vanessa and Lynn Redgrave?
14. In which series did Alan Davies travel Europe with a video camera?
15. Who became the caretaker of the community centre in *Coronation Street* in 1983?
16. Who played Mr. Peabody in *The Jewel In The Crown*?
17. On *Spitting Image* who was portrayed as a slug?
18. Which quiz show were Paddy Feeny and Geoffrey Wheeeler question masters on?
19. Euston Films was an offshoot of which TV company?
20. Who hosted *Trick or Treat* with Mike Smith?
21. What type of correspondent for the BBC was Michael Cole before he went to work for Mohammed Al-Fayed?
22. What was the first theme music to *The Sky at Night* called?
23. Which ITV region is the largest in terms of area?
24. Which actor appeared in *Dixon of Dock Green* and *Grange Hill*?
25. Which part did Mrs Gene Roddenberry play in *Star Trek: The Next Generation*?
26. What was Anne Robinson's job on *Breakfast Time*?
27. Which former *Coronation Street* star played Liz in *Bloomin' Marvellous*?
28. What was the name of Brenda's daughter in *Bagdad Cafe*?
29. Which show was originally called *These Friends of Mine* before taking on its star's name?
30. In *All In The Family* what was Archie's daughter's name?

QUIZ 24　Who's Who 1

LEVEL 3

Answers: see Quiz 23, page 231

1. Who is Mrs Adrian Edmondson?
2. Who played Plautus in *Up Pompeii!* and co-founded *Private Eye*?
3. Who was interviewing Kenneth Tynam when he famously used the 'F' word for the first time on British TV?
4. Which actor links the 80s sitcom E/R and the 90s medical drama ER?
5. Which Earl has presented *Miss World*?
6. What was the occupation of *Mastermind* champion Christopher Hughes?
7. Which star of *Brideshead Revisitied* shares a birth date with sports commentator Brendan Foster?
8. Which talk show hostess has a daughter called Allegra?
9. Which actress is the moher of presenter Emma Forbes?
10. What was the profession of Sir David Frost's father?
11. Ex-BBC man Martin Bell became MP for which constituency in 1998?
12. Rowan Atkinson is former student of which University?
13. What occupation did *Hi De Hi!*'s Paul Shane have on leaving school?
14. Which future Hollywood star played Angela Reid in *Emmerdale*?
15. How is TV actress Joyce Frankenberg better known?
16. Where does Roseanne have a tattoo of a pink rose?
17. What is Anthea Tuner's middle name?
18. Bruce Forsyth has only one of which organ?
19. Which TV star fled from the play *Cell Mates* because of stage fright?
20. Which *Whose Line Is It Anyway?* star is a black belt at judo?
21. Gary Webster of *Minder* was a county player in which sport?
22. Which sports commentator won the Manchester Mile in 1949?
23. Who produced a fitness video called BLT Workout?
24. Anneka Rice was removed from which famous London venue in 1997?
25. Frank Muir was Rector of which university from 1976 to 1979?
26. Which TV star duetted with David Essex on *True Love Ways* in 1994?
27. Who was the first woman on *This Is Your Life* when it transferred to ITV in 1969?
28. Which British comedienne played Emily Winthrop in *The Simpsons*?
29. Which writer and actor was David Niven's batman in WWII?
30. Which soccer side does Clive Anderson support?

ANSWERS

Pot Luck 5 (see Quiz 23)

1. Charlton Heston. 2. Angela Thorne. 3. *Game On.* 4. Geoff Hamilton. 5. Martin Tupper.
6. Jeannie. 7. Sarah Chalke. 8. Henry Cooper. 9. Kenneth Cope. 10. Detective sergeant.
11. *Watchdog.* 12. Patricia Routledge. 13. Rachel Kempson. 14. *One For The Road.* 15. Percy Sugden. 16. Peter Jeffrey. 17. Kenneth Baker. 18. *Top Of The Form.* 19. Thames TV. 20. Julian Clary. 21. Royal correspondent. 22. *At The Castle Gate* by Sibelius. 23. Grampian. 24. Nicholas Donnelly. 25. Nurse Christine Chapel. 26. TV critic. 27. Sarah Lancashire (Raquel). 28. Debbie. 29. *Ellen.* 30. Gloria.

LEVEL 3

Answers: see Quiz 26, page 234

1. Which show hosted by Cheryl baker and Rose King helped people to realise their fantasies?
2. Who was the original host of *The Golden Shot*?
3. *You Bet!* was based on a game show from which country?
4. Who replaced Michael Aspel as presenter of *Child's Play*?
5. Who originally shared the chair of *What's My Line* with Eamonn Andrews?
6. Who hosted the 70s quiz game *Whodunnit*?
7. What were the two colours on the basic *Blockbusters* answer board?
8. *The Pyramid Game* was presented by who?
9. Who chaired *Ask Me Another*?
10. How many times a week is *Supermarket Sweep* shown on ITV?
11. What did Michael Miles ask contestants to do in his TV quiz?
12. How many contestants start in *Pass The Buck*?
13. Who was the train-driving *Mastermind* champ?
14. How many homes were featured on each episode of *Through The Keyhole*?
15. Which ITV game show consisted of teams of people with the same occupation?
16. Which two Michaels have chaired *Give Us A Clue*?
17. Who asked the questions unseen in the first series of *Winner Takes All*?
18. Which Joe hosted *Face The Music*?
19. Cleo Rocos was the assistant on which game show?
20. Who was the original host of *Stars In Their Eyes*?
21. Which quiz required contestants to pick odds when answering questions?
22. Max Bygraves preceded whom as presenter of *Family Fortunes*?
23. Who was Richard Wilson in *Cluedo*?
24. What question – the title of the game show – did Noel Edmonds ask?
25. Who was the most northerly team on the very first *University Challenge*?
26. What had to be linked on *Connections*?
27. Which quiz show was presented by Loyd Grossman?
28. Which game show did Annabel Croft star in after *Treasure Hunt*?
29. What was the prize to avoid on *3-2-1*?
30. In which show do the contestants compete in four zones?

Answers: see Quiz 25, page 233

1. What was the name of the late 70's *Blue Peter* series featuring John Noakes?
2. Who discovered Worzel Gummidge at Scatterbrook Farm?
3. Who helped Daddy Woodentop in his garden?
4. Who narrated *The Magic Roundabout* when it was revived by Channel 4 in the 90s?
5. In the children's comedy *Metal Mickey* which character built Mickey the robot?
6. On *Swap Shop* what was the pet dinosaur called?
7. Who was 'General Manager' of the *Saturday Superstore*?
8. Which ex *Bread* star presented *The Movie Game for children*?
9. How many episodes of *Postman Pat* were originally made?
10. The company that produced *The Snowman* also created a *Beatles* cartoon. Which one?
11. What was the *Magpie* mascot called on the show of the same name?
12. What was Mr Magoo's first name?
13. Which young actor starred as *Young Sherlock* in the 1982 Granada series?
14. Who provided the voice of Badger in the 1983 animated version of *The Wind In The Willows*?
15. The fantasy adventure serial, *The Box Of Delights*, was based on whose original stories?
16. Whose regular adversary was Lieutenant Decker?
17. What were Boss Hogg's christian names in *Dukes Of Hazzard*?
18. Which Deputy kept law and order in Mississippi?
19. What was the name of the eagle in the *Muppet Show*?
20. Who wrote *The Little Princess* which was serialised on TV?
21. Who played the beast in the 1988 TV adaptation of *Beauty And The Beast*?
22. What do *the Munsters* keep in the coffin near their front door?
23. Who was Mork's son?
24. Whose friends are Annie and Clarabel?
25. Where did Mr Benn live?
26. Who played the side-kick Pancho on TV?
27. For how many years was *Magpie* broadcast on TV?
28. How many series of *The Flowerpot Men* were made?
29. In which series did the dolphin, Splasher, appear?
30. What was the name of the first dummy to have its own TV show?

Quiz & Game Shows 2 (see Quiz 25)

1. *My Secret Desire.* 2. Jackie Rae. 3. Holland. 4. Ronnie Corbett. 5. Gilbert Harding. 6. Edward Woodward. 7. Blue and white. 8. Steve Jones. 9. Franklyn Engleman. 10. Three. 11. *Take Your Pick.* 12. Twelve. 13. Christopher Hughes. 14. Two. 15. *Busman's Holiday.* 16. Michael Aspel and Michael Parkinson. 17. Geoffrey Wheeler. 18. Joe Cooper. 19. *Brainstorm.* 20. Leslie Crowther. 21. *Winner Takes All.* 22. Les Dennis. 23. Rev Green. 24. *Whatever Next?* 25. Leeds (v Reading). 26. Letters. 27. *Relative Knowledge.* 28. *Interceptor.* 29. Dusty Bin. 30. *The Crystal Maze.*

Answers: see Quiz 28, page 236

1. In which 60's comedy series were the characters Buddy Sorrell and Sally Rogers?
2. Who succeeded Mr. Grainger as senior salesman, Gentlemen's Department, Grace Brothers?
3. In *GBH* which character played by Michael Palin was headmaster of a school?
4. Who played Marjory in *Talking Heads II*?
5. Which children's series featured Mr. Zed and starred Garry Miller?
6. Who succeeded Anneka Rice on *Treasure Hunt*?
7. What was the last round on *The Krypton Factor*?
8. What kind of dealers were on *Play Your Cards Right*?
9. In which children's series did Ant McPartin appear?
10. What surname do the Chuckle Brothers share in real life?
11. What rank is Worf in *Deep Space Nine*?
12. In which sitcom do Sally and Tommy Solomon appear?
13. Who were the resident band on *Six Five Special* in the late 50s?
14. Who was Ray's brother in *Grange Hill*?
15. Who was the housekeeper in *Father Ted*?
16. *Men Behaving Badly* star Leslie Ash was born on the same day as which royal?
17. Radio and TV actress Lucy Davis is the daughter of which comedian?
18. What university studies do David Baddiel and Vanessa Feltz have in common?
19. What colour are Jane Seymour's eyes?
20. Who was described as 'A bowling alley reject' in the 1989 Blackwell's Worst Dressed Women List?
21. How is TV funny man Robert Nankeville better known?
22. Paul Shane was junior champion in which sport?
23. Which soccer side does Danny Baker support?
24. Where did Hughie Green serve in WWII?
25. Which actor released a solo album *Heart and Soul* in 1990?
26. Which knight has appeared on *Baywatch*?
27. Which astronomer appeared on the BBC coverage of the first moon landing?
28. Which profession did Janet Street-Porter train for before embarking on a TV career?
29. What was the western Hero Cheyenne's surname?
30. In *Z Cars* who was Fancy Smith's partner?

LEVEL 3

Answers: see Quiz 27, page 235

1. Which comedian created Frank Doberman?
2. Which character does Brian Wilde play in *Last Of The Summer Wine*?
3. Which hospital featured in *Surgical Spirit*?
4. Gerald Kaufman was portrayed as which film character on *Spitting Image*?
5. What was the name of Frank Spencer's neighbour played by Glynn Edwards in *Some Mother Do 'Ave 'Em*?
6. Which martial arts expert made a guest appearance on *Friends*?
7. The telephone girl on *Laugh In* was played by which actress?
8. What do Rhoda, Phylis and Lou Grant all have in common?
9. How had the ghost Yetta died, in *So Haunt Me*?
10. What business did the Cunninghams run in *Happy Days*?
11. Name the two writers of *Porridge*?
12. What is the name of Michael J Fox's character in *Spin City*?
13. In *On the Up* what was Mrs Wembley's usual response when offered a drink?
14. Who played Whipper Cone in *Ally McBeal*?
15. What was the name of Rachel Davies' character in *Making Out*?
16. Whose husband was played by Alun Lewis in *Birds Of A Feather*?
17. Clare Kelly played which part in ITV's *The Cuckoo Waltz*?
18. What was the name of the BBC comedy about the trials and tribulations of the ATS?
19. Who starred as Mollie Sugden's other half in *My Husband And I*?
20. Which actress played Ingrid in *Porridge* and *Going Straight*?
21. Whose alias was Professor Wallofsky?
22. Which *Waiting For God* star could be seen as Betty Sillito in *A Bit Of A Do*?
23. On RWT who were Dirk, Ron, Stig and Barry collectively?
24. What was *Captain Butler*?
25. Who played the one-armed odd-job man, Albert Riddle, in *Robin's Nest*?
26. What is Dave Allen's real name?
27. Which comedian's daughter appeared in *Watching*?
28. Which of the *Young Ones* was played by Adrian Edmondson?
29. Who was the female presenter of *Nice Time* with Kenny Everett and Jonathan Routh?
30. Chris Collins took his stage name from which member of his dad's pub dominoes team?

Answers: see Quiz 30, page 238

1. What was Kylie Minogue's character's job in *Neighbours*?
2. Which long standing *Coronation Street* actor was a skilled stuntman?
3. Who was Cliff Barnes sister in *Dallas*?
4. Which actor played Sarah's father in *Eastenders* and Travis in *Blake's Seven*?
5. Who was Jack Ewing's old business partner in *Dallas*?
6. Which two series did Kylie Minogue appear in before *Neighbours*?
7. In which city did the Carringtons live?
8. At which studios is the *Eastenders* set sited?
9. In *Coronation Street* what was Jack Walker's hobby?
10. What were the names of the two families which featured in *Soap*?
11. What was Dave Crosby's nickname in *Brookside*?
12. What was Des Clark's occupation in *Neighbours*?
13. In *Neighbours*, how was Des' wife Daphne killed?
14. Which *Coronation Street* actress is a patron of the Manchester Taxi Drivers Association?
15. Dorothy Burke was the headmistress in which Australian soap?
16. Which soap star produced a fitness video called *Secrets of Fitness and Beauty*?
17. How was *Neighbour* Kerry Bishop killed?
18. Which Robinson was manager of Lassiters?
19. Who in *Coronation Street* met her death after being hit by a bus?
20. Who played Clayton Fallone in *Dallas*?
21. Which actor John plays the evil Nick Cotton?
22. Who were Cheryl Starke's twins in *Neighbours*?
23. Which *Hollyoaks* star recorded *When I Need You*?
24. Actor Guy Pearce played which *Neighbours* character?
25. In *Hollyoaks* what was the name of Mandy Richardson's brother?
26. Which character was played by Linda Gray in *Dallas*?
27. Which *Spice Girl* appeared in *Emmerdale* as an extra?
28. In which soap did Demi Moore find fame?
29. Who was the second actress to play Fallon in *Dynasty*?
30. What was the name of Jacqui's club in *Brookside*?

QUIZ 30 Drama 4

LEVEL 3

Answers: see Quiz 29, page 237

1. Where was the play *No Trams To Lime Street* set?
2. F-Troop was based at which fort?
3. Who was *Lovejoy's* motorbiking sidekick?
4. The drama *Thin Air* concerned the running of what?
5. Who was *A Perfect Spy*?
6. In which series did Suzi Kettles appear?
7. Which drama series was inspired by the life of Margo Turner whose story had been researched for *This Is Your Life*?
8. Who was the blind mentor in *Kung Fu*?
9. *The Fall Of Eagles* was the story of which European Royal family?
10. Which daughter of a star of *The Good Life* played Mary Bennet in the 1995 *Pride and Prejudice*?
11. Whose family seat was Brideshead Castle?
12. Who was the only American actor in the *Colditz* cast?
13. Which newspaper editor was played by Ed Asner?
14. In which city was *Family Affair* set?
15. In *The Bunker* who played Adolf Hitler?
16. *The Secret Army* was set in which country?
17. In which series featured Bradley Hardacre?
18. Donald Pleasance and Denholm Elliott starred in which drama about a newspaper?
19. Who played Virgil Tibbs on TV?
20. Who played Gorse in *The Charmer*?
21. In which series did a steel-worker, Harry Perkins, rise to become Prime Minister?
22. Who wrote *The Glass Menagerie*, adapted for TV in 1974?
23. Who starred as journalist Mitch?
24. The television play *Amy* concerned which famous female?
25. Which US writer created *The Moneychangers*?
26. Joanna David featured in the title role of which adaptation of a du Maurier novel?
27. Which Python starred in *GBH*?
28. Who played Trampas in *The Virginian*?
29. In which series did we meet the character Gordon Shade?
30. Who did Deborah Kerr succeed as *A Woman Of Substance*?

Soaps 4 (see Quiz 29)

1. Car mechanic. 2. Bryan Mosley (Alf Roberts). 3. Pam Ewing. 4. Brian Croucher. 5. Digger Barnes. 6. *The Henderson Kids, The Sullivans*. 7. Denver. 8 . Elstree. 9. Bowls. 10. The Campbells and the Tates. 11. Bing. 12. Bank manager. 13. In a car accident. 14. Liz Dawn (Vera Duckworth). 15. *Neighbours*. 16. Joan Collins. 17. She was shot while trying to save some chicks. 18. Paul. 19. Ida Barlow. 20. Howard Keel. 21. John Altman. 22. Brett and Danni. 23. Will Mellor (Jambo). 24. Mike. 25. Lewis. 26. Sue Ellen. 27. Mel B. 28. *General Hospital*. 29. Emma Samms. 30. Bar Brookie.

ANSWERS

Answers: see Quiz 32, page 240

1. Which naturalist presented *The First Eden*?

2. What did Bette Midler try to get Parkie to do live on TV?

3. GP Barry Brewster was the subject of which series on BBC1?

4. About which islands did Prince Philip present a documentary in the 60s?

5. Who presented *An Englishman's Home*?

6. Which TV celebrity explored *Castles Abroad*?

7. On which mountain did Mick Burke, a BBC cameraman, meet his death?

8. The funeral of which statesperson was the subject of *The Valiant Man*?

9. What is *News At Ten's* claim to fame?

10. Which Labour Shadow Cabinet minister moved to Sky?

11. What was the title of the very first documentary about custom and excise officers?

12. Who introduced *Living With Waltzing Matilda*?

13. Why did ITV fail to show coverage of the Queen's Silver Jubilee?

14. *The Most Dangerous Man In The World* highlighted the events of the assassination attempt on which public figure in 1981?

15. *This Year's Blonde* was about whom?

16. Who was seen on TV making a public speech during a Wembley pop concert in 1990?

17. Which TV presenter sang the hit song *Shifting Whispering Sands*?

18. *Global Village* was presented by who?

19. Muriel Gray hosted which show about fashion?

20. In which year did Judith Chalmers start presenting *Wish You Were Here*?

21. Who presented a series about wine on Channel 4?

22. Who made the mistake of trying to sing an Elvis hit at the end of *Viva Elvis*?

23. Who did Anna Ford replace as a BBC newsreader?

24. Which documentary was about the writer Georges Simenon?

25. Name the sixties early evening programme presented by Simon Dee.

26. Where were cameras allowed for the first time during the Coronation?

27. Which ship featured in *Sailor*?

28. What did celebrity Fred Dibnah do for a living?

29. Which news programme was the first to announce the appointment of Margaret Thatcher as leader of the Conservative Party?

30. On which consumer programme did Esther Rantzen make her TV debut?

Answers: see Quiz 31, page 239

1. Which Goon presented *Highway*?
2. In which series were Oliver and Simon antique dealers?
3. Who presented *Clapperboard*?
4. Who was Chester Tate's wife in *Soap*?
5. How are George Logan and Patrick Fyffe better known?
6. Which early evening programme was presented by Michael Barrett?
7. In *Dangermouse*, what was Penfold's first name?
8. Where do *The Jetsons* live?
9. Which daytime show moved from Liverpool docks to London?
10. Which game show did Jimmy Tarbuck go on to present when he left *Winner Takes All*?
11. Who was William Devane's character in *Knots Landing*?
12. What was Grandma Walton's first name?
13. Who named Lucy Ewing 'The Poison Dwarf'?
14. Which of the cast of *Three Of A Kind* had her own U.S. series?
15. In which series did Liza Goddard take over a captain's role from Una Stubbs?
16. In which series was the local newspaper 'The Daily Slate'?
17. Which series has had three Robinsons as presenters?
18. In which futuristic series was the character Admiral Nelson?
19. What was TV presenter and scientist Dr Pike's christian name?
20. At which sport did presenter Suzanne Dando represent Britain?
21. What was the surname of TV presenters Jess and Paula?
22. Where would you find Dollies and Cue Cards?
23. Which Australian character had a husband Norm?
24. On whose chat show was Harry Stoneham musical director?
25. What was the name of the deputy in *Gun Law*?
26. Which satirist had a hit with *The Ballad Of Spotty Muldoon*?
27. Which actor/singer connects *The Upper Hand* to *Dynasty*?
28. Who played Dr Thorpe in *Only When I Laugh*?
29. In which series was there a detective named Harry Hawkins?
30. Leonard Rossiter played a detective sergeant in which series?

QUIZ 33 # Comedy 6

LEVEL 3

Answers: see Quiz 34, page 242

1. How was William White better known?
2. What is Rebecca's surname in *Cheers*?
3. What was Vivian studying in the *Young Ones*?
4. What was 'Robin's Nest' in the sitcom of the same name?
5. Who created The Baldy Man?
6. Which actress appeared in *Bread* and *A Taste Of Honey*?
7. Who starred as entrepreneur Richard De Vere?
8. Which *Laugh In* star had a UK hit in 1968 with *Here Comes the Judge*?
9. Who played Bishop Len in *Father Ted*?
10. What was the name of Dorien's husband in *Birds Of A Feather*?
11. Which long running comedy series came to an end with the episode *Goodbye, Farewell And Amen*?
12. Which Australian stand up comedian styles himself as the Beige Sensation?
13. In which series did we meet The Phantom Raspberry Blower Of Old London Town?
14. Which comedian opened a folk club called The Boggery in Solihull?
15. Which actor links *It Ain't Half Hot Mum* and *Last Of The Summer Wine*?
16. Who plays Norm in *Cheers*?
17. Noel Dyson appeared as which character in *Father, Dear Father*?
18. Who provided the music on Kenny Everett's *Making Whoopee*?
19. Which pseudonym did Reginald Perrin assume when he attended his own funeral?
20. Where is Frasier's apartment in *Frasier*?
21. What type of car did Joey drive in *Bread*?
22. When *Fawlty Towers* was shown in Spain, what nationality did Manuel become in order not to cause offence?
23. What was Judi Dench's first TV comedy series?
24. Ashley and Elaine were the main characters in which ITV sitcom?
25. Who presented his *Laughter Show*?
26. For whom did the Fonz stand in during the phone marriage to Lori Beth?
27. In total, how many TV series of *Monty Python* were transmitted?
28. In *A Kind Of Living*, The Beasleys came from which town?
29. Johnathan Ross, Mel Smith and Griff Rhys Jones hosted which 1989 telethon?
30. In which US comedy did Corporal Henshaw appear?

ANSWERS

Music & Variety 3 (see Quiz 34)
1. *Love and Fury* (The Tornadoes). 2. 1987. 3. *It's Now Or Never*. 4. Arlene Phillips. 5. *The Hot Shoe Show*. 6. Tom O'Connor. 7. Roy Walker. 8. Middlemiss. 9. *Kiss Me Kate*. 10. Gerorge Chisholm. 11. *Kiss Me Quick*. 12. Benny Hill. 13. Johnny Todd. 14. ATV. 15. Billy Crystal. 16. Doug Ross. 17. Andre Previn. 18. *All Creatures Great And Small*. 19. Andy Williams. 20. Janice Nicholls. 21. Madge. 22. *The Generation Game*. 23. Bob Monkhouse. 24. *Strike It Lucky*. 25. Paul Shane and Bob Monkhouse. 26. Peter Cushing. 27. Paul Daniels. 28. David Copperfield. 29. Billy Smart's. 30. Gheorghe Zamfir.

Answers: see Quiz 33, page 241

1. What was the original theme tune of *Juke Box Jury*?
2. In which year did the BBC remove *Whistle Test* from their schedule?
3. The tune of which Elvis song was used to sell ice cream?
4. Who founded the dance group, *Hot Gossip*?
5. Bonnie Langford was the lead female dancer in which TV show?
6. Who presented *Wednesday Night At Eight*?
7. Which of The Comedians hosted a quiz show featuring popular sayings?
8. Which Jayne presents the *O-Zone*?
9. What was the first musical film shown on BBC2?
10. Which trombonist featured in a comedy spot on *The Black And White Minstrel Show*?
11. Which Elvis record did The Beatles predict a hit when they appeared on *Juke Box Jury* in 1963?
12. Whose creation was Fred Scuttle?
13. Which folk song was the basis for the famous theme tune to *Z Cars*?
14. Which ITV company presented *Saturday Spectacular*?
15. Who hosted the 1998 Academy Award Show from Hollywood?
16. Who was judged by Radio Times as the sexiest male TV doctor?
17. Which composer appeared with Morecambe and Wise on Christmas Day 1971?
18. Which series was voted by Radio Times readers The Best TV Drama Of All Time in 1998?
19. Whose popular shows introduced British audiences to *The Osmonds*?
20. Whose catchphrase on *Thank Your Lucky Stars* was "Oi'll give it foive"?
21. Which *Neighbours* character appeared with Dame Edna Everage?
22. Which show features a conveyor belt of prizes?
23. Which game show host did we have *An Audience with..?*
24. 'Hot Spots' are a feature on which game show?
25. Who sang the theme music for *You Rang M'Lord*?
26. Which horror actor worried about being paid as a guest on Morecambe and Wise?
27. Whose magic show featured 'The Bunko Booth'?
28. Which comic has the same name as a Dickens character?
29. Which circus was a television holiday favourite?
30. Who recorded Doina De Jale, the theme song for *Light of Experience*?

Answers: see Quiz 36, page 244

1. Which female character was shot in the Queen Vic but survived?
2. In *Eastenders*, who was imprisoned for embezzlement?
3. Which former *Coronation Street* actress was mayoress of her home town Blackburn?
4. Who owns the video shop in *Hollyoaks*?
5. Who was cast as Amanda Woodward in *Melrose Place*?
6. Name the former *Eastenders* female star who also appeared in *Get Well Soon*.
7. Which actor played Jim Robinson in *Neighbours*?
8. Which soap star produced a fitness video called *Rapid Results*?
9. Todd Carty plays which soap character?
10. Which former *Emmerdale* star has also been *Doctor Who*'s assistant?
11. Name the author of *The Thorn Birds*.
12. What was the nickname of Dirty Den's cellmate?
13. Which soap based in a fashion house has a valuable sounding title?
14. Which *Last Of The Summer Wine* actress appeared as Doris Luke in *Crossroads*?
15. What was Ian Bleasdale's character in *Take The High Road*?
16. In *Angels*, who starred as Nurse Jo Longhurst?
17. Which *EastEnders* star recorded *Subterranean Homesick Blues*?
18. Which Avenger appeared in *Coronation Street*?
19. Exactly how many episodes of the short-lived BBC soap, *Eldorado*, were broadcast?
20. Which BBC soap commenced in 1985?
21. What is the marital connection between Pat Wicks and Cathy Mitchell?
22. In which soap did Alec Baldwin find fame?
23. Which Queen did the Street's Alma Baldwin portray on film?
24. Who was Sue Ellen's sister in *Dallas*?
25. Who had an affair with both David and Simon Wicks?
26. Sophia Loren was reputedly the first choice for which role in *Dynasty*?
27. Who in *Coronation Street* had a star named after his wife?
28. Which former star of *Brookside* played Poppy Bruce in *Emmerdale*?
29. Which Albert was Valerie Barlow's uncle in *Coronation Street*?
30. Which *Dynasty* star duetted with Bing Crosby on *Let's Not Be Sensible* in 1962?

Pot Luck 8 (see Quiz 36)

1. Varley. 2. Maddie. 3. Michael Grade. 4. The Academy Awards. 5. Bessie. 6. Niece.
7. Psychiatrist. 8. Diane Keen. 9. The High Street. 10. Paul Merton. 11. Newcastle. 12. Chief
O'Brien. 13. Jaye Griffiths. 14. Les Dennis. 15. Miranda. 16. *The Dick Van Dyke Show*. 17. *Local
Heroes*. 18. Nancy Bartlett. 19. Harriet Thorpe. 20. *The Simpsons*. 21. *Kiss Kiss Bang Bang*.
22. Channel 4. 23. Sebastian. 24. American Football. 25. *A Grand Day Out*. 26. Wishbone.
27. *King Of The Hill*. 28. Antiques, including toys and teddy bears. 29. Anthony Newley. 30. Peter
Dimmock.

QUIZ 36 Pot Luck 8

Answers: see Quiz 35, page 243

LEVEL 3

1. What was the chimney sweep's name in *Camberwick Green*?
2. Who was Alex and Virginia Hayes' daughter?
3. Which former Head of Channel 4 was born on the same day as Lynn Redgrave?
4. Billy Crystal won an Emmy in 1998 for hosting which annual event?
5. What was the name of Lord Belborough's steam engine in *Chigley*?
6. What relation, if any, is *Bramwell* star Jemma Redgrave to actress Vanessa Redgrave?
7. What was Lilith Crane's profession in *Cheers*?
8. Who was the *Foxy Lady* played by?
9. Where did Helen give birth in *The Brittas Empire*?
10. Whose show had a regular sketch set in a newsagent and tobacconist's kiosk in an Underground station?
11. Kate Adie is a former student of which university?
12. Who was the Head Engineer on *Star Trek: Next Generation*?
13. Which star of *Bugs* played D.I. Sally Johnson in *The Bill*?
14. How is TV presenter Leslie Heseltine better known?
15. What is the name of Hollin and Shelly's baby in *Northern Exposure*?
16. In which 60's sitcom did Richard Deacon play Mel Cooley?
17. Which series featured Adam Hart Davis seeking out inventors and inventions?
18. What was Sandra Bernhardt's character in *Roseanne*?
19. Who played Fleur in *Absolutely Fabulous*?
20. Side Show Bob featured in which cartoon series?
21. Which cinema magazine programme was presented by Charlie Higson?
22. On which channel was the motoring series *Driven* transmitted?
23. What is Rowan Atkinson's middle name?
24. Bill Cosby was offered a professional trial in which sport?
25. In which episode did Wallace and Grommit go to the moon?
26. Who was Paul Brinegar's character in *Rawhide*?
27. In which cartoon series are the neighbours called 'Khan'?
28. What kind of expert is Bunny Campione?
29. Which actor, singer, songwriter made a guest appearance in *Eastenders* as a used car dealer?
30. Who was the original presenter of *Sportsview*?

Answers: see Quiz 38, page 246

1. Where was *Tumbledown* set?
2. In *Bonanza* what was the name of Adam's horse?
3. What was the name of the TV series of the works of Jean-Paul Sartre?
4. In which city was *St Elsewhere* set?
5. In country was *The Regiment* set?
6. *The Fugitive* was inspired by which Victor Hugo novel?
7. What was Dame Peggy Ashcroft's character in *The Far Pavilions*?
8. Name the first Western series to be transmitted in full colour.
9. In which series about gambling did the Dragon Club feature?
10. Who wrote the novel *Anna Karenina*, adapted for TV in 1961?
11. Who played Chrissie's wife in *Boys From The Blackstuff*?
12. What was the first name of the butler in *Upstairs, Downstairs*?
13. Which town was featured in *Sunset Strip*?
14. Who wrote *Lace*?
15. Who starred in *Luke's Kingdom*?
16. What is the character Harry Lime better known as?
17. Robert Powell played which John Buchan creation on TV?
18. Which role did David Suchet play in Reilly Ace of Spies?
19. What was the name of the chimp on *Fantasy Island*?
20. Who starred as the *Mayor of Casterbridge*?
21. Who had *Have Gun Will Travel* printed on business cards?
22. Which 70's drama showed a Russian doll in its opening credits?
23. *The Onedin Line* was set in which city?
24. Who starred opposite Timothy Dalton in *Sins*?
25. How much money did Ken Masters win in a power boat race in *Howard's Way*?
26. What royal adornment featured at the start of each episode of *An Age Of Kings*?
27. What was the title of the BBC series dramatising the life of Lewis Carroll?
28. Who in *The Winds of War* was nicknamed 'Pug'?
29. The play series *Armchair Theatre* began life on BBC. With which TV company did its existence end in 1974?
30. Who starred as Sarah in *Upstairs, Downstairs*?

Answers: see Quiz 37, page 245

LEVEL 3

1. Who was responsible for sport on *Saturday Superstore*?
2. What is the main colour of the Dukes' car, the General Lee?
3. In which series did Mr Turnip appear?
4. On which mountains was the 1950s series *William Tell* made?
5. Which cartoon character says "Heavens to Murgatroyd"?
6. What was the name of the pet tortoise on *Blue Peter*?
7. Whose arch enemy is Grotbags?
8. Who starred in *The Storyteller*?
9. In *Fun House* how was the discovery of a star prize announced?
10. Which TV celebrity hosted *Wizbit*?
11. Who managed the *Partridge Family*?
12. Whose friends are Henry and Gordon?
13. In which year did *Sooty* first appear on TV?
14. In *The Muppets* who was the original voice of Miss Piggy?
15. In *Mork and Mindy*, what was the Orkan expression for 'Goodbye'?
16. Whose barrel organ provided the theme music for *The Magic Roundabout*?
17. According to the theme music, Davy Crockett was born a mountain in which state?
18. Which cartoon character is "the biggest clown in town"?
19. Who was the seventh Dr Who?
20. Which TV hero had a friend called Bear?
21. Which two cartoon characters attended Bedrock High School?
22. Where does Captain Ze live?
23. What was the name of *Tarzan*'s orphan friend?
24. What was the name of the seal in *Stingray*?
25. What musically links *William Tell* and the *Lone Ranger*?
26. In *Terrahawks*, of which planet was Zelda the Imperial Queen?
27. Who sang the theme for *Davy Crockett*?
28. Who sang the theme song for *Robin Hood* in the 1950s?
29. Which house was located in Minnesota?
30. Ace reporter Huxley was what animal?

LEVEL 3

Answers: see Quiz 40, page 248

1. *Car 54* was based at which New York precinct police station?
2. Who grasped his ears before transmitting back to his planet?
3. The US comedy, *Tabatha*, was a short-lived spin-off of which other series?
4. Which actress connects *Man About The House* with the game show *Crazy Companions*?
5. What is Bill and Ben's surname in *Two Point Four Children*?
6. Which actor connects *Poldark* and the comedy *Dear John*?
7. Which ostentatious character did Peter Blake play in *Dear John*?
8. Robert Llewellyn played the part of a robot with a conscience in which series?
9. Who made a guest appearance as the Duke of Wellington in *Blackadder The Third*?
10. In which sitcom would you find the Cafe Nervosa?
11. Which house did Hester and William rent in *French Fields*?
12. Within which show did *The Fresh Prince of Bel Air* appear in the UK?
13. Who played Phoebe's twin sister Ursula in *Friends*?
14. What was Bernard Hedges' nickname in *Please Sir*?
15. Who was Jethro's sister in *The Beverley Hillbillies*?
16. Name Bilko's camp commandant at Fort Baxter.
17. Who was the pianist in *It Ain't Half Hot Mum*?
18. What were the names of the female characters played by Les Dawson and Roy Barraclough?
19. Who played the harrassed mother in *The Cabbage Patch*?
20. What was the name of the doctor played by Robin Nedwell In *Doctors In The House*?
21. Which of the *Golden Girls* played Sly Stallone's mother?
22. The *Three Of A Kind* trio consisted of Lenny Henry, Tracy Ullman and who else?
23. Who links *Do Not Adjust Your Set* with *Open All Hours*?
24. Who appeared in both *Porridge* and *Fraggle Rock*?
25. Fred Gwynne starred in which police comedy?
26. Who starred in the comedy *Atmosphere*?
27. In *Happy Days* who belonged to the Leopards Lodge?
28. Which TV comic politician had a wife called Sarah?
29. George Logan is better known as which female comic?
30. Who was the comedienne behind Gayle Tuesday?

QUIZ 40 Sci - Fi 2

LEVEL 3

Answers: see Quiz 39, page 247

1. Who was Broomfondle's colleague in *The Hitchhiker's Guide to the Galaxy*?
2. Which ship had a subservient computer called Slave?
3. When Lister tried to install Kochanski's holodisc in *Red Dwarf*, what happened?
4. Which system in *Babylon 5* was known for being a place where First Ones lurked?
5. What terrorist organisation did *Voyager's* Commander Chakotay belong to?
6. Along with Frohike and Byers, who completes the Lone Gunmen?
7. Who was the American star of *UFO*?
8. Who was the technician who aided *Sapphire & Steel* in two adventures?
9. Who did Roy Thinnes play?
10. What race was Odo in *Star Trek: Deep Space Nine*?
11. Who played Wilma Deering?
12. What needed to be special about Sydney's computer in *VR5* to let her enter her dreamlike virtual worlds?
13. Who played Starbuck in *Battlestar Galactica*?
14. In which series were alien bodies found during the excavation for an Underground extension?
15. What designation did Richard Mayhew eventually earn in *Neverwhere*?
16. What was the name of the reporter investigating *The Incredible Hulk*?
17. The Enterprise is which class of starship?
18. *Lois and Clark* is the sequel to which series?
19. How old was *Doctor Who* supposed to be?
20. What was the name of Jack's jilted wife-to-be in *Ultraviolet*?
21. In *Land Of The Giants*, what was the name of the dog?
22. What colour was also the name of Captain Scarlett's boss?
23. In *The Day of the Triffids*, what blinded most of the population?
24. Who did *Joe 90* work for?
25. What was Stringfellow Hawke's brother called?
26. Who was finally revealed to be *The Prisoner's* Number One?
27. Which goddess is Hercules' most dedicated enemy?
28. In *TekWar*, what is Tek?
29. Who was Steve Zodiac's girlfriend?
30. Like KITT, *Knight Rider* Michael Knight had an evil double. What was his name?

QUIZ 41   Pot Luck 9

Answers: see Quiz 42, page 249

1. Which ex-PM was born on the same day as Python Eric Idle?
2. Richard Wilson aka Victor Meldrew was awarded an honorary doctorate by which university?
3. What is the theme for *Blue Peter* called?
4. Who did Griff Rhys Jones replace in the *Not The Nine O'clock News* team?
5. What was the name of Brian Wilde's character in *Porridge*?
6. Which 'Man Behaving Badly' narrated *Red-Handed*?
7. Who links *Scrapheap* to *Red Dwarf*?
8. Who presented the quiz show *Pass The Buck*?
9. What does Mark Freden talk about on *GMTV*?
10. Which US comedienne has her own C5 chat show?
11. Who on Channel 5 is *The Antique Hunter*?
12. How is Ray Burns better known?
13. Who said 'What a beautiful pair of knockers' on *Blue Peter*?
14. Who presented *Bookworm*?
15. Melanie and Martina Grant assist Pat Sharp on which game show?
16. Mike Yarwood had soccer trials with which clubs?
17. Which former page 3 girl presented the game show *Fort Boyard*?
18. Which Gladiator produced a fitness video called *Summer Circuit*?
19. Joanna Lumley and Jennifer Saunders were asked to edit which UK magazine?
20. Which medal did commentator Kenneth Wolstenhulme win in WWII?
21. What was the subject of the *Grange Hill* song *Just Say No*?
22. Who played a womanising PR man in the 70s sitcom *Casanova*?
23. What was Miriam Stoppard's profession?
24. Who originally was the voice of Mr. Kipling in the cake ads?
25. What was the name of the series where Robbie Coltrane was a Majestic?
26. Which TV star duetted with Barbra Streisand on *Till I Loved You* in 1988?
27. Which actor has played Captain Hillio, Butler and The Governor in Doctor Who?
28. Which financial programme was presented by Maya Even?
29. Who had a ventriloquist's dummy named Chuck?
30. What kind of food was advertised by Alf Roberts?

Answers: see Quiz 41, page 249

1. Where was ITV's first soap *Sixpenny Corner* set?
2. Which *Dallas* star was born the same day as musician Stephen Stills?
3. Who married Mike Baldwin in 1990 in *Coronation Street*?
4. Which *Home and Away* star recorded *Love and Kisses*?
5. In which soap did Ellen Burstyn find fame?
6. Which EastEnder once played Mrs Eckersley in *Emmerdale*?
7. Who did Irma Ogden marry in *Coronation Street*?
8. Which part did Gandhi star Ben Kingsley play in *Coronation Street*?
9. Which *Eastenders* actress became Mrs Nick Love in 1998?
10. Which ex-soap star played Christine Keeler's mother in the movie *Scandal*?
11. Why did Victoria move to the Rovers Return in *Coronation Street*?
12. Which former *Emmerdale* star played Harry Hawkins in *Softly Softly*?
13. Which character did Patricia Brake play in *Eldorado*?
14. Which future soap star became the youngest winner of *New Faces* when she won in the mid 70s?
15. Who did Frank Barlow work for?
16. 'Sugar La Marr' in *Coronation Street* went on to play whom in *Bread*?
17. Ross Davidson alias Andy in *EastEnders* was an international in which sport?
18. Which ex-Albert Square favourite wrote a book *My East End*?
19. With whom did Eddie Yeats lodge in *Coronation Street*?
20. Which Street actress's real name is Shirley Ann Broadbent?
21. Who has played Al Simpson in *Home & Away*, and Doug Willis in *Neighbours*?
22. What was surname of *Neighbours* doctor Clive?
23. Which star of *Dallas* was a singer with the Seattle Opera?
24. Which father and daughter appeared in *Coronation Street* in 1998 as father in law and daughter in law?
25. What sort of toys does Peter Baldwin, once Derek Wilton, collect?
26. In *Neighbours* who originally played Scott Robinson?
27. Which Dr Who assistant turned up in an Italian restaurant in Walford?
28. Which ex *Brookside* actress's autobiography was called *Hold on to the Messy Times*?
29. Which *Heartbeat* star played Mickey Malone in *Coronation Street*?
30. Who was Paul Robinson's second wife in *Neighbours*?

Answers: see Quiz 44, page 252

1. *Hadleigh* was set in which county?
2. What was Anthony Quayle's character in *The Strange Report*?
3. Which character's residence was Melford Park?
4. Why was the *Big Breadwinner Hog* removed from the screens in 1969?
5. Which character did Nyree Dawn Porter play in *The Forsythe Saga*?
6. What was *The Prisoner's* number?
7. Which secret agent featured in *Wet Job* in 1981?
8. Who starred as Napoleon Solo?
9. In which drama did an antiques dealer lead a double life as a secret agent?
10. Who wrote the pilot for *London's Burning* but not the series which followed?
11. Name the BBC's twice weekly drama which was the first made by them in colour.
12. How many of Rockcliffe's Babies were female?
13. Which *Upstairs, Downstairs* star was the real life wife of Dr Who Jon Pertwee?
14. Which actor, famous as Fagin in *Oliver!* has starred in *The Avengers*?
15. Who played Lola Lasagne in the *Batman* TV series?
16. Which actress who played *Moll Flanders* in the 90s once starred in *Grange Hill*?
17. Which series was based on *Butch Cassidy and the Sundance Kid*?
18. Which comic went straight in *One Fine Day*?
19. Which Dame starred as Queen Mary in *Edward And Mrs Simpson*?
20. What was the follow-up series to *Bouquet Of Barbed Wire*?
21. Which TV doctor lived in Tannochbrae?
22. What did Hine do for a living?
23. What Fleet Street first was played by Francesca Annis in *Inside Story*?
24. What did Glenda Jackson have done to her hair in order to play Queen Elizabeth I?
25. *Wagontrain* was a spin-off of which film?
26. Who helped save Douglas Motors in the 80s?
27. *Lou Grant* was Editor of which newspaper?
28. Who did Peter Egan play in *Lillie*?
29. Which group of soldiers was imprisoned in Stalag 13?
30. Which drama commemorated the 20th anniversary of JFK's death?

QUIZ 44 Comedy 8

LEVEL 3

Answers: see Quiz 43, page 251

1. In which US comedy did the characters Lenny and Squiggy appear?
2. In *Mr Ed*, what did the horse always call Wilbur?
3. Whose catchphrase was 'Say goodnight Gracie'?
4. Who played the lodger in *Goodbye Mr Kent*?
5. Which ex Goodie was born on the same day as Michael Howard?
6. Who presented the comic play *The Fly*, in which the genes of a hooligan were mixed with those of a video director?
7. In *Please Sir* what was the name of the headmaster?
8. Benny Hill made an appearance in which comic musical film about a car?
9. Whose daughter was Clare in *After Henry*?
10. Which comic starred in *Bingo Madness*?
11. Sergeant Bilko's first name was what?
12. What was Blanche's surname in *The Golden Girls*?
13. John Cleese was awarded an honorary doctorate of which university?
14. David Jason married Gwen Taylor in which comedy?
15. Who starred in *Split Ends*?
16. What is the name of Dame Edna's husband?
17. *Comic Relief* was first televised in which year?
18. Which gang did the Fonz belong to?
19. Which of the *Goodies* had a starring role in *The Bubblegum Brigade*?
20. Name *Deputy Dawg's* two sidekicks.
21. What was the name of *Monty Python's* giant hedgehog?
22. Who played Alf's son-in-law?
23. Which comedian wrote the autobiography *Sweet And Sour Labrador*?
24. Which *Last Of The Summer Wine* star appeared in *No Frills*?
25. Which comic/writer/presenter appeared naked in *Who Dares Win*?
26. Which comic series was banned from caricaturing Mickey Mouse?
27. From which service had Harvey been demobbed at the start of *Shine On Harvey Moon*?
28. In which 1980s comedy did the Dinky Doos feature?
29. Which comedian has four initials, J.P.M.S?
30. In which year did Ronnie Barker retire from TV?

ANSWERS

Drama 6 (see Quiz 43)

1. Yorkshire. 2. Adam Strange. 3. Haleigh's. 4. Due to complaints of excessive violence. 5. Irene. 6. Six. 7. Callan. 8. Robert Vaughan. 9. *The Baron*. 10. Jack Rosenthal. 11. *The Doctors*. 12. Two. 13. Jean Marsh. 14. Ron Moody. 15. Ethel Merman. 16. Alex Kingston. 17. *Alias Smith And Jones*. 18. Dave Allen. 19. Dame Peggy Ashcroft. 20. *Another Bouquet*. 21. Dr Finlay. 22. Arms salesman. 23. Fleet Street's first female editor. 24. It was shaved. 25. *Wagonmaster*. 26. *The Chancer* (Steven Crane). 27. The Los Angeles Tribune. 28. Oscar Wilde. 29. *Hogan's Heroes*. 30. *Kennedy*.

LEVEL 3

Answers: see Quiz 46, page 254

1. Who walked out on an interview with David Dimbleby when asked about royalties from an autobiography?
2. Robin Hall and Jimmie MacGregor were singers on which current affairs programme?
3. Cliff Michelmore first presented *Holiday* in which year?
4. Shortly after commentating on which state occasion did Richard Dimbleby die?
5. Who travelled around the world to present the documentary series *Civilisation*?
6. What was newsreader Anna Ford's claim to fame?
7. Which two newsreaders presented the very first *News At Ten*?
8. What did *Omnibus* replace as BBC's arts programme?
9. How did Frank Muir describe Joan Bakewell?
10. Which Scottish pop star had his own chat show in the early 1980s?
11. What did Reginald Bosanquet's father invent in the sporting world?
12. What was *News Review*'s claim to fame when it was introduced in the mid-60s?
13. Which crimestopper is known as *Whispering Grass*?
14. Which BBC news programme was first broadcast in 1953?
15. What did Grace Jones hit Russell Harty with on his show?
16. Who succeeded Brian Walden as presenter of *Weekend World*?
17. Name the documentary made by Granada about the Beatles' visit to New York.
18. *Fame Is The Spur* featured which political party?
19. From which hospital was *Hospital* broadcast?
20. What was *This Week* renamed for one year in its 30+ year run?
21. What kind of shop did newsreader Kenneth Kendall open on retiring from TV?
22. What was Robert McKenzie's very last political documentary before he died?
23. Which presenter was a co-founder of *TV-AM*?
24. What was the name of the mini-series about Martin Luther King?
25. *The Rough Guide* travel series formed part of which BBC2 programme?
26. *The Stars* was the sequel to which series?
27. Trevor McDonald was awarded an honorary doctorate of which university?
28. To whom did Prince Charles admit he spoke to plants?
29. Who won an award for her reports from Libya?
30. Why was Prince Edward in the headlines in 1987?

Answers: see Quiz 45, page 253

1. Chris Tarrant was born on the same day as which star of *The Jewel in the Crown*?
2. *Stars and Garters* featured which female singing star?
3. Angus Deayton had a soccer trial with which club?
4. Which Dr Who served on HMS Hood in WWII?
5. Which 1960s western series featured a stern wheel paddle steamer?
6. What was Sonny Jim's real name in *Coronation Street*?
7. Which Australian singer appeared in *The Newcomers*?
8. Who was the scout in *Wagon Train*?
9. Which *Mastermind* drove a train for the London Underground?
10. On which day did *Watch with Mother* feature *Andy Pandy*?
11. Who played Jodie Foster's father in *Paper Moon*?
12. Which duo co-wrote and starred in *Chelmsford 123*?
13. Whose neighbours were Fred and Ethel?
14. Who is taller – Jill Dando or Claire Rayner?
15. Which TV comedian had the number plate COM 1C?
16. Which *Neighbours* actor appeared in the film *L.A. Confidential*?
17. If Christopher Connelly was Norman who played Rodney?
18. Which luxury did Esther Rantzen choose on *Desert Island Discs*?
19. Actor Robert Brown appeared as which spymaster on film?
20. Which Italian Countess hosted the Eurovision Song Contest?
21. What was Thora Hird's autobiography called?
22. In which soap was there a character named George Holloway?
23. Who wore pink bow ties on *Call My Bluff*?
24. Which cowboy had the surname Layne?
25. Who composed the music for *Victory At Sea*?
26. What was *Honey Lane*?
27. Which of her possessions did Janet Street Porter sell at auction in 1997?
28. What was the alternative name of the television western series *Sugarfoot*?
29. Which soccer side does actor Robert Lindsay support?
30. Which giant actor appeared in *The Army Game*?

Answers: see Quiz 48, page 256

1. What was the name of *Rupert Bear*'s elephant friend?
2. What was the first children's programme on BBC2?
3. In which city did *Ollie Beak* live?
4. Which Western star always wore a black hat?
5. Which ranch did Gene Autry own?
6. On which river did the town of Tickle lie?
7. Who always ended shows with the words "Bye, bye, everyone. Bye, bye"?
8. In which country was *Elephant Boy* set?
9. Who commanded *Stingray*?
10. Why breed of dog was *Scooby Doo*?
11. Who created the *Cisco Kid*?
12. Which legendary pirate's girlfriend was called Peggetty?
13. Who spoke the language Oddle Poddle?
14. Which adversaries of the Suntots cause pollution?
15. In which comedy were the Kravitzes the next door neighbours?
16. On which island did the Doozers reside?
17. Kissyfur was what kind of animal?
18. What was the name of Gomez Addam's pet octopus?
19. Which superheroine "makes them look like a bunch of fairies"?
20. Which ex-pop singer presented *Puddle Lane*?
21. What does Fred Flintstone wear on his feet?
22. Which London tourist attraction did a *Blue Peter* presenter once climb on TV?
23. Which rap artist was the first to have a cartoon series?
24. What did Davy Crockett call his rifle?
25. Who did the Soup Dragon live with?
26. In the *A-Team,* what was Face's real name?
27. Who wrote about *Eric the Viking*?
28. Which children's TV presenter was lead singer with Kenny?
29. Which soccer side does Timmy Mallett support?
30. Who made up the *Space Sentinels* with Mercury and Astria?

LEVEL 3

Answers: see Quiz 47, page 255

1. In *Coronation Street* what was Eddie Yeats' C.B. handle?
2. In which hospital is *The Young Doctors* set?
3. Which soccer side does Liz Dawn – alias Vera Duckworth – support?
4. Where is *A Country Practice* located?
5. Which *Neighbours* actress played Rosie in *Sons And Daughters*?
6. What was Maggie Clegg's husband's name in *Coronation Street*?
7. Who did Stan Harvey marry in *Crossroads*?
8. What did Philip Martin do for a living when he first appeared in *Neighbours*?
9. In *Coronation Street* who had a sister Debbie who moved to Southampton?
10. Which *Neighbours* character was engaged to Shane Ramsey?
11. How was Clive dressed when he almost sabotaged Des and Daphne's wedding in *Neighbours*?
12. What was J.R. Ewing's number plate on his car?
13. Who divorced Audrey in *Coronation Street* because of her affair with Ray Langton?
14. Who had a sister Maggie in *Coronation Street*?
15. Who stabbed Ray Krebbs in *Dallas* in 1988?
16. What was Rachel's surname in *Eastenders*?
17. What was Hattie Tavernier's mother's name in *Eastenders*?
18. Who ran the grocery side of the post office & corner shop in *Coronation Street*?
19. Who sent a rude valentine card to a teacher in *Brookside*?
20. Who in *Eastenders* visited Jan to persuade her not to see Dennis Watts again?
21. Who in *Eastenders* inherited the laundrette in 1992?
22. Who occupied a flat in the same premises as Alan & Jenny Bradley in *Coronation Street*?
23. Who did the electrical wiring that caused the fire at *Coronation Street's* Rovers Return?
24. In *Coronation Street* what business did Maggie Dunlop own?
25. In *Eastenders* who tried to sabotage Ozcabs?
26. In *Neighbours* who was Joan Langdon's fiancee?
27. Who did Saheed make obscene phone calls to in *Eastenders*?
28. Which star of *Dallas* appeared in *The Eagle Has Landed*?
29. Who links *Space Precinct* to *Knot's Landing*?
30. On which day did Mark Fowler in *Eastenders* tell his parents that he was HIV positive?

Answers: see Quiz 50, page 258

1. Of which Gang Show was Jim Davidson formerly a member?
2. Which actress starred in *Piggy In The Middle*?
3. *Let's Be Frank* starred who in the title role?
4. Which comic actress had an imaginary friend called Marlene?
5. Harry H Corbett owned a corner shop in which TV series?
6. Who plays the word-confounding policeman in *'Allo, 'Allo*?
7. *Please Sir* was set in which area of London?
8. Which patriot had pictures of the Queen and Winston Churchill hanging on his wall?
9. Which soccer side does comedian Bernard Manning support?
10. Which star of *Yes, Minister* was a conscientious objector in WWII?
11. Which actor, famous for a successful sitcom, released a solo album *What Is Going to Become of Us All* in1976?
12. Which part of his body has Dave Allen lost part of?
13. Who played Milo O'Shea's mother in *Me Mammy*?
14. Who played Alf Garnett's wife?
15. Jane Asher competed for the same man with Felicity Kendal in which series?
16. On whose show did Susie Butcher play the muddled anchor woman?
17. What number was Bilko's Formula to remove wrinkles?
18. In the 1970s remake of the *Rag Trade* who took Reg Varney's original part?
19. In *Watching* which male character's surname was Stoneway?
20. Bob Buzzard was a doctor in which BBC comic series?
21. What kind of restaurant was above the *Cheers* bar?
22. Who played Fletcher's wife?
23. What colour was Adrian Edmondson's hair in the *Young Ones*?
24. What is the name of *Monty Python's* theme music?
25. Who did the *Auf Wiedersehn Pet* gang call Erics?
26. Which male comic starred in *Going Gently*?
27. Who were the first two *Ab Fab* stars to appear on *Friends*?
28. Carol Royle and Simon Cadell starred together in which comedy?
29. In which US comedy did Potsie feature?
30. Which actress did Anton Rodgers marry in *Fresh Fields*?

ANSWERS

Pot Luck 11 (see Quiz 50)
1. *Cyborg.* 2. Martin Bell. 3. Dutch. 4. Gibbons. 5. Martin Clunes. 6. *We Can Work It Out.*
7. Bernadette O'Farrell. 8. Brenda Blethyn. 9. Aviation. 10. *Dempsey and Makepiece.* 11. Jimmy Tarbuck. 12. Robert Wightman. 13. *Lou Grant.* 14. The Brick. 15. Oasis Publishing. 16. Leonard Nimoy. 17. Gloria Hunniford. 18. Wolverhampton. 19. Alessi. 20. Joan Greenwood. 21. Jerry Stevens. 22. Penelope Keith. 23. Jonathan Dimbleby. 24. Mike Smith. 25. Commander Chakotay. 26. *Brookside.* 27. Squadron Leader Rex. 28. Luton Town. 29. World Illustrated. 30. Beavis and Butthead.

QUIZ 50 Pot Luck 11

Answers: see Quiz 49, page 257

1. Which book was the basis for *The Six Million Dollar Man*?
2. Which former BBC war correspondent became an MP?
3. What nationality was Carla, played by Kylie Minogue, in *The Sullivans*?
4. What is chat show host Leeza's surname?
5. Which star narrated the *Rottentrolls*?
6. Which consumer programme was presented by Judy Finnegan?
7. Who was the first actress to play Maid Marian in *The Adventures Of Robin Hood*?
8. Who starred in *The Labours Of Erica*?
9. What was the subject of the 1980 series *Diamonds In The Sky*?
10. In which series did Tony Osoba play Det. Sgt. Chas Jarvis?
11. Who presented *Winner Takes All*?
12. Who succeeded Richard Thomas as John Boy in *The Waltons*?
13. In which 80's US series was there a photographer named Dennis 'The Animal' Price?
14. What is the name of Holling's bar in *Northern Exposure*?
15. What was the name of the publishing company in *Executive Stress*?
16. Who played The Great Paris in *Mission Impossible*?
17. Which Irish presenter shares a birth date with Bobby Hatfield of *The Righteous Brothers*?
18. Sue Lawley was awarded an honorary doctorate by which university?
19. Gayle and Gillian Blakeney played which twins in *Neighbours*?
20. Who played the landlady in *Girls On Top*?
21. Who was the host of *TV Quiz*?
22. Who played a lady MP in *No Job For A Lady*?
23. Which Dimbleby presented *First Tuesday*?
24. Who hosted *The Funny Side*?
25. Who is second in command of the Voyager in *Star Trek: Voyager*?
26. Presenter Paula Yates made a guest appearance in which soap?
27. Who did Tim Woodward play in *A Piece Of Cake*?
28. Which soccer side does Nick Owen, formerly of Good Morning With Anne and Nick, support?
29. Which fictional magazine featured in *Shirley's World*?
30. Who duetted with Cher on *I Got You Babe* in 1994?

ANSWERS

Comedy 9 (see Quiz 49)

1. *Ralph Reader's Gang Show*. 2. Liza Goddard. 3. Frankie Howerd. 4. Beryl Reid. 5. Grundy. 6. Arthur Bostram. 7. The East End. 8. Alf Garnett. 9. Manchester City. 10. Paul Eddington. 11. Jon Le Mesurier. 12. Finger. 13. Anna Manahan. 14. Dandy Nicholls. 15. *The Mistress*. 16. Victoria Wood's. 17. Formula 7. 18. Christopher Beeny. 19. Malcolm's. 20. *A Very Peculiar Practice*. 21. A seafood restaurant. 22. Patricia Brake. 23. Orange. 24. Liberty Bell. 25. Germans. 26. Norman Wisdom. 27. Jennifer Saunders and June Whitfield. 28. *Living Without George*. 29. *Happy Days*. 30. Julia McKenzie.

LEVEL 3

Answers: see Quiz 52, page 260

1. In *King's Royal*, what was the company producing?
2. In *The Rockford Files* how much did Jim Rockford charge per day?
3. What was the name of James Bolam's character in *When The Boat Comes In*?
4. Which actor portrayed Disraeli in *Edward The Seventh*?
5. Which series based on Arnold Bennett's work was ITV's longest-running drama in 1976?
6. What sort of journalist was Lytton in *Lytton's Diary*?
7. Which part did John Hurt take in *I, Claudius*?
8. In *Roots*, which part was played by John Amos?
9. *Spend, Spend, Spend* told the story of which football pools winner?
10. What happened to *The Professionals* in the very last episode?
11. Who starred as Moses in the 1970's?
12. Jeremy Irons, Christopher Blake and Peter Davison vied for the attentions of Mel Martin in which 70s adaptation of an H E Bates novel?
13. Who requested changes to the script of *Tumbledown*?
14. In which state was *Laramie* set?
15. What was the Manageress's name as played by Cherie Lunghi?
16. Where did Frank and Tessa marry in *Love Hurts*?
17. In which women's prison was *Within These Walls* set?
18. Who published *Nanny* under a male pseudonym?
19. In *First Among Equals* which political party were elected to power?
20. Which character did Francesca Annis play in *Edward VII* and another 70s series with her name in the title?
21. Which moviestar of the late 90s played Pte. Mick Hopper in *Lipstick on Your Collar*?
22. In which country was *Fields of Fire* set?
23. Who played Anthony Blunt on TV?
24. What was the name of Leslie Grantham's character in *The Paradise Club*?
25. Who portrayed Donald Campbell in *Across The Lake*?
26. Which actress found a cream cracker under her settee in *Talking Heads*?
27. Which family did Mrs Bridges cook for?
28. Which political figure was played on TV by Faye Dunaway?
29. Which *Blue Peter* presenter appeared in *Fallen Hero*?
30. How long was Marlon Brando's appearance in *Roots, The Next Generation*?

Crime 1 (see Quiz 52)

1. Galloway. 2. Darren McGavin. 3. Chief Superintendent. 4. Dave Creegan. 5. Superintendent Albert Tyburn. 6. Amanda Donohoe. 7. Sparta. 8. Chicago. 9. Amanda Redman. 10. *Miami Vice*. 11. Cousin Tel. 12. Iolani Palace. 13. David Lynch. 14. *Highway Patrol.* 15. Kevin McNally. 16. *Cracker.* 17. Noel Harrison. 18. Sylvia Costas 19. John Creasey. 20. A blue lamp. 21. Paul Moriarty (George Palmer). 22. Det. Insp. Purbright. 23. *Hill Street Blues.* 24. Harry Morgan. 25. Hartley. 26. Maverick. 27. Michael Medwin. 28. Leslie Ash. 29. Reece Dinsdale. 30. He was a lawyer.

ANSWERS

Answers: see Quiz 51, page 259

1. Who did Burnside replace in the CID?
2. Who played Carl Kochak in *The Night Stalker*?
3. What rank was Spikings in *Dempsey and Makepiece*?
4. Which character did Robson Green play in *Touching Evil*?
5. Which character did Trevor Eve play in *Heat of the Sun*?
6. Who played the bisexual British attorney in *LA Law*?
7. Which Mississippi town was In the *Heat of the Night* set?
8. Where were the outdoor scenes of *Hill Street Blues* filmed?
9. Who is Beck?
10. In which U.S. crime series did Phil Collins make a guest appearance as a criminal?
11. Who was Hazell's sidekick?
12. In *Hawaii Five O* where was the seat of the Hawaiian government?
13. Who starred as Gordon Cole in *Twin Peaks*?
14. Broderick Crawford appeared in which 1960s crime series?
15. Who played Jack Taylor in *Chiller*?
16. Judith Fitzgerald was a character in which crime series?
17. Which English actor was *The Girl From UNCLE's* sidekick?
18. Who was the public defender in *NYPD Blue* before she married Andy Sipowics?
19. Whose novels were *Gideon's Way* based on?
20. What was above George Dixon's head outside the station?
21. Which 90s EastEnders star played Jake Barratt in *The Gentle Touch*?
22. Which detective did Anton Rodgers play in *Murder Most English*?
23. In which series did Pizza Man appear?
24. Which *Dragnet* actor appeared in *M*A*S*H*?
25. In *Juliet Bravo*, where was the police station?
26. Which western spoof did James Garner star in before he became investigator Jim Rockford?
27. Who played *Shoestring's* boss?
28. In *Cat's Eyes*, who starred as Fred?
29. Who plays Charlie Scott in *Thief Takers*?
30. What did *Matlock* do for a living?

Answers: see Quiz 54, page 262

1. What relation is ER's George Clooney to 50s songstress Rosemary Clooney?
2. Simon Mayo and Timmy Mallet both attended which university?
3. How is TV funny lady Joan Molinsky better known?
4. What is Robson Green's middle name?
5. Which political interviewer was South of England show jumping champion in 1964?
6. IWhich TV presenter produced a fitness video called *Fit For Life*?
7. Which soccer side does sports presenter Jim Rosenthal support?
8. Which TV presenter used to be in a group called Memphis 5?
9. Which husband and wife TV stars had the number plate 8 DEB?
10. What was Dawn French's profession before becoming famous?
11. Which TV presenter once held the title Miss Parallel Bars?
12. Which job did Jeremy Beadle once have in a circus?
13. Which pianist and sometime Countdown 'expert' was born the same day Rachmaninov died?
14. What is Clive Anderson's profession?
15. Who scripted the first series of *Blackadder* with Rowan Atkinson?
16. Which Australian hosted *The Big Breakfast* with Zoe Ball?
17. Who played keyboards with a rock band called Fine China?
18. Who played the Emperor Nero in the acclaimed *I Claudius*?
19. Who famously ditched her ring and fur coat but kept her VW Golf?
20. Which actress is president of the Dyslexia Institute?
21. Which TV presenter is Lord Puttnam's son in law?
22. Who made her TV debut in 1989 in *The Big World Cafe*?
23. About whom did Kitty Muggeridge say "he rose without trace"?
24. Who shot to fame as Polly in *The Camomile Lawn*?
25. Who became the BBC's youngest ever scriptwriter aged 21 in 1980?
26. Who wrote the theme song for *Hearts of Gold*?
27. Who played Max de Winter opposite Emilia Fox in *Rebecca*?
28. Who played Rhett Butler in the TV sequel to *Gone With the Wind*?
29. On which show did Julia Carling parody Princess Diana in the operating theatre?
30. Which interviewer was described by an interviewee as 'the thinking woman's crumpet gone stale'?

Music & Variety 4 (see Quiz 54)

ANSWERS

1. Vanessa Mae 2. David Soul 3. Topo Gigio 4. Phil Collins 5. Parkinson 6. Jack Jones 7. 'Everyone we meet' 8. The Brit Pop Awards 9. Julie Felix 10. The Ed Sullivan Show. 11. Raw Sex 12. The *Andy Williams Show* 13. Rock Follies 14. Whispering 15. *Six Five Special!* 16. The 80's hit was released by Kim Wilde whose father, Marti, co-presented *Oh Boy!* 17. *The Hot Shoe Show* 18. *My Kind of People*. 19. The theme to *Hazell* 20. 1990 21. *My Music* 22. *Song By Song* 23. Harry Secombe 24. Petula Clark 25. At The Palace 26. Roy Hudd 27. *Hotel Babylon*. 28. Andrew and Julian Lloyd Webber 29. Roger Daltry 30. Apple Films.

QUIZ 54   Music & Variety 4

LEVEL 3

Answers: see Quiz 53, page 261

1. Which young female violinist featured on *Top Of The Pops*?
2. Which U.S. TV cop sung on *Top Of The Pops* apart from Kojak?
3. What was the mouse puppet on *Sunday Night at the London Palladium* called?
4. Which singer hosted a show where fans could ring and request songs to be sung?
5. On whose chat show did Sammy Cahn accompany the host?
6. Who sang the theme to *Love Boat*?
7. Who did the Monkees get the funniest looks from?
8. Which music awards were co-hosted in 1989 by Sam Fox?
9. Name the female folk singer on *The Frost Report*.
10. Which US variety show was originally called *The Toast of the Town*?
11. Roland Rivron was one half of which comic musical duo?
12. Donny Osmond made his first regular TV appearances on which show?
13. In which series did we first meet *The Little Ladies*?
14. What is the nickname of the former *Whistle Test* presenter, Bob Harris?
15. On which show did Adam Faith make his TV debut?
16. What is the connection between the 80s hit *Kids In America* and the 50s show *Oh Boy!*?
17. Wayne Sleep starred opposite Bonnie Langford in which TV dance show?
18. Which talent spotting show was hosted by Michael Barrymore?
19. Maggie Bell hit the charts with which detective theme?
20. Pavarotti sang the theme for the World Cup Finals in which year?
21. Steve Race hosted which music programme?
22. Julia McKenzie starred as a singer in which musical programme?
23. Which musical Mr Pickwick went on to receive a Knighthood?
24. Who was the star of the 50's series *Pet's Parlour*?
25. TV comics Harry H Corbett and Wilfrid Brambell met royalty where according to their chart hit?
26. Who explored *Halls of Fame*?
27. Which music show did Dani Behr present after *The Word*?
28. Who composed the music for the *South Bank Show*?
29. Which pop star took the role of McHeath in *The Beggar's Opera* on TV?
30. The Beatles TV film *Magical Mystery Tour* was made by which film company?

Answers: see Quiz 56, page 264

1. Joanna Lumley was awarded an honorary doctorate of which university?
2. Where did the live, real-time Christine Kochanski join the *Red Dwarf* team from?
3. What is John Cleese's real name?
4. Which ex *Gladiators* presenter is a karate black belt?
5. Which soccer side does actor John Alderton support?
6. Which luxury did Helen Mirren choose on *Desert Island Discs*?
7. What was the name of William Shatner's Doberman Pinscher dog?
8. What was the female resistance worker's name in *'Allo 'Allo*?
9. Who played the female bank manager in *Joint Account*?
10. What was the TV version of *The Clitheroe Kid* called?
11. Who was Gail Emory's cousin in *American Gothic*?
12. In which series is the local paper *The Lochdubh Listener*?
13. Which service did Anthea Turner work for before she found media fame?
14. Who presented the new *Candid Camera*?
15. Which character in *Reckless* used a dog sled team in his attempt to return to his ex-wife to tell her she was making a mistake about remarrying?
16. Which star of a 70s adventure Sci-Fi series was a former Miss America?
17. In which year was TV naturalist Sir David Attenborough awarded his knighthood?
18. On *That's Life*, what was the name of the little old lady who became an overnight star after being interviewed in the street?
19. What was the name of the office boy in *The Slap Maxwell Story*?
20. Who played George Drummond in *The Drummonds*?
21. Who kept the score on *Bullseye*?
22. Which entertainer died on the same day in 1990 as Muppet creator Jim Henson?
23. Harry Mudd was a character in which sci-fi series?
24. In *This Is David Lauder*, what was Lauder's job?
25. What was the name of the series in which Tony Wilkinson experienced living rough?
26. Sally Jones was the sports presenter on which breakfast programme?
27. Who welcomed viewers on the opening night of BBC 2?
28. What was *Hooperman's* first name?
29. What did Rollo and Bedrock do for a living?
30. Sheila Gish played which characters in *Small World*?

Comedy 10 (see Quiz 56)

1. Leonard Rossiter. 2. She plays the piano. 3. The second series. 4. An eye doctor. 5. Galton and Simpson. 6. Sue Pollard. 7. A poet. 8. Cannon and Ball. 9. A chauffeur. 10. Sgt Bilko. 11. *'Allo, 'Allo.* 12. Dubois (Benson was his first name). 13. Paul Shane. 14. Leslie Ash. 15. *Cuckoo Waltz.* 16. Warden Hedges. 17. Marigold. 18. Lenny Henry. 19. Harrap. 20. Dudley Moore. 21. *Chalk and Cheese.* 22. Carla's. 23. Selling used cars. 24. *M*A*S*H.* 25. Stan Butler. 26. Harry H Corbett. 27. Bernard Hedges. 28. Malcolm. 29. Eli. 30. *Take Three Girls.*

LEVEL 3

Answers: see Quiz 55, page 263

1. Who played the title role in *Tripper's Day*?
2. What does Victoria Wood have in common with Les Dawson apart from being a comic?
3. For which series of *Blackadder* did Ben Elton first become a co-writer?
4. What was Ralph Malph studying to be in *Happy Days*?
5. Which duo wrote the scripts for *Steptoe and Son*?
6. Which *Hi De Hi!* star used to be in a group called Midnight News?
7. What was Jonathan Morris's character in *Bread* aspiring to be?
8. Who were originally called the Harper Brothers?
9. What did Jim Davidson play in *Home James*?
10. The character Joan Hogan was whose girlfriend?
11. In which comedy did Colonel von Klinkerhoffen appear?
12. What was the surname of the Tate's butler in *Soap*?
13. Which singing comedy star appeared as an impresario in *Very Big Very Soon*?
14. Which star of a sitcom quartet was a backing singer for Smiley & Co?
15. In which ITV comedy did the married characters Chris and Fliss Hawthorne feature?
16. Who nicknamed Captain Mainwaring Napoleon?
17. What was Winston's nickname in *In Sickness And In Health*?
18. Who created the DJ Delbert Wilkins?
19. What is the surname of dad and daughter Simon and Samantha, in *Me and My Girl*?
20. Who is taller Ronnie Corbett or Dudley Moore?
21. In which ITV comedy did Michael Crawford play a cockney in a gentrified street?
22. Whose ex-husband is called Nick Tortelli in *Cheers*?
23. To what end did Roy Kinnear use his power in *The Clairvoyant*?
24. This classic comedy was based on the novel by Dr Richard Hornberger. What is it?
25. What was the name of Reg Varney's character in *On The Buses*?
26. Who starred in *Mr 'Aitch*?
27. What was the name of John Alderton's teacher character in *Please Sir*?
28. What is Mrs Merton's 'son' called?
29. What was the name of Jimmy Jewel's character opposite Hilda Baker's Nellie Pledge?
30. In 1969 actresses Liza, Angela and Susan were the trio of stars in which series?

LEVEL 3

Answers: see Quiz 58, page 265

1. What relation in *Neighbours* was Harold Bishop to Joe Mangel?
2. Who was Joe Mangel's niece, a secretary, in *Neighbours*?
3. Who did Den catch with Angie in their sitting room in *Eastenders*?
4. Who did Percy Sugden lock in Hilda Ogden's shed in *Coronation Street*?
5. Which *Coronation Street* star recorded *Where Will You Be*?
6. Who left Brookside Close for a job in Wolverhampton?
7. In *Eastenders* while working at The Meal Machine who did Hattie fall in love with?
8. Which luxury did Leslie Grantham, formerly Dirty Den, choose on *Desert Island Discs*?
9. Who opened a hair salon in Rosamund Street and employed Elsie Tanner?
10. Which two different characters has Beverley Callard played in *Coronation Street*?
11. In *Emmerdale* which Esholt inn was originally used as *The Woolpack*?
12. Which councillor stopped the tarmacking of *Coronation Street*?
13. Which happened first, JR's shooting or Meg Richardson leaving *Crossroads*?
14. Who helped the Street's Emily in Gamma Garments to take care of the Gamma Man?
15. Who was the first soap star to receive an honour from the Queen?
16. In which series was soap's first test tube baby?
17. Who took Deirdre in with Tracy after she was made homeless?
18. Which BBC boss was responsible for introducing *Eastenders*?
19. Which famous soap actress was Cherie Booth's step mother?
20. How is actress Sylvia Butterfield better known?
21. What was the name of the dog saved by the Robinson's after an accident in *Neighbours*?
22. Who first persuaded Helen in *Neighbours* to exhibit her paintings?
23. In *Dynasty* who kidnapped Fallon's child?
24. In *Coronation Street* who punched Billy Walker on the nose when he was fired?
25. In *Dallas* what was Stephen Farlowe's nickname?
26. Who died from a fall from Alexis's balcony in *Dynasty*?
27. What was the name of Den Watt's girlfriend in *Eastenders* played by Jane How?
28. Which ex-*Eastender* was lead singer with Milan?
29. In *Brookside* who lived with the Jackson's before moving in with Pat and Sandra?
30. Who was Blake Carrington's half sister in The Colbys?

LEVEL 3

Answers: see Quiz 57, page 265

1. Which fictional character invented the "cartoonerator"?
2. Who provides the voice for Penelope Pitstop?
3. What kind of animal was Nobby who introduced *Ghost Train*?
4. Which boy found *Stig of the Dump*?
5. Of what was Davy Crockett the king, according to his theme song?
6. Which family had a dog called Simon?
7. What did the *Lone Ranger* make his mask from?
8. Who presented *Stay Tooned*?
9. Who narrated *The Perishers*?
10. Who owned a racehorse called Nooky?
11. Who hosted *Cuddles and Co*?
12. Who were the two young friends of *Worzel Gummidge*?
13. What was the first children's show Zoe Ball presented on terrestrial TV?
14. Which Spice Girl turned down the offer of hosting a cable children's show before finding fame with the band?
15. In which series did Ed Sullystone make appearances?
16. What was the name of *Secret Squirrel*'s partner?
17. Which means of transport featured in the children's game show, *Fun House*?
18. As a ghost where did Arthur English live?
19. Whose friends were Mad Jack and Nakuma?
20. What did *Tiswas* stand for?
21. Who were the two creators of the *Muppets*?
22. What colour was *Rainbow*'s George?
23. In which year was the *Multi-coloured Swap Shop* first broadcast?
24. What does Ermintrude have in her mouth?
25. What type of spot did Emma Forbes first present on *Going Live!*?
26. Pip Hinton could be seen singing on which Friday children's show?
27. Who first narrated *The Magic Roundabout*?
28. Who played The Riddler in *Batman*?
29. Which puppet was said to be modelled on comic actor Terry-Thomas?
30. David Jason helped present which 1960s children's show?

QUIZ 59 Pot Luck 13

LEVEL 3

Answers: see Quiz 60, page 268

1. Which programme would you connect with Jonathan Routh?
2. How is TV actor Donald Wayne better known?
3. Which horror actor's voice is heard on Michael Jackson's *Thriller*?
4. How many words were there according to the name of the game show hosted by Ray Allan?
5. Who briefly replaced Paul Merton on *Have I Got News For You*?
6. How is Geoffrey David Nugent better known?
7. Who played Matlock?
8. Hugh Laurie of Jeeves and Wooster fame won an Oxbridge blue for which sport?
9. Name the two stars of *Executive Stress*?
10. Where in France did Penny reunite with Vince in *Just Good Friends*?
11. Which luxury did Bob Monkhouse choose on Desert Island Discs?
12. What does 'breaking the fourth wall' mean in TV terms?
13. In which series did Richard Eden play a unconventional lawman?
14. Which soap powder did the star of *Cracker* advertise?
15. Which spoof police series features a Captain Trunk?
16. Which show featured the Whirly Wheeler with tragic consequences?
17. Where is Chris Evans' home town?
18. Who did *The Equalizer* work for?
19. Who shot to fame after the 1994 Eurovision Song Contest?
20. What is the first round on *A Question Of Sport*?
21. Who tried to teach Pauline Quirke and Linda Robson to sing in *Jobs For the Girls*?
22. What breed of dog was companion to the detective Cluff?
23. Which TV company produced *First Tuesday*?
24. Which was the first production company to produce *The Big Breakfast*?
25. Who presented Channel 4's religious series *Canterbury Tales*?
26. Who is the doctor in *Hamish MacBeth*?
27. Which humorist's autobiography was called *Unreliable Memoirs*?
28. Who played Solly in *It Ain't Half Hot Mum*?
29. In *GBH*, what did GBH stand for?
30. Which soccer side does Nigel Havers of *Dangerfield* support?

ANSWERS

Drama 8 (see Quiz 60)

1. M M Kayes. 2. *The Onedin Line.* 3. Blair Brown. 4. *The Jewel In The Crown.* 5. *The Love Boat.* 6. Robert Shaw. 7. *Shadowlands.* 8. Kizzy. 9. Texas. 10. Toranaga and Ishido. 11. Omar Sharif. 12. How *Green Was My Valley.* 13. Ian Richardson. 14. A psychiatrist. 15. *Gunsmoke.* 16. Dr. John McUre. 17. *Cat On A Hot Tin Roof.* 18. Anthony Valentine. 19. Alan Bates. 20. Dennis Potter. 21. *The Country Diary of an Edwardian Lady.* 22. Willy. 23. *Z-Cars.* 24. Francesca Annis. 25. *Blind Justice.* 26. *Gunsmoke.* 27. A tennis coach. 28. Sean Bean. 29. Ossie Whitworth. 30. *War And Remembrance.*

Answers: see Quiz 59, page 267

1. *The Far Pavilions* was based on whose novel?
2. In which series did the ship *Charlotte Rhodes* feature?
3. Who played Jacqueline Kennedy opposite Martin Sheen's JFK?
4. In which series did the policeman Merrick appear?
5. How was the Pacific Princess otherwise known?
6. Which Jaws star appeared in *Buccaneers*?
7. In which drama did Joss Ackland portray C S Lewis?
8. Who was Chicken George's mother in *Roots*?
9. In which state did *Rawhide* commence the trail?
10. Who were the two Japanese rivals in *Shogun*?
11. In *Harem*, who starred as a Sultan?
12. Stanley Baker and Sian Phillips starred together in which Welsh drama?
13. Who played Nehru in *Mountbatten, The Last Viceroy*?
14. What was Herbert Lom's profession in *The Human Jungle*?
15. The Longbranch Saloon featured in which Western?
16. Who created *Cardiac Arrest*?
17. Which television version of a Tennessee Williams play did Robert Wagner and Natalie Wood appear in?
18. Which star of Callan appeared in *Colditz* as a German officer?
19. Which actor won a BAFTA for *An Englishman Abroad* in 1982?
20. Who wrote *Lipstick On Your Collar*?
21. What was the series based on the life of Edith Holden?
22. Which character did Peter Lupus play in *Mission Impossible*?
23. In which 60s police series was there a sergeant named Twentyman?
24. Who played Madame Bovary in the 70s drama series?
25. In which drama series did Jane Lapotaire portray a barrister?
26. In which Western did the feisty Kitty Russell appear?
27. What did Bill Cosby pretend to be in *I Spy*?
28. Who played Mellors to Joely Richardson's *Lady Chatterley*?
29. What was the name of the vicar played by Christopher Biggins play in *Poldark*?
30. What was the sequel to *Winds Of War*?

Answers: see Quiz 62, page 270

1. In which comedy would you hear the words "I hate you Butler!"?
2. Who presented Q5 on the BBC?
3. On which series did the *Monty Python* team first appear together?
4. Which *Likely Lad* starred in *Dear Mother... Love Albert*?
5. Who played Jeeves opposite Ian Carmichael's Wooster in 1985?
6. Which *Eastender* played the original old moo in *Till Death Us Do Part*?
7. Which sitcom star wrote a biography of John LeMesurier?
8. On which show did Caroline Aherne develop her Mrs Merton character on TV?
9. The comedy *Please Sir* was inspired by which 60's British film?
10. Which comic starred in *No, That's Me Over Here*?
11. In which series did Donald Sinden and Leslie Phillips play vicars?
12. Who was Thora Hird's husband in *Meet The Wife*?
13. What were the full names of *The Likely Lads*?
14. Which film was based on *The Army Game*?
15. What did Richard Branson do to show his displeasure when interviewed by Clive Anderson?
16. Who starred in Up the Elephant and Round the Castle?
17. Bernard Manning hosted which social club on TV?
18. Who played Mike Channel on KYTV?
19. Who created Captain Kremmen?
20. In *Last Of The Summer Wine* which character claimed to have been a corporal in the army?
21. Who went from *Are You Being Served* to *Take A Letter Mr Jones*?
22. Which show featured Down Your Doorstep?
23. Where was Ain't Misbehavin' set?
24. What occupation did Anton Rodgers have in *May To December*?
25. Who played Mavis to Les Dennis' Vera?
26. What was the name of the heavy metal band created by *The Comic Strip*?
27. What did Ralph Bates' character do for a living in *Dear John*?
28. Who played *The Climber*, the bakery worker with a high IQ?
29. Which play did *The Dustbinmen* develop from?
30. What did Liza Goddard's character do for a living in *Roll Over Beethoven*?

Answers: see Quiz 61, page 269

1. Who charted the history of *The Viking*?
2. The horse racing documentary *Royal Champion* featured which royal?
3. Who presented *The Duke's Award*?
4. What was the subject of the programme *In The Club*?
5. Who sponsors the ITV Weather nationally?
6. In which year was Prime Minister's Question Time first televised?
7. What have Peter Jay, Brian Walden and Matthew Parris got in common as far as television is concerned?
8. What did gardener Harry Dodson restore on TV?
9. Which other politician joined Austin Mitchell in the presentation of a Sky chat show?
10. Why was there much TV attention in the Solent in October 1982?
11. Who was known as St. Mugg?
12. *Lost Worlds, Vanished Lives* was presented by who for the BBC?
13. What did *Man Of The World* do for a living?
14. Who sent postcards from Rio and Chicago?
15. From which town does Michael Parkinson originate?
16. Political interviewer Peter Jay is the son-in-law of which former PM?
17. Who retired from reading the *News At Ten* in 1991?
18. Which music accompanied *This Week*?
19. Who presented *A Prime Minister On Prime Ministers*?
20. Which current affairs programme was described as The Window On The World?
21. Who was the very first guest on *Wogan*?
22. What did *Day To Day* change its name to?
23. Which political reporter guested in *Blackadder*?
24. How was *Home Town* known on the radio?
25. Who took in a *Grand Tour* for his last TV series?
26. Who was the first presenter of *Nationwide*?
27. Who were the presenters of ITV's *Animal Roadshow*?
28. What kind of tree did David Bellamy go up?
29. The interior of which London building was first televised in 1969?
30. What was the name of Derek Nimmo's chat show?

Answers: see Quiz 64, page 272

1. Where did Tracy Hobbs work at *Crossroads*?
2. Who abducted Vicky Fowler in *Eastenders*?
3. In *Peyton Place* who died of a cerebral haemorrhage after a fight with Rodney Harrington?
4. Which Neighbours star recorded Don't It Make You Feel Good?
5. Who gave Derek Wilton a lift back from a coach trip to London in *Coronation Street*?
6. Which soap star advertised Cinzano with Leonard Rossiter?
7. Which character appeared in the first scene of the first episode of *Coronation Street*?
8. What was Ethel's middle name in *Eastenders*?
9. What was the name of the nightclub where Alan McKenna saw Fiona sing?
10. Who died in *Crossroads* just before she was due to marry Benny?
11. Who shared a flat above the corner shop with Doreen Lostock in *Coronation Street*?
12. Who was Todd Fisher's mother in *Sons and Daughters*?
13. Who was Blake's best man at his wedding to Alexis in *Dynasty*?
14. In *Eastenders* what was Debbie Bates' former husband's name?
15. In *Neighbours* whose part has been played by three different actresses, including Sasha Close?
16. Who was Rita Sullivan's first husband in *Coronation Street*?
17. Who in *Dallas* left South Fork when Julie Grey died?
18. What was the date of the *Crossroads* fire?
19. What is Tracy Barlow's middle name?
20. Who was Dot Cotton's grandson in *Eastenders*?
21. Which festival was Emmerdale Farm part of in 1979?
22. What was the name of Ian Beale's loan business in *Eastenders*?
23. In whose house was Lynne Johnston found murdered in *Coronation Street*?
24. Who in the *Colbys* married Prince Michael of Moldavia?
25. Which doctor fell in love with Krystle Carrington in *Dynasty*?
26. Who in *Coronation Street* moved into Len Fairclough's house?
27. Who was Debbie Wilkins' partner in *Eastenders*?
28. Who was shot at Ewing Oil in 1984 by Katherine Wentworth?
29. Which ex-Eastender began her career as a backing singer with Mari Wilson?
30. In *Crossroads* who ran a travel agents after their marriage?

LEVEL 3

Answers: see Quiz 63, page 271

1. Which soccer side does John Motson support?
2. Which luxury did Harry Enfield choose on *Desert Island Discs*?
3. Who did Eamonn Holmes nickname Miss Tippy Toes?
4. Who played Harley Gage in *The Equalizer*?
5. Which TV presenter married hairdresser Stephen Way in 1998?
6. Who made her TV debut as Dennis Potter's Christabel?
7. In which city is *Robocop* set?
8. Which 'Caligula' was also 'Quentin Crisp'?
9. Which male has worn the most make up on *They Think It's All Over*?
10. Which former BBC Governor received a peerage in 1991 and writes detective novels?
11. Who owns KBHR , the radio station, in *Northern Exposure*?
12. What were the first names of The Snoop Sisters?
13. Magrathea featured in which series?
14. Who investigated in the TV series *Cover Her Face*?
15. Who plays Denise in *The Cosby Show*?
16. Who played the wife of Potter?
17. In *George Washington*, who played the title role?
18. Who played chief suspect Sir William Gull in *Jack The Ripper*?
19. Who played table top games in *Late Night Line Up*?
20. Who was Thora Hird's character in *In Loving Memory*?
21. Who worked as a waitress at Mel's Diner?
22. Who starred with Peggy Mount in *You're Only Young Twice*?
23. Which Scotland Yard cop was played by Boris Karloff?
24. What was the title of the TV equivalent of *Desert Island Discs*?
25. Robert Hardy played a member of what in *Jenny's War*?
26. Who served the tea at Emu's Broadcasting Company?
27. Which John assisted Pinky and Perky?
28. E.G. Marshall was a regular in which 60's American courtroom series?
29. The character Willie Melvin featured in which comedy?
30. Which Dr. Who appeared in *War and Peace*?

LEVEL 3

Answers: see Quiz 66, page 274

1. What was the name of Spock's father?
2. Which actress starred as *Alice In Wonderland* and also played a *Dr Who* companion?
3. Who plays Jadsir Dax?
4. Who created – and wrote much of – *Babylon 5*?
5. Who was the Bionic Man's boss?
6. Name the first actress to play Catwoman on TV?
7. Which sixties sci-fi series featured Dr Peter Brady?
8. Which celebrated *X-Files* episode portrayed Mulder and Scully as Men In Black?
9. What is the name of William Shatner's character in *TekWar*?
10. Which actor plays *Voyager's* hologrammatic doctor?
11. What stigma does *Space: Above and Beyond's* Commander McQueen labour under?
12. Who plays the professor in *Sliders*?
13. What is *Robocop's* name?
14. What was Dayna's speciality in *Blake's 7*?
15. Where did Marshall Teller live?
16. What is required to regenerate otherwise dead vampires in *Ultraviolet*?
17. Who played Toby in *Doomwatch*?
18. Where was the first Floating Market held in *Neverwhere*?
19. Which actor led the fight against the invaders in *The War of the Worlds* TV series?
20. In which season did Kryten join the regulars on *Red Dwarf*?
21. In *The Tripods*, how was the practice of implanting mind control devices known?
22. What make of car did *Automan* drive?
23. What type of bomb was at the center of the crisis in *Whoops! Apocalypse*?
24. How many adventures did *Sapphire & Steel* have?
25. Who was the creator of *The Incredible Hulk*?
26. Who was the producer of *Buck Rogers in the 25th Century*?
27. Who played Tasha Yar?
28. What was the weak spot in KITT's protective bodywork?
29. When was *1990*, starring Edward Woodward, broadcast?
30. Who played *Max Headroom*?

QUIZ 66 Comedy 12

Answers: see Quiz 65, page 273

1. Who tried to remove inflated condoms from the college courtyard in *Porterhouse Blue*?
2. Denis Waterman starred opposite who in *Stay Lucky*?
3. In the *Not The Nine O'Clock News* team who did Griff Rhys Jones replace?
4. Which royal did Beryl Reid provide the voice for on *Spitting Image*?
5. What was the surname of the Major in *Fawlty Towers*?
6. Which MP represented the fictitious constituency of Haltenprice?
7. Which *That's Life* contributor wrote Executive Stress?
8. Who played Dinsdale Landen's mistress in *Piggy In The Middle*?
9. In Fawlty Towers, what was Polly's surname?
10. Which real life PM made a guest appearance in a special edition of *Yes, Minister*?
11. Who played Thora Hird's nephew in *In Loving Memory*?
12. Who starred as *Potter*?
13. Who led the Tooting Popular Front?
14. Who won awards with *M*A*S*H* in the roles of director, writer and cast member?
15. What was *George and Mildred*'s surname?
16. Which Arthur and Queenie took the lead roles in *Yus My Dear*?
17. What was the surname of the character, Selwyn, played by Bill Maynard?
18. Who connects *Rising Damp* and *A Kind Of Living*?
19. Who was Grandma trying to find a mate for in the *Beverley Hillbillies*?
20. Who was *The Lad Himself*?
21. Which US female title character told us she was born in December of 1941 at the beginning of her show?
22. Who the sang the song '*Ello John, Got A New Motor*?
23. Who was Spike Milligan talking about when he described him as 'One of the greatest clowns the world has ever seen'?
24. In which BBC series did the character Elaine Nardo appear?
25. Who was the commander of Bilko's Fort Baxter?
26. Who was known as Mr Parrot Face?
27. What were the three children called in The Fosters?
28. In which series did Richard Briers play a vicar?
29. Who created Slack Alice?
30. Who was suffering *Life Without George*?

Sci-Fi 3 (see Quiz 65)

1. Sarek. 2. Deborah Watling. 3. Terry Farrell. 4. J Michael Straczynski. 5. Oscar. 6. Julie Newmar. 7. *The Invisible Man*. 8. Jose Chung's From Outer Space. 9. Bascom. 10. Robert Picardo. 11. He was biogenetically engineered and tank-bred. 12. John Rhys-Davies. 13. Alex Murphy. 14. Making and using weapons. 15. *Eerie, Indiana*. 16. The blood of a 'live' vampire. 17. Robert Powell. 18. Battersea Power Station. 19. Jared Martin. 20. 3. 21. Capping. 22. Lamborghini Countach. 23. Quark bomb. 24. Six. 25. Stan Lee. 26. Glen A Larson. 27. Denise Crosby. 28. There wasn't one. 29. 1977-78. 30. Matt Frewer.

QUIZ 67 Drama 9

LEVEL 3

Answers: see Quiz 68, page 276

1. Who portrayed Rupert Murdoch in *Selling Hitler*?
2. *Connie* was set in which city?
3. In which Western did actor Raymond St Jacques appear?
4. Who wrote the Channel 4 series Melissa?
5. The controversial series *A Time to Dance* was written by whom?
6. What was Robson Greene's profession in *Reckless*?
7. Which Woman's Own fashion editor's first novel eventually became a Channel 4 blockbuster mini series?
8. Which character did Joss Ackland portray in *Shadowlands*?
9. Who played Albert Campion?
10. Which Eastender starred in *Winners and Losers*?
11. Which Swedish actress played Hedda Gabler in 1963 on TV?
12. For which production in 1976 did Mick Jackson win the BAFTA for direction?
13. In which drama series was there a nuclear plant named Northmoor?
14. Which part did John Cleese play in BBC TV's production of *Taming Of The Shrew*?
15. In which 1990s series is *Danse Macabre* the theme music?
16. Which John Osborne play did Jack Lemmon star in as Archie Rice?
17. What was Rosemary Leach's character in *Jewel In The Crown*?
18. Who played Campion's manservant?
19. Which crime series featured George Sewell and Deren Nesbitt?
20. Which series first starred Alfred Burke as a private detective?
21. Which series starred Kenneth Haigh as Joe Lampton?
22. Which 1971 series of plays featured greed, jealousy, and other sins?
23. Which family featured in *A Family At War*?
24. In which Jane Austen story did Ann Firbank play Ann Elliot?
25. Which American tough guy actor appeared with Liz Fraser in *Man And Boy*?
26. What was the 1970s political thriller series set in the future?
27. Name the 60s crime series featuring the Royal Canadian Mounted Police.
28. In *I, Claudius*, who starred as Caligula?
29. Where is the base of *The Flying Doctors*?
30. In which character Harold Pinter play, adapted for TV in 1987, did the character Godberg feature?

Children's TV 7 (see Quiz 68)

1. 'Turn off your television set and go do something more interesting instead'. 2. Johnny Ball. 3. Billy Bunter. 4. Gaby Roslin. 5. Anthea Turner. 6. Rowlf the dog. 7. *The Wombles.* 8. Terry Wogan. 9. *Andy Pandy* 10. Four. 11. *Rainbow.* 12. *Billy Bunter.* 13. Huw Wheldon. 14. Ian Holm & Penelope Wilton. 15. Susan Dey. 16. John McGeorge and Larry Harmon. 17. *Supergran.* 18. Wrexham. 19. Mickey Dolenz. 20. Patricia Driscoll. 21. *Hong Kong Phooey.* 22. *The Fairly Pointless Show.* 23. Moosylvania. 24. Yellow & green. 25. Robin Hood. 26. Tomato ketchup. 27. Dr Tiger Ninestein. 28. With the Horn Resounding. 29. Nero 30. On the ceiling.

ANSWERS

QUIZ 68 Children's TV 7

Answers: see Quiz 67, page 275

LEVEL 3

1. What did the *Why Don't You?* team oddly ask you to do during their theme tune?
2. Who presented *Think of a Number*?
3. Which 50s show was shown twice daily – for children and later for adults?
4. Whose first TV job was presenting *Hippo* on Sky's Superchannel?
5. Who has hosted *Up2U*, *Blue Peter* and *Going Live*?
6. Who played piano on the *Muppet Show*?
7. With which children's characters is Mike Batt associated?
8. Who narrated *Stoppit and Tidyup*?
9. Which programme was the vety first on *Watch With Mother*?
10. How many Z's are there in *Sooty's* magic spell?
11. Which show did the actor who played Detective Constable Scatliff in *Z Cars* go on to present?
12. Who did Mr Quelch try to keep under control?
13. Who hosted the children's talent show, *All Your Own*?
14. Which husband and wife team played Pod and Homily in *The Borrowers*?
15. Which member of the *Partridge Family* appeared in *L.A. Law*?
16. Who provided the voices of the cartoon *Laurel and Hardy*?
17. Which heroine wore a Tam-O-Shanter?
18. Which soccer side did *Blue Peter's* Tim Vincent support?
19. Which former pop star produced *Metal Mickey*?
20. Which Patricia read the *Picture Book*?
21. Which super-sleuth masqueraded as a "mild-mannered janitor"?
22. What was the subtitle of the show *Do Not Adjust Your Set*?
23. Where did Bullwinkle live?
24. What colour are Big Ears' trousers?
25. Archie Duncan and Alexander Gauge played the friends of which 50s hero?
26. Which food accompaniment brought *Count Duckula* back to life?
27. Who was the leader of the *Terrahawks*?
28. How did *Eric The Viking* wake up the Gods?
29. What was the name of the caterpillar in *Dangermouse*?
30. In which unusual place did Jumblie sleep?

ANSWERS

Drama 9 (see Quiz 67)

1. Barry Humphries. 2. Nottingham. 3. *Rawhide*. 4. Alan Bleasdale. 5. Melvyn Bragg. 6. A surgeon. 7. Barbara Taylor Bradford (A Woman of Substance). 8. C. S. Lewis. 9. Peter Davidson. 10. Leslie Grantham. 11. Ingrid Bergman. 12. *Threads*. 13. *Edge of Darkness*. 14. Petruchio. 15. *Jonathan Creek*. 16. *The Entertainer*. 17. Aunt Fenny. 18. Brian Glover. 19. *Special Branch*. 20. *Public Eye*. 21. *Life At The Top*. 22. *The Ten Commandments*. 23. The Ashtons. 24. *Persuasion*. 25. Telly Savalas. 26. *The Guardians*. 27. R.C.M.P. 28. John Hurt. 29. Coopers Crossing. 30. *The Birthday Party*.

276

Answers: see Quiz 70, page 278

1. In *City Lights*, what did the lead character aspire to be?
2. Who starred opposite Ian Hendry in *The Lotus Eaters*?
3. Who wrote and directed *Jessie*?
4. Who made an *Enquiry into the Unknown*?
5. Which sci-fi series features Jump Gates?
6. What was Howard Rollins character in *In The Heat Of The Night*?
7. Where did Maddie Hayes meet her future husband?
8. Who was known as Soapy in *Rumpole of The Bailey*?
9. In whose show did PC Monkhouse appear?
10. Who did *Banacek* work for as a detective?
11. Who played the lead in *Testament of Youth*?
12. What was the name of the series featuring the female private eye, Claire McGarron?
13. Which soccer side does Michael Palin support?
14. On *The Fame Game*, who introduced new comedians?
15. Which TV personality started her career on Hong Kong radio?
16. Who was the central figure in *The Power Game*?
17. In which series did Gary Coleman play Arnold?
18. Who hosted *Here to Stay*?
19. What was the name of the dog in *The Thin Man*?
20. Who links *Angels One Five* and *The Importance of Being Earnest*?
21. In *The Mogul*, who played Driscoll?
22. Who starred in the comedy, *The Melting Pot*?
23. *Laverne and Shirley* were played by which actors?
24. Whose sister was Ophelia Frump?
25. Name the duo who presented *Something to Treasure*, a series about collecting?
26. What was Carlos first job in *Crossroads*?
27. Which bookmakers featured in the TV drama *Big Deal*?
28. Sue Ingle presented which wildlife series?
29. Who played Ali in *EastEnders*?
30. In *A Sharp Intake of Breath*, who starred opposite David Jason?

Answers: see Quiz 69

1. Who first lived in the bungalow in *Brookside*?
2. Who did Ken Barlow have an affair with in 1972 in *Coronation Street*?
3. Who was Blake Carrington's manservant in *Dynasty*?
4. Which *Brookside* star recorded *Whose Love Is It Anyway*?
5. At what address was Reg Cox's body found in Albert Square in *Eastenders*?
6. Which ex *Coronation Street* actor turned impresario is a director of Everton FC?
7. Who modelled for Alex Ward in *Dallas*?
8. What was the name of Punk Mary's daughter in *Eastenders*?
9. Which EastEnder appeared on a Sammy Davis Jr Special with Mandy Rice-Davies?
10. In *Dallas* who was Lucas Wade's daughter?
11. Which star of *The Lovers* played Janice Langton in the Street?
12. In *Brookside* who lived in France with Lucy Collins?
13. In *Crossroads* who was Adam Chance's best man?
14. Who was Ian and Lofty's partner in their knitwear business in *Eastenders*?
15. What was the name of Harry and Concepta Hewitt's son in *Coronation Street*?
16. What did Shane Ramsey do in *Neighbours* before his accident?
17. Which soap actress who shares her first name with her character has a husband who wrote scripts for *Emmerdale*?
18. Who in *The Colbys* was Alexis' partner in South China Sea Oil?
19. Which star of *Minder* played Graham in *Eastenders*?
20. Which Street star made his first TV appearance from Olympia in 1946?
21. Which former soap star presented *The Saturday Banana* with Bill Oddie?
22. What did *Crossroads* change its name to in 1987?
23. Who did Paul Morgan defend in a manslaughter case in *Dallas*?
24. Which one of the Corkhills in *Brookside* was an electrician?
25. Who in *Coronation Street* had been awarded the Military Medal?
26. Whose attempted murder was Cliff Barnes arrested for in 1984 in *Dallas*?
27. Who ran a Kissogram business from the Queen Victoria in *Eastenders*?
28. How did Adam try to kill Jeff in *Dynasty*?
29. What was Burt's alien substitute's name in *Soap*?
30. Angie left Albert Square for Majorca with whom?

Answers: see Quiz 72

1. What is Johnny Logan's *Eurovision* claim to fame?
2. Which comic was the manager at Revolver?
3. Where was *Fame* set?
4. What was *Russ Abbot's Madhouse* previously called?
5. Which weatherman was a hit on *Top Of The Pops*?
6. Which song did French and Saunders sing with Bananarama?
7. Who presented *The Roxy*?
8. Paul McCartney recorded which soap theme?
9. According to the theme song what could you have a fish in *When The Boat Comes In*?
10. Which Jane portrayed Edith Piaf on TV?
11. Which pop show moved from Manchester to London?
12. Peter Cook sang a ballad about whom?
13. Who plays the piano on *Whose Line Is It Anyway*?
14. Ron Grainger composed the music for which popular BBC Sci-Fi series?
15. Who was the voice of Robin in the Muppet's hit song *Half Way Down The Stairs*?
16. In which decade did the *Grand Ole Oprey* first reach UK screens?
17. Who had a recording label called Rodent?
18. Which TV personalities/DJ's released their version of *It Takes Two, Baby*?
19. Who sang the *Postman Pat* theme song?
20. Which band first released *All Right Now*, used to sell chewing gum?
21. Whose daughter is Julie, formerly in the pop group Guys And Dolls?
22. How many adjudicators were on the talent show, *New Faces*, each week?
23. Waylon Jennings sang the theme for who?
24. Who starred in *No Excuses* as a rock singer?
25. On which show did the Beatles make their TV debut?
26. Which UK conductor was the subject of a 1980s drama?
27. Musician Richard Stilgoe first appeared on TV in which current affairs programme?
28. On *Ready, Steady Go* what was singer Millie dubbed?
29. Who sang *Back Home* on *Top Of The Pops* in 1970?
30. Which TV personality was called Mr Guitar?

Answers: see Quiz 71, page 279

1. Which two pub landladies have been played by Dervla Kirwan?
2. Who connects *The Army Game* with *Dad's Army*?
3. Who was Laverne's comedy partner?
4. Which sitcom writer was born Romana Barrack?
5. *Last Of The Summer Wine* is set in which real life Yorkshire town?
6. In which series did Griff Rhys Jones and Mel Smith first team up after leaving *Not The Nine O'Clock News*?
7. Dawn, Jennifer, Ruby and Tracey were collectively what?
8. What is the first name of the father in *Bread*?
9. Which doctor was played by Richard Wilson in *Only When I Laugh*?
10. Tim Brooke-Taylor played which character in *Me And My Girl*?
11. On which show did Harry Enfield make his TV debut?
12. The catchphrase "Very interesting – but stupid" is associated with which series?
13. Which of *The Golden Girls* was born in Sicily?
14. Who created the character Old Scrunge?
15. What connects *Dad's Army* to Hattie Jacques?
16. At the end of whose show did Janet Webb usually steal the thunder by singing?
17. Who did Alec meet and marry after acting as her divorce lawyer?
18. Which comedian's 1991 autobiography was called *Still On My Way to Hollywood*?
19. Who was the star of *Cool It*?
20. What did Bilko do for a living after leaving the army?
21. Who played in *The Glums* on TV?
22. Name the comedy centred on the goings on in the Salvation Army?
23. What was Paul Nicholas' job in *Close To Home*?
24. In which comedy did the agency Maggie's Models feature?
25. What did Julie Walters train to be before her show business career?
26. In *May To December* which TV lawyer does Alec wish he could emulate?
27. What was the name of Larry Grayson's fictitious postman?
28. What was the nickname of the amiable police officer in *Sykes*?
29. Which armed service featured in the 1970s series *Get Some In*?
30. What happened to the President's brain on *Spitting Image*?

LEVEL 3

Answers: see Quiz 74, page 282

1. What was the name of Penny's boss in *Just Good Friends*?
2. Who starred as the doctor in *Enemy at the Door*?
3. Who was the star of *Colin's Sandwich*?
4. Where did the characters of *The Glittering Prize* meet?
5. What four letters did *TJ Hooker* have on his uniform?
6. In *Mork and Mindy*, Mindy's father owned what kind of shop?
7. What was the name of Ronnie Corbett's wife in *Now Look Here*?
8. What was Max in *The Bionic Woman*?
9. In *The Water Margin*, how many knights were reborn to fight tyranny?
10. Who held two nurses hostage in *Brookside*?
11. Which 1969 comedy paired John Fortune and Eleanor Bron?
12. In *Moonlighting*, what was Bert Viola's middle name?
13. On which talent show did singer/impressionist Joe Longthorne make his TV debut?
14. Which *Carry On* regular appeared in *Shillingbury Blowers*?
15. Who played the neighbour in *George and Mildred*?
16. Which actor played Kuba in *Casualty*?
17. In *Crossroads*, which comedian drove Meg Mortimar to her wedding?
18. Who owned the circus in the 1950s series *Circus Boy*?
19. In *Auf Wiedersehen Pet*, who played Wayne's German girlfriend?
20. In *Quincy*, who owned the bar Danny's Place?
21. Which New Zealand-born actress starred in *Zodiac*?
22. What is the name of Bob and Terry's local pub in *The Likely Lads*?
23. In which country was Joanna Lumley born?
24. What was the registration number of *The Saint*'s car?
25. Who played the title role in *Ellery Queen – Whodunnit*?
26. Who succeeded Jeremy Beadle as presenter of *Chain Letters*?
27. Name the writer of *Open All Hours*.
28. What did Peter Davidson run in *Holding The Fort*?
29. In which year was the *Grand National* first televised?
30. Who ran *The New Globe* in *Falcon Crest*?

Answers: see Quiz 73, page 281

1. Which character did Helena Bonham Carter portray in *Arms And The Man*?
2. Who wrote *The Glittering Prizes*?
3. Who is Vanessa Redgrave's acting sister?
4. What was the 1970s series about an arms salesman starring Barrie Ingram?
5. In which series did Margaret Lockwood play a barrister?
6. Which 1970s series featured crime stories by late Victorian writers?
7. Who performed excerpts from Shakespeare named collectively *The Ages Of Man*?
8. Which part did Alan Bates play in *The Mayor Of Casterbridge*?
9. Who starred with Stanley Baker in *How Green Was My Valley*?
10. What was the series about a crime-detecting clerk created by Edgar Wallace?
11. Who was the Victorian detective played by Alan Dobie?
12. Which series starred Phyllis Calvert as a journalist?
13. What was the name of the series starring John Stride as a solicitor?
14. Which series starred Ronald Fraser as an ex-colonial returning to Britain?
15. In which series did Stanley Tucci play Richard Cross?
16. Who played Carol White's husband in *Cathy Come Home*?
17. In *Roughnecks* where is the rig Osprey Explorer?
18. In which series did Siobhan Redmond portray Det. Maureen Connell?
19. What was Det. Isbecki's first name in *Cagney and Lacey*?
20. What was the original play that the series *Boys From The Blackstuff* was based on?
21. What was Grandpa Walton's first name?
22. In which drama series was there a Dr. Monica Broome?
23. In which series did Robert Culp and Bill Cosby play Government agents?
24. Who did *Callan* befriend in Wormwood Scrubs?
25. Which mini-series featured Lord Toranaga?
26. Which series featured a special with Terry aboard the Orient Express?
27. Which Gentle Touch actress appeared in *CATS Eyes*?
28. Which series was the forerunner of *The Power Game*?
29. What was the sequel to *The Winds Of War*?
30. Who starred on ITV as Sherlock Holmes in 1975?

LEVEL 3

Answers: see Quiz 76, page 284

1. *Ruff 'n' Reddy* were what types of animals?
2. Which 80s series was based on the Alan Parker film of the same name?
3. After eating a particular fruit, what alter ego did Eric become?
4. Which satellite channel was established in the USA in 1977 as CBN Satellite Service?
5. What was James Adams better known as?
6. What was the name of the spacecraft on *Get Fresh*?
7. In *Lost In Space*, how many children were there?
8. What did Evil Edna look like in *Will O'The Wisp*?
9. In *Voyage To The Bottom Of The Sea*, what was the name of the Admiral?
10. Whose invincible friend was called Moggie?
11. Who had a computer called TIM?
12. The cartoon series *Droids* was the spin-off of which film?
13. What is *The Flintstones'* daily newspaper?
14. What was the full name of *Top Cat's* sidekick Benny?
15. Who played the title role in *John Silver's Return To Treasure Island*?
16. What kind of animal is children's TV presenter Scally?
17. In which year was the cartoon *Rocket Robin Hood* set?
18. What was the name of the *Beverley Hillbillies'* bloodhound?
19. Which children's favourite hosted *The Joke Machine*?
20. Name the oldest Womble.
21. Who presented the game show *Finders Keepers*?
22. How much did Matthew Corbett pay his father, Harry, to secure full ownership of *Sooty*?
23. Who was the storyteller in *The Hot Chestnut Man*?
24. Which star of Kula Shaker is the great nephew of the lady who appeared with *Muffin the Mule*?
25. What was the subject of the 1950s children's series *Rex and Rinty*?
26. Who replaced Michael Rodd as presenter of *Screen Test*?
27. Which children's series was inspired by Monica Dickens and featured Arthur English?
28. What was Southern TV's adventure series starring Wendy Padbury?
29. Who was the sheriff of *Four Feather Falls*?
30. What was Madeleine from *Bagpuss*?

Answers: see Quiz 75, page 283

1. Who played Debbie Wilks in *Eastenders*?
2. Who dyed Lofty's hair in *Eastenders* causing it to turn green?
3. Who did Eddie Yeats meet from *Coronation Street* in prison?
4. Which soccer side does Johnny Briggs alias Mike Baldwin support?
5. What was Krystle Carrington's former surname?
6. Whose death in *Crossroads* was Benny suspected of?
7. Which *Emmerdale* star recorded *Just This Side of Love*?
8. What as the name of the pyramid selling scheme that Derek Wilton was involved in?
9. In *Emmerdale* what was the name of the Greek restaurant in Hotten?
10. Which *Casualty* star played Will Thurley in *Brookside*?
11. Who in *Neighbours* was Madge's youngest brother?
12. What was the name of Des' son in *Neighbours*?
13. Who moved into Brookside Close in the first episode?
14. In *Eastenders* who acted as midwife when Sue Osman gave birth to Ali Jr?
15. What nationality was Andy O'Brien in *Eastenders*?
16. Who in *Dallas* raped Lucy Ewing?
17. In Emmerdale where was Annie Sugden when she was trapped by fire?
18. Which *Eastenders* character was played by David Scarboro until the actor's suicide?
19. Who died in *Crossroads* just before her marriage to Benny?
20. Who became Des Barnes' housekeeper when she lost her job at the cafe in *Coronation Street*?
21. What was the name of Renee Bradshaw's brother, who was in the army?
22. The deaths of Albert Tatlock and Stan Ogden occurred the same year as which *Coronation Street* star's departure?
23. Which *Crossroads* wedding took place the same year as Ray and Deirdre Langton's?
24. What number did Elsie Tanner live at?
25. Which football club was the subject of *United!*?
26. What was the first English language serial to come from Wales?
27. What was the setting for the 70s series *Rooms*?
28. Where did Mark first meet Gill in *Eastenders*?
29. Which baby died in his cot in *Eastenders* in 1985?
30. In *Emergency Ward 10* which doctor and nurse were real-life husband and wife?

LEVEL 3

Answers: see Quiz 78, page 285

1. In *Sorry*, what did Ronnie Corbett's character do for a living?
2. Name the husband and wife who worked together in *Forever Green*.
3. Whose sidekick is Madge Allsop?
4. When *Spitting Image* was repeated in 1991, what was the series called?
5. Who played Dermot in *Men Behaving Badly*?
6. Who did Cliff live with in *Cheers*?
7. Who wrote *It's Ulrika* for Ulrika Jonsson?
8. Who played the eponymous space-bound housewife in *Come Back Mrs Noah*?
9. Who played the hard up landlady in *All at No 20*?
10. Which German officer was keen on Rene in *'Allo, 'Allo*?
11. Which *On The Buses* actor appeared in *Beggar My Neighbour*?
12. In which LWT series did James Beck play the title role?
13. What was Col. Blake's christian name in *M*A*S*H*?
14. Which sitcom featured Louie, Alex and Latka?
15. Pat Phoenix and Prunella Gee were feuding landladies in which sitcom?
16. Which sitcom star was married to *Are You Being Served?* writer Jeremy Lloyd for just four months?
17. Who played Nellie Pledge's brother in *Nearest and Dearest*?
18. Which actor was *Comrade Dad*?
19. In which series did Jennifer Saunders play multiple roles?
20. Which sitcom starred Simon Cadell and Carol Royle?
21. In which series did Maria Charles play Maureen Lipman's mother?
22. In which series were Beryl and Geoffrey courting?
23. Who was the banker in *The Beverley Hillbillies*?
24. Where did Herman Munster work?
25. Which character did Hylda Baker play in *Nearest and Dearest*?
26. Who in *Please Sir* was his 'Mother's Little Soldier'?
27. Who links the *Professionals* to *The Cuckoo Waltz*?
28. In *May to December* what was Miss Flood's married name?
29. In *Dad's Army* who was in charge of the Eastgate platoon?
30. Who played the title characters in *Pat and Margaret*?

Answers: see Quiz 77, page 285

1. How was performer Wladzir Valentino better known?
2. Who links *Potter* and *I Didn't Know You Cared*?
3. Who played a mad furniture designer in *Maelstrom*?
4. What was the name of the hospital in *Dr Kildare*?
5. In *The Strange Report*, who played Adam Strange's American assistant?
6. What was the name of Michael Caine's character in *Jack The Ripper*?
7. Who was the TV critic on *Saturday Night People*?
8. How was the character Ronald Bird better known?
9. Who played Bill Fraser's mother in *Flesh and Blood*?
10. Which Olympic medalist was a team captain on *Sporting Triangles*?
11. Which TV announcer was described as having 'a bubbling voice of captivating quality'?
12. Who presented *The Late Late Show*?
13. Which actor played the pilot of *Blue Thunder* in the TV series?
14. Who links *Who Dares Wins* to *The Refuge*?
15. Who helped protect Penelope Pitstop from The Hooded Claw?
16. Who played John Wilder's wife in *The Power Game*?
17. In which series might you meet Captain Apollo?
18. In *Hot Metal*, who used the phrase, 'Her Majesty's Press…'?
19. In which madcap series did Eccles and Bluebottle feature?
20. From which city was *Open Air* broadcast?
21. Where was *Banacek* set?
22. In which show might you have heard all about beautiful downtown Burbank?
23. What was the name of the agency in *Me And My Girl*?
24. What was the name of the family in *Not in Front of the Children*?
25. Who created *The Black and White Minstrel Show*?
26. Who was the presenter of *Tree House*?
27. Which actress was George Cole's wife in *Blott on the Landscape*?
28. What kind of shop did Jan Howard run in *Howard's Way*?
29. Who was the creator of *Hopalong Cassidy*?
30. Name the star of *Later Starter*?

Comedy 14 (see Quiz 77)

1. Librarian. 2. John Alderton and Pauline Collins. 3. Dame Edna's. 4. *Spitting Back.* 5. Harry Enfield. 6. His Ma. 7. Vic Reeves. 8. Molly Sugden. 9. Maureen Lipman. 10. Lt. Gruber. 11. Reg Varney. 12. *Romany Jones.* 13. Henry. 14. *Taxi.* 15. *Constant Hot Water.* 16. Joanna Lumley. 17. Jimmy Jewell. 18. George Cole. 19. *Happy Families.* 20. *Life Without George.* 21. *Agony.* 22. *The Lovers.* 23. Mr. Drysdale. 24. At a funeral home. 25. Nellie Pledge. 26. Frankie Abbott. 27. Lewis Collins. 28. Tipple. 29. Captain Square. 30. Victoria Wood and Julie Walters.

ANSWERS

LEVEL 3

Answers: see Quiz 80, page 288

1. Who was known as 'The Voice Of America'?
2. Who wrote *Jacob's Ladder*?
3. Brian is actually Brian Walden's middle name. What is his first name?
4. Who held a TV interview with Prince Andrew and Lady Sarah Ferguson prior to their marriage?
5. Which newsreader appeared in *Doctor Who* as himself in 1966?
6. Who presented *Chronicle* for the BBC?
7. Which newsreader helped us trace family trees in a series on the subject?
8. What is TV's longest running wildlife series?
9. What would a TV journalist mean if he mentioned the acronym ENG?
10. Who presented *All Our Yesterdays*?
11. Who presented *Monitor*?
12. What was the Queen's youngest son's programme about the Duke of Windsor called?
13. What was the subject of *The Epic That Never Was*?
14. From where in Hampshire is there televised an annual Air Show?
15. Name the ITV 1970s series on the plight of the South American Indians?
16. Which subject was featured in the documentary *The Hardest Way Up*?
17. Who took part in the BBC documentary *Girl Friday*?
18. Who presented *Pioneers Of Modern Painting*?
19. Who UK news presenter interviewed Saddam Hussein just before the Gulf War in 1990?
20. Which country was the subject for the documentary *Edge Of Blue Heaven*?
21. Who narrated the fly on the wall series *Love And Marriage*?
22. Who presented the daytime *City Hospital*?
23. Which newsreader has written a book called The Loch Ness Story?
24. Which late pop singer named 'The British Elvis' featured in an *Omnibus* documentary?
25. Who accompanied Rory McGrath on a *Holiday to California*?
26. Who presented *The Car's The Star*?
27. Who narrated *Fraud Squad*?
28. Which newsreader advertised Cow & Gate baby food as a child?
29. What was the rock in *Death On the Rock*?
30. In which city is the Adelphi Hotel featured in the BBC documentary *Hotel*?

Answers: see Quiz 79, page 287

1. Who was the manager of a football team in the soap *Dynasty*?
2. Which comic wrote the golfing comedy, *The 19th Hole*?
3. Which film theme was used by the BBC for the 1996 Olympics?
4. What did Kent Walton commentate on on *World of Sport*?
5. Which crimestopper presented a TV series about the card game bridge?
6. Which BBC sports commentator was married to an Olympic long jump champion?
7. Jimmy Greaves previewed films on which breakfast programme?
8. Who was only the third soccer player to win the BBC *Sports Personality of the Year* after more than 40 years of the award?
9. Which former pentathlete is now known for her holiday trips on TV?
10. What nationality was the first winner of *European Superstars*?
11. Which was *World Superstar* competitor Bob Seaman's event in the Olympics?
12. Which music was used by the BBC for the 1998 World Cup?
13. Which football team did BskyB bid £635 million for in 1998?
14. Where is the British Grand Prix now televised from?
15. Which former Chelsea manager commentated for the BBC in 1997?
16. Which former Goalkeeper is a football presenter for ITV?
17. Who was former sports reporter Ross McWhirter's twin brother?
18. Who first read the football results on *Grandstand*?
19. Which jockey was a team captain on *Question Of Sport*?
20. Henry Longhurst was the BBC commentator on which sport?
21. Where were the Summer Olympic Games of 1960 televised from?
22. Which 1500 metres champion is a commentator for ITV?
23. Which former Olympian organises the London Marathon?
24. Which boxer appeared as a damsel in a Shakespearean sketch?
25. Joe Brown was often featured in televised outside broadcasts. What is his activity?
26. Which actor attempted Everest in a television film?
27. Who presented *Match of the Seventies* in 1995?
28. Who was the BBC ice hockey reporter?
29. What sport did Jim Neilly commentate on?
30. What event was watched at midnight by 18.5 million people – the largest ever audience at this time of day?

Answers: see Quiz 82, page 290

1. Who was Lockhart in three police drama series?
2. Which soap actor played a Det. Sergeant in *No Hiding Place*?
3. Who played Telford in *Telford's Change*?
4. Which actor first shared a *Z Car* with James Ellis?
5. Which future Hollywood star played Nancy Astor's playboy husband in the 1982 BBC2 series?
6. In which 1993 TV adaptation of a Jilly Cooper novel did Patrick Ryecart star?
7. Which James Bond starred opposite Stefanie Powers in *Mistral's Daughter*?
8. Who played Mrs Bennet in *Pride and Prejudice*?
9. Which ITV comedy drama set in London spanned 15 years between 1979 and 1994?
10. Which mother and daughter have played Max de Winter's second wife in separate productions of Rebecca?
11. Whose dramatised Jane Austen's *Persuasion* for TV and changed the ending?
12. Who was the lesbian in *Drop The Dead Donkey*?
13. What was the name of Robert Lindsay's political character in *GBH*?
14. Which LA Law actor starred in *The Tommyknockers*?
15. Who was seen in silhouette in the introduction of his television plays?
16. Which Hollywood star played Trevor Eve's mistress in *The Politician's Wife*?
17. What was the name of the Falklands veteran in *Tumbledown*?
18. Which character did Allyce Beasley play in *Moonlighting*?
19. Sir Guy Of Gisburne featured in which TV series?
20. Which English actress appeared in L.A. Law as C.J Lamb?
21. In which Bronte drama did Tara Fitzgerald play Helen?
22. Which wife of impresario Eddie Kulukundis starred in *The Grand*?
23. Which actress's real name is Ilynea Lydia Mironoff?
24. Who said, "you might very well think that, but I couldn't possibly comment"?
25. In which series was Ron Smollet a bobby?
26. Willy Armitage was a character in which action series?
27. In '92 which drama had the highest ratings then for a costume drama?
28. Which Lady Nunn played TV detective Anna Lee?
29. Who is the doctor in *Ballykissangel*?
30. Which Oscar winner played Woodrow F. Coll in *Lonesome Dove*?

Answers: see Quiz 81, page 289

1. Who wrote the documentary *Talking Pictures*?
2. In *Bewitched*, what objects did Aunt Clara like to collect?
3. Who played Oliver Douglas in *Green Acres*?
4. Who explored public toilets on *Forty Minutes*?
5. What was the subject of the documentary *444 Days ... And Counting*?
6. In which show did the main character use a flashback machine?
7. How many series of *Fawlty Towers* were made and broadcast?
8. Which show had the slogan, 'Sit tight in your chair, and we'll take you there!'?
9. In *Space*, who played Norman Grant?
10. Which director created the TV series *Peter Gunn*?
11. In which series did the puppet Larry Dart appear?
12. Who played the professor in TV's *King of the Rocket Men*?
13. In *The Lovers*, what was it that Richard Beckinsale loved but his girlfriend hated?
14. In which BBC show, hosted by Bruno Brookes, did children compete against their teachers?
15. What were the names of the orphaned twins in *The Family Affair*?
16. In *The Mistress*, what kind of shop was owned by the lead character?
17. What was the name of the character played by Penelope Keith in *Sweet Sixteen*?
18. In which show did Dick Van Dyke make his TV debut?
19. Which TV cop was in the crew of *Blake's Seven*?
20. Who presented the documentary *The Planets*?
21. Name the sport which featured in *Playing For Real*?
22. What was the title of *Danger Man* changed to in America?
23. Who links *Poldark* to *Surprise, Surprise*?
24. An outbreak of which disease was the subject of the drama *The Mad Death*?
25. In *Executive Stress* what was the surname of Caroline and Donald?
26. What was the sequel to *The Little House on the Prairie*?
27. Who in 1971 played the role of Casanova on TV?
28. What did Barbara Flynn's character do for a living in *Open All Hours*?
29. Who starred opposite Peggy Mount in *The Larkins*?
30. Which actor was Dale Winton named after?

1. What is the acting connection between Gilly Coman and Melanie Hill?
2. In which comedy series did Natasha Pyne and Ann Holloway appear as sisters?
3. Which series starred Irene Handl and Wilfred Pickles?
4. What was the title of the programme about a joke-telling contest between comedians?
5. Which soccer side does Jo Brand support?
6. Who played Albert in *Albert and Victoria*?
7. What was the title of the ATV show starring Marty Feldman?
8. Who scripted his Channel 4 sitcom *Blue Heaven*?
9. Which comedian played Johnny McKenna in *The Detectives*?
10. What was Jean Stapleton's role in *Bagdad Cafe*?
11. What are Mr. Humphries forenames in *Are You Being Served*?
12. Which henpecked husband in a sitcom is in real life a former husband of writer Margaret Drabble?
13. What was Lilith's maiden name in *Cheers*?
14. What was *Ellen*'s character's surname?
15. In *'Allo, 'Allo* what was Herr Flick's first name?
16. Whose parents were Rita and Les in *Just Good Friends*?
17. What was the title of entertainer Paul O' Grady's TV series?
18. Which sitcom features Majors Healy and Nelson?
19. Which actor from *Casualty* was Dawn French smitten by in *The Vicar Of Dibley*?
20. What is Dec of the duo *Ant and Dec* surname?
21. In *Dead Ernest*, what was Ernest's profession before he died?
22. Who played the large lodger in *The Big One*?
23. Who played Beryl in *Beryl's Lot*?
24. Which BAFTA award winning actress starred in *The Labours Of Erica*?
25. Which of The Three Degrees starred in *The Land Of Hope And Gloria*?
26. Who was the star of *Dora*, a 1970s sitcom?
27. Where was the sitcom *Down The Gate* set?
28. Who replaced Cicely Courtneidge as Stan Butler's mother in *On The Buses*?
29. Who played Pippa in *One Foot In The Grave*?
30. Who starred as photographer *The Magnificent Evans*?

ANSWERS

Soaps 12 (see Quiz 84)

1. William Tarmey (Jack Duckworth). 2. Dean Sullivan (Jimmy Corkhill). 3. Vodka and Tonic. 4. Black Forest Clinic. 5. Richard and Esther Shapiro. 6. Tony Warren. 7. Helicopter accident. 8. Monday 9. Larry Grayson. 10. *The Mikado*. 11. Grant Mitchell. 12. Mike Baldwin. 13. Poodle. 14. Lowestoft. 15. Clive Gibbons. 16. Gill. 17. Elaine Paige. 18. Maggie Clegg. 19. Mark Jennings. 20. Sickle Cell. 21. Braddock County. 22. The Weatherfield Gazette. 23. Adam Chance. 24. The police suspected her of stealing a car. 25. John James and Emma Samms. 26. Ralph Hardwick. 27. *The Practice*. 28. *Emergency Ward 10*. 29. Christopher Beeny. 30. Raul.

LEVEL 3

Answers: see Quiz 83, page 291

1. Which soap actor conducted the Halle Orchestra in 1989?
2. Which Brookside actor played Sam Jackson in Radio Merseyside's *The Merseysiders*?
3. What is Rita Sullivan's favourite tipple?
4. Which German soap was first shown on Channel 4 in 1988?
5. Which husband and wife were co producers of *Dynasty*?
6. Whose autobiography was called *I Was Ena Sharples' Father*?
7. How did Jock perish in *Dallas*?
8. *Coronation Street* is broadcast on which days?
9. Who appeared as Meg and Hugh's chauffeur on their wedding day?
10. Which Gilbert & Sullivan opera was playing on Derek's car radio as he died in *Coronation Street*?
11. In *Eastenders* who had an affair with his mother-in-law?
12. Who is Amanda Barrie's character in *Coronation Street* married to?
13. What breed of dog was Rowley in *Eastenders*?
14. Reg Holdsworth left for a supermarket where when he left the Street's corner shop?
15. Who almost sabotaged Des and Daphne's wedding in *Neighbours*?
16. Who did Mark Fowler marry in 1992 just before she died in *Eastenders*?
17. Which musical star played Caroline Winthrop in *Crossroads*?
18. Who was Betty Turpin's sister in *Coronation Street*?
19. What was the name of Krystle's former husband in *Dynasty* whom Alexis was accused of killing?
20. From which disease did Lloyd Tavernier suffer in *Eastenders*?
21. In which county was Southfork ranch?
22. Which newspaper did Ken Barlow purchase and then resell?
23. Who was manager of the *Crossroads* health centre?
24. Why was the Street's Sally stopped by the police during her driving test?
25. Who were the two actors who returned to *Dynasty* after *The Colbys* ended?
26. In *Brookside*, who met Madge through a lonely hearts ad after his wife died?
27. In which soap did the Castlehulme Health Centre feature?
28. What was the first soap to be transmitted twice a week on ITV?
29. Which *Upstairs Downstairs* actor appeared as the youngest son in The Grove Family?
30. What was the name of The Ewing's butler?

Who's Who 3

Answers: see Quiz 86, page 294

1. What relation was ex Channel 4 Head Michael Grade to the late Lord Lew Grade?
2. What is sports presenter Bob Wilson's middle name?
3. Who was the only woman in the 1980s to win the BBC *Sports Personality of the Year* on her own?
4. Which soccer side does Roy Walker support?
5. Which presenter used to be in the group Jet Bronx and the Forbidden?
6. Who married Peter Hook in Las Vegas in 1994
7. Who was the first co presenter of *Surprise Surprise* with Cilla Black?
8. Which actor is the son of Margaret Thatcher's Attorney General?
9. What was the name of David Furnish's TV profile of Elton John?
10. Which star of sitcom and theatre made her TV debut opposite John Gielgud in *The Mayfly and the Frog*?
11. Which TV couple met on the set of *Ballykissangel*?
12. In 1990 who founded Animal Line with TV writer Carla Lane?
13. Whose memoirs were called *Stare Back and Smile*?
14. What was the only part of Nicholas Lyndhurst visible in his first TV appearance?
15. Who famously appeared in ads for Tesco chasing chickens in France?
16. Who played *Globelink's* Dave Charnley?
17. Which presenter is the daughter of a veteran radio newsreader Clive?
18. Who hosted the quiz *Gagtag*?
19. Who launched the cable TV station L!VE TV?
20. Which was the first show hosted by Anthea Turner to have her name in the title?
21. Which magician's wife wrote songs for *That's Life*?
22. Which journalist and TV personality is Lady Nicholas Lloyd?
23. Which actress is the mother of Sam West?
24. Which TV presenter wrote a book called *Rock Stars in their Underpants*?
25. Who first hosted the quiz show *Home Truths*?
26. What is Yorkshireman Timothy West's middle name?
27. Who's autobiography was called *Dear Me*?
28. Which Suchet brother is older?
29. Which actress is the wife of writer-director Mike Leigh?
30. Which TV personality has children called Betty Kitten and Honey Kinny?

QUIZ 86 Children's TV 9

Answers: see Quiz 85, page 293

1. Who presented *Full House*?
2. Which children's information show was presented by Harry Fowler and Kenny Lynch?
3. What was the children's S.F. series starring Spencer Banks?
4. What were the names of Mickey Murphy's children in *Camberwick Green*?
5. In *The Flintstones* what was Wilma's vacuum cleaner made from?
6. Who devised and hosted the first *Children's Royal Variety Show*?
7. Which male presenter first joined Fred Dinenage for *How 2*?
8. In which children's comedy did Witchiepoo feature?
9. What was Hokey Wolf's fox friend called?
10. In *Ivor the Engine*, which station did Dai look after?
11. Which company did Oliver Postgate and Peter Firmin set up?
12. Who held the record for reading most stories on *Jackanory*?
13. Who was the female regular on *Do Not Adjust Your Set*?
14. Which children's TV series celebrated its 40th birthday in 1998?
15. What was the name of the cartoon puppy created by William Timyn?
16. Which Captain Marryat story was a 1998 Sunday evening serial?
17. Where can you see *The Rugrats* on a Saturday morning?
18. What is BBC's award-winning children's series featuring crazy inventions?
19. What was the name of *The Worst Witch*?
20. In *The Jetsons*, where did George Jetson work?
21. What was the name of BBC2's children's poetry series?
22. Which well known puppet character was purchased on Blackpool Pier in 1948?
23. Which children's art and craft programme was presented by Neil Buchanan?
24. Which US group were the first major guests on *Jim'll Fix It*?
25. Who was the Most Special Agent for World Intelligence Network?
26. Who was the first female presenter of *Newsround*?
27. Who played William when Richmal Crompton's stories were first adapted for the small screen?
28. Who hosted *Young Krypton* in 1988?
29. Who was the first producer of *Dr Who*?
30. What was the animated series of *Lassie* called?

Who's Who 3 (see Quiz 85)

1. Nephew. 2. Primrose. 3. Fatima Whitbread. 4. Blackpool. 5. Loyd Grossman. 6. Caroline Aherne. 7. Christopher Biggins. 8. Nigel Havers. 9. Tantrums and Tiaras. 10. Felicity Kendal. 11. Stephen Tomkinson and Dervla Kirwen. 12. Linda McCartney and Rita Tushingham. 13. Joanna Lumley. 14. Hands. 15. Dudley Moore. 16. Neil Pearson. 17. Gaby Roslin. 18. Bob Monkhouse. 19. Janet Street-Porter. 20. *Turner Round the World.* 21. Victoria Wood. 22. Eve Pollard. 23. Prunella Scales. 24. Paula Yates. 25. Steve Wright. 26. Lancaster. 27. Peter Ustinov. 28. John. 29. Alison Steadman. 30. Jonathan Ross.

Answers: see Quiz 88, page 296

LEVEL 3

1. Which character was played by Harold Bennett in *Are You Being Served?*
2. What was the name of the family who featured in *A Kind of Loving?*
3. Which actress was *Dressing For Breakfast?*
4. In which Western series did the Chinese cook Hop Sing appear?
5. Who played Winston in *The Lenny Henry Show?*
6. Who links Adam Smith and *The Norman Conquests?*
7. In which soap did Michael Ranson play a doctor?
8. What is the stage name of TV actress Phyllis Bickle?
9. In *MPF Circus*, who was heard to demand 'Your lupins or your life!'?
10. What was the name of the father in *The Lacey Family?*
11. In *St. Elsewhere*, what did Luther keep as a pet?
12. Who starred in *The Nearly Man?*
13. Name the actress who played two characters in *Take the High Road.*
14. Which famous singer sang the theme for *Baretta?*
15. What positions did G'Kar and Molari hold aboard *Babylon 5?*
16. Name the TV detective who drove a 1959 Peugeot 403?
17. What was Ironside's first name?
18. Who was the star of *Codename Kyril?*
19. In *The Green Hornet*, what did the hero call his car?
20. Which presenter wrote the theme song to *The Marriage?*
21. At which club did Big Jim apparently hang out?
22. Which comic actor appeared as John Watt?
23. In *Take Me Home*, who played the taxi driver?
24. Which comic played the country singer called Fat Belly Jones?
25. The soap *United* used the facilities of which real football club?
26. What is a 'Jeremy Beadle' in the *Dictionary of Cockney Rhyming Slang?*
27. In *Porridge*, who played the judge who ended up inside?
28. Who was the original presenter of *Watchdog?*
29. Who hosted *ORS 85?*
30. Name the actress who links *Another Sunday* and *Sweet FA* to *Coronation Street?*

LEVEL 3

Answers: see Quiz 87, page 295

1. Which of the *NYPD Blue* cast won an Emmy in 1998 for Outstanding Supporting Actor in a drama series?
2. Which Dame played Mrs Danvers in the 1990s *Rebecca*?
3. What was the occupation of Sam Elliot's character Doug in *Mission Impossible*?
4. Who shot to fame as Ladislaw in the BBC's *Middlemarch*?
5. Which octogenarian played Violet in *Waiting For A Telegram*?
6. For which two series did Emma Thompson win best actress BAFTAs two years running?
7. In which drama series did *The Grand Turk* play a British Frigate?
8. Which character in *Soldier, Soldier* was played by Jonathan Guy Lewis?
9. Who was David Haig's character in *Talking Heads II*?
10. What was Eileen Atkins character in *The Hand Of God* by Alan Bennett?
11. Which billionaire was played by Tommy Lee Jones in a US Drama?
12. Who was Beatrice's sister in *The House of Elliot*?
13. Who was Richard Bradford's character in *Man In A Suitcase*?
14. In which police series would you find Detective Inspector Roy Galloway?
15. Which 1998 drama had a budget of £12million and was filmed in the Black Sea?
16. What relation is Ruth to Peggy in *Where The Heart Is*?
17. Which *Reckless* star had her film debut as a handmaiden to Liz Taylor in Cleopatra?
18. Who played Rosemary in *Nights In The Gardens Of Spain*?
19. On which series was there a pet named Tricky Woo?
20. Teraise and Ollie feature in which BBC1 children's series?
21. Which Victorian Detective was played by John Barrie?
22. Which of *The Troubleshooters* was an expert on the English longbow?
23. Which Sir Lancelot married Rita Fairclough?
24. Who had a fear of flying in *The A Team*?
25. Where was Louisa Trotter's hotel?
26. Who was Captain Frank McNeil's bald lieutenant?
27. Who played Georgina Jones in *Adam Adamant*?
28. What was Susan Jameson's role in *When The Boat Comes In*?
29. Which Roman Emperor had a speech impediment in a Robert Graves series?
30. In which series was the hero referred to by his teacher as Grasshopper?

1. In which sitcom did Ian Carmichael play a single foster-father?
2. Who played the landlady in *All At Number 20*?
3. Which title did William Melvyn have in *All Gas And Gaiters*?
4. Who played Bev Harris in *Roseanne*?
5. In which programme did Philip Drummond adopt two brothers?
6. In which sitcom did Meredith Baxter Birney play Elyse Keaton?
7. Who links *Duck Patrol* to *One Foot In The Grave*?
8. Which actress from *You Rang M'lord* had dated Prince Andrew?
9. Which distinguished film actor appeared in the sitcom *Young At Heart*?
10. Which company produced *Drop The Dead Donkey*?
11. Which star of *Mona Lisa* appeared in *Thick as Thieves*?
12. In which series did Claire Buckfield succeed Claire Woodgate as Jen?
13. Which *Saint* appeared in the sitcom *Tom, Dick and Harriet*?
14. Who appeared in *Family Ties* as Laura Miller?
15. Which *Dad's Army* actor was the star of *My Old Man*?
16. What was the name of Nicholas Lyndhurst's character in *The Two Of Us*?
17. Who was Corporal Henshaw's sergeant?
18. In which series was there a butler named Dubois?
19. Which female film star's name was adopted by Alf Garnett for his son-in-law?
20. What was the name of Terry's sister in *The Likely Lads*?
21. What was the name of the cowboy builder in *Fawlty Towers*?
22. Where did E.L. Wisty sit in his sketches?
23. Who played Maureen Lipman's secretary in *Agony*?
24. Who played Laura Petrie in a U.S. comedy series?
25. What was the comedy series starring Robin Askwith and Brian Glover?
26. Who was Ronald Forfar's character in *Bread*?
27. What was the 1950s series starring Bebe Daniels and Ben Lyons?
28. Who played Hans in *'Allo, 'Allo*?
29. Which football team does Frank Skinner support?
30. In which series did Fletch attain his freedom?

Answers: see Quiz 89, page 297

1. What is the name of the BBC's 24-hour television news service?
2. In which country is the ITV magazine show *Lunch In The Sun* based?
3. Philippa Forrester introduces which BBC1 science and technology series?
4. The Channel 4 series *Deals On Wheels* dealt with which type of car market?
5. Who was the comedian who explored *Great Railway Journeys* with the BBC?
6. On which channel did we meet *Vets In Practice*?
7. Archaeologist and historian Julian Richards asked us to meet whom on BBC2?
8. With which subject is the BBC series *Ground Force* concerned?
9. In which country was TV traveller and reporter Alan Whicker born?
10. Michael Wood led us in the footsteps of which ancient Emperor on BBC2?
11. What nationality is presenter Eamonn Holmes?
12. Which Scottish soccer star hosts a BBC chat show with Fred MacAulay?
13. Which barrister hosts a talk show?
14. What UK motorway was featured in ITV's *Motorway Life*?
15. The Sunday evening topical discussion show *Heart Of The Matter* is hosted by who?
16. Which former Tory Prime Minister was profiled in BBC2's *A Very Singular Man*?
17. Who made the controversial 70s documentary *Yesterday's Men*?
18. Which former *News at Ten* presenter hosted CBS's *West 57th Show*?
19. Who was the presenter of *Person To Person* in the late 1970s?
20. Name the former Nationwide reporter who presented *Sin On Sunday*?
21. Who won a BAFTA award in 1969 for his coverage of the Vietnam War?
22. Who examined the consumer battle between Pepsi and Coca Cola?
23. Which Russian did Malcolm Muggeridge spend *A Week With..* in 1982?
24. Who narrated the documentary *Nagasaki – The Return Journey*?
25. Which news programme was the first to have two newsreaders?
26. Mike Scott was the original host of which ITV talk show?
27. Which of the *Game For A Laugh* team presented *Good Morning Britain*?
28. Who presented *Midweek*?
29. What replaced *Tonight* on BBC1 as the evening news and current affairs programme?
30. *An Ocean Apart* was presented by who?

LEVEL 3

Answers: see Quiz 92, page 300

1. Whose wedding did Walter Lankersham interrupt in *Dynasty*?
2. Which early *Eastender* was diagnosed as having Multiple Sclerosis?
3. *Crossroads* actors Terence Rigsby and Norman Bowler had previously appeared together in which police series?
4. What did Alf Roberts help to conceal in the cellar at The Rovers Return?
5. When Rita originally appeared in *Coronation Street*, what assumed name did she use?
6. Who played Annie Walker's son in the Street?
7. Which soap actor sang with a group called *Take Ten*?
8. How much money did Ivy Brennan give to Mike Baldwin to help settle the gambling debts of her husband, Don?
9. What were the first three surnames Valene had in *Knot's Landing*?
10. In which soap did Kylie Minogue play the part of Char?
11. Which Carrington was named after her wonderfully blue eyes?
12. In *Dallas* who married the same man on two separate occasions?
13. Jeff and Doreen Horton are which *Coronation Street* child's grandparents?
14. In *Coronation Street*, who won a night out with Mike Baldwin in a raffle?
15. Which newspaper was owned by Alexis in *Dynasty*?
16. Who first sang the *Neighbours* theme song?
17. Who did *Lovejoy* play in *Dallas*?
18. Who owned The Diner with Ailsa in the early showings of *Home and Away*?
19. In *The Colbys* whose baby was adopted at birth?
20. Who was the Baldwins cleaning lady in *Coronation Street*?
21. At which soccer side's ground was action filmed for *United!*?
22. Who played neighbour Joyce Harker in *The Newcomers*?
23. In which soap did Sly and Serena appear?
24. In *The Colbys* how did Jeff almost meet his death?
25. Which former President's wife had a role in *Falcon Crest*?
26. Who did Stan Richards play in *Emmerdale*?
27. Who was referred to as Queen of the Soaps?
28. Who owned The Southern Cross Ranch?
29. Who gave Frank and Pat Butcher fluffy dice as a wedding present?
30. Who spoke the first and last ever words in *Crossroads*?

Answers: see Quiz 91, page 299

1. *Victorian Values* was written and presented by who?
2. Who starred opposite Denis Lawson in *That Uncertain Feeling*?
3. In *Peyton Place*, who owned a bookshop?
4. What did Nicky Henson wear around his neck in *Fawlty Towers*?
5. What was the name of the harassed Captain in *Car 54, Where Are You*?
6. What was the name of the newspaper in *Hot Metal*?
7. In *The Heroes*, who played Paddy McDowell?
8. Who starred in *Sledge Hammer*?
9. What did Luke Mae run in *Flamingo Road*?
10. Who played the school teacher in *P'tang Yang Kipperbang*?
11. Dan Fixx was a character in which soap?
12. Name the regular comedian in *The Funny Side*.
13. In which series did James Bolam play a priest?
14. Who was the voice of *Bugs Bunny*?
15. Frank Bough of *Breakfast Time* fame won an Oxbridge blue for which sport?
16. What did Kate and Allie have in common?
17. In which soap was Councillor Muldoon a character?
18. Which real-life agony aunt assisted in the creation of the comedy *Agony*?
19. What was the name of Vince's mother in *Just Good Friends*?
20. Who assisted Bruce Forsyth on *You Bet*?
21. Barry Ryan's mother appeared on *Spot The Tune* – what was her name?
22. Who links *Fame is the Spur* and *Jewel in the Crown*?
23. How much did it cost to stay for a weekend on *Fantasy Island*?
24. The western *Bronco* was a spin-off of which other western series?
25. Sister Jefferies was a character in which soap?
26. Who starred as *The Marksman*?
27. Desmond Llewellyn appeared on TV as the owner of which farm?
28. Name the host of the quiz *Get Set, Go*.
29. In *Small World*, who wrote poetry?
30. What was the name of the Indian character in *Casey Jones*?

ANSWERS

Soaps 13 (see Quiz 91)
1. Blake and Krystle Carrington's. 2. Colin Russel. 3. *Softly, Softly.* 4. A greyhound. 5. Mrs Bates. 6. Kenneth Farringdon. 7. William Tarmey (Jack Duckworth). 8. One thousand pounds. 9. Ewing, Gibson, Waleska. 10. *The Henderson Kids.* 11. Krystle. 12. Su Ellen. 13. Tommy Duckworth. 14. Hilda Ogden. 15. The Denver Mirror. 16. Barry Crocker. 17. Don Lockwood. 18. Bobby Simpson. 19. Monica Colby's. 20. Hilda Ogden. 21. Stoke City. 22. Wendy Richard. 23. *Dallas.* 24. By inhaling paint fumes. 25. Ronald Reagan's ex-wife Jane Wyman. 26. Seth Armstrong. 27. Noele Gordon. 28. Clayton Farlow. 29. Charlie Cotton. 30. Jill.

Answers: see Quiz 94, page 302

1. Which songstress recorded the theme to *Howard's Way*?
2. Arthur Daley featured in which single by the Firm?
3. Which group recorded the single *TV*?
4. Which former Playboy centrefold presented *The Word* aged 17?
5. What was Chris Evans first pop series, on Sky?
6. Who composed Cilla's 1960s theme song *Step Inside Love*?
7. How are Charles Hodge and David Peacock otherwise known?
8. Which famed pop 1950s pop show was broadcast for only one year?
9. Freddie Davies won *Opportunity Knocks* – what was his nickname?
10. What was the subject of the series *Applause, Applause*?
11. Who appeared as Hylda Baker's brother in a sitcom and was partnered on stage by Ben Warris?
12. How many Royal Variety performances did Morecambe and Wise appear in together?
13. Singer and actress Debbie Allen appeared in which series set in a stage school?
14. The GoJos featured in which Irishman's variety show?
15. On which show was there a feature called *Sofa Soccer*?
16. Who hosted the BBC New Comedy Awards for 1998?
17. Who recorded the theme for *Linford's Record Breakers*?
18. Which solo entertainer ended his shows by singing *May Each Day*?
19. In which year did Brotherhood Of Man win *The Eurovision Song Contest*?
20. *Elgar* and *Debussy* were films made for *Omnibus* by whom?
21. Which TV and musical star is the son of the lead singer with 50s band *The Southlanders*?
22. Which actor recorded an album called *Down Wind with Angels*?
23. Boxer Freddie Mills appeared on which ground-breaking music programme?
24. Which music show is sponsored by a soft drinks company?
25. *The Flower Duet* from Lakme by Delibes was used by which arline in an ad?
26. Where did the first *Songs of Praise* come from?
27. On which show did the host have a built in ashtray in his armchair?
28. Which former Bonzo Dog Doo Dah Band member hosted a comedy music show?
29. What was Leonard Sach's title on *The Good Old Days*?
30. Which Italian-American singer had his show on the BBC preceding *Sportsview*?

LEVEL 3

Answers: see Quiz 93, page 301

1. Who was the boxer in *Taxi*?
2. Who played 'Excused-Boots' Bisley in *The Army Game*?
3. From which medium did the sitcom *An Actor's Life For Me* originate?
4. Who played Prunella Scales' mother in *After Henry*?
5. Which agony aunt co-wrote *Agony*?
6. Which man lived in the flat above the Ropers?
7. What was the name of the series featuring Richard Briars and Prunella Scales?
8. Who did Lesley Dunlop replace as Zoe in *May To December*?
9. In which country was *Me Mammy* set?
10. Which other character did Max Baer Jr. portray apart from Jethro in *The Beverley Hillbillies*?
11. What was Monsieur LeClerc's first name in *'Allo, 'Allo*?
12. Who joined Punt and Dennis in *Me, You and Him*?
13. In which series was Francois Pascal an English student?
14. What was Paula Wilcox's surname in her series playing a single mum?
15. What was Miss Lancing's first name in *The Brittas Empire*?
16. Who wrote the *Carry On Laughing* Christmas Specials?
17. Which doctor presented *The Pink Medicine Show*?
18. What was Noel Howlett's position in *Please Sir*?
19. *Prisoner and Escort* was the pilot for which sitcom?
20. Who played *Farrington of the FO*?
21. Which breed of dog was the family pet in *Father, Dear Father*?
22. Who played Lenny Henry's dad in *The Fosters*?
23. In *Frasier*, how did Martin Crane become an invalid?
24. Who played Frances De La Tour's husband in *Every Silver Lining*?
25. The actress who played Michael J. Fox's mother in *Back To The Future* plays a cartoonist in which sitcom?
26. Which surreal series featured a book editor named Martin Tupper?
27. What was Ernie Pantuso's nickname in *Cheers*?
28. Which sitcom character once owned 'Buy The Book'?
29. Which comedian Eric was the oldest – Idle, Morecambe or Sykes?
30. What do Jerry and Phil do in *The Larry Sanders Show*?

LEVEL 3

Answers: see Quiz 96, page 304

1. Which children's channel did Warner Amex found in the US in 1979?
2. Who designed the *Blue Peter* logo?
3. Who created *Ollie Beak*?
4. What was the last word of the Pink Panther song?
5. Which character from *Noel's Houseparty* had a No.1 Hit in 1993?
6. What is *Buffy*'s predestined role?
7. What was the name of Ivan Owen's vulpine puppet character?
8. What creature was Musky in *Deputy Dawg*?
9. Which former Olympic Champion hosts *Record Breakers*?
10. Who ran the TV station PPC TV?
11. Who was the pianist on *Play Away*?
12. Which school featured in *Press Gang*?
13. In which cartoon series did an elephant called Shep appear?
14. Which character did Alexander Gauge portray in *The Adventures of Robin Hood*?
15. Ant Jones featured in which children's series?
16. Which BBC children's series lead to the biggest toy success of 1997?
17. Who are Bart Simpson's favourite cartoon characters?
18. Which female puppet appeared on the *Rainbow* after Geoffrey left?
19. The producer of *Roobarb and Custard* likened the cat and dog relationship as that between which two comedians?
20. Who played the headmaster in *Teenage Health Freak*?
21. Who was Dr. Bunsen Honeydew's assistant?
22. Which future soap star played Gerry in *Going Out*?
23. What type of creature was Colonel K in *Dangermouse*?
24. Where in *Camberwick Green* would you meet Captain Snort?
25. Which spaceship crew did Miss Piggy belong to?
26. On which channel was *Pob* broadcast?
27. Tim Brooke-Taylor, Harry Enfield and Enn Reitel were the voices for which children's series?
28. Who were the stars of *The Quack Chat Show*?
29. Who created Henry the cat?
30. How is Theodore Geisel better known?

LEVEL 3

Answers: see Quiz 95, page 303

1. In *Airwolf*, what was Hawke's first name?

2. What colour did western character Adam Cartright always dress in?

3. In which decade was the series *South Riding* set?

4. Which talent show was hosted by Arthur Askey?

5. Snarky and Friegle were members of which gang?

6. Which family featured in *All at Number 20*?

7. In *Return of the Antelope*, what was The Antelope?

8. What was Sid's surname in *Bless this House*?

9. Who created *The Dustbinmen*?

10. Abby Urquhart appeared in which soap?

11. Who presented a *Guide to the BBC*?

12. In *Auf Wiedersehen Pet*, who got tattooed?

13. Who had two heads in *The Hitchhiker's Guide To The Galaxy*?

14. What did Reginald Perrin call his shop?

15. Where does Helen Mirren have a tattoo of a pair of crosses?

16. Who was the star of *Murder of a Moderate Man*?

17. In which sci-fi series was Roj the leader?

18. Who played Carol in *Mister Ed*?

19. Who did Samantha Egger Portray in *Ziegfeld: The Man and His Women*?

20. *Family Fortunes* was based on which US quiz?

21. Who was called 'The Snow Queen' in *Wish Me Luck*?

22. Wilfred and Mabel presented which *Jim'll Fix It* forerunner?

23. In *Dallas*, what was the name of Southfork's maid?

24. What was the name of John Thaw's character in *Home To Roost*?

25. Who was the presenter of *The Rock and Roll Years*?

26. What did *The Avengers* call their boss?

27. Which quiz was hosted by Angela Rippon?

28. What is the name of the dating game show hosted by Claudia Winkleman?

29. *All Our Yesterdays* was originally presented by who?

30. For which comic actor did Bob Monkhouse write gags?

LEVEL 3

Answers: see Quiz 98, page 306

1. Which series starred Kate O'Mara on a North Sea ferry?
2. In which series was there a detective named Pepper?
3. Who played Professor Quatermass in the 1950s on television?
4. Which mini series had 130 million viewers on its first transmission?
5. Who played Ted Danson's wife in *Gullivers Travels*?
6. Who created *The Baron*?
7. Whose first stage play *Talent* was adapted for TV in 1979?
8. Who played the governor in *Within These Walls*?
9. What was Susan Hampshire's role in *The Pallisers*?
10. What was the sequel to *Bouquet of Barbed Wire*?
11. What did Kathleen Harrison's Mrs Thursday do for a living?
12. Which star of *The Bill* since its 1983 pilot is a qualified scuba diving instructor?
13. Who was Roger Smith's character in *77 Sunset Strip*?
14. In which film did PC George Dixon first appear?
15. Who created the police series *87th Precinct*?
16. In which series did John Hillerman play Higgins?
17. Which member of Spandau Ballet appeared in *Supply And Demand*?
18. Walter Winchell narrated which crime series?
19. Which adventure featured characters Wilde and Sinclair?
20. Who was Roddy McMillan's character in *Hazell*?
21. In which country was Ben Hall an outlaw?
22. What was the name of the Yorkshire detective played by Leslie Sands?
23. Who starred in both *The Protectors* and *Howards Way*?
24. Who played *Big Breadwinner Hog*?
25. Which area of London was featured in a Neil Dunn Wednesday Play?
26. Which Avenger played a footman in *Upstairs Downstairs*?
27. What was Alan Wheatley's character in *The Adventures of Robin Hood*?
28. What nationality is Leo McKern?
29. Which Oscar winner played a PC in *Z-Cars*?
30. I which series did Lynn Darby play the girlfriend of a petty criminal?

LEVEL 3

Answers: see Quiz 97, page 305

1. In *Eastenders*, how was Café Osman previously known?
2. Who replaced Hilda Ogden as cleaner at the Rover's Return?
3. Which guitarist played the theme music to *The Thornbirds*?
4. What was Gillian Taylforth's autobiography called?
5. Which two villages have been used for Beckindale?
6. In which soap did the town of Braddock appear?
7. What is the connection between Brian Rix and *Emmerdale*?
8. Which mountains were on Hilda Ogden's wall?
9. The character Dr Bywaters featured in which soap?
10. Who narrated *The Waltons*?
11. *Market In Honey Lane* was set in which UK city?
12. In *Albion Market* what was singer/actress Helen Shapiro's occupation?
13. Who won a Golden Globe in 1984 for playing Angela Channing?
14. Name the first US soap to appear on British TV.
15. What soap would you be watching if the cast were Angleton New Town?
16. Who played Scott Robinson before Jason Donovan?
17. What was the surname of the family which featured in *Newcomers*?
18. Which soap was based on a novel by Robert Wilder?
19. In *Dallas*, what happened to April while on honeymoon with Bobby Ewing?
20. Which Doctors were based in Coopers Crossing?
21. The Denver-Carrington Corporation belonged to who in *Dynasty*?
22. In *Soap* what was Chuck?
23. When Meg Mortimar sailed away from *Crossroads* on route to New York, which ship did she sail on?
24. Which soap actress's real name is Patsy McClenny?
25. In the *Brookside* siege how many people lost their lives?
26. To which country did Elsie Tanner move to from *Coronation Street*?
27. Who were Miss Ellie's grandchildren in *Dallas*?
28. Which soap star played D.I. Monk in the first series of *Birds of a Feather*?
29. What was Charlene's occupation in *Neighbours*?
30. When Bet Lynch wanted to go to Spain to work who lent her the airfare?

Answers: see Quiz 100, page 308

1. The long running programme about TV, *Did You See...?*, was hosted by whom?
2. Which founder member of BBC's *Breakfast Time* team left the weather spot to go to *Sky News*?
3. Which BBC reporter was at the scene of the Iranian Embassy Siege?
4. Who introduced *Just Another Day*?
5. Marion Foster was a presenter on which BBC lunchtime programme?
6. Who had to cut his news bulletin short because he was unwell?
7. How are Moira Armstrong and Pamela Armstrong related?
8. Which twice weekly Thames show was presented by Mavis Nicholson?
9. Which Bob co-hosted *Open Air*?
10. Which soccer side does GMTV's John Stapleton support?
11. Who presented *Newsround Weekly* when it was introduced in 1977?
12. Trevor McDonald wrote biographies of which two cricketers?
13. What were the interviewers in the series *We Want An Answer*?
14. Which weekly programme reviewed the outpourings of Fleet Street?
15. *A Week In Politics* was broadcast by which channel?
16. Tom Mangold specialised in reporting on what?
17. On which Scottish news programme did the *Tube's* Muriel Gray make appearances?
18. Which newsreader wrote the novel *Chasing The Dragon*?
19. Which newscaster was the first to present a programme for the retired on Channel 4?
20. *Now Get Out Of That* was hosted by which former *Nationwide* reporter?
21. Whose books include *Cats in the News* and *Dogs in the News*?
22. On which channel could *News View* be watched?
23. Who links *Crimewatch UK* to *Daytime Live*?
24. Which Natalie appeared on *Open Air*?
25. *Split Screen* was presented by who?
26. *Taking Liberties* was introduced by who?
27. According to the title of the series, David Lomax reported on what kind of matters?
28. Susan Rae went from Radio 4 to which BBC morning programme?
29. Helen Rollason presented which evening news programme?
30. Who did Gillian Reynolds replace as presenter of *Face The Press* on ITV?

LEVEL 3

Answers: see Quiz 99, page 307

1. Which actress famous for sitcoms played Nellie Harvey in *Coronation Street*?
2. Who first played Rose in *Keeping Up Appearances*?
3. Who was Bernard Woolley Private Secretary to?
4. In which 1970s sitcom did Wally and Lily move from a gypsy caravan to a housing estate?
5. Which comedy partnership appeared in *Running Wild*?
6. What is the sheep's name in *A Close Shave*?
7. Which comedienne starred in *Murder Most Horrid*?
8. In which sitcom did Cannon and Ball appear as security officers?
9. What was the ITV sitcom set in a public convenience?
10. In which U.S. sitcom is there a Father Mulcahy?
11. Who was created by two school friends in *Weird Science*?
12. John Inman starred in which comedy set in a seaside rock factory?
13. What did Mel Smith study at Oxford University?
14. Whose autobiography was called *Arias and Raspberries*?
15. *Basil The Rat* was an episode in which comedy series?
16. Where was *The River* set?
17. Which of the *Friends* had a girlfriend called Janice?
18. In which series are Carter and Stewart city employees?
19. What was the name of the newspaper in *Foxy Lady*?
20. Who was the founder of *The Simpsons'* home town?
21. In which sitcom did Wayne Knight play Officer Don?
22. Which state did *The Fresh Prince Of Bel Air* come from originally?
23. What is Zoe's occupation in *May To December*?
24. Who played the Duke of Edinburgh's father in *Blackadder*?
25. What was the name of Felicity Kendal's character in *Solo*?
26. Who created *Rutland Weekend Television*?
27. Who was Michael Medwin's character in *The Army Game*?
28. Who played Aulus Paulinus in the Roman spoof *Chelmsford 123*?
29. What was Dan Conner's hobby that became his business in *Roseanne*?
30. Who played Daisy in *The Dukes Of Hazzard*?

QUIZ 101 Pot Luck 22

Answers: see Quiz 102, page 310

LEVEL 3

1. What was the name of the dog-like character in the cartoon *Will O' The Wisp*?
2. Where did Sharon and Elsie work?
3. Who presented the children's show *Going a Bundle*?
4. Angela Down played which character in *Take Three Girls*?
5. Who chaired *Ask Me Another*?
6. *The Day The Universe Changed* was presented by which BBC science expert?
7. Which reporter met a lost tribe in Brazil in 1970?
8. What was Cash's surname in *Cash and Cable*?
9. Alf Garnett's son-in-law lived in which city?
10. Who hosted the show *Running Late*?
11. Which impressionist starred in the 1960s show *Three of a Kind*?
12. What did Geoffrey do for a living in *The Lovers*?
13. Who links *The A-Team* and *Chopper One*?
14. Hayley Mills played Tilly Grant in which series?
15. What kind of hat did the detective Mr Rose wear?
16. In which series did Professor Popkiss appear?
17. What was the name of the playwright in *An Englishman's Castle*?
18. Which pop singer starred in the TV mini-series *Blood And Orchids*?
19. Who played the title role in *The Travels of Jaimie McPheeters*?
20. Sharon Duce played a gambling addict's girlfriend in which 1980's series?
21. Bill Conte wrote the theme tune for which soap?
22. Which character did Tony Selby play in *Get Some In*?
23. What was Chris's job in *The Cuckoo Waltz*?
24. Who starred as The Snoop Sisters?
25. In which city was the World War II drama *And a Nightingale Sang* set?
26. Who links *Wings* to *Piece of Cake*?
27. Who did Rosie Tindall meet at the start of *No Strings*?
28. What was the full name of the character played by Windsor Davies in *Never The Twain*?
29. The drama, *Shalom Salaam* was set in which city?
30. Which game show was co-hosted by Wie Wie Wong?

ANSWERS

Children's TV 11 (see Quiz 102)

1. Julia Sawalha. 2. Una Stubbs. 3. *Rupert Bear.* 4. Patricia Hayes. 5. *Stopit And Tidyup.* 6. Dedication. 7. Richard the Lionheart. 8. *The Hobbit.* 9. A doctor. 10. *Josie And The Pussycats.* 11. Tom of T.H.U.M.B. 12. Mike Reid. 13. Rolf Harris. 14. Marshall Thompson. 15. Sir Basil and Lady Rosemary. 16. A bow tie. 17. Connie Booth. 18. Shari Lewis. 19. Vicky Licorish. 20. Mark Curry. 21. Four. 22. Red and yellow. 23. *SuperTed.* 24. Alberto Frog. 25. Bella and Ursula. 26. Simon Groom. 27. *Follyfoot.* 28. *The Adventures of Twizzle and Torchy.* 29. Michael Bentine. 30. Knightmare.

Answers: see Quiz 101, page 309

1. Which future sitcom star played Lynda Day in *Press Gang*?
2. Who played Mrs Plugg in *Morris Minor's Marvellous Motors*?
3. Ray Brooks narrated the stories of which character?
4. Who narrated *Gran*?
5. Which children's series was narrated by Terry Wogan?
6. According to the first *Record Breakers* theme song what did you need to be a record breaker?
7. Name the future king played by Dermot Walsh.
8. *The Return Of The King* was based on which book?
9. What was the profession of *Ramar Of The Jungle*?
10. Hanna-Barbera created which cartoon all-girl band?
11. What was the name of the tiny spy in the cartoon *King Kong*?
12. Which future soap star presided over *Runaround*?
13. Who was Koojee Bear's human companion?
14. Which actor starred as *Daktari*?
15. Who owned the garden in *The Herbs*?
16. What does BooBoo wear around his neck?
17. Who in 1980 played *Little Lord Fauntleroy*'s mother?
18. Who had a puppet called Charlie Horse?
19. Which female presenter was in the coffee shop in *Saturday Superstore*?
20. Who presented *Blue Peter* and *Screen Test*?
21. How many daughters were there in *The Little House On The Prairie*?
22. What were the colours of the two teams in *Cheggers Plays Pop*?
23. Victor Spinetti provided voices for which superhero cartoon?
24. Who was conductor of the band in *Bod*?
25. What were the names of *George Of The Jungle*'s two girlfriends?
26. Which *Blue Peter* presenter was once arrested on assignment in Japan?
27. On which farm did Christina Rodska appear?
28. What was Gerry Anderson's first TV series called?
29. Who created *The Bumblies*?
30. In which show would Treguard warn contests "Temporal Disruption occurring!"

LEVEL 3

Answers: see Quiz 104, page 312

1. What is the family link between *Up The Junction* and *Cathy Come Home*?
2. Who parked the cars in *77 Sunset Strip*?
3. Which lawyer's christian name is Horace?
4. What was Patrick Duffy's name in *The Man From Atlantis*?
5. Who played No. 1 in *The Prisoner*?
6. In which county was Paul Dangerfield a GP?
7. Which German series featured the story of a U-boat and its crew?
8. Carol Drinkwater and Lynda Bellingham both played which role?
9. Which late private detective was played by Ken Cope?
10. In which series is there a pub named Fitzgerald's?
11. Who played Captain Pellow in ITV's *Hornblower*?
12. In *The Man From UNCLE*, who wore the number 11 on his badge?
13. What was Eric Porter's character in *The Forsythe Saga*?
14. On whose book was *The History Man* based?
15. Who played Inspector Alleyn in the pilot for the subsequent series with Patrick Malahide?
16. Who played Sgt Fletcher in the Miss Marple series before becoming another detective's sidekick?
17. In which town was *Capstick's Law* set?
18. Which Douglas sister did Steven Crane have an affair with in *The Chancer*?
19. In *Kennedy*, who portrayed Bobby Kennedy?
20. *Gentlemen And Players* was set in which business world?
21. Which star of *The Men's Room* is the niece of actor Christopher Lee?
22. Which actor in a long running drama series wrote a book called *Vet Behind the Ears*?
23. Caine was what type of priest in *Kung Fu*?
24. What or who was Fred in *The Duchess Of Duke Street*?
25. Which drama used 1,000 Yugoslavian Territorial Army members as extras?
26. In which drama did The Rana of Blithar appear?
27. Who starred as Richard Gaunt in *The Regiment*?
28. Who played Danny in *Fame*?
29. In *Marcus Welby MD*, who played the doctor's assistant?
30. *A Piece Of Cake* featured which of the armed forces?

LEVEL 3

Answers: see Quiz 103, page 311

1. Which early *Eastender* tried to commit suicide by takin an overdose of pills?

2. Who did Vera Duckworth buy the *Coronation Street* window cleaning round from?

3. In which soap did the newspaper the New Globe appear?

4. Which Dallas star duetted with Andy Gibb on *All I Have to Do Is Dream* in 1981?

5. What was the name of the *Prisoner: Cell Block H* theme tune?

6. In which village might you have found Sergeant McArthur keeping law and order?

7. Who played Titus Semple in *Flamingo Road*?

8. Who did Dirty Den call Princess?

9. In which soap did the Carnation Killer leave a white carnation at the scenes of his crimes?

10. In which fictitious town was *Dynasty* set?

11. Who was the second soap victim (after Valerie Barlow) to die from electrocution?

12. Who did Richard Chamberlain play in *The Thorn Birds*?

13. Which 1960s soap did the *'Allo, 'Allo* actress Carmen Silvera appear in?

14. What was the name of the racecourse owner in *Falcon Crest*?

15. Which character left Albert Square to go to university in East Anglia?

16. Which creator of *Knot's Landing* shares his name with a UK radio and TV personality?

17. In *Eastenders*, who was Pete Beale's first wife?

18. The Green Lantern takeaway featured in which soap?

19. The TV tales of whom are based on the novel Spender's Mountain?

20. What was Helen's hobby in *Neighbours*?

21. Which *Eastenders* character shares his name with a football manger sacked in favour of a Frenchman?

22. Which former *Brookside* star married photographer Sven Arnstein?

23. Which actress was spotted by Larry Grayson who cast her as Dot on his TV show?

24. Who in real life has dated 'Beth' and 'Maxine' from two different soaps?

25. Which *Dynasty* star released a single *Don't You Need* in 1979?

26. What were the names of Tom's two children in *Howard's Way*?

27. What occurred during the wedding ceremony of Cecile Colby and Alexis Carrington?

28. In *Coronation Street* what kind of animal was Lucky?

29. In *Eastenders* Dot Cotton only drinks alcohol at what time of the year?

30. How many people were killed in the Rovers Return fire?

Drama 14 (see Quiz 103)

1. Author of *Junction* Nell Dunn married *Cathy* author Jeremy Sandford. 2. Kookie. 3. Rumpole. 4. Mark Harris. 5. Patrick McGoohan. 6. Warwickshire. 7. *Das Boot*. 8. Helen Herriot. 9. Marty Hopkirk. 10. *Ballykissangel*. 11. Robert Lindsay. 12. Napoleon Solo. 13. Soames. 14. Malcolm Bradbury's. 15. Simon Williams. 16. Kevin Whately. 17. Bowdale. 18. Victoria. 19. John Shea. 20. City finance. 21. Harriet Walter. 22. Christopher Timothy. 23. A Shaolin (Buddhist) Priest. 24. The porter's dog 25. *War and Peace*. 26. *The Far Pavillions*. 27. Christopher Cazenove. 28. Carlo Imperato. 29. Charles Brolen. 30. The RAF.

Answers: see Quiz 106, page 314

1. Which painter advertised Flash?
2. Who played Dr Jake Ramorey in *Friends*?
3. What was Paul's occupation in *Ever Decreasing Circles*?
4. Which stand-up comic wears large collars and carries many pens in his top pocket?
5. Who links *Second Thoughts* to *Faith In The Future*?
6. What was Derek Nimmo's character in *Oh Brother*?
7. Which sitcom star produced a fitness video called *Let's Dance*?
8. The character Kirk St Moritz appeared in which comedy series?
9. Which football team does June Whitfield support?
10. To whom did Clive Anderson say "there's no beginning to your talents"?
11. Who wrote and sang the theme song for the 70s sitcom *No Honestly*?
12. What was Alec Callander's young wife's name in *May to December*?
13. Which character was the bigoted American *Archie Bunker* based on?
14. Which character's girlfriend was played by Donna from *Eastenders*?
15. In which series did Uncle Mort appear?
16. Who played Mr Big?
17. Dermot Kelly was which comic's sidekick?
18. In *Beggar My Neighbour*, who played the well-off couple?
19. In which series did R. S. M. Brittain appear?
20. Who was the star of *Idiots Weekly, Price 2d*?
21. The Cemetery Gates were on which bus driver's route?
22. What was the first name of Keith Barron's character in *Duty Free*?
23. Who starred in *L For Lester*?
24. Who was the star of *Now – Something Else*?
25. What was Harry McGhee's character in *The Worker*?
26. Sheila Burnett could be seen on which stunt series?
27. What was the name of the cousins in *Perfect Strangers*?
28. How many sons did David Jason have in *A Bit Of A Do*?
29. Steve Nallon provided the voice of which Prime Minister on *Spitting Image*?
30. In *Only Fools And Horses* what had been Uncle Albert's rank in the merchant navy?

QUIZ 106 Pot Luck 23

LEVEL 3

Answers: see Quiz 105, page 313

1. Margaret Savage was a principal dancer on which show?
2. Who bigamously married Emily in *Coronation Street*?
3. In which year was the House of Lords first televised live?
4. Humphrey Burton introduced which annual youth competition?
5. What was the middle name of MP Alan B'Stard?
6. In which series did Angela Thorne play an overseas diplomat?
7. Pamela Sue Martin played which youthful detective on TV?
8. Who links *Danger UXB* and *Tutti-Frutti*?
9. Who did *The Champions* work for?
10. Which agency did Maddie and David run?
11. What was the name of the Detective Inspector in *The Men from Room Thirteen*?
12. Who played Bat Masterton in *The Adventurer*?
13. In *The Price*, who starred as the husband of Harriet Walter?
14. Which actor has '100% Blade' tattooed on his arm?
15. Who created the *Blue Peter* cartoon, *Bleep and Booster*?
16. In which city is Anglia TV based?
17. What was *Gentle Ben*?
18. Angus is Angus Deayton's middle name, what is his first name?
19. Who hosted *Babble*?
20. Old Ned was the gardener at which manor?
21. Who played Paddy in *The Rag Trade*?
22. Who narrated *The Poudles*?
23. What were the real names of Amos and Andy?
24. How did *The Magnificent Evans* make a living?
25. In *WKRP In Cincinnati*, who starred as a Doctor?
26. Where did Ewart Plimmer work?
27. Which star of *The Upper Hand* has a brown belt at judo?
28. Who starred in *The Consultant*?
29. Who played a caped crusader in *Adam Adamant*?
30. In which city did *Mork and Mindy* live?

ANSWERS

Comedy 19 (see Quiz 105)

1. Karl Howman (Jacko). 2. Joey. 3. Hairdresser. 4. Harry Hill. 5. Lynda Bellingham. 6. Dominic.
7. Richard Wilson. 8. *Dear John*. 9. Wimbledon. 10. Jeffrey Archer. 11. Lynsey de Paul. 12. Zoe.
13. Alf Garnett. 14. *Mr. Bean*. 15. *I Didn't Know You Cared*. 16. Peter Jones. 17. Arthur Hayes.
18. Reg Varney and Pat Coombs. 19. *Alfred Marks Time*. 20. Peter Sellers. 21. Stan Butler's.
22. David. 23. Brian Murphy. 24. Rory Bremner. 25. Mr Pugh. 26. *Candid Camera*. 27. Larry and
Balki. 28. Two. 29. Margaret Thatcher. 30. Stoker.

HOW TO SET UP YOUR OWN
PUB QUIZ

It isn't easy, get that right from the start. This isn't going to be easy. Think instead of words like; 'difficult', 'taxing', 'infuriating' consider yourself with damp palms and a dry throat and then, when you have concentrated on that, put it out of your mind and think of the recognition you will receive down the local, imagine all the regulars lifting you high upon their shoulders dancing and weaving their way around the pub. It won't help but it's good to dream every once in a while.

What you will need:

- A good selection of biros (never be tempted to give your own pen up, not even to family members)
- A copy of *The Best TV Pub Quiz Book Ever*
- A set of answer sheets photocopied from the back of the book
- A good speaking voice and possibly a microphone and an amp
- A pub
- At least one pint inside you
- At least one more on your table
- A table

What to do:

Choose your local to start with, there is no need to get halfway through your first quiz and decide you weren't cut out for all this and then find yourself in the roughest pub in Christendom 30 miles and a long run from home.

Chat it through with the landlord and agree on whether you will be charging or not, if you don't then there is little chance of a prize for the winners other than a free pint each and this is obviously at the landlord's discretion – if you pack his pub to bursting then five free pints won't worry him, but if it's only you and a two others then he may be less than unwilling, as publicans tend to be.

If you decide on a payment entry keep it reasonable, you don't want to take the fun out of the quiz; some people will be well aware that they have very little hope of winning and will be reluctant to celebrate the fact by mortgaging their house.

Once location and prize are all sorted then advertising the event is paramount, get people's attention, sell sell, sell or, alternatively, stick up a gaudy looking poster on the door of the bogs. Be sure to specify all the details, time, prize and so on – remember you are selling to people whose tiny attention span is being whittled down to nothing by alcohol.

After this it is time for the big night, if you are holding the event in the 'snug' which seats ten or so you can rely on your voice, if not you should get hold of a good microphone and an amplifier so that you can boom out your questions and enunciate the length and breadth of the pub (once again, clear this with the landlord and don't let liquid anywhere near the electrical equipment). Make sure to practice, and get comfortable with the sound of your own voice and relax as much as possible, try not to rely on alcohol too much or "round one" will be followed by "rown' too" which will eventually give way to "runfree". Relax with your voice so that you can handle any queries from the teams, and any venomous abuse from the 'lively' bar area.

When you enter the pub make sure you take everything listed above. Also, make sure you have a set of tie-break questions and that you instruct everybody who is taking part of the rules – and be firm. It will only upset people if you start handing out impromptu solutions and let's face it the wisdom of Solomon is not needed when you are talking pub quiz rules; 'no cheating' is a perfectly healthy stance to start with.

Finally, keep the teams to a maximum of five members, hand out your answer papers and pens and, when everybody is good and settled, start the quiz. It might not be easy and it might not propel you to international stardom or pay for a life of luxury but you will enjoy yourself. No, really.

ANSWERS

Part One

1 _____

2 _____

3 _____

4 _____

5 _____

6 _____

7 _____

8 _____

9 _____

10 _____

11 _____

12 _____

13 _____

14 _____

15 _____

16 _____

17 _____

18 _____

19 _____

20 _____

21 _____

22 _____

23 _____

24 _____

25 _____

26 _____

27 _____

28 _____

29 _____

30 _____

ANSWERS

Part Two

1 _____

2 _____

3 _____

4 _____

5 _____

6 _____

7 _____

8 _____

9 _____

10 _____

11 _____

12 _____

13 _____

14 _____

15 _____

16 _____

17 _____

18 _____

19 _____

20 _____

21 _____

22 _____

23 _____

24 _____

25 _____

26 _____

27 _____

28 _____

29 _____

30 _____

ANSWERS

Part Three

1 _____

2 _____

3 _____

4 _____

5 _____

6 _____

7 _____

8 _____

9 _____

10 _____

11 _____

12 _____

13 _____

14 _____

15 _____

16 _____

17 _____

18 _____

19 _____

20 _____

21 _____

22 _____

23 _____

24 _____

25 _____

26 _____

27 _____

28 _____

29 _____

30 _____